AT THE FRONT

DEDICATION

For André, Annemarié, Martin, Bruwer and Mariana

AT THE FRONT

A General's Account of South Africa's Border War

Jannie Geldenhuys

JONATHAN BALL PUBLISHERS

JOHANNESBURG & CAPE TOWN

First published in 1994 in hard cover by
Jonathan Ball Publishers (Pty) Ltd
under the title *A General's Story*.

This edition first published in trade paperback
with the new title *At the Front* in 2009 by

JONATHAN BALL PUBLISHERS (PTY) LTD
PO Box 33977
Jeppestown 2043

ISBN 978-1-86842-331-6

Translated and edited by Willem Steenkamp
Design by Triple M Design, Johannesburg
Maps by A1 Graphics, Pretoria (By courtesy of J L van Schaik Publishers, Pretoria)
Set in 10.5/14pt ITC New Baskerville Std
Printed and bound by CTP Book Printers, Duminy Street, Parow, Cape

CONTENTS

PREFACE TO THE SECOND ENGLISH-LANGUAGE EDITION

When I first wrote this book, between December 1990 and January 1992, I did not set out to research and produce a history. Instead I committed to paper an account of what I had experienced. The book was published in Afrikaans in 1993, entitled *Dié wat wen – 'n generaal se storie uit 'n era van oorlog en vrede*, followed in 1994 by the English version, *A general's story – from an era of war and peace*.

It was an uncomfortable time to write a story like this, because on 2 February 1990 South Africa had taken a quantum leap into the future, and in the weeks and months that followed the situation and the thinking changed faster than in all the previous years and decades.

I have not modified that original story for this edition in any substantial way. Changes relate mainly to structure rather than content, although here and there are minor explanatory additions for the benefit of a newer and wider potential audience, a few small corrections have been made and I have added a final chapter and various new annexures.

But it remains what it was: a story about life. A story about people, about friends and enemies: people who opened up the way ahead and people who went down that new path; about great people who turned out to be small, and small people who turned out to be great.

*　*　*

There are people who would like secretly to think that we were beaten on the battlefield during what is now popularly called the 'bush war'. Even at this latest time of writing, 2007, they are still fossicking about in the embers of a war which is now past and long since burnt out. They hunt for defeats and hidden misdeeds by the winners, and look for angels and forgotten glories on the side of the losers.

They are a pathetic sight in their suits of sackcloth and ashes. The last shoot-outs of the Cold War ended in 1988 – two decades ago. It is time for everyone to accept the facts.

The global Cold War was an intertwined conglomeration of politics, propaganda campaigns and warfare. In southern Africa the shooting war ended in 1988 with a wave of Cuban defeats in the Angolan bushlands. And in Europe, hot on the heels of these events at our back door, the political war ended with the collapse of the Berlin Wall and the disintegration of the Soviet Union.

Fables
A couple of decades after the fact, one wishful thinker after another, in books, newspapers, magazines and radio and TV programmes, is engaged in revealing alleged secrets and intrigues which belong in the realm of fables. They claim that we lost the bush war against the Cubans, and that we left behind great numbers of South African soldiers and combat aviators in shallow graves, and concealed mass burial sites of our victims near the erstwhile border base of Eenhana in Namibia … All ancient and nonsensical propaganda stunts which are being dished up for a new audience.

Facts
No nation, and that includes the Cubans, would tolerate the execution by firing-squad of its best army general (General Arnaldo Ochoa

x

Sanchez) just after the bush war, especially not when the general commanding their air force had just fled to Miami, Florida.

It is common knowledge that if more than 40 South African combat aircraft had been shot down in Angola, aircrew and all, and more than 1 000 troops killed – as was alleged in the *Beeld* newspaper – the voting public would have rebelled, and the then South African government would have fallen. (Incidentally, it is a delicate matter to talk lightly of casualties, and in a radio interview I requested that we wait for the reaction of the next of kin of all the dead who were supposed to be buried in 'shallow graves' in Angola to discover the truth. There was no reaction to this suggestion, although the accusations continue.)

The 'mass graves' in Namibia were, ironically enough, the tragic consequence of the United Nations peace-keepers' dereliction of duty at the end of the bush war. They were supposed to protect the cease-fire agreement from insurgent infiltrators. They did not, despite the fact that we gave them early warning of what was happening!

So at the beginning of April 1989, there was another outburst of fighting, the so-called 'Nine-Day War', when a large number of SWAPO infiltrators contravened the cease-fire agreement and in the process suffered heavy losses – the result being the mass graves at Eenhana. The South African police and air force helicopters saved the situation. The dead insurgents were buried under UN control and in full view of the media and the public. There was nothing secret about it, and if it was denied (as the media allege) by someone like Martti Ahtisaari, the former 'Special Representative' of the UN Secretary-General, he was either playing very recklessly with the truth or simply telling ordinary blatant lies.

It is ironic that in 2007 one must still rely on an unamended manuscript of yesterday's events to find the bracing truth behind today's panel-beaten lies. The first-hand eyewitness truth is available, and I am very proud of the fact that the first edition of this book remains one of the best original sources of truth about the war.

It is also highly regarded by Dr Chester Crocker, United States Deputy Secretary of Foreign Affairs for Africa, who was the neutral facilitator of the final negotiations between the Republic of South Africa, the USSR, Cuba and Angola. Crocker calls it the work of 'a professional's professional'.

The political situation

I retired as Chief of the South African Defence Force on 31 October 1990, just after the end of the Cold War. My book contains my life-story, but it is especially a personal witnessing of South Africa's experience of the Cold War between 1970 and 1990. I participated in that war in key positions of leadership, authority and responsibility, from the beginning to the end.

One of the Cold War's great episodes was the story of South West Africa's constitutional development to independence. From my perspective the United Nations and its stubborn, muddle-witted commissioner, Sean McBride, played no significant early role; much later, the single greatest and unnecessary mass killing of the entire story took place on 1 April 1989 as a result of the dereliction of its much-vaunted 'Special Representative', Martti Ahtisaari.

It is true that the Western 'Big Five' (the USA, Canada, the United Kingdom, France and Germany) achieved some breakthroughs at first, but later their wilfulness caused a 10-year delay in South West Africa's international constitutional development.

SWAPO, the South West African People's Organisation, made its external contribution to independence, but its then leader, Sam Nujoma, is still suspected – along with Ahtisaari – of complicity in the deaths caused by his organisation's violation of the ceasefire in April 1988.

It is not my style to praise politicians, but a revolutionary war is a political war, and if there were political heroes in this matter, they were John Vorster, Prime Minister of South Africa; P W Botha, Vorster's successor and later State President of South Africa; Dirk Mudge, the Namibian political leader; and Ronald Reagan, President of the United States.

Initially Vorster indicated the new political direction for South West Africa with the guideline 'South Westers themselves must decide about their future', which in the modern democratic dispensation meant one person, one vote. Dirk Mudge then took the lead in turning Vorster's guideline into reality.

The Big Five promoted the UN Security Council's Resolution 435, which was supposed to arrange for South West Africa/Namibia's independence ... but did not.

In turn P W Botha accepted the resolution, but wisely refused to give permission for its implementation, for which he was severely taken to task at the time. But the resolution demanded the withdrawal of all South African forces from Namibia, while making no corresponding provision about the withdrawal of Cuban troops in Angola, who outnumbered the South African military presence by more than two to one.

The presence of the Cubans, some of the proxy troops Cuba deployed all over the world in those days (as long as the Soviet Union's money and will held out), would have disturbed the balance of power and created a situation of great danger, and so Botha made their withdrawal a condition for ours.

The courageous Mudge knew, during those first few days of revolutionary violence in SWA/Namibia, that the time was not ripe for independence. A couple named Walters had been cruelly murdered at Okahandja in the presence of their children; other victims of political murder included Minister Philemon Elifas in 1975, Minister Toivo Shiyagaya in 1978, the prominent political leader Clemens Kapuuo in 1978, Minister Shikongo and Chief Minister (Pastor) Cornelius Ndjoba in 1980, as well as more than 20 tribal chiefs.

On the one hand, the winds of disappointment kicked up by the events in new African states which had swiftly received independence after 1960 fostered little enthusiasm for an acceleration of the political process. On the other, many uninformed people and wishful thinkers believed, or wished in their heart of hearts, that revolutionary violence would triumph in Namibia. But it did not.

The military situation

The South African Defence Force and the nascent SWA Territory Force had the task of making possible the fulfilment of the constitutional development process. This meant that they had to prevent a violent revolutionary take-over by creating and maintaining stability, order and security.

The first hot episode of the Cold War in the then South West Africa was Blou Wildebees (Blue Wildebeest), a combined police–SADF preemptive operation which took place at Ongulumbashe on 26 August 1966. Operation Blou Wildebees symbolised a particular period of 20 years in South Africa's counter-insurgency campaign over Namibia, a period during which we took the lead.

The 'Nine-Day War' proved that P W Botha had been right, and had rescued the situation by anticipating what would happen. One can imagine what the result would have been if some of the 52 000 Cuban troops in Angola had become involved in this disgraceful cross-border foray in their customary manner of that time.

A large chunk of history was written between the operation at Ongulumbashe in 1966 and the mass burials at Eenhana in 1989, and I have recorded it in this book.

But to return to politics. Abroad the Western Five and the UN caused 10 years of political stagnation through their stubborn refusal to accommodate Botha's reasonable objection. Internally, Mudge played a leading role in 10 years of significant domestic constitutional development.

Then the next hero appeared on the scene: Ronald Reagan. He accepted Botha's position and ended the stalemate. His Secretary of State, George Schulz, and Schulz's super-diplomat, Chester Crocker, concluded a peace settlement and ceasefire agreement (the Geneva Protocol) which had the UN's sanction.

This time a Cuban withdrawal *was* included, just as Botha had wanted; that was the spark which eventually led to the salutes being fired over an independent Namibia.

Those who won

The Afrikaans version of this book, as I have mentioned, was and is entitled *Dié wat wen* (Those who win). There is a reason for that title. During the 1970s and 1980s I had to listen with monotonous regularity to statements, especially by foreign journalists, that a country under attack from a revolutionary force with Soviet support, and on top of that the active participation of the Cubans, did not have a hope! But they didn't really know us then, and so what they anticipated did not happen in Namibia and South Africa.

In the Angola of 1988 the South African alliance's victories over the Soviet/Cuban forces at the Lomba River and the Techipa region were the last nails in the proverbial coffin of the Soviet-led Cold War. After that Cuban troops vanished from the international scene and the Soviet Union decamped from Eastern Europe. Neither the Cubans nor anyone else marched through the streets of Windhoek or Pretoria, as had been predicted.

To a large extent our successes can be ascribed to the fact that we never sat back and waited to be attacked. We always took the initiative and carried the struggle to the insurgents, as in the case of Ongulumbashe, despite all the criticism that resulted.

That is why Namibia and South Africa bore almost no scars of war when their respective movements towards political settlements began.

It was all worth the effort, and it was the proud attainment of all those in South African uniform – those who won.

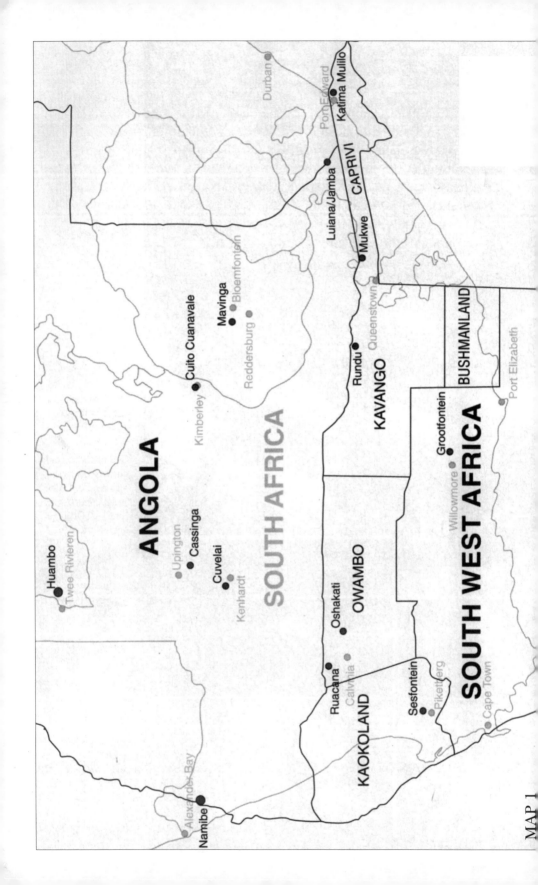

MAP 1

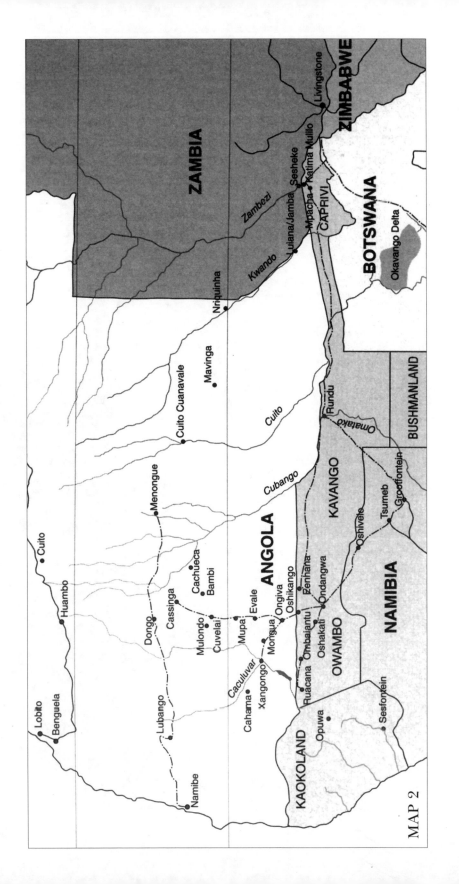

MAP 2

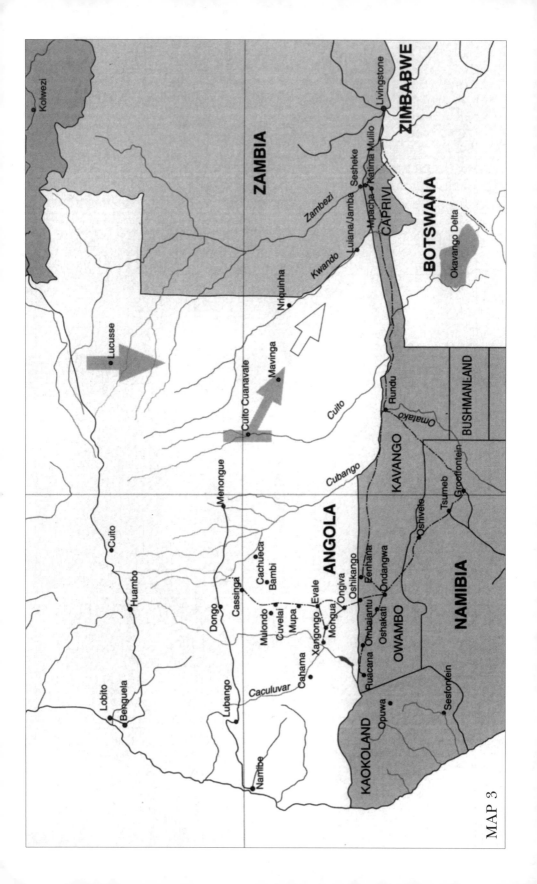

MAP 3

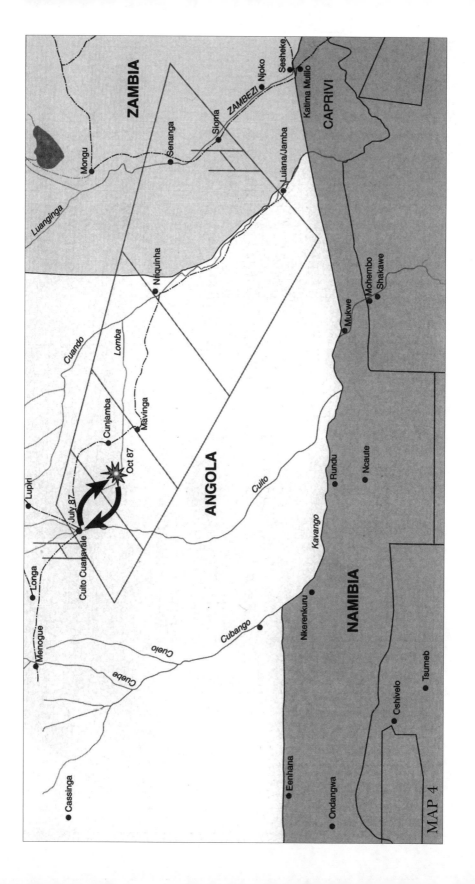

MAP 4

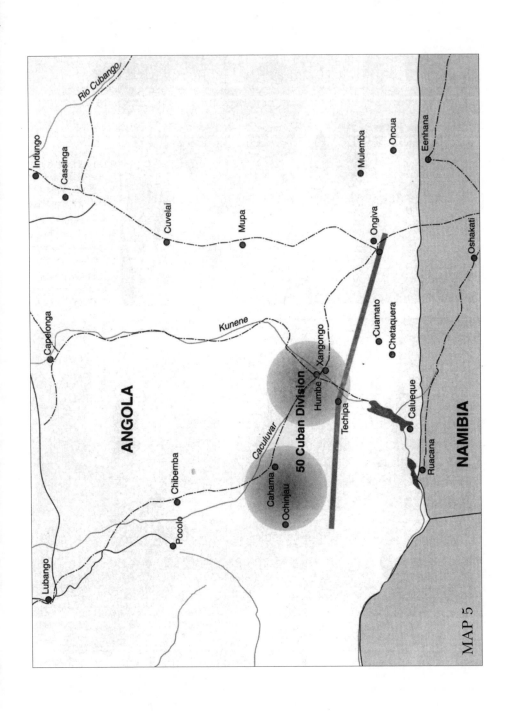

MAP 5

CHAPTER 1

THE END AND THE BEGINNING

The ABC of war and peace – fortune and misfortune

'I warn you, we are on the brink of a devastating war!' The warning was issued by my Cuban counterpart, General Ulises Rosales Del Toro. Seated next to him was his staff officer, who was also acting as his interpreter. At my side were General Neels van Tonder and my personal staff officer, Brigadier Johann Sonnekus.

It was 4 May 1988, and we were sitting in a small, sparsely furnished private lounge in Brown's Hotel, London. The occasion was an informal meeting during the Angola/South West Africa negotiations. We had been attending the first in a long series of drawn-out peace-making conferences.

During this conference the leader of our delegation was super-diplomat Neil van Heerden. Other members of the team were Dr Niël Barnard of National Intelligence and Derek Auret of Foreign Affairs.

The leader of the Cuban delegation was Jorge Risquet (whose beard, incidentally, had earned him the nickname of Oom Kaspaas – a character in a South African comic strip.) His team included Señor Carlos Aldana Escalante and General Rosales.

The Angolans' team was led by their Minister of Foreign Affairs,

Afonso van Dunem, assisted by the Deputy Minister of Defence and Chief of Staff, General Antonio dos Santos Franca, better known as Ndalu; according to certain observers, such as Fred Bridgland, the Cubans and Angolans were really part of the same delegation.

Chester Crocker, the United States Assistant Secretary of State for Africa, acted as chairman. We suspected that the Russian envoy, Anatoliy Adamishin, was waiting somewhere in the wings, and this suspicion later proved to be correct.

When we were adjourning on 4 May, at the end of the conference, I received a personal message from Rosales: he wanted to talk to me. Privately.

He started our informal meeting in the small lounge by saying that he wasn't threatening me and that he merely wished to warn me. But then, for almost half an hour, he told me through the interpreter that the Cubans had been mustering a large force comprising their best troops, and that they were concentrated in the south-west of Angola, just north of the South West African (now Namibian) border. They were ready for us. Not even the Namibian border would stop them.

In effect he was saying: If you do not use this opportunity to make peace and if you do not fall into line, you are in for a big war – a war that will destroy you.

He was calm, but very serious. He talked without notes, in measured words and sentences. Now and again he would move forward slightly and widen his eyes to accentuate the gravity of his words. He ended in a tone that said: I've had my say, what do you think?

I met his eyes. What did I see – challenge and expectation, hope and ... fear?

It was drizzling outside. A thousand and one thoughts were racing through my mind. He had mentioned war and peace in the same breath as if they went hand in hand. But peace and war are poles apart. However, negative and positive poles will attract one another – the threat of war and the hope of peace. I thought of our troops in Angola and South West; of *Blackmail or War* by Genevieve Tabouis. Was Rosales serious? Would they invade South West Africa? Did Fidel Castro aim to crush the South African forces decisively and so bring an end to the war? Was it blackmail?

My feeling was that the Cubans were trying to bluff their way out of the defeats that their alliance had suffered on the battlefield, and at the same time bluff their way into a strong negotiating position at the conference table. We did not have to allow ourselves to be intimidated. Suddenly the picture of Foreign Minister Pik Botha in action on a particular day about four years earlier came into my mind's eye.

*   *   *

Foreign Minister Pik Botha was the leader of the South African delegation during a round of negotiations between South Africa, Angola and the United States in Lusaka on 13 February 1984. The venue was the Mulungushi Conference Centre, which had been made available to us by President Kenneth Kaunda. The aim was to negotiate a cessation of hostilities. It was just after the end of South Africa's Operation Askari in Angola. We had actually already withdrawn, but had had to return, crazy as it might seem, to negotiate our withdrawal. But the negotiations comprised more than that. The talks eventually led to the Mulungushi Declaration and the Lusaka Agreement, over which a joint monitoring commission would play watchdog.

Mr Botha, his aides, my accompanying officers and I had met in advance to discuss how we would conduct the discussions in Lusaka, and Mr Botha had decided on a certain approach.

The negotiations began. One must remember that Pik Botha was a super diplomat de luxe – the longest serving Minister of Foreign Affairs in the world at that time. He was a man who could think on his feet. He was flexible. He was unpredictable. He came up with surprises. He often surprised his own side. That day he would do it once again.

Before the formal conference was opened he had had informal talks with the other parties (this was not an unusual procedure), and his superb insight into the mood of the opposition had made him abandon the approach that had been decided upon earlier, something I was unaware of.

When the conference started I sat doodling in my notebook, because I thought I knew what Pik Botha was going to say. But when he took the floor, his deep, resonant voice captivated every person present. He took the entire audience on a journey into the past in a compelling and passionate speech. He spoke of how the South African republics had

3

resisted the might of Great Britain, the strongest military power in the world at that time, for three years from 1899 to 1902 ...

The rest of the conference is history. An agreement was successfully concluded. I accept part of the blame.

*　*　*

It was this episode that came to mind four years later in London. I stared intently at Rosales ... and then pulled a 'Pik Botha' on him.

I, too, spoke to Rosales of the Boer War. In the process I reminded him that Cuba was a small island, far away from the African continent. Waging a war thousands of kilometres away from home was extremely difficult and expensive. And if they should now dare to set one foot across the border to take us on, on our own turf – we, who for three years had braved the mightiest power in the world – it would be the blackest day in Cuban military history.

Despite his threat, Rosales was not militarily impolite. Neither was I. Waging war and making peace involve the unravelling of many intrigues. One dare not allow oneself to be intimidated or conned. But one should never take reckless risks either. One must remain calm, calculated and responsible.

I believed that Rosales felt the same, and that is why I said to him: 'Let's not be unsporting; let's forget about threatening each other, and let's concentrate on the issue at hand.'

And that was what we did from that day on. That grey London day was the beginning of the end of a long journey. It was a journey along roads and through crossroads that took us through good fortune and misfortune, joy and pain, truths and untruths – through an era of storms and quiet. That was the time of the ABC of War and Peace: Angolans, Boers (as SWAPO and the Angolans called South Africans), Cubans. The leading figures included Aldana, Botha, Crocker. Because the journey takes us through war and peace, I would like to devote some thought to those concepts before we go any further.

Peace. We have never understood it, not even in the time of Adam and Eve and the Fall. And even when we think we do, we do not know how to achieve and safeguard it. We keep studying the causes of war, but we

4

remain ignorant of the causes of peace. We learn of love and peace at a tender age, we are taught to cherish love and peace by the church and at school, but generation after generation continues to make peace and war, to love and to hate. The human race managed to work out how to put a man on the moon, and did so; but we have not yet learned how to live in peace with our neighbours. We will probably savour everlasting peace only in Heaven.

War. A certain exceptional aspect of war is ever-present. One does not hear of it often, but if we do not bear it in mind, we may well lose sight of the full meaning of the stumbling-blocks that we encountered on the road to war up to 4 May 1988 in London. It is a phenomenon that can decide the outcome of a war. It was formulated in the previous century by a German student of warfare, Carl von Clausewitz, as *friction de guerre* – the stress of war. In Von Clausewitz's words:

> Everything in war is very simple, but the simplest thing is difficult. The difficulties accumulate and end by producing a kind of friction that is inconceivable unless one has experienced war ... countless unforeseeable minor incidents combine to lower the general level of performance, so that one always fell far short of the intended goal ...
>
> Friction is the only concept that more or less corresponds to the factors that distinguish real war from war on paper ... None of the [military machine's] components is of one piece: each part is composed of individuals, every one of whom retains his potential of friction, [and] the least important of whom may chance to delay things or somehow make them go wrong.
>
> This tremendous friction ... brings about effects that cannot be measured, just because they are largely due to chance ...
>
> Action in war is like movement in a resistant element. Just as the simplest and most natural of movements, walking, cannot easily be performed in water, so in war it is difficult for normal efforts to achieve even moderate results.

This is *friction de guerre,* the stress of war. The accent often falls on 'countless unforeseeable minor incidents' that are 'largely due to chance'. There are people who argue that there is no such thing as 'chance', that everything is caused by something specific. They are right, of course. But in human terms, and for all practical purposes, chance is a fact of life (note that I do not refer here to acts of God, in which I believe).

I can illustrate one kind of chance by using rugby as an example. A rugby ball has an oval shape. A player kicks the ball high into the air. The exact way boot and ball make contact, the effects of air pressure, wind and temperature when the ball travels through the air, the exact manner in which it makes contact with the ground and other factors will make it bounce in a certain direction. But the player merely wants to kick the ball high into the air. He does not intend to make it hop in a specific direction. The ball may bounce in any direction, to the advantage of one player, or the disadvantage of another – this is chance.

I can illustrate another form of chance by using bridge as an example. Once during a game at Oshivelo in the then South West Africa, Johann Sonnekus was dealt the full suit of 13 clubs. The odds of this happening are less than one in 600 000 million. One's planning would never make provision for something with such a low probability. He benefited from it. He was fortunate – it was chance. Johann Sonnekus cannot be praised for the luck that came his way.

In the same way, the rugby player cannot be blamed for the ball that bounces the wrong way. But there are times when one holds someone else responsible for a chance happening. However, the degree of culpability is sometimes so small as to make it excusable in human terms.

Take the player for whom the ball bounced the wrong way: An opponent grabs it and scores. Something of this nature can happen to anyone. The more players in the team, the greater the possibility of accidents happening to a number of them, which could result in a weaker team winning a game against a stronger side. We tend, however, to conveniently identify and tag excusable mishaps when they cause opponents to score points, but we don't really take notice of those which do not lead to points, the cumulative effect of which can be just as decisive as the more obvious 'blunders'.

Injury to a key player in a strong team, a player skidding on a wet patch, a ball hitting the crossbar and bouncing back, errors of judgment by the referee – all these cases of 'bad luck' often lead to a team losing the advantage. It is then that we say that we were beaten by the bounce of the ball; that we just had bad luck; that that is the way things happen. Or we say we made too many mistakes; the team that makes the least errors is the one that wins; or that the opponents made better use of their opportunities – the team that takes advantage of its chances is the team that wins. However, we should not forget that the element of chance, *friction de guerre,* was also present here.

That is sport. But in war there are other aggravating factors. War is not a game you play on a standard tennis court or rugby field – you may even have to fight for the terrain you selected for battle. The teams do not play with the same standard cricket bat. If you want to use a wider bat, that's your decision. And if your opponent chooses to hurl an iron ball at you, he is free to do so. And people shoot at each other. To kill. To destroy. To conquer.

And when a battalion fights, there are a thousand individuals each of whom can 'slip on a bad patch', who can 'fumble while the ball bounces the wrong way', who may 'tighten the wrong screw'. Perhaps this is what a British officer meant when he told me in 1960: 'In a future war, I suppose we'll muddle through to victory again!'

There is the chance that anything can go wrong with any one of 1 000 men in a task force. If you like, call it Murphy's Law (which states that if anything can go wrong, it will) or *friction de guerre;* it doesn't matter. If you and those with you suffer more than your fair share of mishaps caused by chance, you are in danger of losing.

The outcome of a few excusable 'blunders' can be frightening. Jeff Dewar says that 99,9 per cent effectiveness, let's say 0,1 per cent *friction de guerre* in South Africa, could mean two unsafe aircraft landings every week, 1 600 pieces of mail lost by the Post Office hourly, 2 000 faulty medical prescriptions per year and 1 000 cheques posted against the wrong accounts daily.

One can scarcely imagine what might happen in a war involving military equipment, weapons, ammunition, explosives – and an enemy.

Everyone I have encountered on the road of peace and war, through good fortune and misfortune, will confirm this: seniors, equals and juniors; commanders and their staffs; warrant officers, non-commissioned officers and troops; men and women in uniform and in civvies; people of all races, members of the Army, Air Force, Navy, Medical Services and Special Forces; people of South Africa, South West and Angola from all walks of life who made a contribution in whatever part of southern Africa or wherever – each had had the potential to have been unlucky. They have had experiences that only those who have had similar experiences will understand. They have learnt what separates real war from the war game. They have suffered the strains of all those countless unforeseen incidents which make the simplest of acts difficult in war.

And so now I come to the beginning of the beginning – the story leading up to 4 May 1988 and thereafter.

CHAPTER 2

FIRST STEPS TO KNOWLEDGE

Style is good, but it's better to win

This story begins in the 1930s, amid threats of war and promises of peace – a time of drought, depression, misery and unemployment. Young people were looking for work, amongst others at the railways and in the ranks of the 'SSB', as it was referred to in both English and Afrikaans, the Special Service Battalion.

The SSB was a very special unit, unique in South Africa's military annals. Established as one of the tools by which South Africa could drag itself out of the unemployment and malaise caused by the Great Depression, it rapidly built a towering reputation for itself as the smartest and most efficient regiment in the then Union Defence Force.

I was born on 5 February 1935 on the farm Dansfontein in the Kroonstad district, the second son of Barend Petrus (Ben) and Anna Geldenhuys. I became aware of the concepts of war and peace early on in my childhood. Old photographs still remind me of how my father and other farmers played at soldiers, as it were, as members of the local Defence Rifle Association. But I was imbued with the message of peace and love, especially from my mother, the finest person I have ever known.

The first few years of my life were peaceful. The worst thing that happened to me was when, as a toddler, I pushed a .22-calibre cartridge into our car's cigarette-lighter socket. It exploded and the sharp edge of the cartridge-case stabbed into my right eye. My father was extremely upset, but *friction de guerre* was on my side, and I suffered no permanent damage.

The year 1939 saw the release of David O Selznick's film 'Gone with the Wind', and it was a prophetic title, because in Europe the winds of war were blowing. World War II broke out that year, South Africa declared war on Germany, my father went on full-time duty in the Union Defence Force and we moved to Pretoria. That was the beginning of a nomadic existence as we moved around from one place to another.

It was only much later that I learned about the internal political repercussions of South Africa's decision to go to war. The Prime Minister of the coalition government, General J B M Hertzog, and his supporters were against fighting on the side of Great Britain and wanted the country to remain neutral, but his deputy, General J C Smuts, took the opposite view.

On 4 September 1939 Smuts won the debate on participation by a margin of 11 votes in the House of Assembly, took over the reins from Hertzog and declared war on Germany. My father was a Smuts man, a 'Sap' (a supporter of Smuts's old pre-coalition South African Party). People like him, who joined up and volunteered for service outside the country's borders – in those days no South African soldier could be compelled to serve abroad – wore red tabs on the shoulder-straps of their uniforms.

My father initially served in a mounted regiment and later in the South African Instructional Corps. His family became camp-followers as he was transferred from one place to another until he eventually went 'up North', as going on active service was called. That is why I never played around in the streets of Pretoria like the other children – we moved to Piet Retief two months after arriving there.

The war actually passed me by. However, during that time I learnt other truths, like the story of my little friend Rosalie, whom I met at Piet Retief. At first I spoke to her in Afrikaans, but she never responded, and I concluded that she did not understand Afrikaans. So I tried English. She still did not reply. I wondered whether it was just my kind of English that she didn't understand; but I persevered. But Rosalie was deaf and dumb. It never occurred to me that some people could not hear and therefore could not speak.

One of my father's colleagues was a certain Captain Porky van Rensburg – probably an allusion to his impressive size – who was the adjutant of the regiment. One day the commanding officer and Porky were summoned to Defence Headquarters in Pretoria. Everybody wondered why. On the evening of their expected return some of the officers gathered to have a few drinks while waiting for them to arrive, since they were obviously keen to hear what new developments had taken place.

Then one of the wives appeared and said: 'You don't have to wait any longer, we've just heard over the Zeesen German news broadcast that the Regiment is going to be transferred to Ladysmith.' That was the news everyone had been waiting for!

And so we moved from Piet Retief to Ladysmith, where the regiment was converted from horses to armoured cars while we camp followers stayed in a boarding house inside the walls of an old fort. Porky's son Herman, who was known to everyone as 'Boytjie', or 'Little Boy' – a typically South African blending of Afrikaans and English – now played at war with myself and the other children living at the fort.

I started school in Ladysmith. Here, again, I was given the message of love and peace every morning, when we were gathered in the courtyard for scripture-reading. Sometimes the message was slightly cryptic, though. By the end of the year I was singing along with the other children, rendering the English words into phonetic Afrikaans. One beautiful song, as rendered by me, went:

> *La la la ... einjils seeheeng*
> *La la la ... and muhseemaail*
> *La la la ... sinnirsrekonsaail*

I did not know what it meant. But it was beautiful and full of goodness. Then, many years later, I realised that it was 'Hark the herald angels', and the real version of my phonetic words were:

> *Hark the herald angels sing*
> *Peace on earth and mercy mild*
> *God and sinners reconciled ...*

At Ladysmith I participated in athletics for the first time. Seven of us took part in the 75 yards race. For some reason I took off my shoes but

11

not my socks, and by the end of the race they were flapping around like two sausages. At home I told my mother that I had won seventh place.

* * *

When my father was sent 'up North' we moved to Frankfort, where we stayed with my mother's sister, Aunt Maggie Frohlich, who was the owner of the Good Hope Café and was married to an English-speaking South African of German descent. Here I continued my school career in all seriousness and passed Sub A. But once again I did not fish barbel in the Wilge River or play among the hills of Frankfort with the other children for long, because we soon moved to Bethlehem. My mother, whose maiden name was Bruwer, had grown up in this district, and most of her family still lived there.

Bethlehem is a picture of dams, streams and weeping willows, set against the foothills of the Drakensberg range. It is the world of the sun-gazing girdle-tailed lizards known as the '*Ouvolk*' (Old Nation), of the north-eastern Free State, the '*riemland*': a mosaic of farmlands with maize and potatoes in summer and waving wheat fields in winter, the time when you freeze to death!

By the time I started my second year at school, I had learnt that there were white people and black people; there were people who could speak and people, like Rosalie, who could not; people who spoke but said nothing; people who could hear but did not listen. I had also discovered in Frankfort that some people supported the English and some the Germans, and in Bethlehem I relived the trauma of making new friends.

You would be asked: 'Are you for the English or are you for the Germans?' If your answer was unacceptable you did not fit in, and if you did not fit in you were bullied. As the son of a red tab I preferred to keep my mouth shut. If I had to, I'd say: 'but Jannie Smuts really is quite clever', which seemed to pacify everybody.

I also learned something else: If you were an achiever it did not matter much whether you were for the English or the Germans. I was good at backyard and playground games, and with my new-found lightness of foot – having got rid of the handicap of flapping socks – I also did well at athletics. Now, at last, I could walk to school in peace with the other children, play in the streets of the town and go fishing at Loch Athlone and Loch Lomond.

My mother was a teacher at the primary school. In those days of rationing and petrol coupons she committed what was probably the only crime of her life: she sieved flour to make white bread! If anybody knocked at the door while this crime was being perpetrated, we would all scatter hastily to hide the evidence, although for all we knew it was just a neighbour wanting to borrow the sieve.

During school terms we stayed in the town, but we spent all our holidays and weekends with my grandfather and grandmother, Jan and Annie Bruwer, on their farm 'Davelsrus', which lay at the foot of huge ochre and crimson cliffs between Clarens and Kestell on the other side of the Golden Gate mountains. My best friend on the farm was Matjarapan. I was called Motle. I often wonder what became of him.

At Davelsrus there still smouldered memories of their experiences during the 'English War', as they called the Anglo-Boer War of 1899–1902, and I remember my grandmother telling me about their life in the British concentration camps. In 1989, 90 years after the beginning of the Anglo-Boer War, Padre Dawie Scheepers, a distant relative of mine, brought me a letter that my great-grandfather had written to my great-grandmother during the war:

Ladysmith, 9 November 1899

M M du Plessis
My dearest and never-forgotten wife and children.
  By the Grace of God I am still alive, and I hope you are, too.
  I have received your letter, which, like a drop of cold water, quenched my thirsting soul. My longing for you is so profound that no words can describe it.
  My darling, you must not stop writing to me as long I am still alive, because the thundering of the guns never ceases and every moment could be the last.
  We hope that our circumstances will improve if we achieve victory at Ladysmith.
  Our side has 15 dead and 04 wounded. Tomas is dead. My dearest wife, you write that you are becoming impatient, but you must rather pray.
  Jan is also here, and if he goes back I will ask him to hire a man

13

and send him here. Because I cannot be released from my duties here and we do not know when the war will end, you will have to have the sheep sheared.

All our friends are well and there is so much to write that I do not know what to say.

And if you can perhaps find a man to hire to take my place, you must do so and send him here. It would make me very happy because I yearn for you, my love. I long for you. If only I could be with you for a few hours, I'd be so happy to see your face again. And my children?

How is Koos?

Now I shall end, but never with my yearning heart. My deepest regards, my dearest wife and children.

W du Plessis, Address Bester Stasi Naudé laager

The Boer leaders, incidentally, quickly put a stop to the practice mentioned in the letter of hiring a burgher to take one's place in the commando.

The 'Jan' to whom my great-grandfather refers was probably my grandfather. 'Koos' was probably my Uncle Koos du Toit of Kestell, who used to tell me stories while feeding his lizards on the verandah. He enjoyed reliving the cricket 'test' matches that they, the prisoners of war, had played against the English in Ceylon – or was it St Helena? I also heard about Hans van Rensburg of the Ossewa Brandwag (OB) when the grown-ups whispered about politics. The OBs were secretly planning to sabotage Smuts's war policy. I knew very little about all this and understood even less.

But the song of peace was there, too. During family prayers my mother used to play the piano and we would all sing. Once I was allowed to choose the hymn, so I suggested that we sing the one about the little car that rode over the mountains ... by which I meant 'Oor berge en in dale, en overal is God' (over mountains and in valleys and everywhere is God).

With my cousins also visiting the farm during the December holidays, I experienced all the conflict and competitiveness that children normally indulge in, especially boys. You had to prove that you were a man. A boy didn't feel pain, because he was a boy. A boy didn't cry, because he was a boy. He must be able to crack a whip; he must have a penknife; he must know how to cut riempies (thin leather thongs), milk cows and shoot. You shot with a pea-shooter, a catapult or a clay-stick, and if you shot with a .22 or actually had your own, then you were really a man.

But unfortunately it went further at times. One day at school, during the long break, a friend of mine called Kobus Colyn and I were goaded into a fight. I still believe the bell saved me that day.

I was often the youngest and the smallest, and so I always had to do the dirty work. But I learned fast: as long as someone is in a position to further his own cause, to prove his manliness or to acquire status, he will do just about anything – and then *you* don't have to do it. I found that if I didn't compete with them and left them alone, the bigger boys would cut the riempies and milk the cows. This gave them the opportunity to demonstrate their skills and prove that they were men.

But there are men and men. My brother, Johan, otherwise known as 'Ouboet' (Old Brother, the traditional Afrikaans nickname for the senior male sibling), who was three-and-a-half years my senior, has reminded me of how I once dealt with the well-known Dutch artist and adventurer Hans Seubring, who used to hawk his paintings from farm to farm and school to school.

Seubring was a real *man*, more than seven feet tall, and when we were in the farm outbuilding one day after he had arrived at Davelrus told us that he could do something we could not. We asked him what that was, and he put up his arm and pressed his hand against the ceiling. I took up the challenge and told him that I could do something that he couldn't. 'What?' he asked. And I walked through the door without bowing my head.

Those days we went around barefoot, and because of all the time spent playing without shoes the soles of our feet became hard and tough; so tough that when you had run across a field full of devil's thorn and reached the other side, you didn't sit down to remove the thorns, you just stood and wiped your feet on the grass.

In winter, of course, the skin under our heels and big toes cracked. I didn't realise how unsightly this looked until one day when I was lying on my stomach on the warm cement at the edge of the municipal swimming pool, cracked country-bumpkin feet and all, basking in the sun.

Then a couple of English-speaking girls walked past behind me, and I heard one of them say in disgust: 'Gosh, look at that boy's feet!' I was so ashamed of myself that from that day on I always picked a spot on the grass where I could lie with my soles up against the perimeter wall.

When I started going to high school and had to participate in sport more regularly I could not go to the farm as often and became more of a townie. During some of my school holidays I worked as a night-duty petrol attendant at Oom Frans Furstenburg's Central Garage, which was on the main road to Durban, and here I added a great deal to my store of knowledge about people and human nature.

I always got the jitters when someone told me to 'fill her up', because with the old pumps it was quite tricky work not to spill the last bit of petrol. I discovered that when this happened some of the more obviously well-to-do people would pay me a penny or a tickey (three pennies) short, 'for the petrol you spilt on the ground', whereas when this happened with some people who seemed rather on the needy side they would actually tip me a penny or a tickey.

*　*　*

When the war ended my father, who was a captain by then, was transferred to the Demobilisation Depot in Pretoria. But a short while later he suffered a stroke and died, and my mother moved back to Bethlehem with us.

At Bethlehem I got my first glimpse of important people. That was in 1947, when King George VI, the Queen and the two princesses visited South Africa. The Smuts-supporting 'Sap' newspapers made a fuss of the Royal Family, while the ones supporting the opposition National Party ignored them.

One of the places the Royal Family visited was Bethlehem. This included an appearance at the Goble Park sports stadium, so that everyone could see them, including myself and Emily, our domestic. I remember that the King appeared to be at ease in his neat business suit.

Escorting them in his robe and chain of office was my Standard 6 teacher, Schalk van Niekerk, who was also the Mayor of Bethlehem. Afterwards my mother asked Emily what the King looked like. Very striking, Emily replied. Very nice; she liked the beautiful clothes the king wore, especially the chain!

Johan Steyl, who played rugby for the Free State, taught me mathematics and introduced me to the wonders of music. He was also the commanding officer of our school's cadet detachment, and I was the sergeant-major. He and Appels Odendaal, who played rugby for Eastern Province and Free State, taught me to play the game.

Koot Brits was the teacher who taught me the most about Afrikaans with the least effort. Miss Agnes Holtzhausen, who would later become principal of the Afrikaans Girls' High School in Pretoria, tried to teach me English, and if I am not a modest person it is not for lack of trying on her part. It was only now that I discovered that there was actually no such Afrikaans word as 'sepereiter', the Davelsrus name for the machine which separated the cream from fresh milk – the correct word was 'roomafskeier'. Kiep van Schalkwyk taught me history, and I enthusiastically shared the successes of Garibaldi and Napoleon with him.

I had good friends, especially among the sportsmen. I played in the same rugby team as three boys who later became Springboks: the well-known Tom (Karel) van Vollenhoven, the best three-quarter I've ever seen on a rugby-field, and Bennie van Niekerk, who toured the British Isles and France with the Springbok rugby team in 1960–1961. The third one was Hannes Botha, who later became a South African shot-put champion, professor in physical education at the University of Pretoria and President of the South African Amateur Athletics Union.

My cousin Antoinette, the daughter of my English-speaking South African uncle of German descent, was married to Alberto Claudio Scopetti, a former Italian prisoner of war who had made South Africa his new home, and they now lived in Bethlehem. Scopetti boxed and I keenly followed his example. I was most enthusiastic: on 31 May 1950 Viccie Toweel had beaten Manuel Ortiz of America on points over 15 rounds, making him the new bantamweight champion of the world.

Tom van Vollenhoven still points out that I ran the 220 yards hurdles with style, but that he beat me; on the other hand, I can reply that when it came to boxing I beat him, whether he had style or not (of course, he was small then). Another chap, Johnny McLaren, punched the living daylights out of me, but I was small then as well. Tom taught me that style was good, but that it was better to win.

17

Amongst the grown-ups of the district there were some big names. Doc Danie Craven of Lindley was a legend even then, not just as a Springbok and rugby expert but also as a highly respected military officer during the war. Doctors Tavi du Preez and James Gilliland would both become Deputy Surgeons-General of the Defence Force, and Jakkals Keevey was a rugby Springbok in the team that toured the British Isles and France in 1951/1952.

My earlier contact with military life continued. My brother was in the Citizen Force in the Regiment Louw Wepener, which was headquartered in Bethlehem. The Permanent Force officer at the headquarters was Captain W P Louw, later Officer Commanding Orange Free State Command and, still later, Chief of the Army. One of the Permanent Force instructors in the region was Staff Sergeant 'Umlaut' Lötter; our paths were to cross again much later, when I was in Windhoek and he was the commanding officer of the Grootfontein base.

I matriculated in 1952 without distinctions and without a first-class pass. Not to mention a D in geography. Bad teacher!

CHAPTER 3

MORE STEPS TO KNOWLEDGE

An open mind means wings on your ankles

In 1953, while Bing Crosby's 'Little Boy Lost' and 'Scared Stiff' bleated from jukeboxes all over the country, I began a year of voluntary training at the Military Gymnasium at Roberts Heights (by now it was already 'Voortrekkerhoogte', but at first I still called it by its old name, as my father had done). A year in the Army, I had decided, would give me time to decide what I wanted to do with my life.

The Pretoria railway station looked black and grimy when I arrived from Bethlehem with its clean air. Voortrekkerhoogte looked red and brickish. I felt lost and alone.

The first time out on the parade ground I, the former student sergeant-major, got the fright of my life. When the instructors, Sergeants Eric Pierce and Blackie Swart, formed us up, I didn't even realise they were speaking Afrikaans. Their commands were rattled like machine-gun fire; before I could react to the first burst the next had already been delivered.

A few days later some of us were ordered to report at the parade ground. There Staff Sergeant 'A-Jack' van Zyl informed us that we had been chosen to be the 'vuurparty' for a colonel. 'Vuurparty' literally means 'fire party', and I gathered that we had been detailed to make the fire at some barbecue or other.

As usual he drilled us for a while, just as a warming-up exercise, before we got to the real task at hand. After quite a few sessions of marking time and turning about at bewildering speed, however, I came to the conclusion that he was overdoing the warming-up somewhat. Then suddenly I realised what he was actually doing. He was preparing us to act as the ceremonial platoon which was to take part at a colonel's military funeral, and that included firing a salute over the grave. That was what the 'vuurparty' bit was about – we were going to be a firing party!

The one-year course that I was doing also served as the first year of a four-year officers' course, and it was murderous. The pace was much like the later three months' basic training at the beginning of a national service term, except that it lasted right through the year!

We invented 'taxis', two pieces of blanket, one for each boot, on which you shuffled around the bungalow so as not to scratch the mirror-like black floors. It cut the daily early-morning spit-and-polish ritual by a few minutes. I must say, however, in later years the troops always told me that 'basics' was the best time of their lives that they would never like to repeat.

During this year we were also required to register for two first-year academic subjects at the University of Pretoria, and I tried to play some rugby too. I made the Northern Transvaal Under-19 side as a replacement for the selected fly-half, who was not available, and during the latter part of the season I played for the senior Garrison team (Defence). My first match was against Police. Their team included Fiks van der Merwe, war veteran and Springbok flank forward in 1949, and Hansie Brewis, Springbok fly-half. I was still under 18.

At our passing-out parade at the end of the year, Major General H B Klopper took the salute. He was a piece of living military history – during World War II he had been the commander of the ill-fated South African contingent at Tobruk when it was captured by the Germans.

At the end of the year I decided to complete the full course and obtain a degree, and a small group of us – we were called 'cadets' then – stayed on at the college in 1954 as Course 322G. Magnus Malan, later Chief of the Defence Force and still later Minister of Defence, was then a senior cadet whose group completed the course a few months after our arrival. Constand Viljoen, later Chief of the Defence Force, was a year ahead of us.

By this time I had naturally become quite a bit wiser. For the second time I experienced the issuing of equipment. The staff sergeant read and marked off the items in a book, and the sergeant handed it over the counter.

'Braces, left and right – one and one. Bottles, water – one …'

I grabbed and packed everything away. The seniors were going to tease me for a rookie, I thought to myself, because all my brand-new clothing and equipment still smelled of the quartermaster stores.

'Bottles, water carrier – one. Belts, webbing – one …'

This special quartermaster's language tickled my sense of humour, and I soon found the opportunity to try my hand at it, too. This was when a special Saturday-morning inspection was called by the cadet wing commander, Major Dawid Schalk Pretorius. He was quite a character, a man of imposing appearance who was nicknamed 'Pieringoog' (Saucer-eye), or just 'Piering' because he had the habit of bugging his eyes at whomever he was addressing.

On this occasion Piering wanted to see not only our military gear but also the appropriate civilian clothes – a hat, a dress suit and so forth – which as would-be officers and gentlemen we were expected to acquire. This meant that in addition to presenting our military uniform in the prescribed manner in our rooms we also had to prepare a list of all our civilian clothes, which had to be placed at the foot of the bed so that each man's complete inventory could be checked.

I decided to list my civilian clothes in the quartermaster language, which was still fresh in my mind: 'Braces, left and right – one and one', 'glasses, looking, mirror – one; glasses, looking, mirror, stands – one' and so on. So I prepared my list of civilian clothes in similar vein: shoes, brown leather, civilian, pairs – one; shoes, black, conservative, pairs – one. Flannels, long, gentlemen's, pairs – one. Jackets, sports, sober – one. And so on. ...

My room was the second from the entrance. The major and his entourage walked into the first one, which was occupied by my friend Malcolm Baillie Anderson. The sergeant major shouted: 'Stand by your beds!' and I heard the loud stamping of Malcolm's feet as he came to attention. Bombastic questions were asked and feeble answers given.

Otherwise it was dead quiet, and suddenly I realised that this inspection was a serious affair. This meant that I had certainly gone too far with that list of mine. But it was too late now. There was no way that I could re-do it; and if I moved they would hear me.

When he was done with Malcolm's room, Piering walked into mine with his inspection group. I held my breath as he went straight for my list, picked it up and studied it. Then he turned to the sergeant major:

'Sergeant-major,' he said, 'look at this. Look at what this cadet has written,' and he passed on the list. The sergeant-major stared at it for a long while, marking time. The poor man was probably trying to work out what the major wanted to hear. At long last he muttered: 'Uh ... yes, I see, sir.' I stood dead still.

Then Piering bugged his eyes at me and declared dramatically: 'This cadet is obviously a born soldier!'

* * *

There were other interesting people at the Military College. One was Major Kuno van der Post. He was a dear man, and it is when you understand war and the military that you can appreciate how such a gentle man could feel at home in the Army. I had the pleasure of meeting other members of his family, such as the writer, Colonel Laurens van der Post, and his nephew, Tommy Bedford, the Springbok rugby captain.

Our training at the college was very broad. We were instructed in horse-riding at the Police College, taught to fence by Major Harry Schmidt and given lessons in judo and dancing. In our second year we underwent training in weapons and leadership, and took three further first-year university courses. After that we became second-lieutenants.

There were only eight of us at our passing-out parade. Two other members of our group, Ian Gleeson and Lourens Oosthuizen, would also become generals one day. Later, during my term as Chief of the Defence Force, General Gleeson was my number two.

We stayed on at the college for the second half of the four-year course and completed our second- and third-year university courses as full-time students at the University of Pretoria. The rest of our further military training was done on a part-time basis, on Saturdays and during university holidays.

The academic subjects I liked most, and which later stood me in good stead, were military history, military law, criminal law, law of evidence, international law, geo-politics, political science and economics. What I really learnt, in the words of Benjamin Disraeli, was that 'to be conscious that you are ignorant is a great step to knowledge'. I duly became aware of my ignorance and took a few steps towards acquiring knowledge.

We were the last group to do our academic training at the University of Pretoria. Thereafter the cadets went to the University of Stellenbosch, which led to the establishment of the South African Military Academy at Saldanha Bay.

Various exceptional people at the University of Pretoria made an important contribution to our education, such as At Pelser, F J du Toit Spies and Commandant (Dr) Cassie Bakkes of the History Department; and Jan Lombard, D G Franszen and Gerhard de Kock of the Economics Department (Franszen and De Kock both later became presidents of the Reserve Bank). E F W Gey van Pittius, the professor of political science, was an arch-democrat; it was said that he would *sjambok* you until you also became one. But that was not how I was 'democratised' – I was influenced rather more by his younger colleague, Charles Nieuwoudt. I admired their scientific approach, and I became an enthusiastic free marketeer.

Officers were supposed to be non-political, but there was no way in which politics could remain just an academic endeavour. By this time Dr D F Malan, Jan Smuts's bitter opponent during World War II, who had taken the National Party to power in 1948, had stepped down, but he had been succeeded by Hans Strijdom, and in 1953 there had been a general election. So party politics was on everybody's lips, and the 'red tab' days of World War II had not yet been quite forgotten. Even reading a newspaper at breakfast was no simple matter. If you read the *Rand Daily Mail,* you were a Sap; if you read the *Transvaler,* you were a Nat.

At Voortrekkerhoogte I found myself in a top-class sports community. Piering had been the South African hammer-throw champion before the war; the current champion (and probably the author of his nickname) was Captain Vic Dreyer, who had captained the Springbok athletics team at the 1954 Empire Games in Vancouver – one couldn't help noticing a

continued competitiveness between the two. Vic Dreyer, in turn, was succeeded by Staff-Sergeant Andy Botes. Retired super-athlete Snaar Viljoen
was always to be seen on the sidelines, and so were other Springboks like
the hurdler Poena Malan. John Short, the well-known shot-putter, who
was later to become an athletic coach and commentator, even played
rugby in those days – as a centre! My friend Thaba (-zimbi) du Plessis
became a pentathlon Springbok, and he and Major Harry Schmidt took
part in the 1956 Olympic Games in Melbourne.

For two years I played flyhalf for the Northern Transvaal Under-19
side; and I played club rugby for Garrison during the entire period of
my stay. After Saturday games we were expected to get together at the
Garrison clubhouse for a bit of socialising. Dancing was sometimes part
of the programme, but it was not one of my strong points, so I usually
did the rounds and chatted to everybody.

Inevitably this meant ending up at the bar and drinking beer. That
was the only drink I knew – in those days you ordered a ginger square
if you wanted to be a bit daring, but the men at the club felt ginger
squares were strictly for sissies.

I remember chatting with two of my Under-19 mates during one of
those evenings, noticing that they certainly weren't holding back on
the brandy and Coke, and thinking to myself: 'These chaps aren't serious about rugby. They're only Under-19, and look at them. They'll
never get anywhere.'

Well, it just happened that one was Ollie Ahlers and the other was
Frik du Preez, who was to become one of South Africa's all-time great
rugby players.

It was on the rugby field that I learnt another important lesson about
life – from a soccer player, Sergeant Sheehan-Shepherd. One day, while
we were kicking the ball around, friendly old big-mouth Sheppie saun-
tered up to us and said: 'You rugby guys are stupid. You don't play with
your brains and you don't even know the basic skills.'

Naturally everybody present wanted to crucify him, but he hastened
to add: 'Wait, wait! I'll show you how to kick at goal.'

In those days one would place the ball and walk backwards in a
straight line to measure the distance. The approach preceding the
kick was also in a straight line to the ball and goal posts. But Sheppie
took the ball, placed it on the halfway line, walked a dogleg backwards,

looked at the poles, ran up to the ball along a circular path and kicked it well over the crossbar between the uprights – in his tennis shoes!

Everybody was astonished and embarrassed. And Sheppie was off again with his big mouth: 'If you have an open mind you can do it with tackies, too.'

No rugby player had ever questioned the accepted style of kicking at the goal-posts, yet Sheppie had proved that his way could be more effective, although for some unknown reason a decade passed before it became the internationally recognised technique.

Why hadn't I taken the initiative? In those days one did not easily question accepted rules, especially in a military milieu. Yet, for progress to take place, accepted practices sometimes need to be challenged and replaced where necessary.

Sport played an important role throughout my military career, and I also found it very helpful in studying conflict (it is, after all, itself a form of conflict). And the primary role of the Defence Force, if it cannot prevent a conflict, is to win the ensuing confrontation when the time comes.

* * *

After the course, I and a few others were posted to our first regiments. As a pipsqueak second-lieutenant I arrived at Tempe in Bloemfontein in 1956 and reported to the unit of my choice, 1 Special Service Battalion Training Regiment, the renowned 'ssb' of my youth.

At that stage the ssb had an unusual structure. It had started out as an infantry regiment in the 1930s, was converted to armour during World War II and after the war was re-converted into a combined-arms training unit consisting of a squadron of armour, a company of infantry – B Company, to be precise – and a battery of field artillery. The ssb had a formidable reputation dating back to its formation in the 1930s, and I have always regarded this 'mother unit' of mine as a first-class regiment.

Several shocks lay in wait for me. The first was being told that I was to take over as regimental transport officer. The second was finding out that I had one surplus Sherman tank in stock. What did an infantry second-lieutenant do with a surplus Sherman tank?

Luckily the annual transfers necessitated some reorganisation, and I was transferred to B Company as a rifle platoon commander, so that the surplus Sherman became somebody else's problem. But that brought the third shock – my platoon was actually well over company strength.

My regimental commander was W R (Bossie) van der Riet, a veteran of World War II, and so I learned a lot about waging war in my time at 1 SSB. It was a privilege to train and do military manoeuvres in which all the combat elements – infantry, armour, and artillery – were combined in one force.

There was, of course, also the normal regimental routine: PT at six o'clock in the morning, followed by parades and so forth. On one occasion I was taking the daily early-morning parade with troops of the 1957 national service intake, the place being a newly mown field.

The drill was that at a certain point in the parade I would give the command: 'Remove headdress! Let us pray', at which all present would take off their caps and bow their heads while I read the Lord's Prayer. But this particular morning was slightly different from its predecessors. When I said: 'Remove headdress! Let us pray', I lost control of the dental plate which replaced two teeth, one removed by a recalcitrant Vickers medium machine gun at Voortrekkerhoogte and the other by an unfriendly boot during a rugby game at Oudtshoorn.

It flew out of my mouth and came to rest on the newly mown grass. Fortunately for me nobody noticed my discomfiture, since all heads and eyes except my own were bowed and closed respectively. So I quickly picked up the denture, replaced it, and read the Lord's Prayer.

Unfortunately cuttings from the previous day's mowing, still damp from the morning dew, now stuck to the plate, and I stood there looking like a goat with stalks of grass protruding from my mouth. Thus decorated, I went on to the next part of the parade, which was to shout 'Staff!' at which the staff-sergeant would march up to me and stand at attention while I gave him instructions for the day's training programme. Then I would order him to dismiss the parade. But this was no ordinary staff-sergeant. He was the renowned Frederick George Crumpton, a World War II veteran who was as hard as nails and sported a broom-like moustache.

At my shout of 'Staff!' Crumpton marched towards me with measured tread, pace-stick under his arm, halted, fixed me with his icy gaze and stood without moving a muscle as I gave him the instructions for the day. That done, I said: 'Dismiss the parade!'

Crumpton replied: 'I will comply with your instructions, sir, but before I do so, there's something I should like you to know, sir. I do not mind your reading the Lord's Prayer, sir, but next time you do so – finish your breakfast first ... sir!'

Every intake of recruits produced its own crop of strange incidents. The procedure for receiving the new arrivals was as follows: They were transported from the railway station in town to the Gym Hall in Tempe, where they were lined up in two long rows at the entrance. Inside they were individually enlisted at a number of registration tables and processed. This production line functioned right into the night until all the newcomers had been dealt with.

On one such night during the processing of the 1958 intake a group of sloppy chaps were ushered in by Sergeant-Major Ben Benade. They had obviously been celebrating their last day of freedom before being swallowed up by the Army, so that they were in a careless, jolly mood and seemed not at all interested in lining up properly.

This type of disorderly conduct immediately makes any sergeant-major spring into action. Sergeant-Major Benade shouted them into a state of dead silence and then formed them up neatly behind the other two lines. But when they eventually reached the registration tables their names did not appear on the lists. Their incoherent efforts to identify themselves didn't help.

Any sergeant-major worth his salt knows how to deal with cases of alcoholic incoherence, however, and Sergeant-Major Benade assured the company second-in-command: 'Never mind, Captain, these scallywags are so plastered we won't get anywhere with them tonight. We'll sort them out tomorrow after they've sobered up. In the meantime I'll put them in the cells for the night.' But on being questioned the next morning, the mysterious recruits explained that actually they weren't recruits at all, but residents of a suburb next to Tempe called Toevlug. They had returned by bus after seeing a movie in Bloemfontein, then got off at the stop next to the Tempe parade ground and had been strolling through the base on their way home when they had somehow fallen into the sergeant-major's hands!

Recruits were in the news in those days, thanks to a member of another country's 1958 intake who created quite a media furore when he reported for basic training on 24 March, after which he was turned into a lorry and jeep driver in the armoured corps before being posted to Germany ... none other, of course, than Elvis Presley, blue suede shoes and all. It didn't affect the course of the Cold War, but the world's most famous rookie went on to capitalise on his experiences with the movie 'GI Blues', which also starred the leggy South African-born dancer, Juliet Prowse.

One thing I came to know during my military career was that one's Army pals come and go, but your paths often cross again somewhere in the future. In my company there was a corporal called Herman van Rensburg, who was none other than Boytjie, the son of Porky van Rensburg of the Ladysmith days, with whom I had played at soldiers in the old fort. But now he was no longer Boytjie. He had grown into a sturdy fellow who was accurately known as 'Large'. And among my fellow officers were Lieutenants Raymond Holtzhausen, Charles Lloyd, Dirk Marais and Lourens Oosthuizen, all of whom played a role in my small world at 1 SSB and then at various later stages of my career.

In 1959, my last year at 1 SSB, a number of personalities who would later play important roles in shaping the destiny of southern Africa in the decades to come shot into the international headlines: in particular a guerrilla fighter called Fidel Castro, who occupied Havana on the first day of the new year after the dictator Fulgencio Batista had fled.

* * *

The end of the year brought the first of three new steps in my life, each following rapidly on the other. In December I was transferred to Pretoria and reported in at the South African Military College as an officer-instructor. In January I was promoted to the rank of captain, and on 6 February I married Marié Martins.

I stayed at the college until the end of December 1963, four of my best, toughest and most enjoyable years. One of my colleagues was Captain Dirk Marais, my old friend from 1 SSB, who was now the college adjutant, and I remember an incident from that era which tells one a lot about what sort of man he was.

When Colonel P J Jacobs had been the college's commanding officer he had laid down strict rules about where one could smoke. Then, while attending a conference at the college after his tour had ended, Dirk found him breaking his own sacred edict by smoking a cigarette while walking around outside among the rondavels and main buildings. Dirk accosted the colonel and politely requested him to refrain from smoking in the built-up area. This did not sit well with Colonel Jacobs, who flew into a rage and caused quite a scene. Subsequently Dirk was accused in some quarters of lacking in tact. But he was not. He was simply a decent man who acted according to the rules, regardless of the effect that it would have on his popularity.

Another interesting person who spent some time at the College, and whom I was to run into again, was the unique Jos Rossouw. When Jos joined the Army it was noted that he had a B Phys degree. Since the Defence Force needed people with a knowledge of physics he was sent to Potchefstroom as a new member of the South African Corps of Signals. But it did not go well with Jos at Potchefstroom. He had a few problems with radios and the like – apparently he once depolarised a whole batch of batteries in one shot, which caused considerable fury, and he was prohibited from ever touching Army batteries again. All became clear, however, when it was discovered during this process that his qualification had been misread. 'B Phys' stood for 'B Educationis Physicae'! As a result he was immediately transferred to Major Piering Pretorius's Physical Training Branch.

Jos and I sometimes worked together at the Infantry Branch of the college, and I got to know him well; his lectures often provided a great deal of light entertainment, particularly when he had not adequately prepared for them. On such occasions he would overcome the problem by employing a special technique he had worked out. He would ask himself a question aloud, then provide the answer as well. This technique had its merits, because apart from helping Jos through the lecture, the answer contained the information that the students needed to know.

On a day in January 1961, I remember, I slipped into the back of one of his classes in one of those of wood-and-corrugated iron buildings which had been erected by the British at the beginning of the century as temporary facilities but were still soldiering on. Jos was busy with one of his monologues. 'OK then, what kind of weapon do we get in the

mortar platoon?' he asked, and answered himself: 'In the mortar platoon we get the three-inch mortar.' From there on it went like this:

'What kind of weapon is it? It's an area weapon.'

'What does "area weapon" mean? It's used for bombing a wide
area.'

'What does one shoot at with this weapon? One shoots at enemy
troops in the open.'

Then he went on to the anti-tank platoon:

'And what kind of weapon do we have here? Here we have, among
others, the six-pounder anti-tank gun.'

'And what do we shoot with this gun? Not people ... Why not?'

Here he hesitated for a moment, realising that he had asked a poor
question, then quickly answered: 'Because they duck!'

After that it was the turn of the medium machine-gun platoon:

'Here we have the Vickers medium machine-gun. What is the maximum effective range of this weapon? During direct firing it can shoot
up to a maximum range of 2 800 yards, and during indirect firing up
to 4 500 yards – but then one has to have special ammunition.

'What kind of ammunition must one use? One must have ... Mark 7z
ammunition.' Now Jos hesitated again, then asked me: 'Gellie, old boy,
it *is* Mark 7z ammunition, isn't it?'

'Well, Jos,' I replied, 'now that you ask me, it's actually Mark 8z .'

'Oh yes, of course!' Jos said. 'I'd quite forgotten that we're already
in the new year. It's 1961 now. Last year we spoke of Mark 7z ammunition; this year we talk about Mark 8z ... and if you return to the College next year we'll teach you about Mark 9z ammunition!'

In 1964 Jos moved the Infantry Branch of the College – although not
its wood-and-corrugated iron buildings – to Oudtshoorn in the Cape.
That was the beginning of the present Infantry School, where future
infantry leaders are trained.

In addition to my other duties at this time I was involved, in an im-
personal ceremonial way, with a number of well-known personalities
of the time. On 31 May 1961, for example, I commanded the street-
lining troops in a certain sector of the route along which the first State
President-Designate of the new Republic of South Africa, C R Swart,
travelled to his inauguration.

I was also in command of the guard of honour on 27 January 1960 at Jan Smuts Airport when the then Minister of Foreign Affairs, Eric Louw, welcomed the British Prime Minister, Harold Macmillan; accompanying him during the inspection of the guard was Major-General Nic Bierman, who had also been a rugby Springbok in 1937.

It was during this visit that Macmillan made his famous and much-quoted 'Winds of Change' speech when addressing Parliament. Though not on a reciprocal basis, as I found when I visited his country shortly after his visit, to attend a series of military courses. I left for the United Kingdom on 1 March 1960, travelling in a South African Air Force IP (Important Persons) Dakota. The Dakota was not speedy by modern standards. We refuelled in Windhoek, Bamako, Villa Cisneros, Gibraltar and Bordeaux and had overnight stops in Luanda, Lagos, Dakar, Madrid and Casablanca (to which we had been diverted from Agadir because of a shattering earthquake). Thanks to a loan of £150 from my mother, my wife was able to follow me by sea a month later.

My first course was at Old Sarum, my fellow students including officers from other NATO countries, and dealt with air portability in the Hastings, Beverley and Hercules C130 aircraft. At first I couldn't make out a word of what was being said in lectures, owing to partial deafness caused by a whole week's flying in the Dakota. While I was on this course, the Sharpeville shootings took place, and I felt very far away from home.

I did my second and third courses in aerial photo-reading and counter-intelligence at the British Army's intelligence school at Maresfield. One of our instructors on the counter-intelligence course, a jovial, stocky blond captain named Jones, gave us a challenging theoretical exercise to do, involving a building equipped with a special room where certain important conferences were to be held. Each student was required to devise a plan to ensure the security and secrecy of the conference room, the people using it and the proceedings themselves. It was only later that I found out that the room really existed. It had been the place where Winston Churchill's war cabinet had met ... and our captain had, in fact, been the officer responsible for its security.

The person in charge of the aerial photo-reading course was an unobtrusive little man whose battle-dress bunny-jacket was too big for him. What I didn't know then was that he was the famed Lieutenant Babington-Smith who, with his wife Constance, had made names for themselves as first-class photo-interpreters during the hostilities with Germany. Everyone had been looking for the secret launching bases for the Germans' v1 and v2 launching bases, installations which could handle rockets of unusual tonnage. At some stage during the course of the search they studied the first prints to Merifield's photo-reconnaissance flight over Peenemünde airfield, and, as A J Brookes recounts in his book *Photo Reconnaissance*, Constance Babington-Smith 'found two identical ramps on the north-east edge of the island; and at the foot of one was a "Peenemünde 20" which could clearly be seen to have no cockpit … (They) … had found the flying bomb at last …'

As is so often the case, South Africans were also involved in this episode and proved their mettle. Brookes mentions various South Africans who participated in the whole effort, including Captain Williams and Lieutenant Godden of the South African Air Force in their Mustang IIIs: 'The prints brought back by the two Mustang pilots were so precise that Bomber Command could see exactly where to place their bombs'.

The most important course I did was a long one for company commanders of the United Kingdom and Commonwealth countries at the School of Infantry, Warminster.

The Sharpeville and Poqo incidents remained on people's minds, and this made being a South African a bit difficult at times. One evening in the mess a British officer, probably out of sympathy, joined me for a beer. He told me that in Korea they had always been eager to see which squadron had been designated for close air support, because, he said, they invariably hoped it would be the South Africans of No 1 Squadron SAAF, the Flying Cheetahs. When the Cheetahs gave close support, he said, you actually heard and saw them. It was a heart-warming conversation.

The course comprised lectures, demonstrations and field exercises about nuclear, conventional and unconventional warfare, and the battle-handling of a battalion group. I listened in awe as foreign officers with operational experience discussed combat situations over a glass of beer, not knowing that in later years it would be their turn to make furtive contact with us to learn from our experiences.

I became friendly with a certain Major E K Kotoka of the Ghana Regiment, who, six years later, led the coup that toppled the founder-president of Ghana, Kwame Nkrumah on 24 February 1966. I was back in Pretoria when this happened, and I reported to Military Intelligence that I knew him. They were not really interested because they did not think he would be in power for long. And they were right. In April 1967 Kotoka, now a lieutenant-general, met his end; I seem to recall he was hanged upside down from a tree.

I did not have the opportunity of seeing much of the United Kingdom on this trip and didn't get to Wales, Ireland or Scotland. I did, however, see the South African cricket team in action, and I was there when Springbok bowler Geoff Griffin performed a hat trick, only to be no-balled out of Test cricket forever for 'chucking'. I also saw parts of the 1960 Olympic Games in Rome – where South Africa won one silver and two bronze medals – on television.

My wife and I returned to South Africa in the *Cape Town Castle* in August–September 1960, she in second class and myself in first. This was because one of our fellow passengers was the military adviser at our embassy in London, Colonel D A du Toit, and in those days it was frowned on for an officer on an official trip to travel second class.

Shortly after my return, the country started gearing up for decimalisation. South Africans woke daily up to the voice of Lance James singing the jingles about 'Decimal Dan' and 'Daan Desimaal' over the radio, and on 14 February 1961 the pound became two rands, and twelve pennies ten cents. But greater things were happening on the world stage. The newly minted South African cents had barely lost their glitter when a much brighter star attracted our attention, and that of the rest of the world: Major Yuri Gagarin's first manned space flight, on 12 April 1961.

At this point my friend officer, André van Deventer – of whom more later – offered my wife and me the use of his bungalow in the WAAF (Women's Auxiliary Air Force) camp while he attended a year-long course overseas. We were newly married and financially it was a relief to move into that cheap little red brick matchbox with its compressed wood partitions, which was much like the modest homes in Toevlug, near Tempe.

* * *

33

During 1963, while still on the staff of the Military College, I did the most advanced military course of my career, the Army's Staff Duties course. My brother officer and life-long friend Ian Gleeson had already done the course the year before and moved on. On the SD course I learned how to manage pressure, especially time-pressure, and how to plan creatively. It was general practice to 'bugger the students around', as many of them, some quite senior, described it. For example, the lecturers would set assignments which were due on a specific date and at a specific time – but were of such a nature that the students never had quite enough time to complete them. To increase the pressure the lecturers, or rather the directing staff, the 'DS's', as everyone called them, would visit the students and pretend to be sincerely interested in their progress and well-being; they would also arrange for a college non-commissioned officer to go around to the students with ostensibly urgent return forms which they were required to complete immediately. This, of course, was simply a transparent ruse designed to waste the students' precious time, and many of the course-goers kept their doors locked. But I recognised the value of these methods, although I understood why some students saw this practice merely as a means of harassing them.

One such student – W P Louw from my Bethlehem days – later became Chief of the Army, and prescribed more 'enlightened' training methods for the course. His argument was that the students registered for the course were there to learn, not to be messed around. But years later, when I, too, became Chief of the Army, I issued clear guidelines for a return to the old proven technique, with a few adaptations. I believed it was not good enough simply to teach the student to plan; he should also learn to plan under pressure, even if the pressure was created only by limiting the time allocated for completing an assignment. I had found in my later career that I had less time to solve real problems than I had had to solve the fictitious ones of training courses, when I had thought the time allowed was inadequate.

When Commandant Piering Pretorius was attending the SD course each student had to do a movement exercise by himself. This involved planning to move a division of troops from point A to point B, with all the vehicles, loads and personnel travelling along pre-determined routes at certain times. Such a move involved thousands of men and

34

vehicles, as well as many tons of cargo, and it presented quite a complicated logistical problem, especially in those pre-computer days. And so, with only a few minutes to spare, Piering found himself with several tons of Army biscuits – 'dog biscuits' in the common tongue – which had to be loaded on somewhere.

One of his fellow students, an impish gunner named Major Harry Pierson, said to him: 'Let me have a quick look at your exercise.' He scrutinised it and then said: 'But Dawid, here you have a Rogers tank transporter which is quite empty. It can carry 30 tons – it can easily accommodate a few tons of dog biscuits.' By now the pressure had taken its toll and there was no time left for thinking. Commandant Pretorius barely had time to say 'thank you' before finalising his exercise with the Rogers trailer stacked full of biscuits … It was only after he had submitted his exercise that he realised that the stacked boxes of biscuits would have towered hundreds of metres into the air! Every SD course usually produced a fair amount of humour of this kind.

Whether on course or in reality, one often had to calculate how many of which items must be provided at particular places at set times for certain operations. You had to plan, for example, for the types and quantities of ammunition and supplies you required, and where they were to be dropped off. This was not always as simple as it might sound. For example, how does one calculate how much toilet paper will be needed at a specific time and place? None other than Major Harry Pierson of dog-biscuit fame came up with the formula for calculating the length of the paper required: the number of troops times the number of days, times 'one up, one down, one polish'.

In 1963 I finished the course and thereby concluded my formal training in the Defence Force. It was only much later that the South African Defence College was established to train officers for posts at the highest level of the SADF. Senior officials of some of the other government departments also attended the courses, and within the Defence Force itself provision was made for the Joint Staff Course, or JSC, for the joint training of officers of all the branches of the service. From then on one could not become a brigadier without completing the JSC.

I was the exception to this rule. I was nominated for the course in 1972, but never got there because of other official commitments, namely my appointment as the project officer for the Ratel infantry combat vehicle which was to see so much operational use in the years to come. I regretted not doing the course, but on the other hand the Ratel project stimulated my interest in science, technology, and research and development. And so in later years I was destined to become an unqualified Chief of the Army and later an unqualified Chief of the Defence Force as well.

I now began to attach great importance to certain elements of the traditional military culture. My formative years as a trainee at the Military Gymnasium, a student at the Military College and a young officer in 1 SSB had made a permanent impression on me, and although I contributed enthusiastically towards establishing an authentic South African military culture there were aspects of the British equivalent which I continued to support. For example, that there were certain things which were 'just not done'. Thus it was a disgrace for an officer's cheque to be referred to drawer, and an officer had no right to generate additional income through business dealings. Some of these concepts clashed with modern ideas and often caused me emotional distress.

Something else I discovered was that one does not really master a subject merely by doing a course on it. It is one thing to know the answers to examination questions, but is a totally different thing to understand the subject with deep insight. You start doing that only when you have to teach it to others. I also learned later on that to thoroughly understand the contents of a voluminous memorandum one must be able to summarise it in plain language on one page. This forces one to discriminate between the important and the trivial, to discover patterns and to identify the salient points. There is a certain integrity in simplicity.

I was privileged to have had the opportunity to train students in tactics, battle handling, joint land–air warfare and so forth. It was possible to apply the knowledge and insight that I gained in this way throughout my career. And I later also experienced the real thing.

I became extremely enthusiastic about the doctrine of science. The political analyst Dr Jan du Plessis once explained to me that it is the discipline whereby the assumptions, underlying principles, methods and boundaries of scientific knowledge are explored, and scientific laws and concepts are formulated. In other words, it is the science of science.

I set out to be rational, and I practised it to the extreme – a sure way of becoming a pain in the neck to everyone within earshot.

For example, somebody would say to me: 'I like the northern Transvaal climate', and I would ask: 'Why do you say that?'

He would reply: 'I like it here', and I would comment: 'Yes, but Pretoria is not in the northern Transvaal.'

'Yes, it is,' he would retort, '... isn't it?'

And I would come back with: 'Go and have a look at the map. You'll see that Pretoria is in the southern half of the Transvaal.'

Or at a cocktail party someone would say: 'It really was a scorcher today, wasn't it?', to which I would reply: 'How can you say that? The average maximum and minimum temperatures during the past few days were higher than today's. You would be more correct in saying it was a cool day.'

This is not the sort of attitude that makes one very popular, and I soon discovered that such replies were the quickest way to kill a casual social conversation that was probably started in good faith and with good intentions.

It grieved me no end when decisions were made without proper consideration of the relevant facts and the necessary application of cold logic – in fact, my first experience of having a factual, logical approach trampled underfoot went back to my boyhood. I was on holiday at the farm and wanted to go for a swim in the farm dam at one o'clock in the afternoon, but my grandmother said: 'No, you may not.'

'Why not?' I wanted to know.

'You'll get sunstroke.'

'But I'll wear my mother's wide-brimmed sunhat.'

'That's a good idea.'

'So, may I go?'

'No.'

'Why not?'

'You'll get sunburn.'

'OK, I'll just go for a dip and then go and sit in the shade of the trees.'

'That's a good idea.'

And so it went on, with my grandmother approving every precaution I proposed against sunstroke or sunburn. After she had okayed everything I asked:

'So, can I go now?'

'No.'

'Why not?'

'Because why.'

And that was that.

I have become wiser in recent years and, I hope, have improved my ways a bit. Now, when somebody says to me: 'We're lucky to live in the Northern Transvaal with its wonderful climate,' I reply: 'Yes, if you mean Pretoria, I agree. The far Northern Transvaal becomes a bit hot.'

Small talk is probably a necessary part of one's social life, but it is not my forte. A serious debate is, of course, a different story. One should probably learn to accept that logic has its time and place. Indeed, I have discovered that facts and logic are not the be-all and end-all of everything. There are also other important elements, such as experience and gut feeling. One can try to be clever for a while, but then the wisdom of 'because why' teaches you that nine times out of ten something *does* go wrong when a child goes for a swim in the midday sun.

I tried hard to emulate N P van Wyk Louw's ideal, to be 'someone who had made it his golden rule in life to approach every issue reasonably, to judge fairly, to condemn hesitantly and to regard his own opinion with a touch of humble self-criticism.' An inexperienced person armed with only hard facts and cold logic could find himself on very thin ice. Fortunately I was also in a position to gain the necessary experience.

My first impression of the Army so far had been merely the worm's-eye view of a student and junior training officer. But soon I would get the opportunity to take a bird's-eye view from Army Headquarters; I would also have the privilege of being able to observe conflict closely, and in fact in another country – Angola.

* * *

At the beginning of 1964 I was transferred to the Operations and Intelligence staff at Army Headquarters, where I learned how to write letters and telexes. One of the interesting people I got to know during this time was the first South African pilot to break through the sound barrier in our country – Captain John Inglesby, who did so in a Sabre 352 on 21 September 1956.

On 11 November 1965, on my way to hospital for a medical check-up, I heard the broadcast of Ian Smith's unilateral declaration of independence in Rhodesia. Then on 2 December 1965, having passed the check-up, I succeeded Ben de Wet Roos as Vice-Consul at the South African Consulate-General in the Angolan capital of Luanda. By now there were four of us in our family: Marié and myself, Annamarié, who was almost four, and Martin, who was just over a year old.

In those days Angola was not nearly as involved with the South African situation as it was in later years, but it was the scene of an on-going revolutionary war, and my duty was to study that war.

At the time of my arrival Ben had recently finished acting as the liaison officer during the rescue operation involving a new South African Air Force Buccaneer that had crashed into the sea during its delivery flight from the United Kingdom at the end of October. The Buccaneers were flown out under command of two officers who would subsequently become lieutenant-generals and Chiefs of the Air Force, Bob Rogers and Mike Muller, while Mike Muller's navigator was the later Brigadier Theo de Munnink, who co-ordinated the very successful rescue of those on board the liner *Oceanos* when she sank in 1991.

Buc 417, crewed by Martin Jooste (pilot) and Anton de Klerk (navigator), was in Mike Muller's formation. They ejected into the sea between Las Palmas and Ascension, and were picked up in a successful rescue operation which involved the Portuguese Air Force.

Ben was an exceptional man who knew no cultural bounds or barriers. He had spent his school years at the Helpmekaar Hoër Seunskool and Pretoria Boys' High, and during the early 1950s sported the Murray of Atholl kilt of the Second Battalion, Transvaal Scottish, on a few occasions. He had worked his way up to become an officer, a role in which he excelled, studied law privately and obtained a degree in 1953. He spoke highbrow English peppered with Latin phrases and quotations from Shakespeare, all salted with a typical Voortrekkerhoogte accent.

Ben spoke Portuguese more effectively than any foreigner I knew, although possessed of a very small vocabulary and an equally small concern for grammar. He was exceptionally skilful in using the word 'bloody'; whenever he had trouble finding the right Portuguese word, he would merely substitute 'bloody' and carry on, and everybody knew exactly what he meant. 'Old Bloody Ben', as the Portuguese used to call him, is another person who features later on in my story.

Our Consul-General, Mike Malone, was another remarkable man, both diplomat and soldier – and by his own account the only man ever to have seen a prehistoric animal in the flesh, as opposed to some fossilised bones. His military career started when World War II broke out while he was in Britain on a family holiday soon after matriculating from the South African College School in Cape Town. He volunteered for service, and by 1941 he was second lieutenant of 19 stationed in the Orkney Islands on the north-east coast.

Mike used to tell a strange story about his days on the Orkneys. He found a strange creature washed up on a beach, and according to a book he consulted at the local Kirkwall Library it was a Plesiosaurus, a species which dated back 70 million years. Mike sliced off a piece of its flipper and reported his find to the curator of a museum on the other side of the island. Next day they went over to have a look, but the sea had already reclaimed the beast, and Mike always regretted that he had missed out on the honour of having had a 'Monstrosis Malonii' named after him.

In 1961 Mike captained the Springbok pistol-shooting team in Germany, England and Switzerland, and in 1962 became the founding commanding officer of the first English-speaking commando in Pretoria, the Hillcrest Commando (later the Hillcrest Regiment).

Contact with the Portuguese culture opened a new world to me; they are refined, cultured people who take great pride in their long and illustrious history, and the Portuguese officer as I came to know him was a skilful professional with excellent academic grounding and wide-ranging interests – an outstanding person.

If I had not felt so strongly about my own country, I would have said that Angola was the most beautiful land in the world. Such an abundance of large rivers, cascades, mountains and tropical vegetation would be hard to equal. I realised once again that despite the beauty to be found on other continents, Africa still remained the only one for me; I simply would not feel at home anywhere else.

CHAPTER 4

A LAND BETWEEN TWO DESERTS

Till the rains come

After my experience at Army Headquarters and in Angola – there were now five of us, following Bruwer's arrival on 6 April 1968 – I was ready for the next move, this time to South West Africa.

I arrived at Headquarters South West Africa Command in Windhoek during April 1970. This HQ was militarily responsible for the area south of the Red Line, the boundary set up in the north to control foot-and-mouth disease, which was much feared in cattle-owning South West Africa. This meant that a number of northern areas were excluded from our purview, including all the future hot spots of the 'border war': Kaokoland, Ovambo, the Kavango, western and eastern Caprivi and Bushmanland.

My new commanding officer was my old friend Brigadier André van Deventer. Various of his predecessors – including Fritz Loots, Chokkie Coetzer and Magnus Malan – subsequently became generals, and so did André. I was the 'Colonel G', that is, the senior staff officer responsible for operations, intelligence, training and so forth. According to the 'first among equals' principle, I was also the second-in- command. The other senior officer was the 'Colonel, Commandos and Cadets', responsible for their administration and training – another old friend, Jos Rossouw.

Jos was a wise man – clever, a philosopher, well-spoken. At the same time he was also a practical person and had gained good experience, so I learned a great deal from him. But he provided us with a few lighter moments as well.

Jos, Major Des Radmore and I lived in Pioniers Park, and to get there from our HQ at the old Eros Airport terminal we had to take a dirt road with a level crossing over the railway line to Okahandja. I worried about that level crossing. Every day I reminded myself on the way home: remember the railway line, take care.

One evening the three of us went home in convoy after a social gathering at the HQ, Des driving out in front in his Land Rover, followed by Jos in his dilapidated old green Austin Mini, which made such a terrible noise on any dirt road that it was impossible to hear a thing above its rattles. I came last in my DKW 3-6 Sonderklasse. As we neared the railway line I took my usual look around and noticed that a train was approaching. I wondered what Des would do, and got my answer when he accelerated and crossed the tracks well ahead of the train. Then I turned to the Mini. What was Jos going to do? The answer was nothing. Jos drove on at a steady crawl, neither speeding up or slowing down. In the meantime the train was getting ever closer to the level crossing. I held my breath as Jos and the train began to close in on one another.

Then I let it out in a sigh of relief as Jos crossed the track in the nick of time and the train clickety-clacked past him, right on his tail. By the time its red rear light finally disappeared into the night, Jos was gone as well.

Next day I said to him: 'Jos, you just made it, hey?'

'Yes, err …' he replied, obviously confused by my remark. 'What do you mean?'

'Last night.'

'Oh.'

'Yes, the train.'

'What train?'

* * *

André van Deventer was transferred after a few months. Like those before him, he had made his mark in the territory. But the tracks that
he left in South West were 50 times deeper than those left by any of
his distinguished predecessors. Throughout history one finds military
officers making names for themselves as researchers of repute. Now,
I don't think André considers himself as a researcher, but before he
left South West Africa he discovered the existence of a creature which
at that time was still unknown to science, a centipede which was later
named *Cormocephalus deventerii*. South West Africa Command and even
South West Africa itself are now history, but André's discovery is still
leaving its tracks in the dust of the new Namibia.

André was succeeded by 'Old Bloody Ben', Brigadier Ben de Wet
Roos, whose path had crossed mine many times before and would do
so again in the future. He was, as I have said, an exceptional man. He
was a good judge of human nature and a born leader. He did not acquire his leadership qualities and techniques by studying theory; he
was a natural, spontaneously setting the example, motivating people
and then getting things done. He taught me a great deal about leadership, lessons which I applied until the end of my career.

Everyone respected him, although he was not interested in seeking
to be popular. He believed that it was better to have the confidence of
his people than to ride high on a wave of cheap popularity. Above all
he was a winner, and what he proved to me was that the seemingly impossible could, in fact, be achieved. For example, there was the time
Ben decided that it was time HQ SWA Command won the Chief of the
Army's shooting trophy. To us it seemed impossible. The competition
was too tough; the trophy had always been won by one of the Army's
many prestige units, not by a small HQ like ours. But he willed it. He
believed we could win, in the same way that South Africa's Arnold Taylor got up from the floor on 5 November 1973 in Johannesburg and
knocked out Romeo Anaya in the 14th round to become the new bantamweight boxing champion of the world. Taylor wanted to win, and
so he did. And so did we. We had a simple plan, we worked hard at it
and succeeded.

As the number two at HQ SWA Command I tried my best to serve Ben
well. I impressed on the staff that we should be good followers, and that
our duty was to be honest with our commander. To be honest might

be cruel at times, but it is often also constructive. To be honest behind someone's back is two-faced and is often destructive. I believed then and believe now in expressing my opinions fearlessly and without any ulterior motive, like a certain corporal I came across a few years later at Grootfontein.

As I recall, the then Minister of Defence, Mr P W Botha, visited Grootfontein in 1978. During the customary briefing, Commandant Wimpie Heunis, the technical officer, mentioned that the percentage serviceability of the vehicle fleet was unacceptably low, adding that the problem was the non-availability of reserve vehicle components.

After the briefing Mr Botha, as was his custom on such occasions, walked around the base, asking questions, shaking a hand here and making a comment there. One of the people he spoke to that day was a corporal in the base workshop; the corporal told him what his responsibilities were, and Mr Botha, his hat in his hand as usual, asked him: 'Well now, corporal, what's your position with vehicle components?' The corporal answered crisply and confidently: 'No problem, Minister, no problem at all!'

We all felt rather embarrassed for Wimpie Heunis, who was there as well, listening to the corporal directly contradicting what he had told the minister just a little earlier. But Wimpie quickly chipped in: 'Corporal, tell the minister about the spares.'

'Oh, Minister, spares?' the corporal responded. 'No, Minister, we've got f** all!' Which was a very clear summary of his position.

To come back to the characteristics of a good follower: I believed that once my commander had made a decision it was my duty to support his plan 100 per cent, as if it were my own, even if I disagreed with it. This was easy. However, should the plan fail, it was also my duty to act as if it were my own. And this was not so easy.

But it is not only through good leaders and followers that mutual respect and *esprit de corps* are fostered. Camaraderie develops when people go through hard times together. And it was here that I had my first anxious moments with Ben.

The two of us once visited Commandant Nico Retief's Walvisbaai Commando during an exercise. Early that morning, when our Cessna 185 landed in the desert at his camp the sand was still moist and hard after the previous night's mist. But at take-off time it had become loose after a full day in the sun, and in addition the air was less dense as well. We had to take off in the direction of the Kuiseb River, one of those dry river-beds one finds in South West Africa – actually just a large donga full of sand, rock and bush which generates clouds of dust when the wind blows. Flaps down, the pilot started his take-off run at full speed, but in the soft sand this meant merely crawling along as slowly as Jos's old Mini had done over the railway line. There was no sign of acceleration or lift, and I had a nasty feeling that we were not going to get into the air that day. We chugged along while the river got closer. We chugged even harder and the river got closer still. I had often wondered what it would be like to be in an air crash. Now, it seemed, I would soon not have to wonder any more; I was going to *know*. If I survived, of course.

When we reached the riverbank we were not yet airborne. And then, bang, it happened – we plunged over the edge! With a thud the aircraft landed on a level ledge, fortunately on its wheels. Then suddenly we bounced back into the air and gained just enough height to scrape over the tree-tops. Ben Roos immediately looked out of the window to check whether the wheels were intact, because we still had to land back at Windhoek! They were, and we did. But this incident has lived on in my memories as 'the prang that never was'. I discovered later that the Cessna 185 has a spring-loaded undercarriage – the strut to which the wheels are attached is actually a metal spring bent in the shape of an upside-down V – which is what caused the bounce that enabled us to stagger into the air.

* * *

In April 1973 the Defence Force assumed responsibility for border protection in South West from the police; and in October that year I took over from Ben. It was some time since I had held a command post, and just as the job of second-in-command had been a learning process for me, the experience as a commander at this level stood me in good stead in later years.

My staff and everybody else in Windhoek were wonderfully supportive. In fact, I began to suspect that they had taken my lectures on how to be a good follower too literally, because they always seemed to agree with any new suggestions I put forward. Now, if one does not watch out, one can easily start thinking that everything one does is right. One might forget that by agreeing with their superior, subordinates might only be showing good manners and tact. One might get the idea that one is really as good as some people say, and that is extremely dangerous. To protect myself against this folly I had a routine arrangement with the command sergeant-major, Sergeant-Major Raymond Marshall, to meet every Friday morning for coffee somewhere in Windhoek to talk about command matters.

Sergeant-Major Marshall, I knew, could be quite obstinate and was very straightforward about expressing in his opinions, and that was what I wanted. If he thought I was making a mess of things he would tell me so without ceremony; if he didn't like a new idea, he would be as precise about his feelings as that corporal in the workshop at Grootfontein had been. At the same time he did not go overboard; he was critical but positive, and always presented alternative ways of doing things. So I used to listen very carefully to his proposals, and often abandoned my own plans if his ideas were better. I would give him credit for his suggestions and get on with the job of implementing them.

Raymond Marshall was not the only independent thinker who was willing to speak his mind. At this time my path had crossed once again with that of my old acquaintance, of the Ladysmith fort days, the latter-day Major Large van Rensburg, who was now at Windhoek's training wing.

I made new acquaintances as well on the crossroads of soldiering. One was Captain Charlie Hochapfel and another was his close associate, one Eros. Charlie was an English-speaking South West African of German descent, full of fun, and a good soldier. Eros, on the other hand, was a dog, a local enlistment, so to speak, who had been recruited and trained by Charlie.

Eros was no ordinary canine. He was a guard dog at the headquarters building who had started off as a semi-official member of the Defence Force and from there eventually graduated to full official status, with his own identity card and access to official rations, medical services and other benefits.

Charlie looked after Eros's interests. This included personally instructing the sentries on how to handle his associate. A typical briefing went like this:

'Guys, when you do guard duty at headquarters you'll find a dog there. His name is Eros. Be good to him, make friends. You're going to need him. You'll also find a nice comfortable chair in the hall. At night you sit in the chair with Eros on your lap. You'll fall asleep, of course. So will he. But when the duty officer arrives on his inspection rounds, Eros will wake up and start investigating the disturbance. And by the time the duty officer gets to you, you'll be up and about, too, a watchful and alert sentry. He'll never catch you sleeping on duty!'

Charlie died in action on 24 March 1986 when he and his team ran into an ambush while evaluating live encounters (South Africa was one of only a very few countries in the world where evaluation teams accompanied troops into battle to critically assess their combat skills).

* * *

SWA Command did not consist only of Windhoek and Grootfontein. There was also a military base at Walvis Bay – commanded by my old friend, Colonel Ian Gleeson – at which the main unit was 2 South African Infantry Battalion Group. At that time Walvis Bay was one of the enlisting centres where men reported for national service training. Naturally, during 'intake' the base was a beehive of activity, with some recruits arriving by train, others by bus and car, and still others with their parents.

One day, at the height of the hustle and bustle, there was a knock at Colonel Gleeson's door, and the adjutant came in to announce: 'Colonel, we have another mother with her son wanting to see you.'

'Please show them in,' Colonel Gleeson said. The petitioners entered rather apprehensively and he said: 'Madam, young man, please sit down. What can I do for you?'

The lady sat down timidly on the edge of her chair with her feet together, tightly clutching her handbag on her lap. 'Colonel,' she said, 'my son, I came to ...'

He immediately tried to put her mind at rest: 'Madam, please don't worry. Leave your son here, and I'll personally see to it that he gets prompt and proper attention. Everything will be fine. By the way, where do you live?'

'Walvis Bay,' she said.

'Fine. Go home now, don't worry. You'll hear from us again.' So she went home. The necessary orders were given and a corporal fetched the recruit to process him in and then take him to the quartermaster stores to get his kit. After that, loaded like a pack-donkey with overalls and linen; with braces, left and right – one and one, and belts, webbing – one, the boy was sent off to his bungalow.

A day or two later the mother was there again, wanting another interview. Hesitantly and somewhat anxiously she asked: 'Colonel, where is my son? How long does it take you to register a notification of change of address?'

An embarrassed Ian Gleeson realised that the poor lad had not arrived to report for national service but merely, as was required by law, to hand in his new address. He apologised profusely and had the boy fetched to his office immediately ... But when he was told that he could now go home with his mother the boy vigorously resisted his liberation. By now he had made friends with the other chaps in his bungalow, he said. He was part of a team and very happy with all the new things that were happening to him. He wanted to stay!

Ian Gleeson is a great human being, level-headed and humble and with a good sense of humour; but this time he was red in the face.

* * *

Apart from the Permanent Force members and national servicemen at Grootfontein and Walvis Bay there were also the part-time soldiers, the conventional-warfare Citizen Force men in 24 Brigade and those in the area-protection units of the Commando Force.

This was a whole new world to me, peopled by extraordinary characters, the like of which I have never met again. I could dedicate an entire book to men like Colonel Koot Theron, one of the 'wild men' of the Kalahari in his young days; Piet Mostert, who fought a lion with his bare hands and survived; and the daring members of Commandant Hans Heinrich Otto Denk's 112 Commando Squadron in their privately owned light aircraft. But where would I stop?

Then there were the people and the country itself – previously German South West Africa, then South West Africa and later Namibia. The sun rises over the Kalahari and sets behind the Namib, and the land between these two deserts is a jewel in the hearts of the people of all races who live there. One either loves South West or one hates it. One cannot be lukewarm. It's a tough country, and anybody who doesn't fit in is rejected.

In the past South West was isolated by distance, vastness and lack of communications, which made it a closed society where the people were tough and proud but good in heart. When they worked, they worked hard – and when they played, they played equally hard. A South Wester didn't drive 250 km on a Wednesday afternoon for a game of tennis and then just say goodbye and go back home. Afterwards there was always the '*gemütlichkeit*', a small party. It was a big country with one big family.

Distance was not regarded as important. In 1972, all togged up and raring to go, some friends and I went to Eros airport to fly to Port Elizabeth with Hans Denk for a rugby test against the French, but the weather was so bad that the control tower couldn't clear our flight for take-off on the first leg to Upington. So Max Kessler quickly fetched his car and drove us to Port Elizabeth and back.

South West was and still is pioneer country, a country of sadness and joy … sadness during times of drought, joy when the rains come. One of the old-time pioneers was the legendary entrepreneur Sam Cohen; his son, Jackie, and I were friends, and he told me that his father had always said that in South West, all problems are cut in half as soon as it rains. That was a truth that I will never forget.

Around October the people anxiously start raising their eyes skyward, searching for signs of rain. Everything is barren and dry. Man and animal yearn for water. Clouds loaded with promise gather and hopes run high. Then they disappear without bringing rain. The next day clouds build up again. There is renewed expectation and tension in the air … and then the clouds disappear again. After a few days – or perhaps a few weeks – of this, the tension begins to increase and people become grumpy. Then the clouds build up again and they disappear – again. And if, in an unguarded moment, you say something frivolous, you might find your joke turning into an incident.

I found that it served no purpose to hold Citizen Force and commando conferences between October and January. It was better to wait until the rains came, until all the problems had been halved, until *gemütlichkeit* and good cheer had returned to the hearts of the people. Then you could talk to them and they were prepared to talk to you, and you all worked together.

I will always love South West, but as my mother liked to say: 'Too much of a good thing is not good', and in December 1974 I was ready to go when I handed over to another old friend, Brigadier Dirk Marais, and left for Army HQ, Pretoria.

By now there were six of us – Mariana, or Lollie, as we called her, was two years old. I told my wife I would never be transferred again, that we would have to settle in Pretoria. But I was a bad prophet. Two-and-a-half years later we were back in South West. In that time many pleasant things would come to pass; but also a war.

CHAPTER 5

A NEW ERA OF WAR

'Commandant doesn't really understand the situation'

For the first time in ten years I was back in South Africa. It needed a lot of adjustment. In Windhoek the pace had been slow and the atmosphere congenial. In contrast Pretoria seemed grim and busy. I got the fright of my life driving down Potgieter Street and finding cars overtaking me on both sides without warning.

In South West you were somebody. If you had a breakdown, the first person to pass would stop. In Pretoria you were one of many nobodies. Strings of cars with poker-faced drivers would speed by before someone eventually came to your rescue.

I was not the only South Wester in Pretoria to find the going tough. Early one evening after work I visited a few of my old mates of 112 Commando Squadron who were doing a ground–air co-operation course at the South African Air Force College. Over a glass of beer I asked Max Kessler's brother, Tikklie, who was from the Helmeringhausen country on the edge of the Namib Desert: 'How do you like Pretoria?'

He gave a typical South Wester's answer: 'The first week or so was OK, but now all the greenery's getting a bit much.'

That day, 29 April 1975, produced its own drama. In Fox Street,

Johannesburg, a maniacal security guard at the Israeli Consulate-General named David Protter armed himself with a rifle and staged a one-man invasion of his own workplace. It was not a political act – it later transpired that Protter had had a personal dispute with the consul-general – but the incident caused a tremendous fuss during the 17 hours that went by before Protter was captured and disarmed.

We sat drinking our beer while the pub radio kept us informed about the happenings at the embassy, which was now under siege by the police under the personal supervision of Lieutenant-General Hendrik van den Bergh, head of the Bureau for State Security and one of Prime Minister John Vorster's advisors. All of a sudden Piet Gouws, Thys Rall, Horst Kreitz and Tikklie decided that the news flashes were actually the call of duty summoning them to Johannesburg to oversee the handling of the situation. So, with typical South West African contempt for distance, they got into a car and drove over to Johannesburg. There they went straight to Fox Street and presented themselves to General Hendrik van den Bergh, who was trying to negotiate with Protter by way of a walkie-talkie.

I am not sure what their contribution to ending the siege was, but next morning there was a front-page picture in a leading newspaper featuring the prim and proper Piet Gouws standing right behind General Van den Bergh (who was later, of course, to feature prominently in the early part of the bush war). They were South Westers, and they played the game, whatever it might be!

But for me life in Pretoria was certainly no game. From January 1975 to mid-1977 I hardly touched ground. During a period of two-and-a-half years at Army HQ I had three different jobs, one after the other. I started off as Director, Intelligence (D Int, in Army jargon), then took over as Director, Operations, or D Ops, and then became Chief of Army Staff, Operations, C Army S, Ops.

The traditional attitude of the South African fighting soldier – supposedly not a serious one – requires you to scoff at working in an office at HQ, be it a battalion or a territorial command, but especially if your desk is at Defence Force Headquarters in its complex in Pretoria. Be that as it may, there was one lone star providing some light amid the shadows of bureaucratic gloom – none other than Jos Rossouw. He had been transferred from Windhoek a year before me, and I found myself not just in the same building, but in the office next to his.

Jos's transfer had not watered down his individualism, as I saw when scanning the standard location board on the wall next to the staircase we both used. When an officer left his office on an outside errand, the drill was that he filled in his date and time of departure, destination and time of return. But I noticed that Jos frequently signed out, mostly from 15h00 onwards, to go to a destination given as 'UPM'. He would then not reappear till 08h00 next morning.

I had never heard of a place called UPM, and when it crossed my mind occasionally I tried to find out. The answer would be something like: 'Hum ... haw ... it's ... Uniform Personnel Management'. I suspected that the officers I consulted didn't know themselves but were reluctant to show their ignorance. Then one day I saw it again and remembered to ask Jos himself:

'Jos,' I said, 'what and where is this "UPM" you went to yesterday?'

'UPM?'

'Yes, man, UPM.'

'Oh,' he said. This was a dead give-away. Ben Roos performed miracles with 'bloody'; with Jos it was 'oh'. It had got him out of many a tight spot. But he couldn't fool me.

'Oh, what?'

'It means "Urgent Private Matters!"'

Now it was *my* turn to say 'oh'.

* * *

As D Int I had to establish the Army's organisation for conducting 'Comops', or Communication Operations, the aim of which was to foster harmony between the Army and its units on the one hand and the population on the other. This applied especially to operational areas, since it is difficult to operate successfully in an environment where the locals are not friendly.

Then the Angolan civil war started in 1975.

In terms of an agreement signed in January that year at the Portuguese town of Alvor, the Portuguese transferred power in Angola to a 'Government of National Unity' consisting of representatives of delegates of Agostinho Neto's People's Movement for the Liberation of

Angola (MPLA), Holden Roberto's National Front for the Liberation of Angola (FNLA) and Jonas Savimbi's National Union for the Total Independence of Angola (UNITA).

This interim government was supposed to rule until a general election had been held, with independence taking place on 11 November. But it did not happen that way. Because of its own internal problems Portugal could not or would not exert any real influence during the transitional period. The interim government disintegrated, and with the help of Cuban troops the MPLA soon became the sole rulers in the capital, Luanda. Roberto and Savimbi took to the bush, from where they declared war on the MPLA. Soon Angola was a battleground inhabited by the three organisations' armed wings – FAPLA (the MPLA), ELNA (the FNLA) and FALA (UNITA).

It will be remembered that during those years – the 1960s and 1970s and thereafter – the pattern was for the big powers to take sides and become involved in regional and local conflicts, and they also secured the active participation of their allies. The United States of America was the leader of the 'West' and the Soviet Union of the 'East', and the participation on almost every continent of the Americans with their allies and the Soviets with theirs is common knowledge: Vietnam and Nicaragua are only two examples of what was going on. This is the international 'Cold War' background against which the conflicts of that time must be seen.

In Angola the Soviet Union, supported by Cuba, various East Bloc countries and others, supported Neto and the MPLA, with Cuba supplying most of the troops. America became involved on the side of Roberto and his FNLA, who in turn formed an alliance with Savimbi and his Unita. And so South Africa, with the war on its doorstep, became part of the anti-Marxist alliance. We code-named the South African participation in the war 'Operation Savannah'.

Although I had been in the Defence Force for 22 years by then, I had not always been conscious of war; for all practical purposes I had lived and worked in peace. Now, however, I felt for the first time that I was involved in a war. It was an unreal, uncomfortable feeling, because the South African general public did not know much and went about their daily lives as usual while Angola became engulfed in bloodshed. Nevertheless, it was the beginning of a new era of war. Mr John Vorster was Prime Minister at the time, Mr P W Botha was Minister of Defence, Admiral H H Bierman was Chief of the Defence Force and Lieutenant-General Magnus Malan was Chief of the Army … and I was the Army's D Ops.

Because of the extremely clandestine nature of the operation, especially during the early stages, only the absolute minimum number of senior staff officers were involved in operational control in Pretoria – mainly the directors of operations, who met daily. The nucleus of the group consisted of the Director-General, Operations, at the HQ of the Chief of the Defence Force, Major-General Constand Viljoen, and his own D Ops, Brigadier Wally Black; the D Ops at Air Force HQ, Brigadier Piet Letley; and myself. On the ground at the 'sharp end' was Brigadier Dawie Schoeman, headquartered at Rundu, who as commander of 1 Military Area was tasked to protect the northern borders of South West Africa.

A few things bothered me. One was the vastness of the combat zone. The distance between Bloemfontein in South Africa and Cela in Angola is 2 386 km (1 205 nautical miles), and the distance to Cassinga – which two years later became the main objective of Operation Reindeer – is 1 928 km (1 038 nautical miles).

Another worrisome aspect was the exclusivity of the group of staff officers in Pretoria who controlled the operation. During October–November 1975 I argued strongly that we should implement the normal command and control structures for conducting operations, and revert to the more formal procedures. General Malan supported me. This led to the establishment of HQ 101 task force at Rundu, with General André van Deventer taking over from Dawie Schoeman and assuming responsibility for Operation Savannah.

This happened more than three decades ago – a long time, during which much has been written about the campaign and many arguments have taken place. Two authoritative books about the subject which were published years ago were *Operasie Savannah, Angola 1975-1976*, written by my tutor, Professor F J du Toit Spies, and *Avontuur in Angola: Die verhaal van Suid-Afrika se soldate in Angola 1975-1976* by Commandant Sophia du Preez.

Sophia du Preez says that the aim of Operation Savannah was to ensure 'a well-disposed government in Angola which would not permit

SWAPO bases and which would govern the country free from communist Cubans', the result being 'a tragic success. By means of a blitzkrieg,
a favourably disposed neighbour was placed in control of almost half
of Angola.'

Sam Nujoma's SWAPO, the South West African People's Organisation,
later known as 'SWAPO of Namibia', campaigned for the independence
of South West. Its armed wing was the People's Liberation Army of Namibia (PLAN), whose members infiltrated South West through Angola
and Zambia.

I do not intend to rehash the material contained in the plethora of
publications about Operation Savannah, but would like to share a few
opinions and relate a few personal experiences.

* * *

On 30 October 1975, during the first stage of the operation, I had to
meet with Dr Jonas Malheiro Savimbi, the president of UNITA, at Silva
Porto, the present Kuito. I had met him once before, and it had been
the beginning of a relationship that would last for many years.

On arrival at Silva Porto I met two of my colleagues and friends,
Colonel Des Harmse and Major Nic Visser of 1 Parachute Battalion.
Dr Savimbi had not yet arrived and Des asked me if I would like to ac-
company him on a reconnaissance flight. I said no, because I had come
to perform a particular task, and therefore would rather wait for Dr
Savimbi.

Des and his party returned by midday, we had lunch together and
they invited me along on another flight that that afternoon. This time
I was on the point of agreeing, but asked if it meant that a passenger
with some duty to perform would have to give up his seat for me. The
answer was yes, but that it would not matter too much. But this persuaded me to decline. As it transpired, Dr Savimbi did not arrive that
day. I waited until the last possible moment and then returned to Rundu; before we took off I remarked to someone that Des and the others
would have to be back within the next few minutes or else it would be
too dark for them to land.

They never returned. Shortly after landing at Rundu I heard that
their aircraft had crashed, killing everyone on board – Des Harmse, Nic

Visser, the pilot, Major Piet Uys, and Lance-Corporal Neville Beechie of 1 Special Service Battalion.

Friction de guerre had played a role that day: a fatal one for some, a lucky one for me. The incident shook me, because the Harmses were family friends and we had come a long way together in the Defence Force (a few years later Des's son, Captain Louis Harmse, was killed in action at the Battle of Xangongo during Operation Protea).

Like any other career officer I would have liked to be part of the campaign itself. During the first phases I did go to the combat zone on liaison visits, sometimes with General Viljoen, sometimes alone, as in the case of the trip to Silva Porto to meet Savimbi. I was not the only one, and sometimes these ventures were life-threatening, since warfare does not discriminate by rank or station.

On 3 January 1976 one of the field commanders, Brigadier J D Potgieter, died in Angola when his helicopter was shot down. Next day he was replaced by my friend and former commander, Ben Roos, and a day or two later I was appointed to take over from Ben as Chief of Staff at Rundu. But Operation Savannah was nearing its end. At the time we were well on the way to victory (it only became known later that the Cubans were already planning their retreat at that stage), but that same month I had to radio Ben and tell him that we were going to withdraw and that he had to prepare himself for that event. His response was deathly silence. After a while I called him again. His response was: '... We will abide by the order.'

The turning point of the war that led to the withdrawal of the South African troops was the Clark Amendment, a new law authored by Senator Dick Clark and passed by the US Congress, which forbade military support to any Angolan party for one year, starting in December 1975 (in 1976 it was extended for another year). The South African government's reaction was that it was not prepared to protect Western interests alone.

This was actually Ben's second withdrawal. The first had taken place only a few weeks earlier. Before his involvement in the southern half of Angola he had been at Ambriz in the north, leading a South African Defence Force liaison team attached to Holden Roberto, president of the FNLA.

I agree with Willem Steenkamp's description of Roberto: ' ... Roberto insisted on going his own way. In the end his stubbornness sabotaged

57

not only his own future but, to a large extent, that of Operation Savannah as well.'

Roberto's ambition was to conquer Luanda before 11 November 1975, which made no sense, because his soldiers were inexperienced and his leader group unskilled. I visited Ben at least once, when SAAF C-130s delivered 140 mm guns to Roberto. His mood was not a happy one. Ben complained that Roberto had no sense of delegation of authority; his people would not allow even a Land Rover to be moved without his personal permission.

Ben told me that he had had a serious talk with Roberto and had explained to him how one had to identify operational tasks and allocate each one to a responsible subordinate commander. But when he had finished Roberto said: 'But Brigadier, war is such a serious thing, you can't leave it to the generals.' It was not the first time I had heard this opinion being expressed.

Roberto did not achieve his ambition. He failed disastrously, as will be remembered, and in Luanda the MPLA celebrated Angola's freedom from Portugal on 11 November 1975 as scheduled, exactly 10 years after Rhodesia's unilateral declaration of independence. The full extent of the negative effects of Roberto' s failure would only be realised later.

After the defeat and instant disintegration of the FNLA in the north, Ben and his team were left isolated and apparently forgotten at Ambriz. They travelled to the fishing village of Ambizete, and on 28 November they and their valuable equipment were rescued by the frigate SAS *President Steyn*, commanded by Captain Sam Davis of the South African Navy. Ben and others were flown out to the *President Steyn* in a Puma helicopter crewed by Captain Ben van der Westhuizen and Sergeant B B Smit, while the equipment was ferried out in the frigate's boats. Two days later, on 30 November, Ben and his party were disembarked at Walvis Bay

My good old friend, Colonel Blackie Swart, was a task force commander during this war. One of his Cuban opponents was a formidable man, but in my opinion Blackie had the better of him. Later the Cuban would feature again later in the history of southern Africa and also make the international headline news: Comandante Arnaldo Ochoa Sanchez, about whom more will be told later.

* * *

At Army HQ itself I had a hard time, because, as I have mentioned, during the early stages the whole operation was handled by a handful of people – almost in the manner of a special forces operation. It disturbed me that such an operation was controlled in this manner. I felt that it would have been preferable to conduct the war in the open, with the whole Defence Force involved, and with the public's support.

With the wisdom of hindsight, and seen purely from a military point of view, it could have been to our advantage if the media had been better informed. But I do not intend to blame the politicians. They had their considerations – and military objectives are always subordinate to the overall political strategy. Sitting in my HQ, I did not have to worry about the Clark Amendment or sessions at the United Nations or the Organisation for African Unity. The fact was that the end of World War II had ushered in a new era: most wars are no longer formally declared, and undeclared and clandestine operations like Savannah have become the norm all over the world. The French intervened in Africa in this way, and the United States and the Soviets elsewhere.

After Operation Savannah the approach changed somewhat, and large-scale operations were often conducted more openly than before. We also benefited from the experience in other respects. On 27 January 1976, General Van Deventer said: 'Now is not the time to pat ourselves on the back because of our combat successes in Angola. Our experience must be communicated to those who have not had it. Our leaders have a great task ahead, because we will still be involved in war for a long time to come.'

I organised and conducted the debriefing conferences on the Army's participation in the war. We identified and formulated the lessons we had learnt and planned our follow-up programme of action. We made substantial changes and adjustments which proved invaluable later on. The improvements affected battle techniques and procedures; hardware projects, such as the one that became the 127 mm multiple rocket-launcher; and closer co-operation between different corps of the Army, and between the other arms and branches of the service.

I was proud of the way in which all our leaders at the various levels had proved themselves, and I was just as proud of the South African troops. And when I say troops, I do not refer only to soldiers of the Army, but to all the men in the air and at sea, as well as the medics.

59

South African troops proved once again that they were very resource-ful. But they could also be mischievous, as this Savannah story from Rundu illustrates.

The year was 1975. Because of the sudden stepped-up military activ-ity Rundu was bursting at the seams. The sergeant-major in charge of catering had his hands full in his kitchen, which had been set up in such haste that he didn't even have a proper pantry, so that he had stacked his tinned food all over the place. Somehow he had forgotten what hungry troops are capable of, and a soldier is always hungry, no matter what has gone down his throat. Even if he has just had a proper meal, and possibly even 'seconds', he is never too full, for example, to polish off a tin of condensed milk (I speak from personal experience, since I did the same ... and still do).

The sergeant-major was reminded of this when his tins started dis-appearing. So he made a plan. He went to the quartermaster stores and found himself a few trunks – 'boxes, soldier, steel', in that special quartermaster's language – and secured the tins in them with locks he had scrounged somewhere. But the tins continued to vanish mysteri-ously, as if into thin air, so he made another plan. He went to the lo-cal shop and bought extra-strong locks; every morning he opened the trunks himself, leaving the locks hanging from the hasps, and during the day kept a sharp eye on everything. Then, before going off duty in the evening, he personally closed each trunk and made sure it was securely locked.

Then after a few days he arrived at the kitchen and found when he unlocked the trunks that some tins had disappeared again! The same thing happened next day. And again on the following day. By this time he was at his wits' end, even though he was a seasoned ser-geant-major. How did the rascals manage it? Eventually the story came out. The troops had bought identical extra-strong locks; during the day they waited for the sergeant-major to be momentarily distracted, then swiftly exchanged them for the ones hanging from the hasps. The result was that when the sergeant-major locked the trunks at night, the padlocks he was snapping shut were the substituted ones, not his own. The troops then came back later, helped themselves and replaced the sergeant-major's locks. Then next morning, the sergeant-major would kindly unlock the trunks for them all over again!

The troops' talents were not confined to scrounging food; on operations they showed the same resourcefulness. But even they didn't always have all the answers, as the following anecdote proves.

Soldiers on a routine patrol somewhere in the Kavango, or just north of it, came upon a herd of elephants. The elephants didn't seem to like being disturbed and reacted quite aggressively, either with serious intent or simply as a show of force. The troops were not interested in finding out which it was and took to their heels.

The radio operator decided that his evasive action was being unnecessarily handicapped by the radio he was carrying and promptly got rid of it. It fell to the ground, still sending out the normal hiss of static. One of the elephants took offence at the hissing, and did what any pachyderm worth his salt would do under the circumstances: he trampled the radio until it was suitably flat and silent.

That was the end of the radio, but not of the story. When the quartermaster at Rundu indented for a new radio, Pretoria demanded the old one back. The quartermaster duly sent it back ... in an official envelope!

* * *

Two new groups of troops made a name for themselves. One was Daniel Chipenda's faction of FNLA soldiers, commanded by the fearless Commandant Jan Breytenbach, who formed them into Bravo Group and later 32 Battalion. I developed a special relationship with them which would strengthen during the years to follow.

I also maintained personal contact with the other group, the Angolan Bushman soldiers the SADF recruited under the name of Alpha Group, which later was re-titled 31 Battalion and even later 201 Battalion. The Bushmen were the most marginalised group in Angola, with every man's hand turned against them till they were offered a refuge by the SADF. Like many other people, I found the Bushmen fascinating.

Commandant Delville Linford was their first commanding officer, during the middle and late 1970s, and he once told me of the day he assembled them all to inform them of their forthcoming participation in Operation Savannah.

His speech was translated bit by bit, first into Portuguese and then into the two Bushman dialects spoken by his men. First he announced: 'We are going to war.' Interpret, interpret, interpret. The Bushmen all cheered. Then he said: 'We are going to fight against the MPLA.' Interpret, interpret, interpret. Again the Bushmen cheered. He continued: 'We are going to make war against the MPLA on the side of the FNLA and Unita.' Interpret, interpret, interpret. Silence.

Linford pressed on, however, and finished his speech. But some time after the briefing a somewhat displeased Bushman delegation asked to see him. They told him: 'Commandant, Commandant doesn't really understand the situation ...' Then they explained to him they were going to fight the MPLA, that was so – but they were also going to fight the FNLA and UNITA!

By 27 March 1976 the last South African troops involved in Operation Savannah had already withdrawn from Angola via Ruacana. It became clear later that had Holden Roberto not squandered his advantage, and had the Americans kept up their pressure against Russian intervention, the result might easily have been some form of neutral government in Angola. The actual outcome, however, meant that SWAPO would be able to use Angola as a springboard for renewed infiltration.

*   *   *

Let us turn to the South West African operational area and what was happening there. The SWAPO incursions took a new turn. Many military observers consider 27 March 1976 to be the date on which the insurgency really started in all seriousness. SWAPO was now potentially in a stronger military position than before, because for the first time it had obtained what is more or less a prerequisite for successful insurgent campaigning, namely a border that provided safe refuge.

From SWAPO's point of view the new situation also held certain disadvantages, one being that Nujoma's previous ally, Jonas Savimbi, was now his greatest enemy. This created a problem for Nujoma, since they were both operating in southern Angola. The MPLA also required SWAPO to make manpower available for their campaign against Savimbi. Savimbi, however, was retreating to the remote expanses of the southeast, because he was fighting for the very existence of his movement.

62

PLAN, Swapo's military wing, established an extensive network of training camps and bases in southern Angola, and they stepped up their incursions considerably; as Steenkamp says, 'for the South Africans – short of men, short of equipment, their defence force still struggling to wrench itself free of the decades of neglect that had followed World War II – the situation was immensely worrying.'

The intensity of the border war was still very low, but a series of intermittent contacts, mine incidents and hit-and-run attacks with rockets and mortars increased the casualty rate. During December the actions actually intensified. Reliable reports reached Windhoek that four of the 'front-line states', Tanzania, Zambia, Mozambique and Angola, were supporting a new wave of insurgency planned for early 1977. From early December 1976 PLAN set its sights on traditional leaders who were mostly conservative and well disposed towards the administration. On 7 December Deputy Chief Hausiki Enkaile was murdered by a group of six or seven insurgents and Chief Willipard Enkale's son was abducted and taken to Angola.

On 11 December 1976, Sean McBride, the ageing UN commissioner for Namibia, was responsible for some light entertainment when he told newsmen during an interview in Lusaka that South Africa had assembled 50 000 men, armed with 'sophisticated' weapons such as helicopters, tanks, field artillery and hundreds of armoured vehicles, in forming-up areas in the Caprivi Strip, ready for launching into Angola. The allegation was that South Africa would justify such action by arguing that MPLA and Cuban troops had joined up with PLAN insurgents.

McBride added to the comedy by claiming that the Rhodesian government had built three new air bases, one of which was in Caprivi, and suggested that this indicated preparation for a long drawn-out war. The allegation was obviously ridiculous. In the first place South Africa could not possibly put a force of such proportions into the field without a full-scale and very public mobilisation. Defence Minister P W Botha gleefully grabbed at the opportunity to invite McBride to visit Caprivi and point out the Rhodesian airfield. McBride wisely declined to take up the challenge.

Late in February 1977 Caprivi experienced its first incident since July 1975, when a PLAN group opened fire on a South African patrol base near the borders with Angola and Zambia, wounding three soldiers.

Twelve insurgents were killed during the counter-attacks before they could cross the Zambian border. In the meantime the South African Army's communication operations scheme, its 'goodwill campaign', got off the ground. On 22 March 76 selected national servicemen were withdrawn from other tasks and assigned to teaching duties in black schools in the border area.

On 31 March 1977 Mr P W Botha announced in Parliament that during the two years since 1 April 1975 a total of 231 insurgents had been killed in Ovambo, Kavango and the eastern Caprivi. During the same time the security forces – that is, members of the Army, Air Force, Navy, Medical Services, Permanent Force, Auxiliary Service, Citizen Force, Commandos and National Servicemen including South Africans and South West Africans of all ethnic groupings; Railway police, Police and Tribal police – had lost 33 men and the infiltrators had killed 53 members of the local population. 101 Task Force HQ had been moved from Rundu to Grootfontein during this time, and Constand Viljoen succeeded André van Deventer as the general officer commanding; a while later he was replaced by my old friend from cadet days and later, General Ian Gleeson.

In May or June 1977 I stood in for General Gleeson at Grootfontein so that he could go home on leave, and in the process picked up a marvellous story emanating from its logistics base, which, so I had heard (correctly) was very busy satisfying the increasing demand from further north.

One day a staff officer received a signal from a forward base containing a request for 250 000 sandbags. He had been working long hours under great pressure (one of his extra problems was looking after the refugees from Angola, who needed tents, food, blankets and various other necessities), but despite the stress he remained calm and meticulous, even when faced with this enormous new demand.

So instead of blowing up, he made some calculations, which indicated to him that 250 000 sandbags seemed excessive, insurgency or no insurgency, and he signalled back: 'What do you want to do with the sandbags?'

The forward base promptly replied: 'We want to fill them with sand.'

Life at home continued undisturbed while the war raged in Angola and South West Africa. South Africa was the venue for the Third World Bowls Tournament between 18 February and 6 March 1976. Sixteen countries participated – the most ever. South Africa won every competition. There were 80 000 spectators. At home everybody was glued to their TV sets – then a novelty in South Africa – and Doug Watson became a national hero and a household name.

Things were happening to me as well. In May 1976 I was promoted to major-general and took over from the Korean veteran, Major-General Jack Dutton, as Chief of Army Staff, Operations. But shortly after this the whole command and control structure in South West Africa changed. Up to that stage the Army had been responsible for two areas, the territory north of the Red Line (101 Task Force), and the territory south of it (SWA Command). Now these were drawn into one large area under a single commander, the General Officer Commanding SWA Command. And I was appointed to fill the post.

CHAPTER 6

SOUTH WESTERS MUST DECIDE FOR THEMSELVES

Brother against brother

After standing in for Ian Gleeson at Grootfontein during July 1977 I went back to Pretoria, packed my things and left for Windhoek on transfer, with my wife and children joining me at the end of the year. A move like this is always disruptive: when Annamarié started Standard Nine at Windhoek Hoërskool in 1978 it was her eighth school, in three different languages. But then, there were people who were worse off.

An old friend, Major Lex Krogh, a well-known medical practitioner in Windhoek and a member of the SWA Medical Unit, ushered in my second tour in South West with a story which linked me directly with the past, to the early World War I days when South West was still Deutsch Süd-West Afrika and the South African Forces under General Louis Botha were engaging the Germans. Later he put the story on paper for me.

You are now the first commanding general in South West since Gen Louis Botha. Gen von Trotha of the Herero War was

66

indeed a general, and various German officers who were here since long ago later became generals. But between Gen Botha and you, there has not been another one.

Col von Heydebrech was the original commander of the German Forces. He died after a mortar, built locally by the Germans, exploded. While the surgeon-general, who had been a spectator, had had the decency to die right away, the colonel had four operations before he came to an end. Col von Heydebrech was replaced by Maj Francke – a veteran who was good, but not in the same class. He lacked the necessary dash. He regarded Swakopmund as indefensible and decided to move inland to use the desert in his defence plan.

On Christmas Day 1914 Col Skinner of the Union Forces landed at Walvis Bay. On 3 January 1915 he occupied Swakopmund. On 6 February Gen Botha himself arrived and set up his headquarters at Swakopmund.

Transport for baled grass for the horses and rations for the soldiers was a big problem. But at Swakopmund he picked up another problem – severe diarrhoea. The diarrhoea was probably the well-known gyppo guts. Then there was also gastro-enteritis, mainly among children, treated with egg white. Another disease, of course, was typhoid fever, which was prevented during this war, for the first time in world history, by inoculation. Up to that time more soldiers had died of typhoid than of wounds.

Swakopmund got its name from two Nama words which mean sh*t hole – he who drinks from this water hole will have an upset stomach. We experienced it at school there. Beyond Goanikontes there are many saline springs in the river containing, amongst others, Epsom and Glauber Salts. The general's medical officer must have diagnosed the general's complaint as gastro-enteritis because he recommended egg white, which was unobtainable.

Gen Botha struggled endlessly to find wagons for transporting provisions and fodder. When the decisive battle began, he had only 40 instead of the 400 wagons for which he had begged umpteen times. Although the battle was successful,

the Union Forces continued to be hampered by the shortage
of transport. Later they had 50 mule wagons and 30 donkey
carts to keep 1 300 men and 1 500 animals alive. In the meantime the soldiers had eaten all the oxen used for pulling the
heavy artillery, but fortunately there was no need for artillery
any longer.

Lex quoted Brigadier-General J J Collyer as saying that he found it difficult to understand why Defence Headquarters reacted so poorly to
Botha's pleas, considering that Gen Botha was the Prime Minister of
the Union of South Africa and the commander-in-chief of the forces in
German South West Africa. He also related how General Botha's gyppo
guts were eventually cured: 'A cruiser was sent from Simon's Town with
a few cows, 24 hens and Mrs Botha!'

Botha's medical officer, incidentally, was a major who did not have a
deep regard for discipline. He refused to wear a cap, for example, and
soon resigned. He later became rather better known as the paediatri-
cian, poet and gourmet C Louis Leipoldt.

I did not suffer from gyppo guts, I had no need for cows or chickens,
and I did not have undisciplined poets to deal with. But I had other
problems. We were facing the beginning of a new era for South West,
South Africa and the Defence Force: an era of revolutionary warfare.

*   *   *

The intensity of the conflict had increased considerably since the incident in which Breedt had been shot in the leg near Grootfontein in
1966 and the skirmishes with insurgents at Ogulumbashe in Ovambo
and Singalamwe in the Caprivi during the early years. One has to bear
in mind that, especially after Operation Savannah, the hostilities had
not been of the conventional-warfare type.

In a conventional war a general can move a whole brigade or division
with one command. But this was a counter-insurgency campaign which
consisted of a multitude of small-scale encounters in a 'combat' zone
stretching from Kaokoland in the west to the eastern part of Caprivi,
a distance of more than 1 500 km. Described by many commentators
as a corporals' and lieutenants' war, it was impossible for a general to

oversee every incident. In addition, military action was and always is subordinate to politics. When I left for South West, General Malan gave me specific orders:

- I had to manage the security situation and contain the level of insurgency so that the constitutional process could develop in an atmosphere of stability and peace.
- I had to amalgamate the old SWA Command in the south and 101 Task Force in the north into a new SWA Command with its headquarters in Windhoek.
- I had to establish a defence force for SWA.
- Everything had to be in line with international and internal political developments.

Steenkamp describes my new appointment as one 'which quickly became the most sensitive command position in the SA Defence Force'. I integrated the two military structures and took over from General Gleeson in the north, and in the south from my other cadet-days friend, Brigadier Lourens Oosthuizen, who had succeeded Dirk Marais in the meantime.

Many military officers are obsessed with structural and organisational changes. I have had officers who, to put it bluntly, felt on being given an instruction that they had to re-organise the whole Defence Force before they could do the job. But the desire to re-organise can jeopardise the chances of getting things done.

This anecdote from my friend, Major-General Jack Dutton, illustrates my argument: An outgoing general handed over his responsibilities to his replacement and also gave him three envelopes, with the instruction that when he encountered his first serious problem he was to open the first envelope and follow the enclosed instructions. Subsequent serious problems were to be handled the same way, by acting on the instructions contained in the other two envelopes.

He put the envelopes in his safe, where they stayed until he finally encountered his first real problem and opened the first one. Inside he found a piece of paper which read: 'Blame your predecessor'.

He duly blamed his predecessor and got away with it. Everything then went smoothly for a while. But then he encountered his next serious problem and opened the second envelope. The message contained in this read: 'Re-organise'.

He reorganised. It proved to be such a complicated and time-consuming process that it stifled every other problem. The intermittent hassles had to wait until after the re-organisation. Then came the third big problem. He opened the third envelope and read: 'Prepare three envelopes'.

The tendency to re-organise instead of getting the work done is an ancient disease. The well-known writer and Armscor public relations officer, Bertrand Retief, once produced the following quotation: 'We trained hard, but it seemed that every time we were beginning to establish proper teams we would be re-organised. I was to learn later in life that we tend to meet every new situation by re-organising, and a wonderful method it can be for creating the illusion of progress while producing confusion, inefficiency and demoralisation.' The author of the quotation? The Roman Gaius Petronius, writing in 66 AD.

However, structural changes *were* necessary in South West, *inter alia* to keep the situation in line with the constitutional and political developments. General Malan had made this clear to me.

On the political front, the international initiative concerning South West started to manifest itself in more visible ways. In September 1977 there were negotiations in Pretoria between the South African government and delegates of the Big Five Western powers, the United Kingdom, the United States, France, West Germany and Canada.

Windhoek acquired new political status with the appointment of the first Administrator-General. The Turnhalle Conference, which hosted the negotiations between the leaders of all the population groups and would now function under his guidance, was proceeding well. This was the mechanism that would give substance to the South African government's concept that 'South Westers must decide their own future'.

A new constitutional and political era was heralded by the appointment as Administrator-General of Mr Justice Marthinus Theunis Steyn, to succeed Mr Ben van der Walt. The last of a long line of administrators of South West Africa, Judge Steyn had to apply what was then still merely a broad political guideline. He would have to initiate a democratic process that would result in free and fair one-person-one-vote elections, and at a press conference on his arrival in Windhoek he made his approach clear: 'I am here to stimulate politics, but not to participate in it. At all times I am neutral as far as that is concerned.'

From the Army's point of view the new constitutional dispensation and the implementation of a new political process could succeed only if it (the Army, that is) could provide the necessary security, and in order to accomplish this the existing military structures had to be adjusted. It was essential that there be one integrated structure with its headquarters at Windhoek.

The political climate in which we performed our duties nevertheless remained tough and intricate.

The Turnhalle Conference resulted in a Constituent Assembly and later a National Assembly from which a Council of Ministers was constituted. The reaction of the general public to the political changes was very much in line with patterns forecast by the behavioural sciences experts for such a scenario (and, much later, those who had lived through the South West African process were able to predict the reaction of people to the reform process when it started in South Africa).

I know South West as it was then was not South Africa; I know that there were many differences, and I know that one cannot compare the two. However, there are similarities between the behaviour of different people reacting to the same type of change.

Profound changes always unleash resistance. What comes into play is the so-called RC (Resistance to Change) factor. It creates emotions such as doubt and confusion because one breaks away from the security of the known to face the insecurity of the unknown. Uncertainty causes people to fear for their safety. Change causes divisions between people, polarisation and friction, and the friction can be severe enough to lead to violence.

During September 1977 Dirk Mudge walked out of the ruling white National Party's congress, which resulted in a dramatic split inside the party; A H du Plessis remained the leader of the National Party of SWA and Mudge formed the Republican Party – in South Africa political changes which led *inter alia* to the establishment of the three-chamber parliament had similar results, for example the breakaway of members of the National Party to form the Conservative Party.

Changes normally also lead to alliances and other kinds of group-forming. The Republican Party formed an alliance with parties of the other population groups which was called the Democratic Turnhalle Alliance, or DTA. The National Party of South West in its turn also involved black and brown politicians to form an umbrella organisation, the Action Front for the Preservation of the Turnhalle Principles (Aktur).

Another party was formed by Andreas Shipanga when he returned from exile to South West on 24 August 1978 – he had been one of the founder-members of the Ovamboland People's Organisation, which had been formed early in 1958 in Cape Town, and later became the South West African People's Organisation. His new party, the SWAPO Democrats, became part of the Namibian National Front, or NNF, which was established in April 1977 and included the South West African National Union, or SWANU, Bryan O'Linn's Federal Party and a few more. For some time the NNF was regarded as the largest party left of the DTA on the political spectrum, and just right of SWAPO.

South Africa experienced the same type of political activity in the early 1990s, although it manifested itself in different ways: some parties split, some grouped and re-grouped, and some formed new alliances.

SWAPO itself was not a banned organisation in South West and its political organisation, or so-called internal wing, continued to exist in the new dispensation, while its external wing and its armed organisation, PLAN (People's Liberation Army of Namibia), continued to operate from abroad.

The deeper the political changes cut, the wider the rifts become. Polarisation and friction between parties and groups of parties become more intense. White resistance expressed itself through 'BlankSWA' (WhiteSWA) and the 'Wit Weerstandsbeweging' (White Resistance Movement). Acts of politically inspired violence were committed by radicals from both the left and right extremes of the political spectrum. John Vorster, Theunie Steyn and myself were accused in graffiti on buildings in Windhoek of having sold South West out. Bombing incidents occurred.

South Africa had much the same experience in the early 1990s. Political splits also led to rifts in other fields. The churches and church councils, school advisory boards and agricultural organisations tended to divide along political lines. But wherever you met South Africans and South Westers you would find them joking, even about serious matters.

Dirk Mudge's departure from the National Party Congress led to many people calling him 'the Walker', and on one flight from Windhoek to Johannesburg my sense of humour reared its head when he was given the seat next to mine. When the stewardess took orders for drinks, we both asked for whisky. She returned a while later with two small bottles and asked me: 'I only have Johnny Walker and Bell's. Which would you prefer?'

I couldn't help replying: 'I'd like the Bell's. Please give Mr Mudge the Johnny Walker, it's more his style!'

There were strong emotional concerns among white South Westers which often ended with brothers ranged against brothers and fathers against sons. People threatened each other and sometimes followed their words with action. Someone once said that the fiercest kind of conflict was that between brothers, and I always remembered this. I also heard once that America lost more soldiers during the American civil war than in any other armed conflict, including the world wars, in which they were involved. I mentioned this to a Jewish friend, who remarked: 'Yes, I believe it. This is why the Israelis and Arabs hate each other so much – they're half-brothers.' When there is dissent among Afrikaners it is often the same.

The emotional friction in South West often caused the real meaning of the new vision and the rapid changes which were taking place to become blurred. This was to be expected. But a large number of people also remained level-headed, although in some cases the changes were just too numerous and too rapid to keep pace with and to comprehend fully.

The manner in which the one-person-one-vote elections scheduled for December 1978 were to be conducted was a considerable departure from generally accepted procedures. During national elections the whites had been used to voting for a particular candidate in a certain constituency; now they had to cast a vote for a party at a polling booth, anywhere – and unfamiliar parties with strange names and symbols had appeared overnight.

Not long before the elections I visited an infantry company at Drimiopsis, north of Gobabis. They were brown soldiers of the new SWA Territory Force, or SWATF, that we had established in the area. During a field exercise that afternoon it started to rain, and everyone

73

ran for shelter. There were a few buildings with tiny roofed verandas on to which the troops crammed themselves; jammed in among the soldiers, I heard one of them saying: 'Spread out a bit, you guys, the lightning might strike an innocent person.'

But the story that I really want to tell is about something that happened at an informal party at the end of the visit. An elderly man approached me and struck up a conversation, saying: 'I also want to speak, now.' Before I could reply he complained about the fact that people of all the population groups were being enlisted into the SWATF. I answered him as correctly and politely as possible and explained why this was so. His reaction was: 'I'm just saying.'

But in the course of his 'just saying' he raised another complaint. Why had one of his white employees been called up again for a month or two for border duty? Once again I responded politely and explained why this was sometimes necessary. I added that I respected his right to have his own opinion, but that I could not understand how one person could complain about both issues at the same time; because if you were against the employment of black, brown and yellow soldiers, then you must accept that whites would have to give more of their time for military service.

Anyway, we had a friendly talk and when he had had his say, he added with all appearances of seriousness: 'Now, General, these elections in December; since I can't vote for a candidate any more, can I vote for the Defence Force?' Maybe he wasn't serious and just felt like pulling my leg. But it is so that when change causes confusion, people tend to fall back on traditional values – and they wanted to be able to rely on the Defence Force.

Even after the elections some people still failed to comprehend the extent of the changes brought about by one-person-one-vote politics ... and it was not only the South Westers who had this problem. A number of South Africans involved in the South West situation who occasionally visited the territory, people with the benefit of the insight and understanding usually brought about by distance, allowed themselves to be trapped by the emotional aspects of the politics of the day.

I listened to many conversations that started with a balanced discussion about the future of South West but soon resulted in two groups being formed, one supporting A H du Plessis, Eben van Zijl and Kosie

Pretorius of the National Party and the other backing Dirk Mudge and his colleagues of the Republican Party. It was as if SWAPO and the other parties did not exist. In other words, they had reverted to the tradition-al white politics of the past. The new challenges – independence for the territory under a democratic government – went unseen

One-person-one-vote politics in a country where the electorate crossed colour lines and consisted of voters ranging from highbrow intellectuals to bush-dwellers had different dynamics from the kind of politics with which people had been familiar up to then. What counted was the method of intellectual persuasion. Some voters would make informed decisions after listening to speeches and reading newspaper editorials. Others would be inspired mainly by emotion. Speeches and leading articles would pass them by, and the way they decided to vote would be the cumulative end-result of emotions such as anger and fear, sentiments, nationalistic urges, tradition and ethnic values. This facet of politics is vulnerable to sentimental and emotional incitement and intimidation. Intimidation could even play the main role.

I did not find the going easy; to stay on track you had to be strong: in your belief, in your head and in your heart. But I was not too unfamiliar with the actual circumstances. During the stormy late 1940s and early 1950s in South Africa, as I mentioned earlier, the very newspaper you read first at breakfast at the Military College had been a serious matter because it might be an indication of whether you were a patriot or a 'jingo' – or something close to either.

I dared not leave the office with a newspaper under my arm in case it sent out the wrong political signals. Were I to be seen with *Die Suidwester,* the RP supporters would say I was an NP man and an A H du Plessis sup-porter. In the case of *Die Republikein* I would be branded an RP man and Dirk Mudge supporter – 'boem, schluss, finish and klaar!', to use a typi-cal trilingual South West expression.

* * *

It was the 1940s and 1950s all over again, right down to school level; just as Ouboet and I had had to choose between the Germans and the English at one school after the other, so my children would be con-fronted with: 'Are you for A H du Plessis or are you for Dirk Mudge?'

75

At the Eros Primary School my daughter Lollie was in the same class as Barend Spies, son of the well-known academic, farmer, journalist and story-teller Dr Jan Spies, who also happened to support the DTA. Naturally little Barend was a proud DTA supporter, and once – at the wrong time and place – he announced his sympathies. A bloody nose and a swollen lip soon brought it home to him that not everybody shared his sentiments.

Children can be crueller intimidators than adults, but they are not good at resisting when they are being intimidated. Thanks to my own experiences I had some understanding of what must have been going on in the minds of our own children, who eventually learned to say that they did not vote for either A H du Plessis or Dirk Mudge, they voted for their father, Jannie Geldenhuys.

These were merely some of the stresses of white politics in those days. But other population groups were also suffering from uncertainty, confusion, anger and fear, especially those who were afraid of Ovambo domination and intimidation in general.

None of this had anything to do with me; but I was directly involved in the sense that the Defence Force had to be commanded and managed in such a way that it could achieve its mission in this atmosphere and under these changing circumstances. And apart from its formal task the Defence Force also had an informal role to play, by contributing to calming an unsettled society through its general behaviour, since friction resulting in violence became a security problem. This meant that the Defence Force had to remain as neutral as was humanly possible, and also that the less its members participated in politics, the better. To this end I formulated a few principles for myself.

Firstly, I stayed out of party politics and expected the same of my colleagues. This was not a problem as far as Permament Force members were concerned, since the majority consisted of South Africans who were not personally or emotionally involved in the political situation. And then, of course, Permanent Force members were professional soldiers who were on duty 24 hours a day, so that the official restrictions on political activities could be strictly applied.

It was another matter with the part-time soldiers of the Citizen Force and commandos. The problem here was that they were full-time citizens of the country and only part-time soldiers, with most of them spending no more than five per cent of their time in military service. They were also born South Westers who loved their country. How was one to keep them out of party politics when they had a right and duty to take part in such activities?

There was, of course, the bureaucratic solution: throw the book of rules at them. There had always been proper guidelines and restrictions governing the behaviour of Defence Force members in respect of party politics, but one cannot command by means of pieces of paper. Paper 'talks' only once, but cannot answer questions, whereas people, especially officers and non-commissioned officers, had questions to ask and wanted answers – and one cannot deny any person that human right.

So I developed a formula for the part-time officers. I said that it was their right as citizens to participate in politics. I could not and would not take that away from them. But it was also fair for me to expect extreme circumspection from them in times of unrest and suspicion, so as not to damage the cohesion and effectiveness of the military machine. As 'circumspection' is a vague term, I elaborated as follows: should an officer be politically active, it was his duty to behave in such a manner that the men under his command would not have any reason to complain. They should have no reason to say that they could no longer serve under him because his behaviour caused strife and endangered the unit's *esprit de corps*.

I think this was as fair, just and correct as it was possible to be. And whatever the regulations, one could not find much wrong with such an approach. Furthermore, the responsibility to play watchdog over the officers and non-commissioned officers was passed from my shoulders to theirs. Everyone was now his own watchdog, and his norm became the reaction of the men whom he led and towards whom he had a moral duty.

The second guideline I followed to develop a politically neutral Defence Force was never to address selected audiences, if at all possible. If I addressed a unit, I never separated the South Africans and South Westers, and colour played no part. With regard to the public, it would probably have been easy to talk about the Defence Force if we had had a politically homogeneous audience. It would have been easy to address a purely Herstigte Nasionale Party audience, a DTA gathering, or

77

only NNF people. But if I had any say in the matter, I always addressed mixed audiences, because then I had no choice but to be factually correct and objective.

I can't remember ever inviting politicians of only one party for visits to the operational area. I invited them from the whole spectrum of South West. All briefings and subsequent discussions were conducted with representatives from all the parties. My door was always open for members of any party who needed to discuss military matters with me. I had discussions with politicians such as Sarel Becker of the HNP, Eben van Zijl of the NP, Chief Riruako of the DTA, Reinhard Rukoro, Dr Ken and Othile Abrahams and her sister Nora Chase of SWANU, and Andreas Shipanga of the SWAPO Democrats. I found all their remarks and requests concerning the Defence Force reasonable, and I would like to flatter myself that we did not just listen to them as a matter of courtesy or a gesture of goodwill, but gave serious attention to their comments, then followed up and reported back to them.

Thirdly, I tried to keep all military personnel informed. My term of command coincided with the negotiations between the five Western powers and the UN which would eventually lead to the settlement plan for South West and the UN Security Council's Resolution 435, and after each important political development involving the UN I always organised a formal session to report back. These sessions included feedback on negotiations with the UN's military representatives such as General Hannes Philipp and later General Prem Chand, and I would inform all Permanent Force, Citizen Force and commando commanding officers and their key personnel about events, especially where I was personally involved. These included visits to South West and discussions with Prime Minister and later State President P W Botha, and with Mr Pik Botha, the Minister of Foreign Affairs from 1 April 1977.

Political leaders and newspapers also reported on the political events I dealt with, but of course, they did so in a way that promoted their own policies and viewpoints, creating conflicting perceptions. The commanders needed more neutral interpretations, and I tried to be factual, unbiased, clinical and accurate. After a few of these conferences the commanding officers started enquiring regularly about when the next session would take place, from which I deduced that they were taking them seriously.

All commanders, in turn, had to keep the people under their command informed, and this was not always easy, as I discovered from Commandant Delville Linford after one feedback session with his Bushman battalion. His soldiers had listened attentively, he said, but had ended up confused. The cause of the confusion, they explained to him in a roundabout way, was the numbering of Resolution 435.

They were happy with the school at their Omega base, and with the fact that their children were doing well there, they said; in fact, they had also learnt quite a bit themselves, they added, among other things how to count – 1,2,3,4,5,6,7,8,9,10. But they didn't understand how he could talk about 'Resolution 435. Surely it should be 'Resolution 345?'

The UN Secretary-General at the time was Kurt Waldheim, who obviously had no feeling for Bushman mathematics. His successor, Perez de Cuellar, was more sympathetically inclined. During the run-up to the Gulf War, he and President George Bush accommodated the Bushmen's sense of mathematical progression with Resolution 678. But during 1992 De Cuellar's successor, Boutros Boutros-Ghali, messed up the figures again with his resolution about violence in South Africa, Resolution 765.

At other places similar presentations required just as much patience. An officer in Ovamboland told me about an occasion when a chief and his advisers had come to ask him what was happening. He then gave them a detailed explanation about the involvement of the UN, the position of the Administrator-General, the role of the Defence Force in Ovamboland and all the other things he thought might be of interest to them. But when he had finished, the first question concerned the subject uppermost in their minds: 'When will the primary school's broken windows be repaired?'

That was the nature of South West's political tangle and the attempts we made to prevent the Defence Force from becoming caught up in it. We might have made mistakes, but I doubt if anyone else could have done better under the same circumstances, and I believe our approach was largely successful. By way of proof I could point to several very successful operations conducted by Commandant Stoffel Rothman's commando in the Outjo district, where SWAPO infiltrators several times penetrated the so-called northern white farming area.

During one such operation Commandant Rothman's commando was mobilised, including his mounted platoon, and the 'sitreps', or situation reports, sent through by the commando as per standing procedures tell the story.

It should be explained that a sitrep is sent at regular intervals to the next higher headquarters at prescribed times, and consists of a report that covers the preceding 24-hour period. To keep the sitrep short, index letters are used to indicate paragraph headings: Thus the A represents enemy activities, B deals with 'own forces' activities, C with administrative and logistical matters and D with matters of general interest.

One of the Outjo sitreps my staff passed on to me had the following to say:

A: Unchanged
B: NTR (nothing to report)
C: Unchanged
D: Aktur, DTA and NNF members all well

The dividing line between military activities and politics, however, was not always very distinct, and sometimes caused suspicion and strife.

The Defence Force never performed its duties in a vacuum; the environment in which it operated also featured political policies and opinions. In this regard it could take a noncommittal stand, but there were also political structures which it could not ignore and within which it had to operate, since it served the government of the day.

The Defence Force had contact with the South African government through the normal channels to the Minister of Defence, but also had to have contact with the South West government, and so liaison was established with the office of the Administrator-General.

The usual three levels of government also existed in South West. Examples of second-tier governments were the Ovambo and Kavango administrations. If, as was actually the case, there was a military presence in Kavango, the commanding officer would have to liaise with the Chief Minister of Kavango and his cabinet. If these ministers were DTA members, for example, it did not necessarily follow that the Defence Force was involved in party politics – but people did not always see it like that.

The Defence Force tried to remain as neutral as possible towards the parties, with the exception of SWAPO. SWAPO was not a banned organisation, but its external armed wing (PLAN) did conduct armed activities inside the territory, which from a security point of view branded its members as the enemy.

Part-time members of the Defence Force sometimes tried to persuade me to give them personal opinions and advice on South West party politics. I did, on a few occasions, go so far as to say that one found politicians who identified political issues and would give their views on those issues; and then one found other politicians who identified political problems and would offer their solutions to those problems. I took the second category of politicians more seriously than the first, I said; solutions counted for more than mere opinions, and the only real solution to the South West African political problem would be one that enjoyed meaningful international support.

It was mainly in the south, in towns such as Windhoek, Swakopmund, Keetmanshoop and Mariental, that people became tangled up in the party-political turmoil around them. The people north of the Red Line, on the other hand, at places such as Oshakati, Rundu and Katima Mulilo, were caught up with what was happening on their doorsteps; they were more sensitive to the daily security situation, and the doings of the UN, the AG and such matters almost passed them by.

Until 1977 it was much the same with the Defence Force members. Those in the north were busy with operations and did not concern themselves with events in Windhoek. They had closer ties with Pretoria, and operations were all that mattered. Then, with the integration of 101 Task Force and SWA Command they acquired more balanced perceptions.

The major military effort in South West was focused on Ovamboland – and this was another political nettle. In Ovamboland the Defence Force was fighting against insurgents who laid mines on public roads, set up ambushes, abducted school-children and killed traditional chiefs. During a two-year period from about 1978 to 1979, 23 chiefs and headmen were killed, including the Chief Minister, Chief Filemon Elifas, Minister Toivo Shiyagaya and Minister Shikongo (in South Africa during the early 1990s, especially in Natal, much the same situation prevailed). This climate of hard intimidation had an inhibiting effect on active politics.

81

The Defence Force always regarded insurgency as a political struggle between the government and the revolutionary movement, which made use of terror tactics. The security forces fought the insurgents to maintain order, stability and security, so that politics could be conducted in freedom from organised violence and intimidation. But the government had to wage the political struggle.

I often heard complaints in Ovamboland that the government did not fulfil its responsibilities in waging the political struggle – although, of course, it is quite difficult to determine whether a government conducts such a struggle as a government or as a political party.

SWAPO ran its politics from kraal to kraal, while the government concentrated on administrative functions, but one cannot fight a revolutionary war through administration alone. It is a principle of successful anti-revolutionary warfare that the government of the day must propagate a cause that is more attractive than that of the revolutionaries, and the Ovambo government might have been able to do this, because they were not without political ammunition.

SWAPO said it wanted freedom and independence for South West – which was promised them in the new dispensation; independence in the form of a unitary state; and free and fair elections. The only condition was that they had to lay down their arms, join the new political process as many others did, and contest the elections. This seemed a better way of attaining power than fighting for it.

Judge Steyn and his successors did indeed activate a free democratic process. The December 1978 election was 'indisputably free and fair', conducted under the eyes of a number of Western observers. One can only speculate about what the outcome would have been if SWAPO had accepted the invitation to participate. Be that as it may, I do not want to be drawn into these political arguments and their merits or demerits. The point that I want to make is that whatever the arguments might have been, the Ovambo government failed to capitalise on what had been offered to them.

I often got the impression that the second-tier politicians had been trained in public administration but never really groomed for party politics. Not that there was a total lack of political activity, but it seemed to be conducted through the traditional tribal chiefs and the authorities. And they were no match for the SWAPO political commissars.

Anti-SWAPO party politics in Ovambo had a very low profile. I recall having an interview with a visitor who had travelled to Ovamboland to analyse the situation and then come to see me on completion of his research. To my amazement I realised that he was not even aware of the existence of the party headed by the Chief Minister, Pastor Cornelius Ndjoba!

The profile of international politics did not seem to be much higher than Ndjoba's, although it did eventually result in an agreement.

On 26 September 1977 the conference of the Western Five with South Africa ended without reaching a settlement. During February 1978 Western negotiators were in Windhoek to confer with the various political parties, including SWAPO's 'internal' wing. During the same month Western diplomats held discussions with Pik Botha and Sam Nujoma in New York without any sign of progress. At the end of the month Nujoma made his well-known statement that SWAPO was not interested in majority government, and that the aim of its struggle was to seize power in Namibia.

Then, on 25 April 1978, the South African government formally accepted the Western proposals for a settlement in South West Africa, the agreement which would later achieve formal status through UN Resolution 435.

CHAPTER 7

SOUTH WEST – A WINNING APPROACH

Time does not take sides

Talking politics was in full swing, and so was shooting politics. PLAN was well established in Angola, and its activities increased considerably: during October 1977 a skirmish involving 88 insurgents started 1km south of the border and by the time it was over a few days later had moved more than 20 km into Angola. It was the closest thing to a full-scale battle to take place in South West since the South African invasion in 1915, and at the end two PLAN bases had been destroyed and a third seriously damaged; in all, 61 insurgents were killed, while the security force lost six men.

The customary propaganda claims followed. This was something SWAPO was very good at. On 30 October 1977 Peter Katjavivi stated in London that the South African losses amounted to double figures, and claimed that the encounter had taken place at Ondangwa, 55 km south of the border (in fact Ondangwa was our biggest operational air base in the north). Later Katjavivi also announced that PLAN had attacked our border base at Eenhana, killing and wounding many South African soldiers, driving the rest out of the base and destroying a lot of vehicles and communications equipment.

Apart from the fact that the South African Defence Force was not allowed to conceal its personnel losses, it was also impossible on a practical level. But it was difficult to refute such allegations, and as a result many people believed them. For once, however, these wild allegations suited me well, and the *friction de guerre* was on my side.

Shortly before this incident I had invited a representative group of journalists to tour the border area, including stops at Ondangwa and Eenhana; now, in the wake of Katjavivi's claims, I invited them for a follow-up visit. They were able to confirm that Katjavivi's statement was a lie – one journalist reported that the only change he had observed since his previous visit to Eenhana two months earlier was that the base's chaplain had erected a new signboard pointing the way to the chapel!

And that was not the end of my good fortune. During one of the UN's excursions to South West its delegation stopped at Luanda on their outbound flight. There SWAPO told them the same stories, and when they arrived in Windhoek, General Hannes Philipp, the UN Force Commander-designate, requested that Ondangwa and Eenhana be included in the group's itinerary.

When Philipp and his party arrived at Eenhana they asked the commander, Commandant Anton van Graan, what the name of the base was. When Anton confirmed that it was Eenhana, an astounded Philipp said: 'But it can't be. Eenhana was destroyed!' But he could judge for himself – and he made no further enquiries about Ondangwa.

* * *

In the meantime the area of armed activity expanded eastwards, as far as Caprivi. During November 1977 a potentially nasty infiltration occurred when Zambian soldiers launched a mortar attack on an observation post on the southern bank of the Zambezi and the South Africans retaliated. The result was an hour-long exchange. A few Zambian bombs fell inside the town of Katima Mulilo, but the residents were not unduly perturbed. The town had come under sporadic fire since 1974, so that slit trenches had been dug and sandbags stacked in front of the houses along the Zambezi; an alarm system had also been installed after two similar incidents earlier in 1977.

On 19 February 1978 a group of infiltrators crossed into Caprivi from Zambia, set up an ambush between Katima Mulilo and Mapacha and fired an RPG-9 rocket-propelled grenade at a Land Rover, killing Commandant Bill Poole, Major Dries Els and a Mr De Lange of the Atlas Aircraft Corporation; a fourth occupant, a Mr Mollenbeek of the Armaments Corporation, survived.

On 27 March extensive violence erupted again, starting with the murder of Chief Clemens Kapuuo, leader of the Hereros, chairman of the Democratic Turnhalle Alliance and SWAPO's fierce enemy, who had been regarded by many as a possible future president of an independent South West Africa.

This was the security situation. To win this war, we had to develop a strategy based on sound premises. How was one to go about it? So many factors and considerations came into play. We were definitely not ignorant about the nature of the war. We already had the experience of the acts of violence that had been committed in South Africa by the armed wings of the Pan-Africanist Congress and the African National Congress. In both these cases, however, the nature and extent of the violence were such that the South African Police could take responsibility for curbing it.

Members of the police had also gained experience in counter-insurgency in Rhodesia. In South West the first incidents had occurred as far back as 1966, but once again the frequency had been so low that the police had remained responsible for public safety and internal security.

During 1973 the Defence Force was made responsible for counter-insurgency and the protection of South West's borders, and took over from the police. It was then a conflict of very low intensity which had been interrupted to an extent by Operation Savannah in 1975–1976, but when the insurgency resumed after Savannah the scene had changed.

It had been a while since we had campaigned on this scale. There had been World War II, Korea and Operation Savannah, but officers and other ranks with experience of warfare were hard to come by, and in any case every war is unique. Even during World War II very few South Africans had held senior command positions or served as senior staff officers at a level higher than brigade, and only a few were still available.

During World War II formations and units of the then Union Defence Force had generally formed part of divisions, armies and corps of the Allied forces. The UDF's formations and units fell in with the higher formations' overall planning, fitted into their command and control structures and were served by their logistic systems. Now, however, we had to rely on ourselves to establish the most effective war machine possible, maintained by its own supporting systems. And though we were not in the desert of North Africa or in Europe, we conducted a war from our base area in South Africa to the northern reaches of South West.

While operating in Angola, our troops were deployed over a vast distance. It is 2 440 km by rail from Bloemfontein to Grootfontein; 669 km by road from Grootfontein to Cassinga and approximately 1 900 km by air from Bloemfontein to Cassinga.

In South West we operated across vast areas with a poor infrastructure. In the summer, in the early days, it took a convoy from Grootfontein to Katima Mulilo and back three to four weeks along the Golden Highway; later it took ten days along the new road.

I could now capitalise on my years of training. In South Africa, training in counter-insurgency had started in all seriousness in 1960, and my experience as an instructor in the subject stood me in good stead. My knowledge was complemented by my observations in Angola and the continuous private study I had undertaken about the protracted wars the Portuguese had fought abroad in Angola, Portuguese Guinea and Mozambique. But no ready-made manual existed which could tell a commanding general in South West how to go about his task.

One person whose work was of great value to me was a previous Chief of the Army, Lieutenant-General C A (Pop) Fraser, who had published a study during the early 1960s entitled *Lessons Learnt from Past Revolutionary Wars*; I identified myself with its contents both emotionally and intellectually, and made his ideas my own. Some of his important points were:

- A revolutionary war is a political war.
- The aim of both sides in a revolutionary war is to win the support of the population, their approval, sympathy and active participation.
- The government must win the political initiative by propagating a

more attractive cause than that offered by the insurgents.
- The danger of complacency (a refusal to acknowledge the real situation) must be avoided before and during a revolution.
- The existence of an outstanding intelligence organisation is essential.
- In revolutionary warfare, bureaucratic delays are as dangerous as subversion itself.
- The best counter-measure to a revolution is – good government.

During the years I also developed my own approaches and concepts. Often I could apply them in practice, and they helped me to read intricate situations with understanding and insight.

One such concept concerns the nature of conventional and revolutionary warfare. Conventional warfare is greatly influenced by the exact sciences, technology and military equipment (the commander of the American air forces during the Gulf War described it as a technological war). Insurgency warfare, on the other hand, is influenced more by aspects related to the social sciences; simply put, it is about people, not machines.

In a nutshell, conventional warfare consists of movement and the delivery of fire-power. By concentrating fire-power on the right places at the right time, one can cause enough destruction to win crucial battles and force a final decision. In this way the war can be ended in a short time. This kind of warfare lends itself to centralised command and management.

Insurgency warfare, however, consists of a multitude of small actions. One cannot bring such a war to a quick end through military action because the enemy does not present one with a geographic military objective on which to concentrate fire-power. Command should therefore be decentralised to a large extent. This kind of war will end in a victory for the insurgents when the government forces collapse as a result of continual set-backs over a period; or the population's will to resist is broken down by attrition. The government's forces will win when it can persuade the population that its cause is more attractive than that of the revolutionaries; or the insurgents, after lengthy periods of relentless operations, do not make progress, lose the support of the population, and negotiations become a more attractive alternative;

88

or the insurgents' host country becomes fatigued by its involvement in the war.

If insurgents have access to a safe haven across an international border a military victory cannot be achieved unless the host country can be persuaded, in some way or another, to withdraw its support. Jordan, for example, refused to give the Palestinian Liberation Organisation free access to Israel from its territory. The Israelis also tried for a long time to create a situation that would make it impossible for Lebanon to be used any longer as a launching-pad for terrorist attacks against them. But this is theory. Let us move on to the realities. We had to address certain key questions:

- From a security point of view we had to make a contribution which would enable the political process to succeed in establishing an independent South West with a democratic form of government. What did this mean in practice?
- We had to prevent military adventures and violence from becoming a means to seize power, or unduly influencing political decisions. How could we achieve this?

We found the answers. Flowing from our concept of the management style required for the successful waging of anti-revolutionary warfare, the matter of centralisation and decentralisation of command was amply clarified. In addition, the Chief of the Army, General Viljoen, and his headquarters expected results from us in Windhoek. They, too, issued directives and even initiated operational actions. Yet it was actually the sector and sub-sector commanders and their captains and sergeants who fought the war.

One may justly ask what function the GOC and his staff in Windhoek were supposed to perform between these two levels when the system was based on decentralised command. In fact there was an important role to play, and we played it. In addition to responding to the directives from our higher headquarters we also formulated for ourselves what the Defence Force was expected to achieve in South West. The sector commanders were actually responsible for operations, but we could provide invaluable guidance and support.

We realised that each sector was unique, and tried not to issue instructions of a general nature which were to be followed by all. From the point of view of the overall command level, we looked at the sectors individually. Each had to have its own design for operations. Our concept for managing anti-revolutionary warfare led us to revise the existing directives issued to the sector commanders, as well as the form of their directives to their subordinate commanders.

The formulation of the 'mission' paragraph in the old directives can be summarised as follows: The commander was required to search for and destroy all insurgents in his area of responsibility within the period of his appointment. If it was possible in practice to accomplish such a mission we would leave it at that. But in certain areas of the border that was an impossible task. The infiltrators could always escape into their host countries, Zambia and Angola. Where that was the position, the mission was redefined to the effect that the commander was expected to decrease the level of insurgency in his area to a certain level within a specified time. This could easily be defined by using various parameters.

One could not allow a competent commander who had worked hard and effectively, and substantially reduced terror in his area, to believe that he had failed in his mission simply because he had not managed to wipe out all the insurgents, since this would be highly demotivating. His new mission would be revised periodically; when the set goal had been achieved, the parameters would be scaled up. In this way realistic goals were set. Some commanders reached their new goals time and again, so that in due course it became a realistic mission for them to completely clear their respective areas of all insurgents.

Apart from the matter of directives, and bearing in mind Pop Fraser's lessons, we gave serious attention to our intelligence system. Our intelligence staff officer, Commandant Johann Saaiman, played an important role, and my personal contribution towards improving the system was to transfer many of the trained junior intelligence officers and non-commissioned officers on my staff in Windhoek to the operational areas. The aim was to increase the quality and quantity of intelligence collected at the active spots. One could process more information and provide a better quality of intelligence from the forward areas with fewer staff in Windhoek, rather than the other way round.

We formulated the command directives more realistically and set out to improve the intelligence organisation. The answer to the question of how to go about preventing armed intimidation from negatively influencing the political decision-making was to gain and maintain the initiative.

I held strong beliefs about the concept of initiative. Initiative is of vital importance in conflict and was always an important consideration during our planning cycle. The thrust of the approach we developed was one which I had not come across anywhere else. One first had to find an honest answer to the question: who held the initiative, you or your opponent? And the fundamental truth in an insurgency war is that the insurgent, potentially and often in practice, has the initiative.

Basically, initiative means that when two parties are in conflict and party A takes certain actions which result in reaction by party B, then party A has the initiative. For example, compare sabotage with crime. A criminal who plans to snatch a lady's handbag is the one who selects the time, place and victim. He has the initiative. The same goes for a person who plants a bomb or sets up an ambush. And in a conflict situation the one who has the initiative seldom loses. Put another way, it seldom happens that the one who does not have the initiative wins. It is therefore imperative that ways and means of obtaining the initiative and keeping it are found. One way to do this is to act first, by taking the battle to the insurgent, instead of waiting.

The planning process thus works as follows: if you believe that your opponent has the initiative, you first plan out what to do to successfully counter his expected actions. Then you apply your mind to the question of what else you can do to gain the initiative – if not immediately then certainly in due course – and duly incorporate the answer in your plan.

If you believe that you have the initiative, you first have to decide what it is that you want to achieve and how to go about doing so. Then you ask yourself what your opponent could do to counter your intended action. When you have the answer to that, you augment your plan to prevent him from doing so.

During our planning cycles and normal environmental studies we also identified patterns through which we could develop new concepts and modes of operation. One such pattern was a seasonal phenomenon. The insurgent is less effective during the dry season because water is scarce and he can easily be ambushed at water-points. In addition, the foliage affords him little cover against observation, while the mobility of the security forces is at its best, because during the rainy season he has good cover and enough water. These advantages were exploited by insurgents for deep infiltration into districts such as the so-called white farming areas. They avoided water-holes and used pylons and roads as navigational aids.

Another pattern that we identified was the greater intensity of activities during the time of the full moon, and fall-off in movement during the dark moon.

Statistics may not always seem clearly to reflect these patterns because other factors tend to disturb the picture. In the case of South West, the most important of these was the political factor. Insurgent operations were normally planned specifically to precede or coincide with political events such as relevant sessions of the UN's General Assembly or Security Council, meetings of the Liberation Committee of the OAU and visits by influential persons.

Likewise, our own periodic major cross-border operations also disturbed the general patterns and created ones of their own. North of the border, in Angola, the rank-and-file insurgents were accommodated in detachment bases. They infiltrated from there to operate in areas south of the border which were adjacent to their respective base areas. However, there were also special groups with bases elsewhere who could take on targets at any place south of the border, concentrating mainly on sabotage and mine-laying.

After our strikes across the border, we found that the dislodged detachment insurgents became inactive for some time, while the special groups were usually not disrupted to any great extent by our operations. One could then expect a constant or higher frequency of mine- and bomb-related incidents – relatively simple operations with high propaganda value.

Another pattern that we observed was that our communication operations – which Willem Steenkamp called 'goodwill programmes', and the troops' 'plough-and-plant' programmes – tended to prevent insurgency from starting in an area, but we were less successful in countering it if it had already commenced. However, communication operations did make a valuable contribution in such areas, provided that they were pre-planned as a follow-up action to successful fighting operations.

We also found that the Citizen Force soldiers were more successful in this kind of operation than the national servicemen. A Citizen Force sergeant with a beard, proudly showing around a photograph of his wife and four kids, made a better impression on the head of a kraal than a brave and fit second-lieutenant with down on his chin and a snapshot of his school girlfriend.

The main objective of our strategy was to clean up Kaokoland, Kavango and Caprivi. By achieving this aim, we would reduce the vast area that had been infiltrated by insurgents so that only Ovamboland remained. We could then concentrate our efforts there and fight more cost-effectively. It might have seemed an impossible task, given the circumstances, but in time we managed to do so.

We distributed our available manpower and other resources with this strategy in mind. The men of Sector 10 (Ovamboland), remarked on the 'high' force levels allotted to other areas, for example Caprivi, but eventually we were sufficiently successful to reduce our troops there and increase the force levels in Ovamboland. In addition we carried out a detailed analysis of the numbers of troops we were employing on defensive tasks, such as guard and escort duties, as opposed to those we used for offensive action. This type of operational activity does not, in itself, win a war. It is therefore necessary to limit to the absolute minimum the number of troops deployed for such purposes.

One example of offensive action is the 'search-and-destroy' operation, which can give you the upper hand, and we tried to make more troops available for this purpose. Similarly, we tried to allocate an increased number of troops for night operations, even if it meant using fewer in daylight operations. Likewise, we planned to use more troops in areas just across the border and smaller numbers inside the border, when it was allowed.

General Malan clearly demarcated responsibilities with regard to cross-border operations. A decision to cross the border was a political one for which the government and the Minister of Defence carried the responsibility. The successful execution of the operation was the responsibility of the Chief of the Defence Force. Detailed instructions were always issued. For example, the circumstances under which hot-pursuit operations were allowed, and the restrictions governing them, were clearly defined. The instructions with regard to Angola, Zambia and Botswana differed, and were continuously amended as the political situation changed.

There were times when we were not allowed to operate at all into Angola, or when we could only carry out non-offensive reconnaissance, subject to certain limitations. Sometimes we were allowed to conduct operations in Angola south of a specified east–west line, provided we did not exceed prescribed force levels.

In the last case, if we could 'shift the border northwards' 10 kilometres or so, we could force contact on cadres inside Angola rather than south of the border. In this way we could reduce insurgent incidents inside South West Africa. If we could dominate the area immediately north of the border, fewer troops would be needed for counter-infiltration, border protection and other defensive tasks inside Ovamboland. Thus more troops would be available for offensive operations. One disadvantage of limiting operations to south of the border was that the tracks of insurgents were often detected only after they had committed an undesirable act. Statistics later proved that operations across the border also saved lives.

There were two kinds of cross-border operations: specific operations and general operations. The first kind was a pre-planned operation, in and out, aimed at pre-selected PLAN bases – a pre-emptive attack just before a new wave of infiltration is a good example of this type of action. During such operations we lost, on average, only one man for every 100 insurgents killed.

General operations, on the other hand, were much the same as the area operations we conducted south of the border with the aim of dominating an area and destroying insurgents. In such operations we lost an average of one man to every 30 of the enemy.

In internal operations we lost an average of one to every ten or less of the enemy. However, this was not always the case, since operations in South West and Angola differed substantially from place to place and from time to time. There were many regional variations within the operational area.

The operational area literally stretched from the Atlantic Ocean in the west to Mpalela Island in the east (the point where four countries met — South West, Botswana, Zambia and Zimbabwe), and from the Red Line in the south, the foot-and-mouth cattle disease boundary, to an east–west line approximately 45 km north of the border. Map 1 compares the size of the operational area to that of South Africa. Isolated actions outside this area also took place periodically.

The zone included regions abounding with trees, such as Caprivi; while other areas, such as the southern parts of Angola, consisted of bushveld. There were areas with large rivers, such as Kavango, while others were flat and empty, for example Ovamboland, and areas comprising savannah-type grasslands. Yet other regions like Kaokoland consisted of high mountains and deep valleys. An added complication was that the populations differed from region to region.

There were many reasons why any area's operational designs and techniques needed to be changed from time to time. For example, every time the insurgents adapted themselves to our initiatives we had to come up with fresh tactics and methods to unsettle them and keep them on the defensive mentally.

We often had a mixture of success and failure. Progress would be made in the Kaokoveld, but problems would arise in Caprivi. Or progress might be seen in Caprivi, but the situation would be deteriorating in Ovamboland. In Kavango it could be peaceful today and ominous the next. The bottom line was that what worked in one place did not necessarily work in another, and what had worked in one year would not necessarily work again later on.

I had the good fortune to have been able to observe the whole picture from the beginning to the end, from the lowest to the highest level. I was involved throughout the whole period of the war, and across the whole extent of the zone, and over time we slowly but surely got the upper hand.

A few specific cross-border operations made headlines: Operation Reindeer on 4 May 1978 and Operation Sceptic, or 'Smokeshell' as it is often misnamed, on 10 June 1980. Both were particularly significant. Each, in turn, had a positive influence on the course of the war. In time other cross-border operations further strengthened our position. The cumulative result of all these operations was one of the most successful counter-insurgency campaigns since World War II.

Before providing details of Operation Reindeer, which included the

95

attack on the town of Cassinga, I want to make it clear that in the end it was the general ground and air operations that earned us international acclaim, while the large-scale specific cross-border operations which were aimed at gaining a winning advantage were dramatic and spectacular. Some of these operations, or parts of them, were professional ruses of war, the subjects of books and videos.

However, in my opinion it was the overall effect of the almost unseen but incessant day-to-day general operations that brought us success. It was our sustained general operations that distinguished the campaign from other counter-insurgency wars elsewhere in the world, and it was this that commanded respect. I refer to protection and escort duties, border protection, tracking and follow-up operations, ambushes, search-and-destroy operations and relentless offensive area patrolling on foot and for long periods at a time, as well as nagging pursuits.

My statement can be illustrated with the following example. After we had terminated our support to Renamo, people remained suspicious and asked me why the Mozambican government forces, while still receiving aircraft, tanks, armoured cars and artillery from the Soviet Union, could not force Renamo to its knees without South African support.

We had good intelligence on the operational patterns and battle techniques of the Mozambican forces, and to me the answer was obvious. I always answered that if we had been expected to use tanks and guns against PLAN we would not have known what to do with them. We used weapons such as aircraft and guns with devastating hitting power on only a few occasions during the bush war, usually during specific cross-border operations, when we attacked strongly defended bases, or when we faced the risk of getting involved with Cuban forces and FAPLA. If all other factors remained constant, the war against Renamo could not have been won unless patrolling was kept up every day, day and night, far and wide, on foot and for long periods at a time. The Mozambican forces did not do it. We did.

Another example. After the Lusaka Accord in 1984, we sent out joint patrols with FAPLA. We were amazed to find that the FAPLA men had to operate with only one water bottle per soldier per day. How many kilometres can a soldier patrol on one bottle of water?

It was in this respect that our Citizen Force and Commando Force troops, during the early stages, and after them the national servicemen and Permanent Force soldiers of all branches, made their mark in silent perseverance. This is the South African soldier, the best I know. They had to show guts and stamina, and they did. In this kind of war short-lived excellence does not mean much. Many people, including some who speak with authority, liked to use the popular cliché that time was on the side of the insurgent. It was not entirely untrue. The motive of the revolutionary strategist is to wear down and exhaust its target country by means of ceaseless multiple actions over a long time. And it works. But there is another side to this theory.

I believe that time is neutral. Time does not take sides. Time is on the side of those who make the best use of it. Time can be on the side of the one with the best staying-power, but sticking-it-out strategies can become destructive to all parties concerned. For them to succeed, from the point of view of the anti-revolutionaries, there should be a national strategy, because this line of approach affects the whole population of a country, whose support is essential.

Even revolutionary strategists admit that to start a revolution is easy; the problem is to keep it going to the end. That is why they came up with slogans such as *a luta continua* – 'the struggle continues' – which were used in adverse situations to encourage revolutionaries not to give up or lose interest. Another example of this type of slogan was *vitoria ecerta* – ultimate victory is assured. This was used to motivate fatigued revolutionary forces with promises of guaranteed success.

This phenomenon can also be found in other conflict situations, such as sport. After the second test match against the Wallabies in 1969 Frik du Preez was dropped in favour of André de Wet. Frik's response was: 'Well, we'll just have to take the bicycle by the handle-bars again and push it over the hill.' Frik is a serious man and often comes up with words of wisdom, and this was his version of 'the struggle continues', or '*vasbyt*', as the South African soldiers said – 'hang in there'.

During the same season, in the Currie Cup final between Northern Transvaal and Western Province at Loftus Versveld, Frik persevered. He took the bicycle by the handle-bars and 'dropped, placed and scored', thus regaining his place in the 1970 tour to the British Isles.

I believed that we had to persevere on the winning path. In the long run Soviet Russia could not sustain its efforts in Angola and its support of SWAPO. The moment that it withdrew from the scene, the scales would tip steeply in our favour. I was reminded of the Duke of Wellington's admonition to the House of Lords: 'A great country cannot wage a little war', and stated publicly that Angola would become the Soviet Union's Vietnam. It was reported in the media, and I shall come back to that later.

Speaking of Soviet Russia and Vietnam, SWAPO's affinity for the communist world was clearly demonstrated by the codes and nicknames it used, for example its bases called 'Moscow' and 'Vietnam'. Which brings me to the first cross-border operation that made headlines – Reindeer.

This operation had its run-up before I took over command in South West, and was carried out soon after the amalgamation of 101 Task Force and SWA Command and the establishment of the single HQ in Windhoek.

Ian Gleeson, the last commander of 101 Task Force, and his fellow commanders, Colonel Blackie de Swardt of the Air Force and Commander Colin Harwood of the South African Medical Services, were responsible for the planning before my arrival which eventually led to Operation Reindeer. Therefore, it was decided, they would be in command of the operation, with the fighting elements under Colonel Jan Breytenbach, Commandant Deon Ferreira and Major Frank Bestbier.

Reindeer was launched on Ascension Day, 4 May 1978, and consisted of two parts. One was an aerial and parachute attack on PLAN's most important training and supply base, 'Moscow' (Cassinga), 250 km north of the border. The other part was a simultaneous ground attack by a mechanised force on various forward transit bases in Angola's border area. This included 'Vietnam', a stretched-out complex at Chetequera, 28 km north of the border. The South African military journal *Militaria* later stated: 'Nearly a thousand insurgents were killed in battle and 200 captured, while only six members of the security forces fell. Large quantities of equipment and supplies were destroyed and valuable documents seized. The loss of trained personnel and the effect of the intelligence gathered by the security forces were a great setback from which PLAN never recovered completely.' Among the casualties was one South African paratrooper missing in action at Cassinga.

General Viljoen arrived by helicopter to join the paratroops while they were still mopping up at Cassinga, the plan being that he would leave with the last wave of the helicopters which were to evacuate the assault force. Before they could take off, however, a Cuban armoured combat team from nearby Techamutete arrived on the scene to aid the defenders. But SAAF fighter aircraft attacked the Cuban column and inflicted serious losses, allowing the helicopters to get away in the nick of time.

At that stage this was one of the most daring operations of its kind, and when a group of foreign officers paid South Africa a hush-hush visit not long afterwards they specifically wanted to know how we had planned and executed the Cassinga attack. General Viljoen and a team briefed them thoroughly and factually, after which one of the officers remarked: 'We wouldn't have done it.'

Asked why not, he answered: 'It's too risky. Not even the Israelis would have used, in one day, more than 250 paratroopers and a mobile air reserve of 120 men in an airborne operation on a target 250 kilometres across an international border, and then flown them back in helicopters.'

But the results spoke for themselves. PLAN sometimes fought very well, especially when its members were surprised or cornered, but the Cassinga attack was a jewel of military craftsmanship – and SWAPO knew it.

The operation triggered the normal propaganda claims and counterclaims, but, as Willem Steenkamp wrote at the end of the border war in *South Africa's Border War 1966–1988*:

> More than a decade later, Cassinga is still being touted in some circles as an infamous massacre of the innocents. Claims and counter-claims aside, the South Africans' insistence that it was indeed a military target is reinforced by unfakeable aerial photographs showing the extensive fortifications and the resistance offered by the defenders, which was so stiff and protracted that the paratroopers stayed much longer than they had planned and had to leave the garrison still holding part of the town.

In my opinion it would have been impossible for 250 men to commit the mass atrocities which were alleged without somebody later talking about it out of sheer aversion (almost all of the paratroopers were reservists of the Citizen Force).

*   *   *

To retain a true perspective of what was generally happening in South West at the time, one should bear in mind that while operations continued on a daily basis, there were other meaningful military developments taking place at the same time.

One of my assignments on being appointed in 1977 was to establish a defence force for South West, to be known as the SWA Territory Force, or SWATF. It was a challenge, and I met with a fair amount of opposition; some people were of the opinion that a local defence force was not desirable, while many others thought it simply would not work.

The project certainly stirred the emotion-laden political pot. In South Africa many people regarded the insurgency conflict as a purely South West African concern, and demanded that the South Westers make a maximum contribution to the war. One argument was that members of the South African Defence Force were risking their lives for the benefit of all population groups in South West, and that those groups, irrespective of their race or colour, should also fulfil their obligations.

In South West, on the other hand, some people regarded the conflict as black versus black, and many warned me that it would cause a white revolt if we armed citizens from all population groups. We did, but the revolt never materialised. It may sound ridiculous now, but in those days it was a serious emotional matter.

During the annual Windhoek agricultural show of 1977 Bushman and brown soldiers were scheduled to perform in the arena. I was specifically warned that if these soldiers walked around Windhoek after hours carrying their rifles there would be major problems. But we persisted, and in the end everything went without a hitch.

During that show, incidentally, we experienced real-life incidents reminiscent of the famed Jamie Uys film *The Gods Must be Crazy*, which deals with a Kalahari Bushman making his first acquaintance with Western-type civilisation and its artefacts (including an empty Coca-

Cola bottle thrown out of an aircraft). Naturally, it was an exceptional experience for a Bushman to sit in the Kalahari Sands Hotel's restaurant and be served by whites and Ovambos, and I found them making a strange departure from the drill book when I went to watch them rehearsing for their drill display. Instead of executing proper 90-degree turns to left or right, as the drill book laid down, they were veering away at such an angle that when they continued marching their course took them diagonally across the stadium arena.

Intrigued, I discussed these strange evolutions with their commanding officer, Commandant Delville Linford. In the end the most acceptable explanation I could get from him was that for the first time in the Bushmen's lives they could not see the natural 360-degree horizon, and this disturbed their natural sense of direction. Just like city people sometimes become 'bush crazy' and get lost in the bundu, the Bushmen had, in effect, gone what might be called 'town crazy'.

I tackled the establishment of the SWATF scientifically and tried to steer a neutral course, but the politics of the day did not make it an easy task. We based much of our planning on the principle of decentralisation, so that we took military training to the man instead of the man to the training. Therefore, instead of founding a central training centre, we established a number of units at various places right across the territory, the exact locations depending largely on where we could find the most suitable and cheapest terrain and facilities. This was a particularly valid approach for the infantry, for which there was a big demand.

A principle of this kind of war was to make maximum use of the local population's knowledge of the environment, languages and customs. We needed them mostly in the border areas, which was why we established units in Kaokoland, Ovamboland, Kavango and western and eastern Caprivi. On the other hand, we centralised in the case of those kinds of soldiers for whom there was not such a heavy demand, one example being bandsmen.

There was only one SWATF band, and it was stationed in Windhoek. The bandsmen were recruited from all regions, both urbanised areas and the bushveld. They were a motley crew, more representative of the territory's various population groups than most other organisations that I knew of, and had only one common qualification – not one of them had ever produced a single note on an instrument! And even if one of them had, perhaps, warbled on a jew's-harp or something similar before joining up, it was certain that no one had ever read a single note of sheet music. In spite of this the band performed in public for the first time approximately six weeks after its formation.

A physical training corporal – I think his name was George Moorcroft – was responsible for their general military education, and he did it well. One result was that members of the band eventually won cross-country races all over South West. They were probably the fittest brass band in the world!

The SWATF finally received formal status on 1 August 1980. This meant that to a large extent there were now separate structures for the SWATF and the South African forces in South West. Technically speaking I was now wearing two hats, since I was both GOC SWATF and GOC SA Army Forces in SWA.

We placed the SWATF on a separate account for the purposes of stores and financial accounting, but we continued to fight as an integrated force, using SWATF and South African troops in the same combat formations for operations.

Inevitably, given the political environment of the time, some people accused us of applying a policy of segregation, while others maintained that we were integrating. Those days these two concepts were always used when analysing events – and we had to face the criticism. We explained it as follows: if one formed a unit such as 101 Battalion in Ovamboland, one naturally recruited troops from that area. That was why 99 per cent of the members would be Ovambos. The same applied to Kavango, eastern Caprivi and other places. The composition of a battalion reflected the composition of the population of that area. If someone chose to regard this as forced segregation of ethnic units, that was his opinion. From our point of view it was the natural outcome of military planning and decentralisation.

The critics who welcomed the integration, as they saw it, however, claimed that it was only a smokescreen and that the black members of the SWATF would not be able to become senior non-commissioned officers and officers. These accusations came mainly from foreign visitors, and in due course they were proved wrong. I remember that before independence there were at least one commandant, one major and many junior officers, warrant-officers and non-commissioned officers who were not members of the white population group. There were also many white South Westers in the SWATF who stayed on in Namibia after independence and were enlisted into the new Namibian defence force.

In retrospect it would seem that the formation of the SWATF was not only wise but essential as well, and that it worked. After independence in 1990 various South Westers of different population groups told me it was the best thing we could have done. They said there were many troops, non-commissioned officers, warrant-officers and officers who could be integrated with PLAN. Many people were comforted by the fact that the new Namibian defence force would consist of both organisations, rather than only members of PLAN, because PLAN consisted mainly of Ovambos who had only one political loyalty. I am convinced that the creation and development of the SWATF before independence was a success story. It may still play an important role in promoting future stability in the country.

The SWATF came a long way and was well managed by all who were involved with me and those who came after us. And it had to be productive. The troops who served in Ovamboland during the early years in 1977 and 1978 were mainly Ovambo soldiers and soldiers from South West and South Africa. I regarded it as unproductive to have units such as the company at Otjisondo in Hereroland left out of service in Ovamboland, but my idea to deploy them there was met with a storm of criticism.

Knowledgeable and well-meaning advisers were deeply concerned that it would lead to friction between the Ovambo citizens and the Otjisondo company's Herero soldiers. Nevertheless, I decided to proceed with the project in a well-organised way, and we experienced very few problems.

The military culture is one of a kind. It creates bonds across ethnic boundaries, and its discipline prevents friction that might otherwise arise. I was quite proud of the fact that we succeeded in doing something that even people who could speak with authority thought was impossible; one cannot always blindly accept experts' advice. If the intention, planning and leadership are good, one can make things work. In other words, where there's a will there's a way. Perhaps it also paved the way for the later deployment of external troops in Ovamboland, so that after some time it was no longer strange to see troops of different cultures, for example Kavango and Bushman soldiers, in Ovamboland.

I am not trying to pretend that we never had problems. Everyone involved was careful not to say or do something that might cause friction between members of the different population groups. But spontaneity was not to be suppressed, and naturally blunders were made.

I remember one such incident. There was discord in the ranks of Captain Fourie's Herero Company at Otjisondo, the claim being that white corporals caused dissatisfaction by addressing Herero recruits in an improper manner. To try to sort things out Mr Clemens Kapuuo and I flew to Otjisondo, where we sat at a table in the front of a hall in which the corporals and troops were gathered and listened patiently and objectively to the stories of both the complainants and the corporals.

When one of the corporals put his case he used the expression 'and then the troop got white'. I accepted this as a blunder, although it was an idiomatic expression – meaning soldiers had become argumentative or obdurate – which was used indiscriminately in the SADF by leaders of all races. I'm not sure that everyone present grasped what he was saying, since it did not provoke any reaction.

Mr Kapuuo adopted a calm and fatherly attitude when he delivered a sort of closing address. He gave some credit to the corporals but also cautioned them, and he gave the troops some credit, but at the same time reprimanded them. Then he offered some advice and concluded by saying: 'But now you must remember, this man sitting next to me, Captain Fourie, he is the "baas van die plaas" (the "boss of the farm").' This was, of course, a colloquial descriptive term for a leader in both South Africa and South West, whether the 'boss' in question is actually a farmer or not. It did not evoke any reaction either, and later I heard these troops sing a song, dedicated to 'Mutango (leader) Fourie'. As some of the Herero troops became corporals, the problems disappeared. The troops received the same treatment from the new corporals, but they no longer grumbled. The same happened at other units.

The SWATF had a lion's share in border operations, and by 1982 it was already providing 60 per cent of the manpower in the operational area. In subsequent years the figure increased to 70 per cent, according to *Militaria* journal, and during Protea, the cross-border operation in August 1981, approximately 41 per cent of the soldiers were members of SWATF. Of the South West African troops involved, more than 90 per cent were yellow, brown and black, and in 1989, when its total manpower stood at approximately 30 000 (including a small percentage of SADF members) the SWATF was already stronger than the defence forces of about 40 African states.

Ovamboland's 101 Battalion earned the honour bestowed on it, but I am not taking sides, because when I went to Kavango I was told that 202 Battalion was the best — and in Caprivi I was told, naturally, that 701 Battalion was the best.

This brings me to the SWA Specialist Unit, almost universally called just 'Swaspes' from its initials in Afrikaans. Established at Oshivelo but later moved to Otavi, Swaspes included a fair number of South Africans and was primarily a reconnaissance unit whose task was to locate the enemy and bring other offensive forces into a position to engage them. Swaspes members were all specialist trackers and scouts. Some tracked on foot, others scouted on horseback or with motorcycles, while still others operated as dog-handlers. Sometimes they saw action as combat troops, but normally Swaspes members carried weapons only for their own protection.

One day the Chief of the Army, General Viljoen, said to me: 'Disband Swaspes! They're not cost-effective.'

I knew General Viljoen well. This was his way of finding out whether Swaspes was indeed cost-effective. So I did not agree with him right away. If he was right, Swaspes should be disbanded — I was aware of certain popular perceptions, some of which supported General Viljoen's point of view — but first I ordered an investigation and also went to take a look for myself in order to establish the facts.

At Oshivelo I sat down under a tree to talk to the commander, the horsemen, motorcyclists, trackers and dog-handlers, individually or in groups.

One allegation about Swaspes was that the dogs actually could not do the work they were supposed to do. Now I received some explanations. Earlier on some of the lower-level commanders were somewhat ignorant of the way dogs should be employed. By way of illustration, a dog would be following a trail, and then one of the junior leaders or even the commander would say: 'This dog isn't worth a thing, the spoor is there on the other side, and he is working right here, look!' This may sound ridiculous, but initially some chaps did not realise that a dog does not follow a track visually, he follows the scent, which the wind might have moved away from the spoor.

Some people also expected too much of the dogs because they lacked knowledge and experience. A dog is like a piece of military equipment in the sense that you have to use it with full regard for its capabilities and limitations. A dog cannot work in the hot sun for hours on end. One should use it when, where and for the time that it can work. One does not start shooting on the way to the battlefield. One takes one's weapons to the point where the enemy is and then starts fighting. The same applies to a dog.

This reminds me of a story dating from the early 1970s, when so-called 'profiles' of the different musterings had to be determined so that the allocation of the most suitable national servicemen to the correct ones could be done by computer. A tank driver, for example, had to be under a certain height and possess a certain degree of co-ordination. Then by chance someone asked what the profile of a dog-handler should be. The answer was: The first requirement is that the handler should be more intelligent than the dog!

The men told me how many of their reconnaissance operations were successful, in other words, how many of their operations had led to contact with the enemy. I calculated that it was somewhere between 60 and 75 per cent. This was a good figure, because we specifically wanted to seize the initiative by forcing encounters with the enemy, but actually making contact was one of our biggest problems.

I also paid brief visits to the sector and sub-sector commanders. They confirmed the claims of the troops, although in most cases it was difficult for them to tell how many of the contacts had resulted directly from reconnaissance by Swaspes elements. The reason for this was that the formats for standard operational reports did not necessarily require information as to how the initial contacts had been made; everyone was more concerned with the ensuing action itself. One commander in Ovamboland, however, estimated Swaspes's contribution in making contact with the enemy at about 60 per cent.

The motorcyclists and mounted elements were very successful in cost-effectively patrolling the border road of the so-called 'Cutline'; light vehicles and even light aircraft were also used to patrol the road for signs of crossings. But if they detected infiltration, they did not have the same means to follow up as the trackers, horsemen and motorcyclists.

I reported my findings, and Swaspes was not disbanded.

CHAPTER 8

KATIMA MULILO AND NGANA

Days of sadness and days of good cheer

Katima Mulilo, 23 August 1978. At 20 minutes past one in the morning a sudden bombardment rocked the town when PLAN launched 30 or so 122 mm rockets from across the border in Zambia. A little later Zambian 82 mm and 60 mm mortars followed suit with high explosive and phosphorus bombs aimed at the town and the Wenela border base.

It was a poor demonstration of gunnery which achieved better results than it deserved. The projectiles came down over an area of several square kilometres, and only two of the rockets caused any damage. One damaged a school in the township of Katima Mulilo. The other – one of the very first fired – struck a barracks building inside the base, killing 10 soldiers and wounding 10 more.

The counter-bombardment began a few minutes later after our sound and radar equipment had located the enemy positions. That was the end of the exchange of fire.

It was, of course, a frightening experience for Katima Mulilo's inhabitants. Only people who have experienced a bombardment of this kind can know what it sounds like and what the psychological effects are.

Jannie Geldenhuys takes over from General Constand Viljoen as head of
the South African Defence Force, 31 October 1985. PHOTO: *Paratus*

Above: Ben and Anna Geldenhuys with Jannie (Kleinboet) and Johan (Ouboet).

Below: Davulsrus nestling beneath ochre and crimson cliffs.

Above: First rugby team, Voortrekker High School, Bethlehem (1952), with three future Springboks who attended the school at the same time as Jannie Geldenhuys. *From top to bottom*: Hannes Botha, Tom van Vollenhoven and Bennie van Niekerk.

Right: The 'Winds of Change' visit, 1960. Mr Harold Macmillan, escorted by Captain Jannie Geldenhuys (*front*), General Nic Bierman (*behind left*) and Eric Louw, Minister of Foreign Affairs.

Top left: Staff Sergeant Frederick George Crumpton (*left*) and Lieutenant Jannie Geldenhuys.

Top right: Brigadier 'O bleddie Ben' de Wet Roos (*left*) and Jannie Geldenhuys (1975-76).

Below left: The SWA Territorial Forces on parade.

Below right: Administrator General M T Steyn. PHOTO: *Stefan Sonderling*

Top: Mr P W Botha with Generals Ian Gleeson, Magnus Malan, Jannie Geldenhuys and Constand Viljoen (1977-78).

Below: Ministerial visit, Windhoek (1977-1978). *Left to right, back:* Administrator Ronnie Edwards, General Jannie Geldenhuys, General Magnus Malan and Minister of Foreign Affairs, Pik Botha. *Front:* Judge M T Steyn and Mr John Viall. PHOTO: *André le Roux*

Above: Key officers: Operation Sceptic. *Left to right, back*: Johan Saaiman, Johan Sonnekus, Ken Snowball, Deon Ferreira, André Kotze, Jorrie Jordaan, Des Radmore, Anton van Graan. *Front*: 'Dippies' Dippenaar, Giep Booysen, Witkop Badenhorst, Jannie Geldenhuys, Theo de Munnink, Ollie Holmes, Chris Serfontein.
PHOTO: *Paratus*

Left: Operation Sceptic: Chris Serfontein, Jannie Geldenhuys and Con Crous, veteran SAPA journalist and doyen of the SWA/Namibian press corps.

OPPOSITE
Above: Before the start of an operation.
PHOTO: *Johan Kuus*

Below left: 'Bottles water four, braces left and right – none!'

Below right: Bush camp, Southern Cross Fund swimming pool.
PHOTO: *Stefan Sonderling*

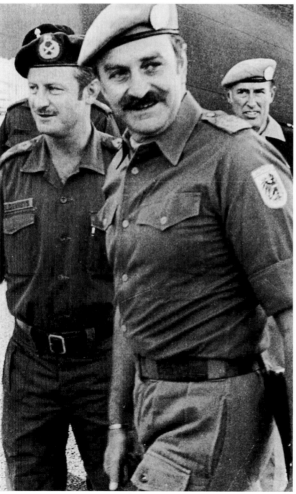

Top: General Prem Chand, the new UNTAG commanding officer is greeted by General Jannie Geldenhuys on his arrival in Windhoek, 1989.
PHOTO: *Stefan Sonderling*

Left: Jannie Geldenhuys and first UNTAG commanding officer, Austrian General Hannes Phillip.
PHOTO: *Argus Africa News Service*

Above: General Jannie Geldenhuys wearing a general's beret displaying the the crossed sword and baton emblem and the Infantry Corps insignia.

This one was a nightmare for the women and children of the village.

When the explosions started, Johnny Henderson of the South African Broadcasting Corporation just happened to be fiddling with his tape recorder, and he placed it on top of his bomb-shelter and recorded the bombardment. I still have a copy of the original, on which the cry of a fish eagle and the anxious howl of a dog can be heard during the brief periods of silence between explosions.

While all this was happening, Major Dirk du Toit showed his mettle. Dirk du Toit was a bachelor, full of wit and wisdom, who had previously been a sports officer in the Cape. When he wanted to rejoin the Defence Force, I took him on a flight from what he described as the shoulder blade of Kaokoland, past the muscle of Ovamboland, the upper arm of Kavango and the forearm of western Caprivi, to the fist of eastern Caprivi. He could choose where he wanted to be posted, and he chose East Caprivi. There he became a father figure for many young wives, their children and the troops, who all affectionately called him 'Oom Dirk', and during the bombardment Dirk showed what he was made of as he drove through the streets in his Ford 250 4x4 with his little dog, Gamat, at his side, shouting words of advice and encouragement to everyone through a loud-hailer.

At first light the sector commander, Commandant A K de Jager, launched the first combat team across the border into Zambia under the command of Lieutenant Harry Holland-Muter. Supported by armed Alouette helicopters, they hit a well-known PLAN camp 30 km north of the Cutline, while shortly after 7 am another team led by Lieutenant Flip Genis crossed the Zambian border as well and engaged the rear elements of the retreating attackers. Within a few hours, too, paratroopers were flown into Zambia.

In Windhoek I had received a radio message from Katima Mulilo a few hours before the bombardment with information about a proposed attack on the town that night. It was actually delivered to me while I was playing host to General Hannes Philipp at an informal farewell by the pool side of the Safari Motel; he and Mr Martii Ahtisaari, the UN Secretary-General's 'special representative', had completed a fact-finding mission and were about to fly out to Europe and the United States.

I had to think fast. Should I or should I not inform General Philipp about the message? There were advantages and disadvantages to either option. Finally I decided to tell him, and did so. Then we left for the airport to see him and the rest of the delegation on their way. Shortly after I arrived home from the airport I received the bitter news of the attack and its results.

Early next morning I left for Mpacha airfield to learn exactly what had happened at Katima. I considered it my moral duty to be there after such a serious incident. I tried my best to keep Judge Steyn away from Katima until we knew exactly what the situation was, but he insisted on going along.

Approximately two hours later we landed at Mpacha and headed for Katima. A grim atmosphere met us. The military personnel and their wives were calm, but it was a bitter experience for all of us, and I had to look them in the eye, explain and answer questions.

While A K de Jager led the follow-up operations we were briefed in detail by his staff officers, Major Koos Muller and Captain Piet de Lange. Although the bombardment had been scattered, they said, one of the very first shots had hit the entrance of a bungalow. The troops had been running for the bomb shelters and trenches, but the rocket had exploded inside the bungalow before all of them could get out.

The follow-up operation continued for several days and nights and eventually involved additional ground troops as well as Buccaneer fighter-bombers and Canberra light bombers. Katima Mulilo and its Zambian counterpart, Sesheke, exchanged fire twice more with artillery and mortars.

On 27 August, four days later, it was over; a confirmed minimum of 20 insurgents had been killed. In terms of casualties inflicted and damage done, our counteraction did not really avenge our losses. But, as Willem Steenkamp later wrote, 'it accomplished a greater purpose: for practical purposes it quashed the insurgency in Caprivi'.

This incident had a wider impact than merely bringing an end to insurgency in Caprivi; it became apparent later that it had made a major contribution towards turning the tide of the war as a whole.

My decision to inform Gen Philipp had been a good one. South Africa had encountered a lot of opposition with regard to its role in South West, and one way of getting at it was to criticise the activities of the SADF in the territory. We had many critics, so that many a time I felt that we could do nothing right, and SWAPO nothing wrong. We were often portrayed as the bad guys and SWAPO as the good guys.

Among our main critics were the UN and its agencies, while others used the UN as a platform for their criticism. We must bear in mind that the General Assembly of the UN regarded SWAPO as the sole and authentic representative of the people of the future Namibia. The outspoken and hostile UN High Commissioner for Namibia, Sean McBride, and his institute were on the UN payroll, and SWAPO was also the UN's most important source of information about South West.

After encounters such as these, the criticism and statements were often as follows:

- It was untrue that PLAN committed loathsome acts. It was propaganda. It might also have been somebody else, for example UNITA.
- It was untrue that PLAN operated from Angola and Zambia. It was propaganda: PLAN operated from bases in South West.
- It was untrue that Angola and Zambia participated in PLAN's armed activities. It was propaganda: South Africa was making these allegations merely to cook up pretexts for carrying out hot-pursuit operations into those countries.
- It was untrue that PLAN attacked civilian targets. It was propaganda: they were fighting against the security forces.
- It was untrue that Swapo did not co-operate in the peace initiatives. It was propaganda: it was the security forces which caused incidents to undermine the peace processes.

It was probably once again *friction de guerre* that I just happened to be talking to Gen Philipp at the exact moment I received the message and so could inform him of the incident straight away, hours before it occurred. When the information became fact, he knew exactly what had happened and 'whodunit'.

This time there was no doubt that PLAN was the aggressor, that PLAN had bombarded a whole village with all its civilian inhabitants, and that PLAN had been operating from Angola and Zambia. PLAN had spoilt the climate for negotiations at the time when Ahtisaari departed to write his report, while the security forces had displayed self-restraint throughout. For once there was no doubt about who the good guys and bad guys were. They knew that it was not a security force trick. At no stage had we tried to wreck any political efforts, and neither were we doing so now. This time it was PLAN, notwithstanding the peace initiatives, which was responsible for the badly-timed incident.

When we informed the media I specifically mentioned to them that we had had information about the attack before it happened. Now, a problem I had experienced in the past was that you were not taken seriously when you told the media about something that had happened and then tried to reinforce your statement's credibility by claiming – without any substantiating evidence – that you had known it was going to happen. This was understandable, otherwise you could report just about anything and demand that the media believe you. But it was a different matter if you could verify the authenticity of your statement by first confiding in a trustworthy person who could provide confirmation. And this time I could verify it, because General Philipp was an honest man who would never deny that I had informed him prior to the attack on Katima Mulilo.

The media's attitude was always that if they were fully informed their reports would be accurate; whereas if they were not, they would be forced to speculate, and the manner in which they speculated became their own business. And now they proved to me that they meant what they said. It turned out to be one of the few occasions on which all the media agreed with our interpretation of an incident; we received intimations of sympathy from the international political world – and we did not provide ammunition for those who preferred not to agree with us.

The way that we handled that incident enabled Mr John Vorster, the Prime Minister, to state his position in strong language to a sympathetic international community. Carel Birkby, military correspondent for *To the Point* magazine, wrote in the 1 September 1978 issue:

> By this time, no doubt, Lusaka had had time to note the uncompromising stance swiftly adopted by Prime Minister John Vorster, Foreign Minister Pik Botha, and SWA/Namibia Administrator-General Judge Marthinus T Steyn, towards SWAPO's murderous intransigence and Zambia's tolerance, or

encouragement, of Nujoma's military basis.

They found swift and unqualified backing by Admiral Thomas Moorer, retired American chairman of the joint chiefs of staff committee, and until he retired in 1974 commander-in-chief of the American and NATO naval forces in the Atlantic.

Moorer, who this week is visiting SWA/Namibia, said: 'When anybody attacks you like SWAPO did, you are thoroughly and absolutely justified in hitting back and knocking the hell out of 'em.'

In the same issue, John Evert said:

> In terms of the political implications of its attack on Katima Mulilo, SWAPO seems to have committed a bad blunder. Its image as a revolutionary force has been dented, the question mark over the willingness to take part in elections has grown, it has embarrassed the Zambian government. And, ironically, it has greatly increased the credibility of the South African government, as regards its commitment to the Western plan and its charge that SWAPO is the main obstacle to the implementation of the plan.

Not long afterwards I was taken to task for having reported to the media that we had had advance information about the attack. It had caused political and psychological embarrassment; people could ask, as John Evert put it, 'why, knowing ... in advance of the impending attack, South African forces did not launch a pre-emptive strike'.

It did not happen every day that the Defence Force was criticised for *not* launching pre-emptive cross-border operations!

It was, of course, a tough question to answer. It was a many-faceted situation, and not all the facets could be controlled. One actually had to have personally experienced the situation at Katima Mulilo and borne the responsibility before one could understand how difficult it was emotionally and intellectually to manage a situation of this nature.

We had a man who was capable of doing so in Brigadier A K de Jager. This kind of stand-off bombardment can be prevented only by dominating the area across the border or by pre-empting enemy action. But Evert provided the right answer to this problem himself: 'South Africa's inaction is justified ... a pre-emptive strike would have resulted in South Africa being branded an aggressor. It would have given SWAPO cause to withdraw from the (settlement) plan, into which it had entered with great reluctance anyway.'

Over a long time prior to this incident we had periodically received information about possible attacks on certain dates, but each time the day had come and gone without anything happening. In between such warnings alarm systems were installed and the troops set to preparing passive defensive measures, for example improving physical protection by building bunkers and other forms of bomb-shelters. But one cannot let people live, month after month, as if such a bombardment could take place at any moment, and we could not let the soldiers in the town live in safer conditions than the women and children.

In areas plagued by insurgency one must always strive to let daily life continue as normally as possible. Bomb shelters had already been erected in schools and homes, and if we had reacted forcefully every time we received a bit of alarming information we would have given the impression that we were panicking. The wives and children of some of the officials might have decided to go back to South Africa, which could have resulted in the collapse of Caprivi's civil administration.

In the meantime, the process of implementing Resolution 435 and the negotiated settlement plan had reached an impasse anyway, and it was decided to call free and fair elections in South West for December 1978 in order to establish a multi-racial constituent assembly.

SWAPO decided not to participate and publicly announced that it was going to launch a plan to wreck the elections. Given the current widespread violence, this threat placed an even heavier burden on the security forces. Many people believed that we would not be able to guarantee the degree of security required for an election in the remote areas of the territory. The fact that PLAN's operations to interfere with the elections were successfully foiled was an exceptional achievement and a feather in the cap of the security forces.

Security-related incidents, however, dragged on, although without great success. On 13 February 1979, 250 insurgents launched an attack on our Nkongo base in Ovamboland, 15 km south of the border, with farcical results. On 26 February the Elundu base was the target of another bombardment, but all the shots went astray. Still, SWAPO declared in London that over a period of three months it had killed more than 300 South African soldiers, destroyed two military bases, shot down two reconnaissance aircraft, damaged 40 military vehicles and seized large quantities of weapons and ammunition.

If a quarter of these allegations had been true it would have been regarded as a national disaster in South Africa. However, even the little bit which was true inspired one to react – and now the opportunity was there. The stand -off bombardment of Katima Mulilo activated the political green light to cross the border, and we made systematic use of the opportunity.

We continued to give intelligence matters much of our attention. Between our withdrawal from Angola in 1976 and Operation Reindeer in 1978 we had had good intelligence, but only about specific potential targets, such as certain PLAN bases and headquarters. Such intelligence enabled us to execute Operation Reindeer, but our general combat intelligence about PLAN's activities, smaller bases, transit bases and infiltration routes was inadequate.

To make things even more difficult, Reindeer's attacks on Cassinga and Chetequera had stirred up a hornet's nest. After their flight and scattering, the PLAN members made many adjustments to their system of bases and changed their patterns. This totally disturbed the intelligence picture we had built up. But Johann Saaiman and his people worked hard. Although certain limitations on our actions were still in place, we were able greatly to improve our intelligence by means of cross-border operations, and so we launched Operations Rekstok and Safraan on 7 March 1979. In actual fact both were components of one large operation, with part taking place in Angola (Rekstok) and the other in Zambia (Safraan).

I remember a story from those days that I would like to share. It concerns Commandant Piet Hall, then commander of the Bushman battalion, which was based at Omega in western Caprivi but took part in operations everywhere to the north, including Zambia.

Towards the end of 1978 I arrived at Katima Mulilo soon after the lucky-draw type Defence Bonus Obligations – the nearest thing to a national lottery the straight-laced government would countenance – had come into operation in South Africa and South West; everywhere people were being exhorted to buy the bonds with the slogan: 'There's a bonus in your future'.

At that time one of the Bushman companies was somewhere out in the bundu in Zambia; a new company commander was expected at any moment, and Piet Hall was filling the gap till the new man's arrival, which was so imminent that Piet was due to be picked up by helicopter the next day so that he could return to Omega before going on leave with his family.

What Piet did not know was that the new company commander's arrival had been delayed. I told A K de Jager that Piet would have to stay where he was until he had been properly relieved, knowing how he would feel when he received A K's signal. But Piet was a man who retained his sense of humour even when the circumstances were difficult, as I discovered next morning, when A K showed me his sitrep for the preceding 24 hours. Cryptic as always, the sitrep's paragraph A (enemy activities) recorded 'Unchanged'. Paragraph B (own forces) was 'NTR', or 'Nothing to Report'. Paragraph C (administration and logistics) said things were 'Unchanged'. But paragraph D (matters of general interest) read: 'THERE'S A BONUS IN YOUR FUTURE' ...

Rekstok and Safraan involved simultaneous attacks on PLAN bases in Angola and Zambia. During an air attack in Rekstok a SAAF Canberra light bomber crashed with the loss of its crew, presumably after being hit by ground fire, but neither operation achieved much in material terms, mainly because the SWAPO cadres had evacuated their bases, some long before time, others at the eleventh hour. The reason why we ended up attacking empty locations was, as I have mentioned, that our intelligence had lost track of some of SWAPO's bases which had been moved after Reindeer.

Naturally the commanders and operations officers made full use of the opportunity to take a dig at the intelligence staff. Colonel J H Vorster recalls a story that one could call 'the Dave Roux incident' which accurately reflects the climate and spirit of the moment:

> Mid-1979, during Brigadier Kat Liebenberg's term of duty as commander of Sector 10, an important cross-border operation was launched from Ovamboland against PLAN targets in

the south of Angola.

After a few days it became clear that the operation seemed not to be very successful, because it appeared as if all the PLAN bases had been evacuated by the time they were assaulted. It almost seemed as if PLAN had received early warning of the operation.

Because of this perception Brigadier Liebenberg temporarily suspended the operation and summoned the commanders to Sector 10 Headquarters.

At 11h00 the atmosphere in the conference hall was tense; because of the failures everyone expected some straight talking from the boss. All became quiet when Brigadier Liebenberg got to his feet, briefly welcomed his commanders and staff officers (and) instructed his intelligence officer, Commandant Dave Roux, to 'tell us where SWAPO is'.

Dave Roux positioned himself next to the map with facial expression and body language saying: 'Yes, yes, always blame intelligence when things go wrong.'

'Good morning gentlemen,' he began. Using a pointer, he indicated an area in western Ovamboland on the map: 'SWAPO was here at Ongulumbashe during 1966, and when General Dillon of the South African Police attacked them on 26 August 1966, they scattered. From that day they started to spread throughout the whole area ... and to this day nobody knows where they are.'

There was dead silence. Everyone anxiously awaited Brigadier Liebenberg's reaction.

After a long silence the Brigadier broke the silence: 'Open the bar!'

The tension disappeared like mist before the sun, and after a beer or two the commanders returned to their units to continue the operation. The next day the first reports of successes started to come in, and in the end the South African Defence Force had concluded another effective cross-border operation in Angola. [Bertrand Retief, *Humor in SA Uniform*]

Everyone was disappointed. As late as the early 1990s, when I was writing the first edition of this book, I often heard colleagues, officers and non-commissioned officers who participated in these operations describing them as failures. I can understand why they thought that way. But this was the perception at the lower level, of the commanders and fighters who tackled operations with enthusiasm and professionalism, and who liked to show results. And so it should be.

However, from my point of view these operations, and the incident of 23 August 1978, were two of the most important turning-points in the war, and afterwards the long-term statistics showed that from July 1979 we began to take the initiative and started to gain on the insurgents, while their position worsened.

Priorities were laid down for every operation. Should one shoot insurgents or capture them? Was this the important thing? Should you destroy enemy equipment or seize it? Should you rather destroy the enemy's military structures? What were your priorities on the ground while you were there? There was seldom time for everything. I laid down the priorities for Rekstok and Safraan myself. Priority number one was to gather operational information and everything else associated with combat intelligence.

One usually collects information in order to plan operations, but sometimes you have to execute operations in order to gather information. Information obtained from these operations enabled us to clear up the enemy picture and to devise new plans for collecting intelligence. We began to ignore supposed enemy positions which we had been researching for a long time and started to focus our intelligence-gathering efforts on places which had never before drawn our attention. If these operations had not taken place we would have remained ignorant of them for a long time. But with our new intelligence we could operate much more effectively.

The statistics that I have mentioned were also released to the media from time to time. During the official opening of the third session of the first Volksraad (Legislative Council) of South West's Rehoboth enclave, I said that PLAN had lost approximately 13 men per month before April 1979; while afterwards the figure had increased to almost 90 per month; this average was sustained for a number of years. PLAN lost 156 during November 1979 and 134 during February 1980.

The number of combat contacts with insurgents increased by 100 per cent from 1978 to 1979. Of these, 85 per cent were initiated and forced by the security forces. The security forces suffered three casualties to every 100 insurgent losses. I am not trying to dress up disappointments as successes by performing tricks with figures. Although I was intellectually satisfied with Rekstok and Safraan, I, too, had hoped for better concrete results. But there was another good reason why I was quietly content with the outcome, and this revolved around the concept of initiative.

Earlier I had propagated the concept that commanders and staffs should brainstorm collectively to find ways of seizing the initiative. The pattern used to be that the insurgent would strike somewhere, and we would react. He would then move away and strike elsewhere, and again we would react. What we wanted was to take action which would persuade the insurgents to react. We could win a skirmish here today, one there tomorrow and one somewhere else the following month, but each would only gain us the initiative locally and temporarily. This was not good enough. We needed plans and patterns that could be forced on our opponent and which would compel him, over a wide area, to react according to our terms. In conventional warfare one could achieve it by the concentration of forces at the right time and place, but in this kind of warfare it was impossible.

It would serve no purpose to concentrate a large force on one of PLAN's many small bases. However, concentration of force as a principle of war could still be applied; instead of concentrating troops at one particular place, they could all be activated at one particular time. So our forces now took the initiative by engaging the enemy in many small actions at the same time by simultaneously attacking a number of bases. This is what we did in the case of Rekstok and Safraan. All the insurgents had to react, and we had them abandoning bases and scattering from the Cunene province of Angola in the west to Zambia in the east. With the added help of other plans, which I will mention later, we started to gain and maintain the initiative.

Just before the start of one of the operations in Zambia I went to draw a few pieces of equipment for myself. One of the young medics present asked me: 'But aren't you a general?' and when I nodded, he said: 'Gee whiz, I didn't know you guys also go on ops!' We were often criticised for doing so. But then at least we knew what was going on. Besides, the enthusiastic reaction of this soldier was more important than the criticism.

The flight engineer of the helicopter to which I had been allocated watched me board the aircraft and then turned to continue the take-off procedure. I found an extra headset, put it on and listened to a conversation that went more or less like this:

'I see we have a pongo general on board.'

'Wonder what the bugger's doing here?'

'Why doesn't he leave the fighting to the troops?'

'Probably wants to show how tough he is.'

And so forth. By the way, when we reached the objective, it turned out to be a lemon – it was empty. Years later, in 1987, after Western Province Defence Force had won the Toyota Rugby Club Championships, I told this story to our team manager, Commandant Os de Waal.

'Yes, General,' he said. 'I know ... I was the pilot.'

These operations caused some embarrassment to other people as well. Commandant L A (Andy) Anderson relates:

> It was during operation Safraan, when our combat team of Eland armoured cars and Buffel troop carriers were hot on the heels of the fleeing cadres. We were keen to make contact.
>
> Suddenly the whole force came to a standstill at a place where we were definitely not supposed to stop. I listened but heard no shots. I heard no explosions either, only incomprehensibly foul words coming over the radio from the leading Eland. The turrets and gun-barrels of the Elands were swung to the sides, while men jumped down from the Buffels and disappeared to either side of the road.
>
> Fine, I said to myself, the drills are working. But there were still no shots – only the unmilitary language over the radio. Something was wrong – very wrong.
>
> I hurried up the dirt road along the convoy of armoured vehicles.
>
> We had reached the Zambezi.
>
> Reaching the front of the convoy, I was met by a scene that could take place only in Africa. My troop commander, a lieutenant, was standing in front of his towering Ratel with its

huge 90 mm barrel practically resting on his shoulder. He was a very unhappy man.

Standing in front of him was a grey-haired Zambian dressed in khaki shirt and shorts, clutching a clip-board and pen. At his side was a small boy holding one of those old tin Flit pumps. Remember them? They were hardly larger than a bicycle pump.

'I don't care who you are,' said the dignified old man, 'this is a Ngana (sleeping sickness) pest control point, and you cannot proceed until all the regulations have been complied with.'

He seemed impervious to the fact that he and the little boy had brought [a] combat team of the SA Defence Force to a halt.

To prevent my lieutenant from having a heart attack I indicated to him that I would continue the negotiations.

'Look here, I've got orders to take this town of Sela and the ferry crossing, and if you do not get out of the way, the armoured cars will drive over you.'

'What town, what ferry?' asked the old man.

In front of me I could see only reeds and a few huts.

'Isn't this place called Sela?'

'Yes, this is Sela,' he confirmed.

Then I realized, for the umpteenth time in my military career, that a map of Africa could well indicate a 'town', but that Africa's cartographers are the most optimistic people in the world.

'Before you go anywhere, Sir, I must insist on carrying out my duties. I shall now spray your vehicles.'

I then realised that the crews of the armoured cars were having themselves a ball watching the show. Grinning faces all over were peeping through the hatches and following our discussions with intense interest.

With the clip-board in his hand the old grey gentleman positioned himself in front of the first armoured car and started to write down its registration number. At the same time his young assistant started to do his bit. He swiftly scrambled up the first vehicle. Reaching the top, he flashed the crew a friendly smile and pushing the spray-nozzle down the hatch, he started to jerk the handle to and fro, pumping with gusto.

With a 'Thank you, Sah' he nimbly climbed down again. The next moment the sneezing men were scrambling through the hatches and landing on the dust road shouting and screaming, eyes tear-filled and gasping for breath.

Without looking back once, the hygiene duo of the Ngana Pest Control not only forced the South African armoured combat team to a standstill, but with the power of justice and order, health regulations and bureaucracy, left every tough and trained armour troop in the convoy standing in the dirt road, coughing and sneezing and wiping tears from [his] eyes.

The old man had done with the last Buffel and walked back to the front slowly with his little assistant.

He stopped and fixed a questioning gaze on me: 'What nationality are you, please?'

When, open-mouthed and more dumbfounded than security-conscious, I failed to respond, he formally announced: 'In any case, you are now free of Ngana and may proceed, but … won't you join me for a cup of tea?' [Bertrand Retief, *Humor in SA Uniform*]

*   *   *

On this English note of high tea in Africa I must mention an international political event which would later have a great influence on southern Africa. On 4 May 1979 Margaret Thatcher became the British Prime Minister.

In the meantime we had worked hard at one of our most important operational objectives, which was to clean up all areas that had been infiltrated by insurgents, until only Ovamboland remained. We gradually managed to do so. In fact, the cleaning-up process had already begun before 23 August 1978, even if it was not then being done specifically as part of a bigger plan.

At that stage small-scale clandestine operations were conducted against PLAN hide-outs inside Zambia, east of the Zambezi. They were carried out very quietly, but ironically demonstrated for the first time the effect of cross-border operations. The complaints of the population in that area became such an embarrassment to Kenneth Kuanda that he forbade PLAN from operating from anywhere in Zambia except the area west of the Zambezi. This in itself was a breakthrough, but infiltration from the area west of the river was still increasing.

Then the incident of 23 August 1978 occurred. This showed Kaunda in a bad light and put him under great pressure. The overt operations following the incident, in addition to Operation Safraan, increased the embarrassment and the pressure, and resulted in his forbidding PLAN from operating against eastern Caprivi from anywhere in Zambia. This was the great breakthrough. It was the end of the insurgency in eastern Caprivi, and the turning-point for the realisation of our plan.

North of the Kavango River and western Caprivi, in the Cuando-Cubango Province of Angola, Jonas Savimbi survived, got back on his feet, was able to build up his forces and began to control the area. UNITA and SWAPO were now arch-enemies. All this resulted in the termination of infiltration from Angola to Kavango and western Caprivi.

At a later stage three groups infiltrated into Kavango, mainly via Ovamboland, and stayed there for some time. They were located and dealt with. There was only sporadic infiltration from Angola into Kaokoland; all these efforts were either rejected, subdued, or resisted and the perpetrators killed. Thus we managed, in a relatively short space of time, to attain our objective of restricting the insurgency to Ovamboland. And it all started in eastern Caprivi on 23 August 1978.

The Caprivians were not lost. The tide had turned and developed its own momentum. CANU (the Caprivian African National Union), which used to be an integrated part of the SWAPO organisation, broke away, abandoned the insurgency struggle, returned to eastern Caprivi and took up normal politics. Its leader, Mishake Muyongo, who had been a vice-president of SWAPO, became the president of the Democratic Turnhalle Alliance.

While all this was happening we continued to search for new ideas about how to force PLAN to react to our initiatives, and then to keep them reacting. We encouraged commanders at all levels to think creatively and innovatively – although innovation must be properly managed. The operational plans resulting from this scheme were called 'fox operations'. To obtain total initiative you had to out-fox your opponents all over and everywhere at the same time. For this reason, innovation had to make its impact over a wide area simultaneously. Every quarter we presented a trophy to initiators and leaders of successful fox operations reflecting wits and fighting spirit in combat.

Some commanders had anticipated the fox operations programme as a natural consequence of their own ingenuity and enterprise, and two of them, Commandant Deon Ferreira, then commander of 32 Battalion, and Major Mossie Basson of the Air Force, were the first recipients of the trophy.

They had established a tactical headquarters at Eenhana, from where they conducted operations in the Angolan border area just north of their position. Troops would be positioned at a selected place north of the border, where they stacked waste oil rags and old tyres. An Alouette III helicopter with smoke grenades attached to it would fly high above the selected area, then after a while dive towards the ground while its grenades released a trail of smoke; as soon as the helicopter reached the pile of wastes and tyres it would turn away and head back to base at very low level, out of sight of the enemy.

In the meantime the ground troops would set the pile alight, sending a column of black smoke into the sky. Then they would take up position, and when the swapo fighters arrived to investigate the helicopter 'crash' they would walk into an ambush on terrain our troops had selected and prepared.

We analysed the technique. Firstly, a visible presence had to be established. Secondly, we had to create an incident that would force the swapo fighters to investigate; and finally we had to be a dominant position to start the fire-fight.

We encouraged the application of this technique throughout the operational area, and it worked. In Zambia Commandant A K de Jager and his Air Force counterpart, Major Vink Hattingh, used two Impala aircraft instead of Alouettes, which were visible from much further away.

One of the Imps would simulate a crash by diving down almost to the ground and flying back home at tree-top level. The other would circle over the area of the 'accident' a few times and then fly back home as well. Sometimes it took the swapo members a bit longer to reach the spot, but the result was always the same. The number of South African aircraft Zambia and SWAPO claimed to have shot down totalled more than the whole SAAF inventory.

Fox operations sometimes also produced unexpected results. There was the case of the carbide-powered orchard cannons, which were used in South Africa's Boland area to scare birds away from orchards or vineyards by firing at regular intervals. We decided that the orchard cannons could be used to create an impression of our presence and to cause incidents which would demand investigation by the enemy.

The cannons were duly ordered, but when I enquired of HQ Sector 10 (Oshakati-Ovamboland) whether it had received the cannons the answer was 'no'. It turned out that the Air Force had refused to transport the carbide because it constituted a safety risk. So I had them sent up by train. But when I enquired a second time, Sector 10 had still not begun its orchard-cannon operations.

I discovered that the cannons and carbide had indeed arrived at Oshakati, and that Commandant Chris Serfontein had personally taken receipt of them. But he had not been fully in the picture, and so, after a quick glance at the labels, he had ordered: 'Give these anti-monster and pestilence devices to the hygiene section!'

Later the orchard cannons were set up along a water pipeline which ended at Eenhana and had been regularly sabotaged by PLAN, so that for long periods not a drop of water reached the base. But the periodic bangs of the cannons, instead of drawing the insurgents to investigate, deterred them to such an extent that now, for the first time in many months, the troops could swim again in the pool donated by the Southern Cross Fund.

As all these operations occurred over the whole of the operational area at the same time, I believe that they made some contribution towards giving us the initiative.

* * *

I cannot conclude the Caprivi story without coming back to General Hannes Philipp. He was a man of indisputable integrity and a dedicated professional soldier of the greatest stature, but he was also a man with a sense of humour. He had a vast repertoire of anecdotes and stories, many of them stories about the eastern European and Scandinavian countries, which he told in a unique way in his delightful Austrian accent. One of these went like this:

> Two elderly Finns are sitting drinking at an inn. One of them fills his mate's glass and his own from a bottle of aquavit. He lifts his glass and says: 'skol', and they drink in silence. Then after a while he reaches for the bottle again and refills their glasses, lifts his and says: 'skol'. They drink. Silence follows, but eventually he pours another round, lifts his glass, looks at his mate and says: 'skol'.
>
> His friend slams his glass down on the table and says: 'Let's get this straight now, do we drink or do we talk?'

I had the impression that Hannes Philipp often found the going tough. He stuck to the codes, the principles and the rules, even when his popularity was at stake. As the force commander-designate of Untag, he was probably regarded as too neutral, too objective and too impartial.

One should not forget that to be regarded as a decent human being in the international community during the late 1970s you had to condemn South Africa and praise its opponents. If you did so, you were normal. If you did not, you were partial to the wrong side.

Which brings me to the eve of the most dramatic operation since Operation Savannah five years earlier – Smokeshell.

CHAPTER 9

SMOKESHELL

Tiffies and postal pigeons

The operation popularly known as 'Smokeshell' (actually its name was 'Sceptic') took place in June 1980. Various events attracted the public's attention during the period leading up to the operation. For example, on 11 September 1979 I told correspondents that while the war was far from over, in my opinion the tide of the security situation in South West had turned (the statistics of the following six months admittedly did not really seem to support my statement); and that same day the Angolan President, Agostinho Neto, arrived in Moscow and suddenly died there, apparently under questionable circumstances.

On 1 October 1979 a new round of negotiations began, when a revised independence plan for South West, formulated by the Western countries, was submitted to Riaan Eksteen, the South African ambassador at the UN. It contained the concept of the so-called DMZ, or demilitarised zone, along the border.

While political activities seesawed, security-related incidents continued to take place, and PLAN's personnel losses maintained a tendency to rise. Of the 6 000 to 8 000 insurgents in Angola and the 1 000 to 2 000 in Zambia, 500 died between May and 18 October 1979. The permanent

SWAPO representative at the UN, Theo-Ben Gurirab, rejected these figures and declared that his organisation was busy re-structuring its forces to intensify the armed struggle. The intensification did not materialise. What did take place was one skirmish after another, with the insurgents still escaping across the border to Angola as before.

The new year of 1980 began with a revival of PLAN activities which were clearly meant to coincide with a visit by the new UNTAG commander-designate, General Prem Chand, to Lusaka to discuss the proposed DMZ.

During February a PLAN group entered South West and ventured far south of the normal operational area, to the Tsumeb–Grootfontein–Otavi triangle, where its members killed two white civilians. The security forces tracked them down and killed 19 for a loss of two men, one of them a Bushman tracker. The pursuit continued, and by the last week of March one more soldier had been killed as well as 11 insurgents, three of the latter by the local inhabitants – two of them were shot by the 15-year-old daughter of one of their victims. The group then changed course and headed back towards Ovamboland.

After the incursion there was a quiet period until May, when the insurgency intensified dramatically. During one contact the security forces lost five men and PLAN 81, while the Ondangwa air force base was the target of a brief mortar attack that caused little damage.

This brings me to Operation Sceptic, better known as Smokeshell. It was the biggest South African mechanised infantry operation since World War II, and its aim was to destroy PLAN's command-and-control centre at Chifufua, 180 km north of the border as the crow flies or 260 km by road.

Operation Sceptic, in a nutshell, was summed up as follows by the military journal *Militaria:*

> [The operation] began with a blitz attack on a PLAN base in southern Angola, but developed into an extended operation as more and more PLAN caches were discovered in the area. Operation Sceptic brought about the first serious clashes with the Angolan forces, FAPLA. Also for the first time contact was made with mechanised elements of PLAN. PLAN lost its forward base facilities and 380 insurgents died. The security forces seized several hundred tonnes of equipment and supplies,

as well as many vehicles. Seventeen members of the South African strike force fell in battle.

Brigadier 'Witkop' Badenhorst, commander of Sector 10 (Kaokoland and Ovamboland), was in command of the operation, which started when Commandant Anton van Graan secured an area across the border ahead of the main body. Then, on 9 June, he was followed by a task force of three mechanised battle groups – Battle Group 10 under Commandant Chris Serfontein, Battle Group 61 under Commandant J M (Dippies) Dippenaar and Battle Group 53 under Commandant Jorrie Jordaan.

At 14h30 on 10 June, following an air strike and a preliminary artillery bombardment, the assault force (Chris Serfontein's Battle Group 10 and Dippies Dippenaar's Battle Group 61) attacked the enemy base area at Chifufua, which we had nicknamed 'Smokeshell'.

Sceptic was supposed to end on 16 June, but as a result of information found at the scene it was extended to bases west of Smokeshell, and ended only on 30 June.

I was at the tactical headquarters on D-Day, 10 June, with a radio receiver Witkop Badenhorst had given me so that I could follow the progress of the battle from H-hour onwards. It was here that I experienced some of the most anxious moments of my life: all because of General Viljoen. I heard his radio going off the air and from the rest of the signals traffic on the net I gathered that something had happened to his Ratel. The seconds and minutes dragged by, and I was eventually told that his Ratel had detonated two anti-tank mines which had been set to explode simultaneously, the resulting explosion tossing him right out of his hatch.

A pattern developed during Sceptic which would be repeated in times to come. It was comparable to what happens when an ant-hill is kicked open. The ants scatter, you search for them around their nest and they lead you to other nests. Smokeshell was the ants' nest. Most of the cadres scattered to find safety at their other bases. Then a combination of area operations, follow-ups and search-and-destroy operations were launched to locate and destroy them.

After the fighting at Smokeshell, Battle Group 10 under Chris Serfontein continued mopping up PLAN bases in the Mulola area, 50 km to the west. There were quite a few stray groups of insurgents in between the various bases, and tons of ammunition and war material had to be located and destroyed or back-loaded.

On 11 June I joined Chris Serfontein, and I spent many days with Battle Group 10. One of my duties, believe it or not, was that of sports commentator. Chris Serfontein tells the following story about what happened on Saturday, 14 June, when his men were scheduled to work through certain PLAN bases and caches:

> The troops were visibly put out when I told them that the starting time of the mopping-up operation would be 15h00. That was when the Springboks' rugby test match against the British Lions in Bloemfontein was scheduled to start.
>
> As General Geldenhuys was with us we dared not postpone the operation. We had to make a plan. Bobby Keller, the signals officer, told me that provided we could use the command vehicle's rear-link radio, he could guarantee that old Gerhard Viviers's commentary would be heard loud and clear, and the men could be kept informed of the battle of Bloemfontein on the command net. The problem was that we had to have somebody with some knowledge of the game to man the rear link. What was wrong with the GOC of South West himself? The nominee agreed and so the mopping-up and the test match could take place at the same time.
>
> This is more or less how it sounded on the command net: 'Two zero, this is nine, you guys must mop up those trenches properly, just now a terro shoots one of you ... the big number nine (General Geldenhuys) says old Gysie has just scored under the posts ... over,' which was followed by an applause equivalent to that of the open stand at the Free State stadium. So it happened that the men reconciled war and rugby.

I went to see Gerhard Viviers in 1991, shortly after his vocal cords had been removed, and told him this story. He could not talk yet, but he responded by scribbling on a piece of paper: 'A chap once told me, "Thanks for the commentary in my vehicle, sir."'

* * *

The news media played an important role in our operations, apart from providing sports commentaries and the like. A large contingent was present during the first battle, the action at Smokeshell. Then, around 12–13 June, shortly after I had joined Serfie and his battle group, I heard someone say that they had all left. I got on to the radio and asked what had happened to them.

Maj Marius KIeynhans, the SWA Command media liaison officer, told me that the journalists had said they had got a good story at Smokeshell which they wanted to file; they also had bosses and couldn't just drive around in the bush hoping and waiting for the next scrap to happen.

I then urgently and seriously ordered him to ask the media corps in Windhoek to send back at least three journalists – one from radio, one from TV and one from a news agency. And so it happened that Con Crous from the South African Press Association, Johan Brits from SWA Radio and Ossie Gibson from RSA TV returned to the bush.

During later years journalists often asked me why we would not allow them to accompany us on operations. This was a valid question, but I could not resist telling them about the above incidents, which proved that we are not as averse to the idea as many people tended to think. Some freelance journalists spent much time with the forces in the bush during operations. Al J Venter was a good example. This man was truly prepared to go anywhere and everywhere, regardless of danger and discomfort.

I left Serfie and his men for a while and flew to Ondangwa with Major Crow Stannard, who was ferrying back material seized during the fighting, then rejoined Battle Group 10 on 22 June. The end of Operation Sceptic was already in sight when we received information that PLAN's mechanised force, which included BTR armoured vehicles and field artillery, was to be found at a place called Tanga Nova. Chris Serfontein decided to attack them with two companies, supported by Captain Budgie Burgers's Impala strike aircraft.

As we moved in for the attack I saw the first mortar bombs fall. I was uncertain whether they were ours or theirs, but I had no time to find out because at that moment my attention was diverted by something very strange. A PLAN member suddenly walked out of the bushes, straight towards our command vehicle – an open-topped Buffel armoured personnel carrier – as we were actually moving between two companies of troops. I did not instantly register what was happening. All I saw was

Serfie grabbing his rifle, jumping up and pointing it, shouting: 'Drop your rifle, drop your rifle!'

If I had been at the receiving end I would have had the fright of my life. Serfie's face was deeply tanned after all the time in the bush under the sun, so that all one saw were two large white eye-balls, and white teeth showing under his bristly black moustache. Only then did I notice the enemy soldier next to our vehicle.

Looking back, the moment was probably not all that dangerous, but it was dramatic enough. Serfie and the insurgent were face to face with only three metres between them, both hanging on to their rifles. The insurgent did not seem to know what he was expected to do, but Serfie's was pointed right at his chest. Then our Ovambo staff-sergeant jumped down and relieved the poor man of his weapon.

Apart from that, it was another fight that never was. The enemy had been occupying a temporary respite area and had made a hasty break just before we got there, so that we had only slight contact with the last of their rear parties.

To my knowledge this was our first contact with PLAN's mechanised force, which attracted international attention many years later (I will come back to that). We seized a great deal of military equipment, including 76 mm field guns, and a stack of documents (which came in handy nearly 10 years later, as I shall relate in Chapter 18). And, of course, that one young man who had been captured by the command vehicle! His name was Smokey, and we grew quite fond of him.

We were not always 100 per cent geared to back-load the tons of seized equipment, but we tried our best. On this occasion, after we had destroyed some of the equipment, we hooked up the guns behind our Buffels, including the command Buffel. The Imps were still overhead, and before we left the general area of the objective I happened to listen to the ground-air radio and suddenly heard one of the pilots say to another: 'I see the Swaps are towing back their guns, let's take a final run and "rev" them a bit.'

I grabbed the radio: 'Stop, stop! There is no enemy here any longer. All the guns you see are now ours!'

* * *

By this time there were not many more bases or insurgents to be tracked down, and on 23 June the settlement negotiations got going again, with Minister Pik Botha ready with certain new proposals.

One night towards the end of June a helicopter came to take me back to the Ondangwa air base and then Windhoek. Next day at Ondangwa, where everyone was clearing out after the operation and I was about to depart for Windhoek, I suddenly saw the 'sharp-nose' men, Commandant Mac van der Merwe's Mirage F1 pilots, scrambling and taking off.

What had happened was that Serfie and his Battle Group 10 had been heading back southwards when they had come under surprise attack from an Angolan force just as they were about to cross the tarmac road from Ongiva to Xangongo.

It was a tough action. Serfie contacted Major Bob King, the leader of Battle Group 10's MAOT (mobile air operations team) on the radio, saying: 'Bob, help!' But he didn't even have to request close support from the air command post at Ondangwa. Colonel Theo de Munnink, commander of Western Air Command, and Commandant Ollie Holmes, the SAAF commander of Sector 10, were listening in to what they later described as the 'long conversation' between Serfie and Bob, and reacted immediately.

The sharp noses attacked the Angolans with 1 000 lb bombs, enabling Serfie to make a clean break, and by 17h30 on 29 June he had completed his withdrawal (Rifleman Paul de Kock was later awarded the Honoris Crux decoration for his courageous conduct during this action, while WOII Schutte, the battle group sergeant-major, received the Pro Merito Medal for keeping wounded soldiers alive by direct blood transfusion while at risk of his life. Later the Ovambo guide commented: 'The Lord looked after us today.'

Sergeant-Major Schutte and Rifleman De Kock were not the only ones who performed excellently. Everyone involved pulled his weight – and bear in mind that everything is more difficult in war, that everyone involved has the potential to slip, and, as I said earlier, to turn the wrong screw.

During Sceptic I learned how well the men who had to 'turn the screws' knew what they were doing when it came to the nuts and bolts level.

During the preparation phase Brigadier Badenhorst suddenly

instructed one Lieutenant Jenkins, commander of the Sector 10 Light Workshop Troop, to repair another eight Buffels which were needed for the operation. It was already late afternoon and Jenkins's 'tiffies', or artificers, were tired after a long day's hard work; but they worked right through the night, so that by first light the next morning the Buffels were repaired, re-sprayed and ready for action. Then the tiffies were told that they would be going along.

Six of them, after working non-stop throughout the night, packed their kit and set off. For two weeks they uncomplainingly kept the wheels turning until they were withdrawn because their 24-month national service term had expired.

The wheels had started to turn for me, too: during the operation it was announced that I would be transferred to Pretoria.

*   *   *

During my tour of duty in South West Africa there had been heavy military activity and I had also been dragged into the domestic and international political scene, so that I was away from Windhoek at least four days a week.

But there had been time for recreation as well. I remember once when I was called away to Pretoria to attend a conference which was scheduled for the Friday before either a rugby test match or a Currie Cup final was to be played at the Loftus Versveld grounds (I hasten to assure my readers that this was pure coincidence). In any case, some friends and I decided to watch the game, so we arranged to meet at the Culemborg Hotel and go on from there in a microbus. The hotel was jam-packed; people drinking beer were standing around in clusters in the bar lounges and other lounges, in the passages, everywhere. All were warming up for the game, exchanging views and speculating over the chances of the two sides

I noticed that one group of rugby enthusiasts standing nearby were whispering among themselves, looking at me, whispering some more and then looking at me again. Obviously they were talking about me, and naturally it made me feel good. Then one of them detached himself from the group, and with the air of a man on a mission steered himself past the other people and headed straight for me, beer in hand.

When he came up to me he said: 'Excuse me, sir, I don't want to intrude on your privacy, but we're having an argument ...'

I was enjoying the situation and told him: 'You're not bothering me at all. Please carry on.'

'We were arguing,' he said, 'about whether you're ... perhaps ...'

'Yes ... Yes?'

'Are you perhaps ... Doug Watson?' he asked.

* * *

One of my last obligations before leaving South West was a trip to Ovamboland to make a speech at a social gathering marking the opening of the Air Force Club at the Ondangwa air base.

I used the opportunity to make what I warned them was an important announcement – namely that a new military unit was to be established. By way of introduction I told my audience about how seemingly outdated technology had suddenly become useful again in the bush war. And considering all the problems we had experienced with telecommunications, I added, we might as well make equally effective use of carrier pigeons and other birds to carry messages.

Everyone present politely concealed their amazement at this radical statement, but they were nevertheless curious to know which of the services, Army or Air Force, would be given responsibility for the bird unit. So I explained as follows: everything that moved on the ground came under the command of the Army, and everything that moved in the air fell under the Air Force; so this new winged unit would be an Air Force operation.

I had already liaised with the Chief of the Air Force, I continued, and had recommended that the key officers to run the new unit were to be Budgie Burgers, Crow Stannard, Mossie (Sparrow) Basson and Vink (Finch) Hattingh ...

Some observers searched diligently for the reasons behind my transfer, but in fact there were none. General Magnus Malan had been appointed Minister of Defence on 7 October 1980; General Viljoen had succeeded him as Chief of the Defence Force, and I had been selected to take over from him as Chief of the Army from 1 November 1980. My headquarters would obviously be in Pretoria.

My service in South West enriched me, and I am thankful for that. I often come across people who tell me that I have been very lucky in my career. I was lucky to have been transferred to South West in 1970, because that is where everything began; I was lucky to have been given command in South West again in 1977, during the amalgamation of SWA Command and 101 Task Force, because quite a few military operations took place during that time which provided me with the opportunity to show my worth. So yes, I was lucky.

But that is not the whole story. It all really started in 1962 at the Loftus Versveld D Field. I was playing full-back for Defence against Tukkies (the University of Pretoria) when I broke my leg just above the ankle and decided to give up rugby and in future follow the game as a spectator.

I then calculated how many hours a month I used to spend on rugby and resolved to put this time to a particular use. I thought about it carefully and first decided, for my own pleasure, to write a book. I started at it straight away, but it took me 20 years to have two booklets published. No big deal.

Secondly, I wanted to learn another language. I decided on Portuguese, as it was the language spoken in our neighbouring territories, Angola and Mozambique, and might come in useful some time or other. I made a start and attended a private class now and then, but concentrated mainly on records and grammar books.

In 1965 I read in a departmental circular that the post of vice-consul in Luanda was vacant. I applied and was appointed, perhaps because I had taken the initiative and learned Portuguese. My term there was extended for one year. But when the possibility of a second extension was raised, I requested to be considered for the annual supplementary transfer list of March–April 1970. In due course, I was told that I would be transferred to Pretoria.

In the meantime, towards the end of 1969, two World War II veteran officers in succession were transferred to Windhoek as Colonel G, but both made representations not to go. The outcome was that, before I could even move to Pretoria, the Chief of the Army had sent me directly to Windhoek, probably because I was available and because my experience in Angola could come in handy.

I would say that my first tour in South West was certainly a factor which contributed to the decision to send me there once again during 1977. I do not think that all was luck. But who can tell? *Friction de guerre* is ever present. Like my first term in South West, my second was also the end of a chapter for me, but not the end of a book.

The Windhoek I said goodbye to was well described by many artists, including poets, among them those who focused on the war. Roy Allen describes the Windhoek of those days like this in the poem 'Bistro', from his volume *Sungong:*

Like a sidewalk of some Paris street,
Gay with bright sunshades,
Coffee-sippers, plastic chairs,
People
Watching
People
Pass –

A dumpy old lady, grey, sits, bejewelled,
Painfully
Penning a
Postcard
To some Munich friend.

The beggar from Ovamboland, wizened and watery-eyed
From too many years of the sun
Is shuffling past

Jo'burg pressmen, beer-fat and pale-faced
Say confidential things into microphone cups
(Perhaps tomorrow's headlines) –
The divorcee, triumphant, ponders her alimony here –
A table away from the SWAPO-D man entertaining New York
    guests –
Heinrich, ex-Wehrmacht, ex-Stalingrad, Ritterkreuz
And still erect goes marching past
As Novicki, the Warsaw architect, talks of Vivaldi
With Aviva – soprano from the opera Don Pascale –

Sarel of security sits there alone
Unreading *Die Republikein* – detachedly carefully,
Watching
People
Passing –
Coffee-sippers
Plastic chairs.
(Scene at a Windhoek outdoor cafe off Kaiser Street, '79)

The 1979/1980 yearbook of the Institute for the Study of Conflict in London described South Africa's military action in SWA-Namibia as 'an outstanding example of a successful counter-insurgency offensive taken at an early stage of the conflict'.

CHAPTER 10

CORRESPONDENTS AND SPIES

Fish eagles and crocodiles

When I left South West I keenly missed my days in the natural wilderness, along with place names like Buffalo, Okavango, Liambezi Lake, Marienfluss and Kunenemund, and also the fish eagles, storks, lions, crocodiles and hippos – the symbols of wild, free nature; to have lived among them had been a magnificent experience.

When I came to South West in 1970 I was a hunter. When I left in 1980, I no longer hunted, although I continued to enjoy (and still enjoy) biltong, dried game sausage and barbequed ribs, as well as 'puff-adder' – a section of large intestine stuffed with liver – and I was still quite willing to tag along on a hunting trip; preferably to advise, beer in hand, during the skinning and cutting up of the meat. But I had found that I could no longer look an animal in the eye and cut its throat.

Then again, facing an animal was one thing and war another; but the single most difficult duty for me was facing a media conference.

The world of correspondents and spies represented one of the interesting phenomena that played a significant role during the 1977–1980 period. This was not part of the chronological factual story, nor of the milestones along the route; but it was like the ever-recurring surges of the sea a captain feels while steering his vessel on its course, or like the behaviour of the weather when a safari continues on its way to its destination.

With the media I always followed three guidelines: if I released information on my own initiative, I gave it to them as a whole. However, if a journalist approached me for information and releasing it was not a problem, I would give it to that journalist, and only to him. And whenever I released information, I tried to give all the facts – which was not always easy, since classified information was usually involved.

There were other problems too. Some of them had no solutions, and one had to live with them. A story from those days illustrates the kind of problems the news media had with me.

The media corps was quite extensive for a territory as sparsely populated as South West: there were representatives from the South West press, consisting of the morning and afternoon newspapers and one Saturday newspaper; the South African press, consisting of morning and afternoon newspapers, Sunday newspapers and magazines; overseas media correspondents; SWA radio; and SABC-TV.

I used to hold regular weekly media conferences, or issue a press statement if there was not enough news to justify a conference on the specified day. Then the morning papers started to complain that we issued the press releases and held the conferences at times that favoured the afternoon press; when we changed that, the afternoon papers complained. All the papers moaned that the radio was always the first to use our information, while the weekend papers, especially the Saturday paper, groaned that we never gave them the chance to be the first to publish security information; the South West press expressed dissatisfaction with what they saw as a favouring of the South African media, and vice versa.

Every complaint had merit when viewed on its own, so I brought about changes to try to accommodate them all. I alternated the conferences, handling them on different days of the week and different times of the day. Embargos ensured that radio and TV news could not jump the gun. But the complaints kept coming in. By way of illustration, the well-known editor Hannes Smith wrote in the 12 July 1980 edition of his paper that 'the Windhoek Observer often violently clashed with the General, particularly because we sometimes suspected him of favouring the South African newsmen and neglecting the local newsmen.'

One day I convened a special media conference and said: 'Come now, elect yourselves a chairman. Decide jointly on which days of the week and on what hours of the day I should arrange my press conferences. If you cannot reach agreement on a fixed day of the week, decide on specific pre-determined dates. I undertake to do exactly whatever you decide.' They agreed and I left them to their conference. It was rather a rash concession, because it meant one forfeited all initiative, but a promise is a promise.

They selected Con Crous of the South African Press Association as chairman. He was an experienced journalist and respected by all, and because he was employed by a news agency he was not a controversial figure. To my surprise I did not receive a speedy recommendation on press-conference times. In fact, I had to make enquiries about the media's silence, and found that there was such a clash of interests among themselves that they could not reach agreement. In the end Con Crous told me to carry on as before.

I had learnt an important lesson: there is no such thing as 'the press'. There are different TV and radio stations, and specific papers and magazines. But the problem had been eased, if not solved.

There were other difficulties too. Hannes Smith said in the same article mentioned above: '... in fact, at one particular military briefing a London spy sat in the ranks of the press, and the General knew it. He concealed his knowledge and only later did seasoned reporters learn why. For this spy was neatly led by the nose and conveyed the wrong information to sources in London.'

It is true that from time to time we had good reasons to strongly suspect certain persons of playing obscure roles, but I cannot now remember any particular incident where I had taken such a course of action. It would seem to be improbable and impractical. However, many years later I did land up in a similar situation, which I shall describe in a later chapter.

Hannes Smith was, by any possible standard of comparison, absolutely special and unique; a fascinating book could surely be written about him. Some people jokingly called him 'crazy Smith', but if he was really crazy, he was wiser in his madness than most of his critics in their state of un-crazy mental equilibrium.

He gave the Defence Force hell. One of his colleagues reminded me many years later of a special confidential briefing to which I had invited the editors and senior reporters. In his next edition Smith reported on the briefing as follows: 'During a strictly off-the-record briefing yesterday, Gen Geldenhuys said that ...' I took it philosophically. In one respect Hannes was like Jos Rossouw; they could both just about get away with murder.

In general I have great respect for the media. They were professional and responsible. I always tried my best to treat them fairly and keep them satisfied. I would like to flatter myself that I succeeded to a reasonable degree, but I must admit that there were favourable factors which made this possible. General Malan delegated the same authority to me as he did to the Chief of the South African Defence Force as regards liaison with the media in South West and the making of general press statements. This was very different from the situation of my counterparts in territorial commands in South Africa. In respect of the release of information specifically concerning operations, I had the same powers in my area of responsibility as the Chief of the Defence Force enjoyed about operations elsewhere. With the appointment of the AG and the separation of South West and South African politics, Pretoria imposed few restrictions on me regarding the media and politics. It meant that I could deal with the media independently.

This brings me to some aspects of the relationship between the military and politics. One should not deduce from the above that there was a firm line between the two. On the contrary, I don't believe one always realises how totally interwoven war and politics became at all levels of society.

In days gone by, peace and war had clear-cut boundaries. During peacetime peoples and states talked to one another and arranged their relations by means of politics and diplomacy. If matters could not be settled in this manner, the parties agreed to differ. To break a deadlock one or both of the parties might resort to violence and declare war. One then overpowered the other, or they destroyed one another. Then they started talking again, and peace was concluded.

Nowadays peacetime and war-time do not follow in such neat phases. Wars are not declared, so that violence and diplomatic politics take place simultaneously. Nations and movements talk while they shoot, and vice versa. This has changed the nature of warfare. In some cases during ancient times two sides would agree that each would appoint a warrior to represent it; the two warriors would fight, and the side whose warrior emerged victorious had won the battle. The duel between David and Goliath is an excellent example. This trend continued for some time.

Dr Cas Bakkes told me once that during the eighteenth century opponents on the field of battle could not always agree as to who would fire the first salvo, and armies sometimes left the battlefield with no contact having been made. At the Battle of Fontenoy on 11 May 1745, Lord Charles Hay, a lieutenant of the 1st Guards battalion, rushed forward before the English and French lines could start firing at each other, took off his hat to the advancing French, bowed deeply and drank a toast to them from his hip-flask. Then he ordered his troops to applaud the enemy with three cheers. After the French had returned the salute and applause, Lord Charles invited them to fire the first volley. The French refused and passed the honour back to the English. The result was that the burst of fire which followed from the English side caused serious casualties in the French ranks.

Customs and traditions have gradually changed. As early as the beginning of the nineteenth century Napoleon very improperly, unsportingly and unceremoniously (by the standards of the time) attacked his opponents from the rear. But since then things have changed even more. The formalities have disappeared completely. War is no longer formally declared. In other words, there can be peace, with politics being practised as usual, but in the meantime fighting is also taking place. The politicians know it, but feign ignorance. Politicians are even hesitant to admit that a situation of armed hostilities has developed, because the first one to announce it is accused of having started it all. One party may try to keep its armed actions quiet and then accuse the other of making war, while the other party will deny it and throw the accusation back at its opponent.

This is the propaganda of the 'good guys' and the 'bad guys'. It is a very unmilitary kind of conduct, but it is politically acceptable. In the old days people declared war openly and drank toasts, now they make war in the dark and sling mud at each other in public. This is what happened in many countries during the past three decades, and there were signs of it in South Africa as well in the early 1990s.

In practice it worked like this from my perspective: the Soviet Department of Foreign Affairs would talk politics and peace, while the Communist Party and KGB incited war. The top people who performed in public would seem to propagate peace, although instructions for subversion and incitement to violence had been issued. The politicians were the masters and integrated the action as a whole. There were political commissars on all levels, even the lowest, throughout the communist military system. Revolutionary organisations supported by the Soviets likewise had political commissars from top to bottom. In Angola, for example, SWAPO had political commissars right down to regional and detachment level. We, on the other hand, followed the Western system, so that the Defence Force had only one connecting point with politics, and that was at Minister of Defence level.

I experienced this situation during my time in South West, especially with regard to propaganda. There is no doubt that in recent decades South Africa convincingly won its military conflicts, although propagandists and those who allowed themselves to be dragged along by their propaganda will, of course, deny it. But be that as it may, one war which we did lose was the propaganda war.

In 1991 I came on an old British pamphlet on the conduct of war which said: 'psychological warfare will be conducted after the outbreak of war by the use of all available means ...' Until the present, this policy has always been applied by totalitarian states and the movements supported by them, with one difference: to them it did not matter whether war had been declared or not. In Western countries, however, the phrase 'outbreak of war' means a formally declared war. But wars are no longer formally declared. Governments therefore never arrive at a point where they enter the propaganda arena, and it is partly because of this difference in approach that the dividing lines between war and peace have become blurred.

With the discussions that later resulted in the 1984 Lusaka Agreement, there were talks about peace while the war was in full swing. The last series of negotiations on a peace settlement in 1988, which resulted in the Cuban troops' withdrawal from Angola and the implementation of Resolution 435 in South West Africa, likewise began long before the war ended.

It could also happen that during one and the same conflict, one of the parties would use propaganda because it considered itself in a position of war, while the other would continue to practise normal politics because it thought that peace prevailed. SWAPO and the MPLA regarded propaganda as a dimension of their struggle, and the propaganda organisation as just another weapon system. We regarded propaganda as a distasteful word and concept without a place in democratic politics.

The SWAPO propaganda embraced certain themes which its practitioners used successfully over a very long time before they were turned upside down, some of them only very recently. To illustrate:

- PLAN *was fighting from bases inside South West.* No such base could ever be pointed out to anybody. With the implementation of Resolution 435 during 1988-1989 not a single UN monitoring officer ever saw a PLAN base inside South West. But SWAPO's claims were believed for many years.
- SWAPO *had about 80 000 refugees in its care.* Over the years we described this figure as ridiculous. It was only with the implementation of Resolution 435 that our counter-claim was accepted; it caused SWAPO great embarrassment when, under UN supervision, only about 30 000 refugees presented themselves. It is easy to understand. If it was the international year of the aged, SWAPO had a large number of old people in its care; if it was the year of the children, SWAPO had a lot of children under its wing; if it was the year of the refugee, it had a lot of refugees. In this way they claimed a lot of aid funds from various sources.
- *The security forces murdered and plundered the local population and looted their towns.* If one or two such cases contained some truth, the other 10 or 20 allegations were also believed. Any useful theme was repeated without interruption until it became accepted as a general perception.

On the other hand, in my experience, all our claims were rejected as untrue. Although we knew that there were advisers of the Soviet Union and its allies present in the Angolan and SWAPO forces, we were seldom believed; analysts insisted on concrete evidence. During Operation Reindeer in 1978 Commandant Frank Bestbier found a Russian's suitcase, containing uniform, documents and all, at PLAN's 'Vietnam' base at Chetequera. Some of these items were displayed to the media. The response was merely that we might have planted them.

Later, during Operation Protea in 1981, two Soviets – Major Yevgenii Victorovich Kireev, chief artillery adviser, and Colonel Joseph Lamonovich, adviser to the political commissar – were killed, and Warrant-Officer Nilolai Pestretsof was taken prisoner. Only then did they believe us – with a shrug of the shoulders.

PLAN abducted people from South West. Few people believed us. But a few days before Operation Reindeer, insurgents hijacked a bus at Olindamba, north of Olushandja in the vicinity of Beacon 6½, kidnapped the passengers and took them to Angola. The bus then got stuck 1.5 km north of the border. The information we released about this incident was received with scepticism. But the kidnapped passengers were found at the Vietnam base after the battle there, and two of them told their story to the media the following day. Even then many people still would not believe it, and told me that we had brainwashed the passengers.

Later, during the implementation of the Lusaka agreement, I experienced similar frustrations. We had reported that members of PLAN were still infiltrating across the border into South West from the area in dispute, in contravention of the agreement. We were not believed. Once we took such a captured infiltrator to the next meeting of the Joint Monitoring Commission and made him available to the Angolans and Cubans for debriefing. They would not talk to him, even if only to manage their own information or to ascertain if he was not in fact a *bona fide* captured insurgent. They simply said he was brainwashed, and that was that.

We obtained proof that Cubans, Angolans and PLAN occupied bases jointly and that PLAN members were wearing Angolan uniforms. Many would not believe us. But after an operation I asked the intelligence officer on the spur of the moment to fetch one of the PLAN prisoners so that the journalists who were waiting for a press conference to start could talk to him; I didn't know who or what kind of a person he was, or what he would say. A foreign journalist questioned him.

The PLAN man spoke freely, and complained that PLAN had discriminated against him. In reply to a question he explained that he was a

Damara and he and the other Damaras were given second-rate rifles, Simonovs, while the Ovambos got the better AK47s. The same journalist then asked him: 'What is that jacket you're wearing?'

'It's a FAPLA jacket,' he replied.

'Why are you wearing a FAPLA jacket?'

'Because FAPLA say that if we're together with them at the same place we must wear FAPLA uniforms, not PLAN uniforms, otherwise the South African forces will attack them.'

During Operation Protea we seized a Soviet operational map of the Xangongo base and its surroundings. On it was annotated in detail the integrated Cuban, FAPLA and PLAN artillery fire-plan. This contributed towards convincing some people of their mutual co-operation

SWAPO leaders always denied that they ill-treated their members in detention, or those assembled for what they called 're-education'. However, when SWAPO returned to South West in terms of Resolution 435, the stories of torture caused a public outcry.

One cannot always blame the media, because in conflict situations the air is so thick with propaganda that even I did not always know what was real and what was not. Was any information based on fact, emanating from reliable and credible sources? Or was everything part of a psychological warfare scheme aiming to scare or influence decision-makers?

However, there was one report which did not leave me with any doubts. That was when the well-known military correspondent, Carel Birkby, reported in *To the Point* on a story about an impending invasion of South West Africa by East German paratroopers operating out of Angola. Some people were anxious about this information, but I rejected it.

> It could have been planted by Moscow. It could have been based on false premises. It could even have been a view sincerely held in some quarters. But whatever its source, [the story] ... was quickly denied last week by defence specialists.

I was one of the so-called defence specialists. Some people were anxious about this information, but I rejected it. But this was not just a wild allegation. Many places, names and facts had been given, some of which were correct, to provide authenticity. Birkby went on to say:

> The reports were neatly patterned. Word was dropped that 'eleven senior generals' from the eastern side of the Berlin Wall had arrived in Luanda. It is correct that a number of officers of general rank were now in Angola as advisers and as observers studying the intermittent activities in an 'interesting' civil war. But a leak to the German newspaper, *Die Welt*, made these professionals sound more ominous. The French intelligence sources cited that five were named and positioned. General Jakanowitz is described as the mastermind planning an invasion. His headquarters are placed in Henrique de Carvalho ...
>
> Vasili Ivanovitz Petrov, described as 'first deputy commander' of the Soviet ground forces, who reportedly advised the Ethiopians and their Cuban aids how to defeat Somalia this year, is reported to have been in Angola. It would be logical for him to take a look at another African scene where internal warfare is going on. Top man in Luanda, where he is close to Pres Agostinho Neto, is Karpov.

Other Soviet officers were also mentioned – Shredin at Lubango, Churopov at Bié, and Gobin at Roçades (later Xangongo).

*   *   *

Other forms of propaganda are also used in revolutionary warfare. General Jack Dutton talked of a multi-dimensional war, one of the dimensions being semantics – the skilful use of words to create perceptions – something SWAPO was very good at. For example, normal PLAN detachments who had been deployed in certain areas of southern Angola, east of the Kunene River, were given names such as 'Ground Forces', 'Air Forces' and 'Naval Forces'. They were nothing of the sort, but it paid good dividends.

SWAPO regularly staged media conferences and issued press releases; one of their well-known spokesmen, Peter Katjavivi in London, used to tell of incidents on the border and then report that SWAPO's 'Air

Forces' or 'Naval Forces' had done this and that and the other. This naturally created the perception that SWAPO had a navy and an air force. Many believed them. It seems crazy, but it is surprising how stupid intelligent people can be – or prefer to be if it suits them.

SWAPO also divided the south of Angola into so-called 'fronts', including the 'Northern Front' and the 'North-Eastern Front'. They also used these designations during press conferences. Once again, this naturally created the impression that they had bases in north and north-eastern SWA.

In the same article in the *Windhoek Observer* I mentioned earlier, Hannes Smith said: 'In a major military briefing some three years ago, Geldenhuys agreed that it was acceptable to him that a Swapo fighter could be called a guerrilla or an insurgent if he fights the security forces, but a terrorist when he attacks a civilian.' This highlights another example of the role played by semantics. Some people used the word 'terrorists' because it suited them, while the majority referred to 'freedom fighters' and 'guerrillas' because it suited *them.*

I was always disappointed when acts of terror had been committed and those responsible were called freedom fighters and similarly glorifying names – a more recent example being the attack on a golf club at King William's Town on 28 November 1992, in which four people were killed and 17 wounded.

I formulated an approach and discussed it with the media: people who committed deeds of terror – such as the murder of Clemens Kapuuo, the planting of the mine on the garage path of the Ovambo Minister of Health, Mr Toivo Shiyagaya, the murder of Mr David Shikongo and the killing of council members and about 24 chiefs during a period of 24 months in Ovamboland – should have been called terrorists. In all other cases where skirmishes took place between armed people and the security forces they could be called guerrilla fighters, if it was so desired.

Many journalists came back and told me that their editors had advised them that it was against their editorial policy and that they could not go along with this formula. Some of them even reported back apologetically, because they agreed that it was a fair policy (the *Rand Daily Mail* was one of the newspapers that did accept it).

I made one mistake with the news media. I was naïve enough to expect accurate and 'positive' reporting and comment. That was unrealistic; I had forgotten that different elements of the media also tried, each in its own manner, to influence political policy. That was their right, and therefore one had to accept 'negative' reporting. But if one was honest with the media, the chances were good that one could also get 'positive' coverage together with the 'negative' type.

I had to take the punch. You could not blame the media, and they could not be blamed if they reported negative statements made by other people. My opinion of the media is described fairly well by Peter Samuel in the *International Freedom Review:*

> Government should try to take the initiative with the media and think positively about it. If the government does not give it a story, it will look elsewhere. Therefore, government should provide spokesmen, keep restrictions to a minimum, and provide all the information it can ...
>
> The media may be rotten messengers at times, but they are not the enemy.

* * *

When I reflect on those days, the name Theunie Steyn always comes to mind, for what he was and how he, too, got stumped by semantics.

I had always heard of the tremendous respect people had had for the President of the Orange Free State of bygone times, Marthinus Theunis Steyn. His son, Colin, had also enjoyed a widespread reputation as an intellectual colossus. And when I got to know Mr Justice M T Steyn, I could better understand everything that I had heard about his father and grandfather. Greatness must run in their blood.

I once attended a function to promote the aims of the Society for the Protection of Endangered Species at which Judge Steyn was the main speaker. I was seated next to Professor Fritz Eloff, professor of zoology, rugby man and nature-lover. Judge Steyn, as I had seen him do before, took out a scrap of paper about the size of a bus ticket, and from the notes on that strip of paper spoke for about an hour and a half.

He began in space, beyond the furthermost solar systems and expanses. He spoke about what was happening there and worked systematically through all the layers of magnetospheres, ionospheres, stratospheres and tropospheres until he reached the crust of the earth. His address penetrated it and ended in the hot, melting masses in the innermost depths of the earth. But before he could get there, Professor Eloff admiringly sighed: 'What a man!'

When Judge Steyn and I arrived at Katimo Mulilo from Mpacha on 23 August 1978, our helicopter was fired on by anti-aircraft guns from Sesheke in Zambia, and I joined him in a bomb shelter. Our own counter-bombardment had begun by this time, and with the sound of field artillery pieces in his ears Judge Steyn – a romantic and a veteran of World War II – looked at me and said: 'Just listen to the music of battle ... It feels like Monte Cassino all over again.'

Piet Voges of Cape Town once told me of a visit he paid to former Minister Frank Waring and his wife Joyce in Bantry Bay towards the end of 1977. The then Prime Minister, John Vorster, was also there, sitting quietly on a swing seat on the verandah. Among the guests were acquaintances of mine, the well-known Windhoek writer Olga Levinson and her husband Jack, and they expressed their appreciation to the Prime Minister for the wonderful person named Theunie Steyn whom he had made Administrator-General. Theunie Steyn was an exceptionally competent man, Jack added.

The Prime Minister listened patiently, then responded in his dry, measured fashion: 'Yes, his father put me in jail.' This had happened during World War II, when Theunie's father, Colin, was the Minister of Justice in the Smuts cabinet. The emergency regulations allowed people to be interned without trial and without interference from the courts, and Vorster was interned at Koffiefontein for his outspoken anti-government attitude to the war.

Judge Steyn completed two successful years in office – even though SWAPO supporters liked to call him the puppet of the Pretoria regime and so forth when he first arrived in Windhoek – and then departed amid all the prescribed official formalities. When he entered the VIP departure hall at Eros Airport, his personal magnetism rippled once more through the crowd of well-wishers. He tapped dignified men on the shoulder and kissed entranced ladies' hands. Then the moment to say goodbye arrived and he walked down the red carpet to the guard of honour, returned its salute and inspected it. At the end of the carpet the Merlin aircraft which was to take him home stood waiting, and at the top of the steps he turned around, removed his hat and waved a last goodbye to the crowd.

This was the signal for the newly formed SWA Territory Force Band to strike up and play him off. The chosen music was ... 'Puppet on a String'.

Friction de guerre strikes people both great and small.

CHAPTER 11

THE BEGINNING OF A NEW DECADE

'The South African government has been shocked'

On 1 November 1980 I took over from General Constand Viljoen as the Chief of the Army. I was to learn fast what this entailed. One lesson came when I attended a party shortly after my arrival in Pretoria. There a woman walked up to me and said: 'Oh, are you General Geldenhuys?' I nodded, and she said: 'How nice. I've seen you on TV, but shame, I didn't know you were such a tiny little man!'

A few months later I invited sports commentator Gerhard Viviers with his wife, Maryna, and rugby heroes Morné du Plessis and Frik du Preez for a visit to the operational area in South West. The troops liked to see people like these, to shake hands with them and have a chat. Morné and Frik would also do a bit of coaching at Grootfontein, Rundu and Oshakati.

They were to arrive in Pretoria on a Sunday; I was to be their host at dinner that evening, where I would say a few words of welcome, and next morning early they would depart for the operational area. By way of preparation I arranged with my public relations officer that from time to time during our normal working hours he and I would stop any soldier we came across and ask him if he knew Frik and Morné, and ask him to say something about them; troops usually come up with good stories, and I hoped to use some of the contributions for a little informal speech with personal and human touches.

On my way to work one morning I arrived at the main gate of Defence Headquarters. For some reason I was dressed in civilian clothes that day, and when the sentry stopped me, in accordance with normal routine, I suddenly remembered the impending visit and my random research effort. So I asked the sentry: 'Do you know who Frik du Preez is, and can you tell me something about him – ?'

'Mister,' he interrupted me, 'before you go any further, you tell me first, who the hell do you think you are?'

I couldn't resist it. So I told him: 'Doug Watson … '

By this time I had learnt many similar lessons in humility.

Anton Rupert, one of the greatest South Africans of our times, said that one should be able to look into the mirror and laugh at oneself; modesty and a sense of humour are useful leadership qualities. But I cannot stand the false humility that some people seem so proud of. One does not brag about being modest. And to be truly humble, you must have self-confidence.

However, we were all small fry. In 1981 a big fish, Ronald Reagan, took over from Jimmy Carter as President of the United States. During the decade of the 1980s he was to play a major role in the new directions that Southern Africa would follow.

* * *

Against this background of soon-to-be-unveiled American diplomatic initiatives, I continue with the story of the operational events in South West and Angola under my successors as GOC SWA Command – first Major-General Charles Lloyd (until the end of 1983) and then Major-General Georg Meiring (until the beginning of 1987). Both were good generals … and Free Staters!

I shall describe their most important cross-border operations first, and then my personal experiences and perceptions. The first series took place under the overall command of Charles Lloyd: Operations Carnation and Protea in July and August 1981, following Operation Sceptic in 1980, resulted in a second confrontation with FAPLA. As a result of the setbacks it experienced during Sceptic, PLAN had moved its bases further north, close to and sometimes among those of FAPLA, to discourage attacks by the South African forces. In addition, PLAN's logistic systems also became completely interwoven with FAPLA's. At this stage FAPLA and SWAPO were co-operating, and FAPLA's air defence system made it dangerous for our Air Force to support our ground troops.

By mid-1981 the security situation in the northern border area of South West had taken a serious turn. The sustained delivery of Soviet arms, continued Cuban support, the stockpiling of vast quantities of weaponry and a build-up of FAPLA and PLAN strengths in southern Angola posed a real threat. In July 1981 a number of contacts with PLAN took place; on 6 July General Lloyd announced that 52 insurgents had been killed during clashes with the security forces over a period of only four days.

This sharp increase in the frequency of skirmishes gave rise to Operation Carnation. Although 225 SWAPO members were killed, Carnation was only partially successful because the operation did not extend further than 25 km north of the border, while the bigger PLAN bases were situated deeper into Angola. But it did create a favourable situation for its successor, Operation Protea.

This time General Lloyd attacked with three task forces and destroyed several PLAN bases and command posts in the area of Xangongo and Ongiva. D-day, 23 August 1981, started with an air attack on a FAPLA radar station and key-points of the Angolan air defence system. On 24 August the ground forces began their advance on Xangongo along three different approaches (see map 2).

It was clear from later information we received that our operation was interpreted as a desire to invade Angola itself; that we had long-range objectives in mind; and that PLAN was merely a secondary consideration. Long afterwards Cuban and FAPLA officers confirmed this to me.

A mechanised force attacked the bases near the town, which also accommodated the regional headquarters of PLAN's 'North-Western Front'. Simultaneously other elements destroyed PLAN bases to the south and south-east of the town. The combined PLAN–FAPLA protection force, which was well settled in and around the town, was driven off after a brief attack on their tanks and infantry. The main force then moved south and east, pushing the FAPLA force at Mongua out of its way.

The attack on Ongiva took place on 26 August 1981. The town was taken on 28 August, after another combined PLAN-FAPLA defensive element had been defeated; as I mentioned earlier, two Soviet officers were killed during this battle and a warrant-officer taken prisoner. PLAN facilities in and around Ongiva were destroyed, and the operation ended on 10 September.

During Operation Protea, the largest mechanised operation by the South African Army since World War II, our security forces lost 10 men, while PLAN and FAPLA suffered more than 1 000 casualties. Included in approximately 4 000 tons of seized equipment were several tanks and armoured cars, a large number of anti-tank guns and about 200 logistics vehicles.

Charles Lloyd's next big operation was Daisy, which started on 1 November and ended on 20 November; just as Operation Protea resulted from the information collected during the preceding operations, so Protea in its turn provided the information that gave rise to Daisy.

A mechanised force penetrated to the deepest point reached since the Angolan civil war, attacking objectives at Bambi and Chetequera. Although no clashes took place with FAPLA's ground forces a number of MIG-21 fighter aircraft had encounters with the South African Air Force and one of them was shot down.

At the beginning of 1982 it became clear that PLAN was preparing to open a new front in Kaokoland, and Operation Super was launched as a counter-measure. Reconnaissance elements of 32 Battalion were sent in to locate PLAN members who were ready to infiltrate the area, and found about 250 of them at an assembly area near the town of Iona, in the south-west of Angola, whence the infiltration was scheduled to begin.

A 75-man force from 32 Battalion under Capt Jan Hougaard was flown to Iona to launch a blitz attack on the PLAN concentration, about 30 being deployed in stopper groups and the remaining 45 forming the main assault force. In spite of their overwhelming numerical superiority, the enemy troops were completely surprised and overpowered.

By the end of the action they had lost 201 dead and Hougaardt's men seized a large quantity of ammunition and weapons. Our total casualties consisted of just two men who had been lightly wounded.

From a professional point of view this operation delivered proof of the excellent combat capabilities of the lower-level commanders and troops.

The next operation, Meebos, was executed during July and August 1982, and consisted of a number of air and ground attacks on PLAN's command and control structures. Of the enemy forces 345 were killed and PLAN's so-called 'Eastern Front' headquarters at Mupa was destroyed before it could be moved. Security forces losses were 29 men, 15 of whom died when a Puma helicopter was shot down.

Charles Lloyd's last operation, Phoenix, in February 1983, was actually an internal action to counter a PLAN cross-border operation into South West. During the first half of February PLAN set off a new wave of infiltrations. On 13 February a 'special unit' of about 1 700 PLAN members, divided into different companies, began its infiltration into Ovamboland. The first important contact took place on 15 February, with 15 PLAN fighters being killed; by the time Phoenix ended on 13 April PLAN had lost 309 men to the security forces' 27, as reported in *Militaria*.

In my opinion Phoenix was an excellent performance in military science terms and the circumstances prevailing in this type of warfare. A defensive counter-insurgency operation of this kind is usually much more difficult than an offensive one. In this case we were concerned with a pre-planned infiltration, taking place over a vast area which was as flat as a table-top and covered in thick bush. The enemy were trained infiltrators, experienced in guerrilla tactics and techniques, and they knew the terrain. To have stopped and contained them, then sent them off with heavy losses, was an exceptional achievement which required professional knowledge, ingenuity, guts and will-power.

At this time my son Martin was doing his national service. He was at the Infantry School at Oudtshoorn during 1983, then joined the Permanent Force and served in 32 Battalion in South West during 1984.

* * *

I come now to my personal experiences and impressions.

During Operation Protea in August 1981 I joined the fighting forces on D-day minus one. There I witnessed the first operational firing of the new 127 mm multiple rocket launchers, or MRLs, from their launching positions; I had a personal interest in this new artillery acquisition of ours because I had also observed the weapon's experimental firing during the project stage a few years earlier. Armscor had researched and developed this system, then made it available to the South African Army in double-quick time to counteract the 122 mm Soviet BM-21 'Stalin Organ' we had encountered for the first time during Operation Savannah. Now we had a weapon system that was better than its Soviet counterpart.

I spent the night at the tactical headquarters. Next morning I arrived at Xangongo after the mopping-up phase of the battle was almost complete; smoke was still curling skywards. The knocked-out Russian T34/85 tanks made me think of the bronze enemy guns that the British had seized during the Crimean War and then melted down and used to mint the famed Victoria Cross.

I immediately radioed Brigadier Witkop Badenhorst, commander of Sector 10, and told him to have one of the tanks recovered to Oshakati; I would tell him why later, I said. He was an outstanding example of the military tradition in the South African Defence Force in terms of which a man says: 'If my captain says make smoke, I make smoke', so his reaction to my cryptic instruction on that winter's day in 1981 made possible the minting of a new South African medal 10 years later. Copper from the shot-out tank formed a small part of the content of the new Southern Africa Medal, which recognised those members of the South African Defence Force and auxiliary services who participated in operations outside the borders of the RSA from 1 April 1976 onwards, in peril of being killed, wounded or taken prisoner.

After that I made a quick visit by helicopter to a place named Peu-Peu to find out at first hand from the commander of the responsible battle group – my old friend from the Sceptic days, Commandant Chris Serfontein – what had happened during the fighting there.

During the helicopter flight to Peu-Peu I saw a soccer stadium in Xangongo which reminded me of a stratagem once used by the OC 32 Battalion, Commandant Deon Ferreira, in the period preceding

Protea. He had been involved in protracted area operations against PLAN in the region immediately north of the border, near Ongiva, and in some strange way had established a sort of long-distance understanding with the FAPLA commander in the town, to the point of actually writing him a letter or two. This personal interaction had prevented unintentional clashes between their forces.

At the time I told Deon once or twice to arrange a soccer game against FAPLA, since we were not really out to pick a fight with them. If General Maritz and Major Edwards could negotiate a ceasefire in 1902 at O'Kiep during the Anglo-Boer war to play a game of rugby, why couldn't Deon Ferreira play a game of soccer against FAPLA at Ongiva? He thought I was joking, and I left it at that.

I knew that when Xangongo was first occupied the commander of the occupying force, Commandant Roland de Vries, had struggled to make proper contact with the local population on an organised basis. Pamphlets had been dropped just before the fighting in the town, requesting the locals to evacuate the area so as to escape injury. They had done so, but now they were hesitant about returning because they did not realise that the fighting was over. So on the way back from Peu-Peu I told Roland de Vries to arrange a soccer game between the South African troops and the locals at the stadium, which I felt would contribute towards normalising the situation and eliminating unnecessary suspicion.

We spent the night in a house which had been used by the Soviets as an office block. It was decorated with posters of the Soviet political structure and photographs of USSR leaders, and its previous occupants had also left behind some vodka and other Russian drinks. Roland de Vries had to leave early the next morning for the next phase of the operation, and my personal staff officer, Colonel Peter Gagiano, and I were also to leave to join Commandant Eddie Viljoen's battle group on its way to Mongua and Mupa. So the job of improving relations with the locals and organising the soccer game was left with Roland's successor, Major Dawid Mentz.

Next morning the town's inhabitants began to return and he set about organising the game. Little did I know where all this would lead. As I later discovered, Xangongo's soccer team just happened to be the champions of Angola's Kunene Province, and its players accepted

Major Mentz's challenge with enthusiasm. As a result, what our men thought was going to be an informal social game turned out to be a proper match with the Xangongo in full club colours; as far as I can remember, Xangongo beat 'Own Forces' 1–0.

For the time being, this was another of those typical make-war-but-don't-say-a-thing operations I described earlier. But at a certain stage – by which time I was already far away – a media contingent was invited to visit the operational scene, and the itinerary included a sightseeing tour of Xangongo and environs. On their way back to the aircraft to depart for their next port of call the journalists happened to pass by the stadium where the game was in full swing. One or two of them caught a glimpse of the activity and requested to be taken there to have a look. That was not a problem. Afterwards, when the news of the operation broke for the first time in the public media, a photograph of this soccer game was given a place of prominence in a number of newspapers.

Now, as happens all over the world during times of war, it is always the other side which shoots first, fights an unjust war, bombards hospitals and schools and mistreats the local civilian population. Protea was no exception, especially during the Security Council meeting of 29 August 1981. The South African Ambassador to the UN, Mr Riaan Eksteen, had to refute accusations of brutality, and on 10 September the Minister of Foreign Affairs and Information, Mr Pik Botha, reacted in a circular of which part read as follows:

> Mention was ... made [by the South African Ambassador] of the fact that during the recent actions against SWAPO terrorists South Africa gave assistance to the local population of Angola in various fields. In this respect the reports of four journalists who had been taken to the operational theatre by the SA Defence Force made a major contribution to confirm the facts given in Ambassador Eksteen's address.
>
> Two of the biggest television networks, for example, during their new programmes later in the evening, screened films of the soccer game between a Defence side and members of the local Angolan population. Precisely this fact was mentioned that afternoon by Ambassador Eksteen in his address.

In the meantime I had arrived at the tactical headquarters at Mupa. Around 27 August Deon Ferreira, Eddie Viljoen, Commandant Vos Benade, Major Smiley van Zyl, the leader of the mobile air operations team, and I were listening to radio conversations, *inter alia* between Lieutenant Thinus van Staden of 32 Battalion and a Telstar (a Bosbok light aircraft which was used as a radio relay station), piloted by Major Vink Hattingh's younger brother.

At this stage Chris Serfontein and his battle group had already attacked Ongiva, while Commandant James Hills was north of the town with three 32 Battalion companies – one of them commanded by Lieutenant Van Staden – which were deployed as stopper groups.

Some of the radio messages had us all guessing. Vehicles and people were moving in Thinus's direction, but at this stage there was confusion over precisely who and what they were. There were reports that they were intelligence personnel who were towing seized vehicles out of Ongiva, and others that they were civilians who had reacted to a warning that they should evacuate the town to avoid becoming involved in the fighting. We tried to make sense of all this contradictory information, but without success.

The 23-year-old Lieutenant Van Staden deserved full marks for calm courage and battle discipline in several extraordinary person-to-person contacts with FAPLA elements in which one or both parties did not know who the other was. This included unorthodox close-range skirmishes which featured hardware such as Soviet BM21 missile launchers, PT76 tanks and BRDM armoured vehicles.

At one stage Thinus and his men heard the noise of approaching vehicles. He reported the information to Telstar and received the reply that they were captured vehicles being brought out of Ongiva by our intelligence personnel. This gave him some peace of mind as two Land Rovers, one white and one blue, came up at the head of some heavy logistics vehicles. Then he noticed that the soldiers in the Land Rovers and other vehicles were all wearing camouflage dress (at that time the standard South African battledress was made of brown 'nutria' material, and only 32 Battalion wore camouflage). He passed this on to the Bosbok but was told not to worry. Later he related: 'Hills told me: "Just show them where to park." As he had to have a better picture of the situation than me, I walked into the middle of the road and pointed to the left. The Land Rovers stopped, the passengers got out and began directing the rest of the vehicles to pull off and stop under the trees.'

At this stage his sergeant discreetly eased up to him and hissed: 'They're FAPLAS!' Thinus realised that the Angolans had mistaken his camouflage-wearing black troops for their own forces, and his sergeant and himself for Cubans. He kept cool, however, and as nonchalantly as possible walked over to the radio to tell the Bosbok: 'Hey, we've got a problem here ...' He was told to withdraw, and what happened then was to make the headlines all over the world. In 1992 Thinus described the event in a manuscript:

> I took one platoon, and when we found the tracks I knew they were too narrow for a tank. We were running along the tracks when we came on a Russian-made Jeep. It was very clean, and I reckoned it was a FAPLA commander's vehicle. I left one section to guard it and continued on the tracks with two sections. We kept finding more and more abandoned vehicles, and I kept leaving troops. We were down to one section when we ran into an ambush from our right. We attacked immediately. We shot three people there. Four others ran north. We shot three more, and the fourth escaped.
>
> The second body I checked was wearing brand-new FAPLA camo, and had a new AK47. When I turned him over I was stunned to see that it was a white man, and I instinctively knew that he was a Russian. I left six more troops there and, with Lt Leon Naudé and two troops, carried on running down the tracks in the dark. Then we saw the two tanks – they were actually PT76's – and I climbed on one with a grenade and listened for anyone inside, but it was deserted. I radioed back to where I'd left the two platoons and told them to come up and guard the tanks.
>
> Lt Naudé, the two troops and I headed back to the RV [rendezvous] to bring a section up. On the way we passed a kraal and detoured slightly out of the way of some bushes next to it. I was leading, followed by Naudé and the two troops. We were about two or three metres from the bushes when we drew fire. We immediately returned fire, advanced and found two

bodies. One of them was white, and he turned out to be the Russian colonel in charge of Ongiva.

I was kneeling, examining the body, when Lt Naudé shouted at someone not to move. I jumped up and looked over the kraal fence to see three bodies in FAPLA uniforms, one still moving. I jumped over the fence and took the weapon away from him, then saw to my horror that the other two were women, both of them dead. The man, a warrant officer mechanic, was uninjured ...

The man was Sergeant-Major Nikolai Pestretsov, who was then taken prisoner. Brigadier Ben Roos looked after him for four or five months, and he was later exchanged for Sapper Johan van der Mescht, a South African PoW held by the Angolans.

Up to this time, most political commentators had doubted our allegations that there were Russian military personnel in remote parts of Angola together with FAPLA and PLAN.

Before Daisy started I had decided to accompany the force from the beginning and, if at all possible, to the end of the operation. Early in November I joined the battle group when it set off on its northward movement. There I was surprised to bump into the freelance journalist Al J Venter. This supported my contention that, if a journalist had the time, the Defence Force was open to the possibility of letting him tag along, even during operations, including cross-border operations.

This was one of the less successful operations. Seen from a professional point of view it was very well executed in terms of doctrine, drills and procedures, and some enemy war material was seized, but few results were obtained because the PLAN members had mostly evacuated their bases before we were able to reach them.

However, although it was a disappointing success – or successful disappointment – Daisy also gave rise to its share of drama and humour.

The battle group moved in 'legs' which extended from one halt to the next; I travelled in Commandant Roland de Vries's command Ratel on the long road to the north, and it was a wearisome journey. The bush was dense and the sand was loose, so that the dust hung thick in the air. Each Ratel carried three key persons: the driver, the gunner and the vehicle commander, each with his own specific duties to perform. The vehicle commander, for example, directed the driver over the intercom, and a typical set of instructions would be approximately as follows: 'No, go left, man! Pass to the left of that tree! No, now right! Watch out for that bloody donga!' And sometimes the language might even have been stronger.

Sometimes the crew members swopped places to break the monotony, so that the driver would become the gunner, the gunner the vehicle commander and so on. This had the potential for unforeseen results. At one of the halts Major Chad Naudé, who was travelling in the Ratel right behind ours with the chaplain for company, came over to say that he had just had an extremely difficult leg. The chaplain had been travelling in his vehicle.

Chad explained when they had changed round before this past leg he had become the vehicle commander and the chaplain took over the driving, after which he asked with a weary smile: 'General, do you know how difficult it is to explain to a chaplain exactly how he should really drive?' I still owe him an answer.

By the time we arrived at the area of the objective I had quietly and confidentially advised Roland several times that in my judgement the Ratels were packed too closely together and should spread out more, especially during stops. There was always a tendency to bunch up and park in straight lines, which made a large number of vehicles a good target, especially from the air.

My main worry was not that we were deviating from textbook doctrine; the real danger was that we were beginning to move out from under our radar coverage. In other words, we could not really expect our own air force to operate against enemy aircraft in that area. At the same time we were moving in under the Angolan radar cover, which made us more vulnerable to the MIGs.

Proof that my caution had not been unfounded was furnished the day after I left the battle group to return to South West, when Major Johan Rankin in his Mirage F1CZ shot down a MIG-21 in that same area, an event which drew the attention of the international media (11 months later Johan again aroused the envy of his fellow fighter pilots by shooting down another MIG in the same general area. On this occasion he was flying escort when his F1CZ was attacked by MIGs).

In the meantime our forces had eventually reached their objective and engaged the enemy, but there was no real fighting and the troops set about the always tiresome task of mopping up the area to collect all the enemy equipment. While this was in progress Al Venter, Major Andy Anderson of Ngana Pest control fame and I were standing together and talking about 20 metres away from a Buffel stacked with enemy ammunition. To my mind some of the ammunition looked the worse for wear, and, in the way that errant thoughts sometime go through one's mind, I asked myself what I would do if this unstable pile suddenly started to explode after all the bumps, heat and friction it had encountered?

One would surely have to get the vehicle away from its position, as there were so many of our own people moving around in its vicinity, including ourselves, and I was just thinking *yes, Geldenhuys, what an embarrassment it would be if you had to drive the vehicle away but couldn't remember how to start it up* when a loud bang shook the air, followed immediately by several more. I was still concerned about whether we were sufficiently spread out against air attack, and my first thought was: *There you have it, probably something coming from a* MIG.

Then, when I did not hear aircraft or see bombs or rockets falling around us, I realised that it had to be something else. And indeed, it was. Rockets and other ammunition lying on that Buffel had spontaneously started to explode one after the other. I had visualised myself taking action in such a situation, but Andy – a man who could think on his feet and did not scare easily – had made the first move. He was already running to the vehicle, which he started up and drove off at great speed to a safe distance while red flames and white and black smoke from the exploding ammunition belched out of the back. For risking his own life to save those of others he was later decorated with the Honoris Crux.

The next trans-border operation, Askari, took place in 1983, just after Georg Meiring had taken over from Charles Lloyd. Towards the end of 1983 it became clear that PLAN was preparing for a large-scale infiltration early in 1984. The new GOC launched Operation Askari on 6 December 1983 with a number of ground and air attacks aimed primarily at disrupting PLAN's logistical infrastructure. Four mechanised battle groups of 500 men each attacked specific targets, while small infantry groups simultaneously executed area operations in the border region.

Inevitably FAPLA forces also became involved in the fighting, although the concentration was on the insurgents. The biggest clash with FAPLA took place on 3 January 1984, when PLAN's headquarters and base five kilometres from the town of Cuvelai came under attack. FAPLA's 11th Brigade and two Cuban battalions came to PLAN's assistance but were beaten off with a loss of 324 men; most of the security force's total of 24 dead for the operation died during this encounter.

The officer commanding 32 Battalion at this stage was Commandant Eddie Viljoen, whose call-sign, which was neither very original nor good for radio security, was Echo Victor, or EV. His people called him 'Big Daddy'. I was not involved in Operation Askari, but Eddie came away with many stories to tell, and I would like to re-tell one of them because it is among his best.

When we attacked Cuvelai on 3 January, hundreds of FAPLA soldiers scattered in groups and headed for the safe haven of Techamutete, which they knew was occupied by one of their battalions. One rainy evening around 20h00 a FAPLA lieutenant and his sergeant in search of shelter – when it rains in Angola it really comes down – arrived at the headquarters there and presented themselves to the sentries, who took them to the commander.

He was a sturdy man of medium height, with a stern expression which was made even sterner by a formidable moustache. Around him were the usual headquarters types, including a tall chap with a drooping Mexican-style moustache. The new arrivals were each given a mug of hot coffee and sat down happily, feeling relaxed and safe now that they were back with their comrades.

The comrades were not very chatty, however, and stared silently at them as they sat smoking and drinking their coffee. Eventually the FAPLA sergeant became somewhat fidgety and began whispering to his lieutenant. The lieutenant cleared his throat and asked the comrades which FAPLA unit they belonged to. The comrades replied that they were, in fact, *not* with FAPLA.

The lieutenant cleared his throat again and asked if the comrades were Cubans, then. No, the comrades replied, they were not Cubans either. Now the newcomers sat bolt upright, still clasping their half-empty mugs of coffee, and conferred quickly in whispers. Then the lieutenant – clearly worried by now – asked in a high-pitched voice whether their hosts were perhaps Russian. No, the hosts said, and went back to staring at them, with only the downpour outside intruding on the silence.

By now the newcomers were not only puzzled but deeply afraid, and the lieutenant half-asked, half-pleaded: 'Well, if you're not FAPLA and if you're not Cubans or Russians, are you Germans, then?'

There was no immediate reply, just another tense silence which stretched on as they sat, wide-eyed with fear, and waited for a response. Then the lanky man with the Mexican-style moustache could not contain himself any longer and loudly told them the awful truth: their involuntary hosts were South Africans. The fact was that the commander they had met was Eddie Viljoen himself, and Mexican-style person was Sergeant-Major Koos Kruger, known to his friends and known to his acquaintances as Koos Krokodil (Koos Crocodile) because he had once been attacked by a crocodile which, most unsportingly, had removed parts of his upper leg.

Let 'Big Daddy' explain in his own words how the FAPLA men had committed this grave social blunder:

> 32 Battalion was assigned to occupy the area north of Cuvelai from an easterly direction. We had to launch area operations against the PLAN bases. The aim was to prevent large-scale infiltrations from this area to the south.
>
> We had instructions to avoid contact with the FAPLA battalion at Techamutete, but in the early hours of 23 December, we sent troops to set up an ambush on the road between Cuvelai and Techamutete. When the ambush troops moved in they heard talking and the clanging of equipment. A skirmish followed, and we heard a noise that sounded like elephants breaking through bush.
>
> Then the mystery cleared up; we hadn't had a brush with elephants or a stray group of FAPLA soldiers. We had, in fact, run into an entire FAPLA battalion which was occupying their main defensive position in that area. The whole FAPLA battalion, including its troops in Techamutete, had taken flight and left all their equipment behind. By 09h00 we had three of our 32 Battalion (rifle) companies, an 81 mm mortar section

and all the seized FAPLA weaponry deployed in and around Techamutete.

This is how it came [about] that literally hundreds of FAPLAS who fled to Techamutete were welcomed by the black Portuguese-speaking 32 Battalion troops, dressed in their traditional camouflage. The FAPLAS only realised later, to their surprise, that the men of 32 who now occupied Techamutete were not fellow FAPLA or PLAN members.

Now to return to our headquarters at Techamutete and our two guests: The sound of two tin coffee mugs falling and the two men getting to their feet was all that disturbed the silence. The two half-heartedly looked at their weapons leaning against the wall, but I could see that they were not very keen to make a grab for them at that moment.

The lieutenant then removed the binoculars hanging around his neck and meekly handed them over to me. The scene resembled a ceremony concluding a peace treaty.

Everyone joined in the laughter, which reached a crescendo when the two were escorted to the 'cells'.

It would appear that the FAPLA discipline was not of a high standard, because the FAPLA sergeant accused his lieutenant in the strongest words that his powers of judgment left much to be desired!

Once they had been properly disarmed and debriefed, Eddie saw to their immediate needs and told them they could go ... This time *friction de guerre* was definitely not on FAPLA's side. One might even say the joke was on them.

* * *

Operation Askari was the last operation of its kind when it ended on 3 January 1984; although not intended as anything more than what it was, it convinced the MPLA government that South Africa had to be engaged in discussions about a cessation of hostilities in southern Angola, and some analysts regard this as the most important result of the operation.

The talks in which I was involved were held in Lusaka (this was when Pik Botha delivered his 'Boer War' address I mentioned earlier) and culminated in the signing of the Lusaka Agreement during February 1984, one provision of which was that the South African troops still in Angola after the operation would be withdrawn. In return, Angola undertook to ensure that no SWAPO insurgents, Cuban forces or conventional weapons such as tanks and guns would be allowed in the area evacuated by our forces, the so-called 'area in question' or 'area in dispute'. A joint monitoring commission would oversee the execution of the operative terms of the agreement.

The area was then systematically cleared by zones – first the northernmost part of the area, thereafter the zone immediately to the south of it and then the zone still further south, and so on, until the border was reached. Each zone was tackled only after the JMC had satisfied itself that the previous one had been cleared to the agreement's requirements, so the evacuation was not completed *in toto* until April.

In truth the South African troops involved in Askari had been withdrawn after the operation and had already been south of the border for quite a while *before* the agreement was signed. We had made a public announcement to this effect, but it transpired that the other parties concerned refused to believe us. So we actually had to send troops back into Angola so that we could withdraw them in plain sight to show that we were honouring the agreement!

In many respects the execution of the Lusaka Agreement was one big frustration for me. The signing of the Nkomati Accord a short while afterwards, in which I was not involved, and the signing of the Lusaka Agreement were political successes which resulted in South Africa being seen in a more positive light internationally, and helped to make it possible for the State President, Mr P W Botha, to visit Europe and personally put South Africa's case to other national leaders.

But so far as the actual security situation in South West and Angola was concerned, the Lusaka Agreement was like any other agreement – merely a piece of paper. Whatever is agreed to on paper and duly signed must still be made to work in practice. I had a key role to play in making the Lusaka agreement succeed, and for that I needed patience, tolerance and steadfastness. But history has proved that the agreement made little or no difference to the war and peace situation in Angola.

Sometimes we had intelligence of SWAPO activities in the area in dispute, in contravention of the agreement. But SWAPO could not, technically speaking, violate the Lusaka Agreement as it was not a signatory. It was the Angolan government which had undertaken to see to it that SWAPO did not enter into the area in dispute, and we therefore had to address such information to the Angolans for action. In practice it meant that we first had to submit it to the Angolan component at the JMC for them to pass it on. However, they and others always found one or other argument for simply ignoring the irregularities.

Sometimes, for example, they would allege that our information lacked credibility. If we then presented confirmed and irrefutable information about, let us say, SWAPO members in the area moving north, we would hear at the JMC that it was unnecessary to make a fuss as they were moving north; they were trying to get *out* of the area, and surely there could be nothing wrong with that?

Afterwards we would come up with confirmed information that SWAPO was moving south in the forbidden area; then we would hear again that if they were moving south, they must be on their way to Namibia; of course, we wouldn't want to complain about that, would we!

Then again, if we obtained information that, say, 20 SWAPO members were moving east or west, the excuse would be: Look, there are only 20 of them, do you really want to make a big issue over a measly 20 men?

If we gave them information about 100 SWAPO soldiers in the area they would say: Yes, but those men have not yet received the message; or, which was even more irritating, they would find some argument to the effect that we were really to blame for everything, and that they saw whatever transgression it was in a very serious light.

Nevertheless, we continued to grapple with the JMC's problems, in spite of the fact that our patience was taxed to the extreme. Admittedly, they did agree that certain incidents constituted definite violations of the agreement. These were then registered, but that did not mean that anything would be done about them.

Our reports of irregularities were not intended to embarrass anybody; we did not do it to wreck the agreement or cause delays, and we did not try to play the good-guy/bad-guy game. We merely followed conventional practices and used the mechanisms and procedures established in terms of the Lusaka Agreement, with the purpose of making the agreement work. According to the agreement the area in dispute had to be demilitarised as prescribed. If successfully done, it would have created a vast war-free zone.

During July 1984 we had confirmed intelligence of the presence of troops and specific military hardware such as anti-aircraft guns, anti-aircraft missile systems, radar systems and T55 tanks at Techamutete in contravention of the Lusaka Agreement. We reported it to the JMC in the prescribed manner, and requested that it be officially and formally registered as a violation of the agreement; also that it should be investigated so that corrective action could be taken (special provision had been made in the agreement for joint investigation by SADF-FAPLA patrols in such eventualities).

Once again our information was not accepted, and we could not persuade the committee to investigate the matter. As a last resort we flew a photo-reconnaissance mission over the area on 12 August, went back to the JMC and substantiated our allegations with the photograph. It could not be, and was not, disputed. Then the propagandists turned the issue on its head: the photo-reconnaissance flight was a transgression of the agreement! This caused me no end of frustration. Our information about the weapon systems had been rejected; we had provided evidence of their presence and proved our claims, and now we were in trouble about the way in which we had done it. As a result our complaint was shoved on to the back burner.

The other parties made such a fuss over the flight that it became virtually the main point on the agenda of a meeting between Minister Pik Botha and Minister Rodrigues of Angola. Pik Botha stated South Africa's case as follows:

> The South African action was necessary to investigate reports obtained from SWAPO prisoners of substantial SWAPO activities in the area in question as well as information that the MPLA was in the process of building up its forces in contravention of the spirit of the Lusaka Agreement and the assurances which the United States gave South Africa in January 1984, that Angola would not take advantage of the disengagement process to the detriment of the security of South West Africa.

Because of the importance of these allegations for mutual confidence and the continuation of the Lusaka Agreement, it was considered imperative to investigate these reports.

The South African Government has been shocked to learn that Angola has indeed deployed modern armaments in the area which cannot possibly be used against UNITA and which must therefore be construed as encouragement of and protection for SWAPO's designs to increase its violence against South West Africa and to return to Angola with impunity. South Africa has also learned to its dismay that a major southward movement of SWAPO terrorists through the area in question is at present under way.

The Angolan accusations kicked up so much dust and created such sinister perceptions that the facts disappeared into the clouds of propaganda. But the truth was that they were the culprits: by the end of August the Angolans had been responsible for as many as 63 violations of the agreement, all jointly and formally registered by the two parties of the JMC, as opposed to only three registered breaches by South Africa – one of which was the controversial photo-recce flight.

I personally pleaded that we should form the JMC into a permanent institution and that the area in question should become a peace zone, but the Angolans would not accept it.

Our frustrations will perhaps be better understood if I draw comparisons with more recent events. While we were being branded as the bad guys during 1984, we appealed: but what about the 63-3 points on the scoreboard?! Nothing. In the South Africa of the early 1990s we had a similar scoreboard of breaches of the National Peace Accord; now one could ask again, what about that? Perhaps the Peace Secretariat should have publicised its successes more often.

* * *

During one of the sessions of the JMC I unexpectedly ran into my son Martin, who was involved in the joint South African-Angolan patrolling and participated in other operations as well.

One of the most fearless soldiers South Africa ever produced, Colonel Jan Breytenbach, relates an incident during such an operation:

> At one time a company conducting operations up the Cubango River took Klepper kayaks with them to assist in the evacuation of the wounded or sick. The theory, at least, was that the wounded or sick would be canoed downstream, with a paddler plus a doctor per craft.
>
> The problem was that movement on the tracks and landing sites up and down the river had become dicey because the whole area had been indiscriminately booby-trapped by both UNITA and FAPLA.
>
> The theory was fine, but as the saying goes, the proof of the pudding is always in the eating.
>
> The company was operating upstream at maximum range, when both Lieutenant Martin Geldenhuys ... and a black sergeant became very ill, requiring evacuation. As planned for in such an eventuality a Klepper was assembled and prepared to take the patients downstream that night.
>
> At the last moment a slightly more than just eccentric Lebanese sergeant, an inveterate collector of snakes, handed them a rucksack containing a selection of live ones to take back to Cachueca.
>
> They pulled away from the bank and began paddling, the going, at first, being good. What they didn't realize, though, was that there were violent rapids downstream. Now, shooting rapids in kayaks by daylight can be terrifying enough, but to unexpectedly run into them in pitch darkness is petrifying, and an unfailing recipe for disaster.
>
> When they did hit the rapids, all they could do was to hope that they would not be smashed against the rocks, against which they were cannoning like snooker balls. The inevitable happened, the Klepper overturned and was smashed by the raging waters. The occupants, two of them very sick men, found themselves struggling for their lives to get ashore, their rifles, food, medicine and the radio having sunk to the bottom, while the remains of the canoe had disappeared downstream

along with the snakes – much to the later disgust of their Lebanese owner.

After much buffeting by the turbulent waters, they finally dragged themselves ashore in the calmer shallows below the rapids. All they were left with was the clothes they stood up in and their World War II-style haversacks.

With the radio gone they could not ask for assistance, so they had no option but to painfully bundu-bash their way towards Cachueca, avoiding the river bank because of mines.

Eventually their boots gave in, forcing them to bind their feet with tree bark as a protection against thorns, sharp twigs and branches. After many days of nightmare marching they finally staggered, starving and on their last legs, into Cachueca, clothes falling off their backs and their feet cut to ribbons.

*　*　*

To conclude the JMC saga: after the withdrawal of the South African forces from Angola during April 1985, PLAN exploited the situation and started anew to operate across the border from their bases in Angola. So this time the joke was on us, and the security forces were left with no option but to resume their operations.

During Operation Boswilger, which started on 29 June 1985 and concluded 48 hours later, we followed PLAN members' tracks right to their bases in three different parts of Angola. On the first day 43 were killed and one was captured in 23 separate contacts; on the second day 14 died and four were taken prisoner during 13 skirmishes. Then our force withdrew across the border again.

I conclude my story of this period of the border war with a last flashback to the Lusaka Agreement, and I make no apology for the fact that it involves a joke, because if we had not cracked a joke or two in our journey down the JMC road as we weaved through one frustration after the other we would probably have fallen by the wayside.

Colonel Dippies Dippenaar of Smokeshell fame was the first South African co-chairman of the JMC. He was relieved during April 1984 at Ongiva, the site of the JMC at that stage (it moved from one location to another as zones were cleared) and replaced by Colonel Piet Hall, the former commanding officer of the Bushman battalion in western Caprivi.

There was little signals traffic to Ongiva for a couple of weeks because continuous high-level discussions were taking place which affected the position of the JMC. Finality had not been reached yet, and we were all waiting to hear what would be decided. Only then would we be able to send Piet Hall new instructions.

Meanwhile Piet was feeling very lonely and forgotten, and sent a signal to Army Headquarters asking for guidelines. Army HQ explained the situation to him and told him to wait. Another week or two went by. Piet remained intensely frustrated. I could understand his impatience, since I had had a good taste of it myself.

He complained that PLAN members who had been killed in the area in dispute had been wearing FAPLA uniforms. The Angolans replied that they came from the pre-JMC period. Then, when SWAPO soldiers with brand-new FAPLA uniforms were killed, the Angolans accused us of bad form, because it was 'not in good taste' and 'not in the true spirit of the agreement' to examine such clothing; then they complained that our troops tortured the local population and damaged their property.

Piet complained that when joint RSA-Angolan patrols investigated alleged breaches of the agreement the Angolans ran out of fuel, rations and water before they got to the place to be examined and then could not go any further. He was really down in the dumps, and to keep himself occupied carved Makalani palm twigs with his Southern Cross Fund pocket-knife. The next time he sent his signal directly to me and begged me to tell him what to do.

I replied by signal HLeër (D OPS) 309/1 OP SCLERA DD 1 JUN 84. I told him again that I understood his frustrations, that he must hang in there and that we were still waiting for the results of the negotiations ourselves. He should do as he saw fit; as soon as I knew more I would inform him and send new instructions. Recalling his message from Kavango in 1978, I ended the signal with: 'Don't be too obstinate. Maintain good relations. THERE'S A BONUS IN YOUR FUTURE!'

By way of a postscript: years later, in South Africa around August or September 1992, I was reminded of the tactics the Angolans used at the JMC. In 1992 everyone was praying for peace, preaching against violence, pleading for tolerance and begging for mutual understanding when the African National Congress–SA Communist Party–Congress of South African Trade Unions alliance announced in harsh language that they were going to march on Bisho in the Ciskei to occupy it and insist on the removal of the president.

A variety of sources publicly advised the alliance to desist because it was not in the spirit of the time; it could seriously harm the negotiation process and could create a climate for violence. But on 7 September the alliance went ahead, and, sure enough, violence followed. The Ciskeian security forces fired on the marchers and at least 23 people died, with at least 188 left wounded.

The alliance's immediate reaction was much like that of the Angolans during the JMC's lifetime in 1984–1985: the incident had once again demonstrated that the government of South Africa was not seriously applying itself to creating a favourable climate for negotiations.

CHAPTER 12

INFORMATION AND DISINFORMATION

The 'massacred village' that never was

The cross-border operations up to 1985 were necessary and well executed. I still believed, though, that the accumulated effect of relentless day-to-day operations south of the border was vital for our overall success. These operations continued, and I wanted to know first-hand what was going on.

I wanted to get into the picture at an early stage because Kaokoland was one of the regions we had always wanted to keep free of insurgency and there were definite indications that it was going to be infiltrated. But that could not be done if I remained stuck in my office in Pretoria, so I left for the operational area early in 1982.

Whenever I went on such trips I informed the GOC SWA Command in detail well in advance, and the GOC himself or his representative would then accompany me. I never gave direct instructions to the GOC's subordinate commanders when in the field. On this occasion my personal staff officer could not accompany me and I took along Colonel Johann Sonnekus, a senior operations staff officer at Army Headquarters.

Commandant Chris Bouwer, the commander in Kaokoland, briefed me on the current situation in his area and the region across the border, explaining what the insurgents were up to and what his men were doing about it. He also described what had happened during an enemy ambush shortly before my visit.

I asked further questions. He explained to me that the infiltrators were doing this and that, which the security force planned to counter by doing so and so. Then I asked him: 'Where do they come from?' He told me. My next question was: 'Who is their commander?' That he did not know off-hand, but his intelligence officer, Captain Dave Drew, did: I don't remember the name he gave, but let us say it was 'Jimmy' for the purpose of this discussion.

One might ask what the significance is of knowing the enemy commander as a person. Well, before I continue, I must first sound a warning that I myself should heed: one must always guard against textbook wisdom and clever notions developed theoretically from a distance. Nevertheless, I told him: 'You can't merely study enemy doctrines and techniques, and then adjust your own. Then you make the war a competition between rivals who try to outdo one another at developing better doctrines and techniques. And this is not all that matters. You can't merely say that insurgents do this and that, because they have a commander and a political commissar who consider objectives, targets and actions, and lay down priorities. It was Jimmy who sent infiltrators into that region, Jimmy who possibly even ordered the ambush and who specified approximately where it should be laid. It's not normally the insurgents themselves who decide. The word "insurgents" is a vague collective concept. It's the man, Jimmy, who makes the decisions.'

I asked him to start thinking about what Jimmy would do next.

I am not mentioning this reasoning because Chris needed the coaching. He was a highly competent officer. I am doing so to provide a background for stories I will soon come to.

The next important point which came up during the discussion between Chris and myself was the confirmed enemy presence at a base across the border near Iona. I asked him why he had not, despite all the information available to him, attacked the base, or requested authorisation to do so in the absence of delegated powers, or had it attacked by other own forces if he lacked the force levels. His answer, which had merit, came down to this: the enemy at that base came and went. He and his men had decided to wait for the right moment, when the largest possible number of enemy personnel would be there.

I then gave him a personal opinion, based on a fair amount of experience: it is difficult to determine when that moment will come, and often you only hear of it when it has come and gone. And in addition, your information sometimes dries up for a while, or something unforeseen happens which disturbs the intelligence picture, and then you have to start all over again. If you're sure of your intelligence now, do it now.

Some days after my visit the operation was launched under the command of that experienced bush-fighter, Captain Jan Hougaard of 32 Battalion. Code-named Operation Super, it was a resounding success.

By chance I heard afterwards about what had happened during the time between our visit and the day of the operation. Back in Pretoria, as befits a good staff officer, Johann Sonnekus followed up and enquired from HQ SWA Command what was being done about the enemy base at Iona.

I do not mind if lower level commanders do not accept my advice; their immediate commanders might not like it either, and in any case, one should not try to fight a commandant's war from Pretoria. But when your advice is not accepted, at least you want the assurance that it had been well considered and that there were more or less good reasons why they had decided otherwise. Sonnie's enquiry and the exchange of signals that followed apparently contributed towards finally deciding to launch the operation.

This story illustrates that the degree of influence a commander exerts depends much on the efficiency of his staff officers. As a result of this and other operational incidents I later appointed Johann Sonnekus as my personal staff officer.

A year or so later I found myself in Kaokoland again. The commander there now was my old friend of Ngana Pest Control and Operation Daisy fame, Commandant Andy Anderson, and the pattern of my previous visit virtually repeated itself.

Again I emphasised that an operational commander should make it his personal intellectual aim to outwit his opposing commander: I called it the 'personalisation of operations'. And just as Operation Super had been launched a year earlier, after my visit to Chris Bouwer, Andy conducted a successful operation against an enemy base soon after my departure. As a result, insurgents managed only occasionally to infiltrate Kaokoland, and then just for brief periods.

My visits to Kaokoland were followed by similar visits to Kavango on a few occasions during 1984 and 1985. Colonel Deon Ferreira was now the commander of Sector 20 (Kavango and Bushmanland). At one time there were three groups of insurgents in the Kavango. They had to be removed, because their presence was not in line with our strategy of confining the insurgency to Ovamboland only. But it took time. I went there a few times so that the GOC, Deon and I could put our heads together, and we decided to apply the 'personalisation of operations' concept.

This concept brings me back to the ideas that I had discussed with Chris Bouwer and Andy in Kaokoland: if the name of the commander of the infiltrators operating against them was Jimmy, I expected them to outwit Jimmy. I familiarised many commanders with this line of approach, which simply meant that if at all possible you, the commander, should know the identity of your opposing commander or commanders. Then you must personalise the conflict by asking yourself: Is he going to outwit me, or am I going to outwit him?

In this way one stimulates the commander to think competitively and attain the right frame of mind to beat his opponent by out-thinking him. It becomes a greater challenge when you realise that you have to use your intellectual capabilities to beat your opponent.

Many years later, in 1991, I found that the same old British textbook from which I quoted earlier, *Conduct of War*, supported this concept: 'Battle is a struggle between the wills of opposing commanders. Victory will therefore be dependent upon the personality of the commander, who must be equipped with the right mental and moral qualities to achieve it.'

The discussions on personalisation inspired Deon to adjust his plans for Kavango. He appointed three commanders, to each of whom he allocated a specific enemy commander – known to us by name – and his group as the commander's opponent. Every commander was given the maximum freedom to choose his subordinate commanders and troops, then forge them into an organisation.

The challenge was that each had to out-think his opposing commander. I even promised them a free stay at the Army Foundation's holiday lodges at Umhloti if they were successful within the prescribed time.

That was the end of the insurgents' presence in Kavango; it was clean by 28 May 1985, seven months before the target date of 31 December. The commanders deserved their holiday by the sea at Umhloti! The modest Deon Ferreira always said that the one thing I could lay claim to was my contribution towards cleaning up Kavango.

Another incursion by 26 infiltrators took place on 1 June of 1985, but by 16 June they had all been accounted for, and Kavango was clean again.

*   *   *

In times of conflict one can never get rid of multi-faceted propaganda, and during all these trans-border and internal operations it continued at full blast. One of the propaganda disputes was whether or not there was a PLAN presence in Botswana, as we alleged.

We had released information from time to time of cadres operating in Botswana, and towards the end of 1983 and the beginning of 1984 we specifically stated that their purpose was to open another 'front' against South West Africa from that country. As usual, most political commentators would not accept our word. I speculated that our critics either doubted the accuracy of our intelligence or suspected us of trying to justify a future cross-border operation, in this case into Botswana; or thought we wanted to thwart some political incentive or other through military action. It was, of course, impossible for us to carry out a cross-border operation without political authorisation.

Then, between 22 February and 2 March 1984, three groups crossed the Botswana border, two in the vicinity of the farm Wilskrag and a third at De Hoek. The operation had been organised in Luanda with the aim of launching armed propaganda in Hereroland East and mobilising the population there; some elements were earmarked to infiltrate as far south as Windhoek.

The District Commandant of Police, Col Klopper, and the military sector commander – my boyhood friend, Colonel Large van Rensburg – launched a joint SADF–SAP counter-operation. The Army's component included some unusual elements. In addition to trackers, who naturally played a key role, there were clerks, storemen, chefs and the like who had been trained and organised for combat duties on a contingency basis, specifically for an eventuality such as this one. They were remarkably successful.

Some of the infiltrators were shot dead, two were taken prisoner and the rest were pushed back into Botswana, and the operation confirmed the credibility of our intelligence and our bona fides regarding the PLAN presence in Botswana.

This dispute is yet another example of what I said earlier: that in a conflict situation it is very difficult to distinguish between truth on the one hand and propaganda and various forms of deception on the other. Apart from using information in this way, it is also used as a tactical tool during negotiations to influence the negotiators. Such information could be true, untrue or half true. I have experienced it several times.

The former American Assistant Secretary of State for Africa, Chester Crocker, once told me quite seriously that he had noticed we were building up our forces to attack PLAN in Angola again. He warned me that such an operation at that particular point in time would have seriously detrimental effects. I told him unequivocally that his information was not correct.

He replied that it would serve no purpose to hide the truth, because his people knew what was going on. I reassured him that it was not the case. After all, I was in a position to know that his information was inaccurate. He remained sceptical, and warned that I should realise that they had the capability of knowing these things, and that I should not try to conceal it. From this I inferred that he was hinting that their intelligence services had picked up the so-called build-up on satellite photographs.

I have much respect for Chester Crocker, and also for his negotiating talents, and if he had never played little tricks with information and words he would have been the exception to the rule. To this day I still do not know if he had received the information he mentioned and had believed it to be true; possibly he did believe it and was sincerely worried. In my experience one is never sure in situations of this kind. It might also have been an attempt to provoke me in order to confirm or explode a suspicion. If that was the case, he achieved his purpose, and it did not worry me. Or perhaps it was just his way of discouraging cross-border operations.

Ninety per cent of the troops we used for cross-border operations were soldiers who happened to be serving in the area at that time; for the most part it was only the Air Force which was significantly and noticeably reinforced before such operations. In any case, on the odd occasion when we did step up our air capacity it was not done exclusively with a view to future offensive operations – it could also have been as a deterrent and for defensive purposes.

Crocker's information might have been constructed from inferences the Americans had drawn from bits of information. Quite often we replaced troops and weapon systems with others, and the actual changeover could create the impression of a build-up. I cannot blame them for that. Or perhaps their aerial photographic interpretation was not accurate. One is never sure. Just before Operation Modulêr in 1987, which I will be getting to soon, we received allegedly reliable information that the advancing Cuban-FAPLA forces were not using tanks. But later UNITA and our forces knocked out just under 100 of them.

* * *

Allegations of military atrocities were another example of the manipulation of information for the purpose of good-guy/bad-guy propaganda. When I became the GOC in South West I was bombarded with accusations of this kind. The same thing happened to General Lloyd when he succeeded me. About one or two per cent of these allegations were true; they were investigated, and the odd one resulted in litigation. The problem was that suspicion about the other 98 per cent always remained.

One of the most incredible cases of disinformation became public only in 1989 on publication of the book *In Search of Freedom*, told by Andreas Shipanga to Sue Armstrong. Shipanga was a founder-member of SWAPO; during 1970 he became its Secretary of Information, and in 1972 he began operating from Lusaka. In the chapter entitled 'Information and Disinformation', he relates:

It so happened that about the same time, Dimo Hamaambo, who became the field commander of PLAN after Hainyeko's death, was in town, and he said to me one day: 'You know, on our last incursion into Caprivi we went a bit out of our way and came across a village that had been completely wiped out by the Portuguese. There were skulls and bones and spent cartridges and things all round.'

He showed me some cartridges he had picked up off the ground and an idea struck me. 'Dimo,' I said, 'If I found some journalists, could you take them back to that village saying you were in Namibia?' 'Sure,' he answered.

It was 1972 and I was off on a mission to the Scandinavian countries. In Stockholm I met Per Sanden, a television cameraman, and I said to him: 'Would you like to see a village in Namibia where there's been a massacre?' His eyes widened. 'Is it true?' he asked. 'Of course,' I said, and he jumped at the idea. I told him that when I returned to Zambia, I would seek permission for him to come to Lusaka to talk to us. I told Sam and company of my plan and cabled to Per that he was welcome to come any time.

He and his crew arrived soon afterwards, and we set off for the Caprivi. It was March, and the rains were heavy. Our Russian lorries struggled through the mud towards the front, but at last we made it. Dimo calculated that the massacred village lay about sixteen kilometres inside Angola. As we reached the sensitive zone and prepared to cross the border, I said to the camera team: 'Look, my friends, you're about to go into enemy territory, and for your own security you must take off your wrist watches and give them to the commanders for safekeeping. And hand over all maps too.'

My main worry was that one of them might have a compass or something that would tell them they were not in Caprivi but in Angola. 'Otherwise, you don't need to worry. The guerrillas will protect you,' I said reassuringly. The crew obediently removed their watches and set off with Dimo and the armed soldiers. I had bad stomach trouble and waited behind at the border for them.

In due course Dimo and his charges returned. They had found the village and taken reels and reels of film of skulls, skeletons and gutted houses. We went back to Lusaka, where I produced the old man, whose name was Haingula [Haingula was actually a PLAN member who had been wounded in South West Africa some time before. – JG], saying he was the only survivor of the massacre. Per spoke to him through an interpretcr, and Haingula played his part wonderfully. 'Oh yes, that was my village,' he said as he displayed his wounds.

Next day I called a press conference at which I presented my evidence – the Swedish television film – and got my 'witness', Haingula, to repeat his story. The journalists packed into the conference and the story of the Namibian village 'wiped out by the Boers' spread rapidly across the world.

Of course I expected some response from the South Africans. Pik Botha was minister of information at the time, and he was furious. Later the press came back to me and said: 'Pik Botha says it isn't true.' I replied defiantly: 'Listen, if Pik Botha denies it, ask him and his regime to allow us to take the press to Caprivi under UN protection! I'll be there, and the old man will be there.' It was a gamble. I was afraid that the South Africans might take up my challenge. And what could we show journalists inside Namibia?

In 1987 I discovered how close I had come to being found out. I was in Cape Town; Gen Jannie Geldenhuys and Pik Botha were there too, and I was sitting with them. I had previously told Geldenhuys the story, and he said: 'Mr Shipanga, tell the minister about that massacred village.' As I told Pik the story he got more and more indignant. Then he said: 'You bastard, Shipanga. You know, the whole international press was on to me, and I said I would take them to the Caprivi.'

Apparently when the story first came out Pik immediately questioned the military, who said there was no truth in it. So he flew a pack of journalists to Namibia and loaded them into a Puma helicopter and took them himself to the Caprivi. On the way there, he told me, he suddenly got cold feet:

'I thought to myself, God, these military men can't always be trusted. It just might be true that they have wiped out the village. Then what would I tell these people?' Pik told the helicopter pilot to land somewhere in the bush and say there was technical trouble and they could go no further. 'It scared the hell out of me that we might find such a village, so I aborted the trip!' he said. We all laughed.

Friction de guerre had smiled on SWAPO and Andreas Shipanga had bamboozled everybody. They were good at this type of thing.

One wonders how many such hoaxes later took place in South Africa during the propaganda-filled days of the early 1990s. And, believe it or not, they are *still* popping up, almost 20 years later. In fact, as recently as 2008 the propagandists flourished photographs of bomb-ravaged three-storey buildings of the town of Cuito Cuanavale, taken, so they claimed, after a South African force had been routed by the FAPLA-Cuban-Soviet alliance.

These photographs were most intriguing, for two reasons. Firstly, there was no South African rout at Cuito Cuanavale or anywhere else during the campaign – the only such thing took place along the Lomba River and at Techipa, many weeks earlier, and it was the alliance troops who were routed, not the South Africans. Secondly, there were no multi-storey buildings at the town of Cuito Cuanavale – or any buildings at all, in fact, since there was no such town, just an airfield in the bush.

So what actually happened was that the propagandists took the media, Mr Jacob Zuma, a number of other dignitaries and the whole of Parliament for a ride and made fools of them all, because the true story of what happened at Cuito Cuanavale has been recorded in detail by various objective military historians!

* * *

Something by the Chinese military philosopher Sun Tzu that I had read many years ago helped me to find explanations for many things. Much later, during a conversation with the commander-in-chief of the American forces in Vietnam, General William C Westmoreland, I learned that he had also found answers to his questions in the same writings. He quotes Sun Tzu in his book, *A Soldier Reports:*

Twenty-five centuries ago, Sun Tzu wrote that fighting was the crudest form of warfare. He advised instead:

'Break the will of the enemy to fight, and you accomplish the true objective of war. Cover with ridicule the enemy's tradition. Exploit and aggravate the inherent frictions within the enemy country. Agitate the young against the old. Prevail if possible without armed conflict. The supreme excellence is not to win a hundred victories in a hundred battles. The supreme excellence is to defeat the armies of your enemies without ever having to fight them.'

I identified many actions that our opponents took against us in Sun Tzu's doctrine.

We had a typical Western approach to propaganda and semantic trickery, and it differed quite a lot from that of the communist-orientated countries and those who received their revolutionary education there. To illustrate: at a meeting of the JMC, Angolan Vice-Minister Venâncio de Moura delivered one of the long rhetorical addresses for which he was known, filled with over-worked propagandistic clichés. He talked about the 'Pretoria regime', which had to shoulder the blame for everything, and the thuggish 'UNITA puppets', and so forth.

I pleaded, for the sake of better mutual respect and confidence, that we refrain from using offensive language. His reply was: 'General, we might have agreed at Lusaka to stop shooting, but we have not yet signed an agreement to moderate our language.'

A lesson learned: Just as you have to agree to cease using firearms, you have to reach agreement to cease using offensive words when you deal with people who use propaganda as a weapon.

CHAPTER 13

PROBLEMS AND CHALLENGES

Peace talks and missiles

While Charles Lloyd and Georg Meiring were steering the operational side in South West and Angola, I took up the reins in South Africa to lead the Army. My new term started with a bang, then abruptly went off by fits and starts in different directions, because my field of responsibility was wider and there was more involvement with a greater variety of activities.

I struggled to find my bearings. It was frustrating, because I was keen to tackle the new job, especially since I had a handicap to overcome: I had to get into the picture from scratch. With the exception of two-and-a-half years I had spent 13 years outside the country in Angola and South West; and in that time my predecessors, General Malan and General Viljoen, had brought about many changes in the South African Army. So the bang was like the one from a starter's blank-firing pistol. And it was a false start, because instead of crossing the line and finding my feet and bearings in my new job, I landed up on a side-track en route to Geneva.

I was a member of the South African delegation that went to Geneva at the start of the new year, 1981, to attend a conference, held under the auspices of the UN and attended by the internal parties of South West and SWAPO, the Western Contact Group, the Organisation of African Unity and the BAMTZZ (Botswana, Angola, Mozambique, Tanzania, Zambia, Zimbabwe) states.

The purpose was to compile a timetable for South West to follow in the process to independence. We did not succeed, but for the first time in my life I had the pleasure of having the Organisation of African Unity pay for my cocktails. Just for the fun of it, I did not try to spare the budget.

Back at Army headquarters, and not much further across the starting line, I found myself caught up in an unexpected cross-fire. It seemed that whenever I was not chasing peace I was dispatched to war. When I went to Angola, there was war. When I went to South West Africa there was war as well. And when I was not heading for war, war was heading for me.

On the evening of 12 August 1981 I was driving to Voortrekkerhoogte. I was then president of the Defence Force Rugby Club, and I was on the way to the base's sports grounds to watch Defence play Harlequins. Along the way I passed Admiral Bert Bekker (later to become the Defence Force's number two man), who was travelling in the same direction, from which I correctly deduced that he was on his way home.

After the game I hosted a social for the president of Quins, Jannie Bezuidenhout, their coach, Kitch Christie, and other officials of their club ... We gathered in the clubhouse at exactly the same spot where, 25 years earlier, I had sat sipping a beer and watching Frik du Preez and Ollie Ahlers seemingly damaging their sporting careers by drinking brandy and Coke.

Then I heard an unusual sound through the conversation and the tinkling of ice-cubes. Nobody reacted to it, but I walked away from the socialising and quickly peeped into the gym hall next door, where the dances had been held long ago, to see if any gymnasts were thumping around on their mats in there. But the hall was empty. Then I heard the noise again, and suddenly realised that I had heard it before. I asked somebody to apologise to my guests for absenting myself and then went to the club's office to make a call. After that I headed home to change, because there was work to do.

Back to Bert Bekker. Around 22h00 he heard two explosions,

presumably from a field exercise in progress somewhere on the outskirts of Voortrekkerhoogte, and resolved to talk to the Officer Commanding Northern Transvaal Command next morning about this lack of discretion in carrying out noisy exercises at that time of the night near a residential area.

Then a projectile shot through his garage, just missed his car and hit the room of his housekeeper, Elsie. There it exploded, sending the roof into the air on a column of flames. This was followed by a fourth projectile, which struck the house and destroyed the dressing room next to the main bedroom. Bert was stumbling through the ruins of his dressing room when the fifth and final projectile – like its predecessors, a Russian 122 mm rocket fired from a single-tube launcher – penetrated the roof of the house, ricocheted off the ground in the garden and landed on the terrain of the Army College. The house then burst into flames.

Bert decided not to wait until the next morning and immediately left for the command's operations room to report his discomfort. His two sons, Martin and Shane, took their mother and sister outside and told them to lie down on the lawn, after which they rushed to Elsie's rescue.

In the meantime, having got home and made a few more telephone calls, I drove straight out to Bert's house. If the rockets had struck a little closer one way or a little further the other way we could have been faced with a terrible tragedy. But they had just missed, and it was almost a joke. Like joy and pain, fortune and misfortune had been only millimetres apart; this time *friction de guerre* had been on our side.

It turned out that the rocket attack was the work of Umkhonto we Sizwe (MK), the ANC's armed wing, which over a period of time had a go at the Sasol oil-from-coal complex, the Koeberg nuclear power station and Air Force Headquarters in the Pretoria city centre.

* * *

Thus, when peace and peace talks were not demanding my attention, war and rockets did. But if there was one issue that did not put me off my stride as Chief of the Army it was the rumour that my military career might veer off on a political course.

In South West the Administrator-General, Justice Steyn, had been succeeded by Dr Gerrit Viljoen, who was followed by Mr Danie Hough. Rumours then started to circulate that I was a candidate to take over from him: 'General Geldenhuys, who is an old South Wester, is being tipped to succeed Mr Danie Hough,' as *The Citizen* newspaper had it on 2 November 1982.

I was flattered that I was regarded as a South Wester. Many people thought I was one, probably because I had spent virtually a decade there. But that was as far as it went. General Viljoen had, in fact, once discreetly inquired whether I would accept an invitation to return to South West as Administrator-General. I had said no. I would never have taken a step that would land me in party politics. It simply was not in my nature.

To be a politician you need guts more than a sense of fair play. In any event, the little advice I could remember getting from my father was to stay out of politics. So my answer to General Viljoen was: 'Please, no.' It would mean choosing between soldiering and a political career. I would very much have liked to go to South West, because I loved the country and its people. But I could not consider leaving the Defence Force after 30 years for something like that (incidentally, I still do not know if there really was a possibility of my being invited to be AG).

Amid all this I finally began to find my bearings. Initially there might have been a degree of confusion about my leadership style among the members of the Army's top management, the General Staff. They had become used to General Viljoen's approach and the pace at which he did things during his last two years, when he was probably anxious to get things done in the little time he had left in office.

When I arrived at Army Headquarters I would ask the General Staff what the problem was, after which we would jointly identify it. Then I would ask: Well now, if that is our problem, what are we going to do about it? And then we would sort it out.

They probably said: 'What the heck is wrong with this Geldenhuys? He doesn't know what the problem is, and he hasn't even got solutions.' But as time went by we got to know each other well and, in my opinion, produced good-quality team-work.

I believed that, when embarking on a venture, you should at least found your approach on a practical philosophical base. In search of such bases I always tried to identify the 'basic truths'. It was an approach I had developed after reading somewhere that 'the study of complex problems usually produces simple truths'. The insight gained from these basic truths meant more to me than mere book-knowledge, and it saw me through many difficult situations.

If a meaningful military aspect appeared on the agenda about which the General Staff had no sound elementary philosophy, we developed one. Thus it happened, for example, that we developed a concept of the nature and characteristics of future Southern African operations.

At a later stage we based the Army's Force Development Plan on this concept, which concluded *inter alia* that firepower, tactical and strategic mobility and an optimal night-fighting capability would promote success in current and future conflict. This in turn was later accepted by Armscor as the guidelines for their Technology Development Plan for the Army. So complicated problems truly produced basic truths.

One aspect of the overall strategic approach that I propagated at the General Staff was that the communists' socialist system would collapse. Dr Wim de Villiers had already made this prediction to me on a few occasions. I did not have his knowledge but I believed him because his explanation made sense. I said that the Soviet Union would eventually have to scale down its military involvement in Angola; in the long term it would not be able to maintain its interventions all over the world, far outside its normal sphere of influence.

I propagated this approach quite often. Once, at a conference I was chairing, I noticed that Commodore Dieter Gerhard – later convicted of spying for the Soviet Union – was also present. At this stage I had already been warned that he was suspected of being a spy, which placed me in much the same position as the one I mentioned in an earlier chapter, except that the occasion then had been at a press conference and the alleged spy had been a journalist.

This time I said to myself: *Okay, if it's true, I'll give him something to report on.* So I predicted again that a Vietnam was waiting for the Soviets in Angola. I also expressed these views to correspondents and overseas visitors. Occasionally one of my listeners would react with the observation that it was impossible, because the Soviet Union was so powerful. My reply to that was simply that the United States had been just as powerful when it withdrew from Vietnam.

In the meantime I had requested military intelligence to determine whether the Soviets had begun to show anxiety over the possibility of Angola becoming a problem for them. The intelligence people subsequently reported back in the affirmative. Many years later Professor Willie Breytenbach of Stellenbosch University told me that in 1988 Soviet Africa experts had openly acknowledged at Woodlands Park, London that the signing of the Nkomati Accord in 1984 had been a big embarrassment for the Soviets. This seemed to be in line with Military Intelligence's opinion that the Soviet Union was worried about its seemingly fruitless and prolonged involvement in Africa, and losing its grip.

* * *

Philosophies, however practical, and overall strategic guidelines, however clever, do not win you a war in themselves. Actual problems require real attention, and we had to adjust the Army's organisational structure to make it better equipped to meet current and future demands.

We carried out certain studies on rationalisation, but this was not forced rationalisation whose aim was to cut human resources and money. We had voluntarily undertaken not to increase expenditure and create more posts, but focus on improving effectiveness. For one thing, we grouped certain logistical elements together in one structure under one commander, the SA Army's Logistics Command. For another, we created the Engineers and Signals Formation in the same way.

Then again, Northern Transvaal Command had become unmanageable. It covered a very large area, and the frequency of activities in that area was too high. I got the impression that because of this problem there was a tendency for its headquarters at Voortekkerhoogte to grow ever larger.

We concluded, however, that we should rather decentralise, so we divided it into three commands, the two new ones being Far Northern Command and Eastern Transvaal Command (the command boundaries, incidentally, corresponded with the layout of the national physical development regions the government had proclaimed). These changes were completed a few years later with the establishment of Northern Cape Command, which also fitted into the national plan.

Floods caused havoc in the Eastern Transvaal and Swaziland soon after the two new commands had been established. The GOC Eastern Transvaal Command was already geared to carry out emergency relief tasks, and at the same time he was also instructed to prepare the venue for the signing of the Nkomati Accord. Infiltration, mine incidents and attacks on farms in those areas of the Transvaal now also began to take place, and both commands were capable of taking immediate action.

Our forecast of future developments turned out to be correct. Although initially the implementation of the structural changes and territorial divisions attracted criticism, many people later told me that they could not imagine how it could ever have been otherwise. But the Army does not consist of philosophies and structures. One has to know the Army to understand how it works.

Although the Air Force is totally dependent on the dedication and skills of its people in blue, it tends to be characterised by its strong involvement with the natural sciences, high technology and modern armaments. And although the Navy is equally dependent on its people in white, with their own unique capabilities and human problems, it also relies heavily on high technology and modern armament systems. The Medical Service is an indispensable operational asset, but by comparison it is more professionally, humanely and service-orientated.

The Army, on the other hand, while also using weapon systems with a high degree of advanced technology, is people-intensive, which is why it accommodates the bulk of the Defence Force's personnel. So for us in the Army it was all about people; people whose help we needed to produce results.

At this high level one cannot command troops directly. It is difficult to motivate so many people in such a big organisation on a person-to-person basis.

Firstly, you must know what you want or have to achieve, and how it is going to be done. You must have vision and set ideals, and you must have clarity on the objectives that you want to attain. You have to ensure that your people know all these things and that they are mentally and emotionally reconciled to them. Everyone should know what the goals and basic elements of your plan and your policy are.

Secondly, the organisation should have a culture that embraces certain values. In a nutshell, you have to create an atmosphere in which you and your people will be stimulated to achieve those ideals and objectives.

If there is not enough time, you have to consider and plan these things yourself. But it is better to formulate them by way of a team effort with your commanders, or, at the very least, with your staff.

I am not saying that such a climate was not already in existence, but it had to be tended continuously. There was no continuity in the army, especially at the lower levels; one had to motivate consecutive intakes of national servicemen as well as induct new Permanent Force members.

The Army General Staff and I formulated four objectives in four main fields. They were: the ability to win the land battle, which was the Army's primary responsibility; the morale of the Army; the image of the Army; and cost-effective management, or productivity.

We also formulated the required atmosphere and culture that the Army should have, as we saw it, which we then marketed to its members. General Malan also made important contributions towards creating a culture in the Army in particular and in the Defence Force in general.

He said that problems did not exist, only challenges: 'Replace the word "problem" with the word "challenge".'

It had a good effect. Previously, when I had visited units I would often hear a commander say something like: 'Yes, we have a problem with our vehicles. The serviceability is not even 70 per cent,' or 'Our problem with this intake of national servicemen is that we have over five per cent AWOL (absent without leave).' After the new approach one would arrive at a unit and hear the commander saying such things as: 'We have a few challenges, the first one is to push up our vehicle serviceability figure to over 80 per cent, and the second is to push the AWOL figure down to under one per cent and keep it there.'

It might sound as if we were merely playing around with semantics, but it is not so. A truly new and positive spirit was being promoted.

My time as the Chief of the Army now began to run out, and although we were proud of our successes, I also harboured some personal disappointments.

One of the biggest disappointments was that in five years I had not managed to visit all the commanders and troops. It was an unattainable ideal right from the beginning, as I should have known. There were more than 250 Commando Force units, more than 150 Citizen Force units and more than 100 Permanent Force/National Service units spread over 11 territorial commands in a variety of home bases, operational bases and training bases. But it is a good thing not to have enough time, because it forces you to identify your real priorities. And sometimes you are surprised at the eventual outcome.

I decided to give a high priority to visiting low-profile groups that one is inclined to overlook – the Neglected Groups, or 'neglects', as I called them. I went out of my way to identify such groups and to satisfy myself about their wellbeing – large and well-known organisations can easily take care of themselves, but small and little-known ones are vulnerable.

A large group, especially if there is a degree of cohesion, develops an inherent force that ensures its survival, and units which have acquired public acclaim and possibly boast a long and proud record are inspired by the name they have to uphold. Traditions, values and culture keep military units like the Parachute Regiment, the Cape Town Highlanders and Regiment President Steyn going. They can take the knocks and bumps. There are also relatively small units with built-in strength, because they are independent and have acquired elite status, such as the special forces units.

But then at a territorial headquarters you will find a small bunch of military policemen, a handful of signallers and somewhere else a few chefs and clerks. They are usually sections or groups which have been detached from their main functional group and attached to other headquarters and units. For example, at a parachute battalion you would find hundreds of paratroopers sharing common interests. But you would never find 100 chefs together. They are split up and posted in small sections to larger units. They have a functional manager somewhere in Pretoria, but where they work they may be commanded by, say, an artillery commander who knows nothing about the culinary arts.

'Neglects' may have a feeling of functional togetherness and pride among themselves, but they are not always bound to the others by virtue of a common tradition and culture or *esprit de corps,* and are often dominated by them. But it is really so that the efficient functioning of many organisations usually depends on those who work quietly, unseen and unheard behind the scenes – the chefs, clerks, signallers, mechanics and telephonists. It is they who often find the going tough but who have to continue under their own steam. They often perform splendidly without much recognition. They are the vulnerable ones.

It is when you neglect these good people that *friction de guerre* can turn against you. Of course, you do not miss the chef until there is no food. Of course, you do not think about your signaller until the radio does not want to talk. You forget about the mechanic until your car refuses to go. And then it is too late. You find them, the 'neglects', at all levels of your organisation. They need your attention.

I mentioned two corps for Excellent Service in Army Orders: The Technical Service Corps, especially in respect of the technicians, or 'Tiffies' who rendered operational duties, and the South African Engineer Corps, the 'Sappers', who detected and lifted mines by hand. The Tiffies' citation reads as follows:

> Members of the Technical Service Corps of the SA Army demonstrated, during operations, unquestionable expertise of which they can be justifiably proud. Their contribution towards assuring the mobility and fire-power of the forces was indispensable. They recovered and repaired combat equipment whenever it was necessary, sometimes under the most adverse conditions and even under fire; often with little resources but good cheer and inventiveness as tools.
>
> They proved that mountains can be moved with the right attitude, courage and by doing what you can, with what you have, where you are. For this exceptional quality of the fighting spirit of the Technical Service Corps, their leaders and especially private soldiers in the field, I pay tribute.

Instead of quoting from the Sappers' citation, I present a statistic which speaks louder than words: From 1974 until the withdrawal of the South African forces from Namibia in 1989, the engineers lifted and disarmed a total of 1 743 landmines.

To put this figure into perspective I should point out that we are not talking about conventional warfare, where one finds identified minefields with a high density of mines in a confined geographical area. In that situation one can render hundreds of mines harmless in one effort. What we are talking about now is insurgent mines, which are often singly laid and concealed anywhere in a vast area. If this task had been carried out less successfully the projected repair costs to damaged vehicles could have amounted to R97.44 million. This is important in itself, but the price of lives saved and injuries prevented is, of course, incalculable.

The Sappers on the ground were fantastic. From 1979 to 1989 they 'spooked' 1.13 million kilometres in Sector 10 (mainly Ovamboland), which involved clearing a road by means of a mine-detecting or mine-detonating vehicle, or by a sapper on a motorbike who visually inspected the road for disturbances of the surface.

Over the same period they 'swept' 438 000 kilometres. Sweeping involves making a road or route safe by walking it on foot with a mine-detector, and investigating every alarm signal it sends out by hand. A detected mine must then be destroyed. It was exhausting, nerve-wracking and dangerous work. And they did the same in Sector 20 (Kavango) and Sector 70 (Eastern Caprivi).

It may be that members of the so-called neglected groups reading this book will be surprised to note my interest in them, because it is quite possible that they never saw me. My greatest disappointment was that I did not get to all the places I wanted to. To manage my time was always one of my biggest problems.

Then my ration of time had been expended. On 1 November of 1985, a little more than two months after Zola Budd set a new world record in the 5 000 metres for women with a time of 14 minutes 48.07 seconds, I stopped taking malaria tablets after 20 years and prepared myself for the last and toughest lap of my career, as Chief of the South African Defence Force.

CHAPTER 14

THE END OF A DECADE

Sampie's shocked out of his wits

On 1 November 1985, as the new Chief of the Defence Force, I had every intention of devoting myself to it, body and soul, as had been the case five years earlier when I became Chief of the Army. I do not mean that I wanted actively to represent the Defence Force in the world at large. I wanted to give my best inside the SADF, to make as much contact as possible with its units and members. But it did not work out quite like that – too many other important matters demanded too much of my time – and I still regret the fact that the circumstances made such contact impossible.

Those other matters which kept me from my chosen path included the following:

- When I took over command, the wave of internal unrest that had started in 1984 was already in full swing and would last through 1985 and 1986, and it took up many of my working hours.
- Then, when the unrest had barely calmed down, South Africa became involved in a big war in southern Angola. To visit the combat zone I often had to travel by helicopters and other aircraft, or do

cross-country trips by ground transport.

- The war had not even ended when negotiations regarding the withdrawal of Cubans from Angola and the independence of South West started. Once again I had to travel a lot, this time overseas. I stopped counting when I had been away nine times in eight months – and this did not include the Brazzaville shuttle.
- Cross-border operations against MK targets in countries other than Angola also took place during this period, while operations in South West and Angola continued.
- The negotiations which led to the implementation of UN Security Council Resolution 435, the withdrawal of the SADF from South West and eventually the territory's independence.
- The scaling-down of the SADF during the new post-war era and under the new South African government. Armament projects had to be cancelled and people had to be retrenched.
- A new wave of internal unrest, this time between the black political parties rather than against the government, which began in 1990 after the unbanning of the African National Congress, the South African Communist Party and the Pan-Africanist Congress.

All these and other things competed for my attention, and in between I also had my normal duties as Chief of the Defence Force to perform. The result was that I could not achieve my self-imposed goal of giving more attention to the people in the force.

I am not talking only about the 'neglects'; I did not even see as much as I should have of the big and active branches of the service and their units. It was, and still is, a painful admission to make. I continue to regret, for example, that I could not visit the Navy more often.

The biggest loss, however, was the fact of being too busy to do my real job – to think. If you can't think for an hour a day, you are not of much use to society.

But two factors made everything possible. The first was what one might call the 'Gleeson factor'. My right-hand man was Lieutenant-General Ian Rimbault Gleeson, my Chief of Staff – and I could not have had a better one. When he retired early in 1990 Niel Knobel, the Surgeon General, described him very accurately by quoting Martina Navratilova:

There are winners and there are losers. And if you choose to
be one of the former, the journey through life can be a little
lonely. When you're a winner, you have to set the standard for
excellence wherever you go.

You have to battle against the fatigue, the intimidation, the
human tendency to want to take things a little easier. You have
to be able to come up with, time and again, one consistently
great performance after another. It is gruelling. I don't know
how many people are willing to make the effort. But those few
true professionals you meet along the way help make the journey just a little easier to manage.

The second was the 'Holliday factor'. Sergeant-Major John James
Clarke ('Jan') Holliday was not an ordinary regimental sergeant-major
or even a brigade sergeant-major, he was the Sergeant-Major of the
Defence Force. He had joined the Defence Force in 1944, when he was
just 16 years old, and with his encyclopaedic knowledge of its structure
and workings he kept me up to date with what was happening to those
under me, from the most senior sergeant-major right down to the most
junior private soldier. This international athletics starter – a true professional – walked all the way with me, and together we arrived at the
end of the road.

*   *   *

Let me start at the beginning. In regard to the internal violence, I first
have to draw a distinction between terror and politically motivated unrest that includes violence. By terror I refer, for example, to infiltrators who commit politically inspired murders, lay mines and set other
types of explosive devices. By unrest I mean burning down schools and
administrative buildings, barricading streets, holding unlawful riotous
assemblies and generating mass syndromes that result in violence such
as the 'necklace' killings.

As far as terror was concerned, a new pattern of geographical infiltration routes and acts of terror developed after the signing of the
Nkomati Accord. The infiltration of insurgents from Mozambique into

the eastern Transvaal came to a standstill, and new infiltration routes replaced the old ones. One was through Swaziland, which created unique problems, and the other was through Botswana, which resulted in acts of violence in the western Transvaal border area and elsewhere.

Many people, including myself and the Director-General of Foreign Affairs, Neil van Heerden, tried our best to persuade Botswana to join us in establishing some form of joint security committee, but to no avail. In the meantime the Western and Eastern Cape, the Witwatersrand and Natal experienced unrest incidents, simultaneously or consecutively.

The reverse of this coin was unrest-related violence, which goes hand-in-hand with political change. The successful referendum on the formation of a tri-cameral parliament in November 1983, and its actual inception in September 1984, marked such change. Not everyone would necessarily agree with me, but in my opinion it brought about a major change in the political dispensation that had existed for decades prior to this era.

And political change always brings confusion and conflict. It fanned the emotions of people towards the right of the political spectrum and it unsettled black people, who felt themselves left out in the cold. I do not think it was mere coincidence that we experienced a spell of unrest immediately thereafter, during 1984, 1985 and 1986.

This wave of unrest was politically motivated and was aimed at the governing authorities and the administration. Stone-throwing was not merely the work of unruly school pupils, and the barricading of streets was not just a sign of juvenile delinquency; there was a more significant meaning behind it all.

Revolutionary committees were established, such as the so-called political and military regional committees, and street committees. Street and block commanders were appointed. Forms of 'alternative' structures were organised, with local alternative committees gradually being placed under regional committees, and regional committees under national committees. The aim of all this was to make the country ungovernable and to replace the official administrative structures with alternative ones from the lower levels upwards.

It was a serious situation. The ANC started to spread the word that a 'black Christmas' was going to hit the country in 1986, and that the administration would crumble. One heard this everywhere, from politicians and officials of African countries to people overseas who got their information about South Africa from the ANC.

The application of emergency regulations and the actions of the security forces prevented this, and in the meantime the negotiations, the propaganda and the armed conflict in South West and Angola continued. Let me mention a few of the events we lived through, by way of illustrating the atmosphere of those hectic days.

Early in 1986 the government had to cope with a barrage of protests about its actions in southern Africa; from allegations that it enforced strict border control on Lesotho to complaints that the security forces had launched an attack on an infiltrators' base at Maseru on 20 December 1985. In turn the South African government warned Botswana not to harbour MK insurgents, an allegation which was rejected by President Quett Masire.

Security forces shot dead four insurgents during a hot-pursuit operation in Angola. This happened during a follow-up after a PLAN attack on Ovambo civilians near Nkongo during which one was killed and another wounded. On 9 January 1986, the same day Chester Crocker arrived in Luanda for another round of discussions, a spokesman for the MPLA joined the never-ending war of words with an allegation that a South African force had penetrated 150 km into Angola. And so on and so on: it would be impossible to mention everything.

On 4 March 1986 Mr P W Botha proposed in Parliament that Resolution 435 could be implemented by 1 August 1986, provided a firm and satisfactory agreement could be reached on the withdrawal of Cubans from Angola before that date. Crocker grabbed the opportunity and swiftly arranged discussions with his Soviet counterpart in Geneva to tackle the question of the Cuban presence in Angola, although the resulting talks did not immediately deliver concrete results.

In this atmosphere of propaganda and negotiations, with the clouds of unrest still in the air, a new and big storm started to brew in Angola which would erupt into a thundering outburst of violence only a year later.

The first storm-clouds began to appear when the Angolan MPLA government and its allies began to prepare for a new offensive against UNITA in Savimbi's south-eastern stronghold – the latest of a series of such forays, all of which had failed so far. The man in charge was a Soviet general named Konstantin Kurochkin, a veteran of the Afghanistan war, who arrived in Angola in December 1985.

Large quantities of modern Russian weapons systems were being brought into Angola, including aircraft which had been taken out of Russia's strategic reserve for any European conflict (later Cuba would also pilfer from its reserve). Moscow sent about 1 000 Soviet troops to fill training and command posts, and 2 000 East Germans to boost FAPLA's intelligence and telecommunication services. Approximately 20 000 members of FAPLA, 7 000 from SWAPO and 900 from the ANC's MK armed wing, assembled at Luena and Cuito Cuanavale.

On 9 and 10 August 1986 4 000 UNITA troops, with possibly a couple of hundred South African gunners, attacked Cuito Cuanavale. South African long-range artillery caused considerable damage, and the Angolan troops and their allies were ordered to retreat to Lucusse, Munhango and Menongue.

During August-September 1986 I was taking malaria tablets once more as I went to look at precisely what was happening, and in due course a few of us found ourselves just east of the Cuito River, on the other side of Cuito Cuanavale. Regular bombardments were being brought down on targets outside the town to disrupt the combined FAPLA forces and prevent them from completing their build-up.

During daytime one had to lie low, and one tended to get bored, since it was impossible to sleep all day. It was the typical African bush scene all over again: the 'MMBA', or miles and miles of bloody Africa, as one expression had it. Although it was still winter in August, it got warm enough during the day to make it necessary to wipe the perspiration from your face every now and again, and dust, bluebottles, flies and other insects abounded to make people irritable.

So I told the fellows that what I wanted was an ice-cream; not just any ice-cream; it had to be a decent one, like those one used to get at the Esplanade in Durban; I did not want an icy ice-cream, it had to be a *creamy* ice-cream, served in a parfait glass.

I could see that some of the chaps were becoming quite irritated with me. But – I suppose because they couldn't do much about it – they listened with grim expressions on their faces. I pretended to be unaware of the irritation I was causing and continued to fantasise while swatting at the flies.

'You have to pour flavouring over the ice-cream,' I would say. 'And special flavouring: red raspberry syrup. It runs down the inside of the glass and some of it mixes with the ice-cream. You mustn't be stingy with the syrup. And to make it all look attractive you must put a red cherry, glazed with sugar, on top of it. Condensed drops of water form on the outside of the glass and run down through the mistiness, leaving trails on the glass like rivers on a map. While you feast on this, the ice-cream melts and sinks to the bottom of the glass, where it mixes with the syrup and then goes pink. And then you drink the last bit – bottoms up.'

Later that day the chef, Staff-Sergeant Sampie van der Westhuizen, arrived – and unexpectedly turned fantasy into reality. I spent years hankering for him to write down the story of that afternoon for me. By great good fortune I ran into him again on a visit to 32 Battalion's Pomfret base in the Northern Cape during 1991, and prevailed on him to put it down on paper. Now a sergeant-major, he was in a great hurry, and in no time scribbled it down with a stub of pencil. I was stunned!

Sampie's story reads as follows:

Gee whiz, I was stunned! There I was, on my own and in the middle of nowhere, trying my very best to get a fire going to make some coffee for the general and the others. I was trying to blow some life into it when I heard somebody saying: 'Staff, what's so difficult about getting a stupid little fire going?' I thought by myself, bugger you, you haven't got a clue.

I looked up, and yes, there was no mistake – it was the general. I jumped up but, still trying to find my feet, he told me: 'As you were, please carry on.' With a sigh of relief, I thought by myself: Fortunately he's also a human being. He knows what it's like to try to get a fire started with nothing.

A few other people were hanging around there as well. The water was on the point of boiling when I heard the general say: 'Today I want an ice-cream float ...' And he started to explain exactly what it should be like.

I was shocked out of my wits. 'Yes, General, very well, General, I'll do it, General,' I said to myself in silent response. After I had served the coffee I thought: Okay, there you have it, do what you can with what you have, wherever you are. Here you are, Van der Westhuizen, someplace in the nowheres, but nobody will get you down; you know what you are and what you can do.

Alone once more, I asked myself, was the General only joking or was he serious? But the General had spoken. To hell with it! I grabbed a box of ratpax [dry rations] and looked through the contents. I thought to myself, General, I'll show you! I'm going to do what you ask, no matter what.

Then I saw light. I created my own recipe, which was as follows:

Ingredients
- *instant milkshake*
- *jelly powder*
- *instant pudding*
- *water*
- *jam*

Method
Shake jelly powder, water, jam and instant pudding in bag. Place in hole under tree and cover up with sand. Pour water every ten minutes (after a while it sets, icy cold.)

I opened the bag and tasted. It had worked, it tasted just like ice-cream!

I poured a tin of lemonade into a glass with the mixture on top. I walked over to him proudly and served him. 'General, here is the ice-cream float you asked for.'

I could see that the General was very surprised ...

What Sampie forgot to mention was that he had found a red cherry, probably in a tin of mixed fruit, which he had put on top of the ice-cream – an example of the ingenuity, sense of humour and sense of duty of the South African soldier of that time.

Let me leave the build-up of the offensive against UNITA and Sampie's ice-cream for the moment, because in between both of these things and various others I still had to carry out my normal duties as Chief of the Defence Force. As had happened so often in the past, the old year did not really end and the new year did not really begin. I had no sense of an old era coming to its finish or a new one dawning: there was simply no pause between one and the other. I just pressed on straight from one year to the next with the never-ending office work, answering letters people kept on sending me.

My good friend and colleague, the diplomat André Jaquet – or 'Jackets', if you like – once quoted to me from a letter from General Wellington to Lord Bradford:

> If I attempted to answer the mass of futile correspondence that surrounds me, I should be disbarred from all serious business of campaigning.
>
> I must remind your Lordship that I shall see to it that no officer under my command is debarred by attending to the futile drivelling of mere quill-driving in your Lordship's office, from attending to his first duty, which is and has always been so to train the private men in his command that they may, without question, beat any force opposed to them in the field.

I need not say that I absolutely agreed with Wellington. But it is an unfortunate fact that there is often other work that simply has to be done; work which is also important.

The Nkomati Accord, or perhaps I should say accusations that the Defence Force violated clauses of the accord, was one of the matters which now clogged my 'In' tray, just like Wellington's. As this issue previously fell outside the scope of my responsibilities, I had to study it from scratch.

It is now a thing of the past, but let me state immediately that when the Defence Force was authorised to do so it supported the Renamo movement in Mozambique, but that when this was subsequently forbidden such support was stopped.

For me the allegations were a serious matter, and I gave the matter as much of my personal attention as was humanly possible. After I had perused the mass of information before me and consulted with many people, I was absolutely convinced that no irregularities had been committed, and nothing happened afterwards to indicate that my finding was wrong. Indeed, the possibility that I might have created the impression among my staff that I distrusted them over irregularities still causes me intense grief.

The accusations persisted for a long time after the assistance to Renamo had ceased. I must take my hat off to the Mozambicans in this regard. They applied a principle which I propagate myself for anyone in a conflict situation: Take the initiative, if you can. And they were very good at getting as many people as possible to repeat the allegations for long enough, until they eventually become generally accepted 'truths'.

The way in which Mozambique applied the principle was to accuse its opponent and to keep him under pressure with continued accusations. The opponent then had to use all available time to react to the charges. In the good guy-bad guy competition there is rarely enough time for the opponent to effectively disclose the other party's irregular conduct. You cannot shoot if you have to keep ducking all the time (might this not be what was happening in South Africa during the early 1990s?)

Mozambique was guilty of irregularities. It had unilaterally withdrawn from the joint security commission and ignored the clause of the Nkomati Accord that the parties should moderate their language.

I did get the opportunity once or twice to express dismay over Mozambique's accusations to some of its people in authority. Their reaction more or less came down to this: 'Oh, well, we don't believe all of it ourselves, and you know what the radio and press are like. And we have no control over them. Don't take it too seriously, that's how things go in politics.' And the allegations continued.

There were even some South African civil servants who would not believe that we had ceased to support Renamo. What sometimes happened was that they were also included in delegations which visited Mozambique for discussions in other fields. Their counterparts, who often included politicians, would then protest against the South African Defence Force's 'continued assistance to Renamo', elaborating on the grief it had caused and how it was the source of everything that damaged relations between the two countries.

Our officials often found themselves in unfamiliar political terrain, without reliable security information that would allow them to accurately interpret the charges. It was frustrating, to say the least.

Even before I became Chief of the Defence Force we had offered to set up radar stations to be manned jointly with the Mozambicans to monitor the airspace for violations. They did not accept the offer, but instead continued their allegations that we were undertaking clandestine flights to Mozambique.

At one stage, after we had insisted that they submit examples of the activities of which they accused us, they came up with reams of invented stories. One was that we had dug a tunnel from the eastern Transvaal to the other side of the border, and were using it to replenish Renamo's supplies. But that was one of the mistakes they made. Even people who were staunch supporters of Mozambique rejected this charge as fantasy. And yet the allegations continued.

* * *

There was something else besides the 'In' tray and propaganda that tended to keep me in my office. My new appointment brought me into contact with a world I did not know at all – Parliament – because while it was in session I had to work from my office in Cape Town.

I was not a regular visitor to Parliament. Although I have nothing against it, I went there only when I had to. The parliamentary system is a good one, and one should not make the mistake of thinking that debates are what it is all about. As a layman I would say that more work is done by committees and study groups in conference rooms than in the assembly chamber itself, but the chamber is indispensable.

Inevitably I met interesting personalities in the ambit of Parliament. One such was Mr Koos van der Merwe MP, who told me a funny story about his introduction to it.

On his first day after being elected he had to attend a luncheon, a gathering consisting mainly of English-speaking people. For various reasons he had not slept and he was completely exhausted by all the work and excitement.

Suddenly, but rather vaguely, he thought he heard the master of ceremonies asking: 'Will … fahn duh Murvie please say grace?' Since this was a common mispronunciation of 'Van der Merwe' among some English-speakers, he started to get to his feet, pressing on the table with the palms of his hands to support himself while trying to recall the old

English Bible words like 'thy', 'thou', and 'kingdom cometh'. Then to his surprise and relief he heard somebody else beginning to pray. It turned out that the MC had actually said: 'Will Father Murphy please say grace?'

Another interesting person I got to know better was Mr Vause Raw, the well-known Member of Parliament for Durban Point. A long-time member of the United Party and then of its successor, the New Republic Party, he was usually the party spokesman on defence matters.

He was an invaluable ombudsman for members of the Citizen Force, Commandos and National Servicemen and their families; the reason being that he was a veteran of World War II and knew what it was all about. In fact, he wrote a collection of verse while in uniform between 1940 and 1945, and a poem that particularly struck me was one entitled 'Again':

> He had been home,
> One word
> Spelling a lifetime
> in the endlessness of war,
> And now he was going again,
> Away ...
> To war ...
> Would he return?
> ... No matter now ...
> Brave noble soldier.
> For he was going away
> To war ...
> Again.

I met Mr Raw for the first time in the operational area, when he visited there with other parliamentarians. I flew with them from Rundu to Omega in a Hercules transport aircraft, and when four of us wanted to play bridge (he was one of the instigators), he rapidly produced two decks of cards: one pinkish and the other one light blue. On the back of the cards was a circular emblem with the words: `United Party, Verenigde Party'.

Now, before a game starts I usually check that the jokers have been removed, so I said: 'Mr Raw, please make sure there are no jokers in those United Party packs.'

He replied: 'Don't worry, they went to the Progressive Federal Party long ago.'

*   *   *

My new world was not populated only by parliamentarians; I was also directly involved with people like Commandant Piet Marais, the chairman of Armscor.

Piet Marais was a character with many facets, visible and invisible. He looked like the chairman of a big company, which he was, but he also looked like a Karoo farmer, because he *was* one. He looked prim and proper and serious, but underneath it he was an imp. He could be a wise man – if you were wise enough to notice it.

He earned international acclaim for South Africa as chairman of Armscor, and in 1988 was awarded the Hertzog Prize. At the award ceremony he remarked: 'A South African doesn't scare away from a problem; he panics closer to the problem.'

That was indeed how it happened. When UN Security Council Resolution 418 was passed and an arms embargo against South Africa was set in place, Armscor did not scare away from the problem but panicked closer to it – with stunning results. It produced the best piece of field artillery in the world, the long-ranged 155 mm G5 towed medium gun and its self-propelled equivalent, the G6; the Rooikat armoured car; and a range of sophisticated naval and air force equipment.

He once told me the following story: he was flying from D F Malan Airport in Cape Town to Jan Smuts Airport in Johannesburg. The only parking he could find was far away from the terminal building, and those were the days before airport trolleys. His suitcase was huge and heavy, the kind my mother would have called a portmanteau, and when a porter approached him Piet asked: 'How much will you charge to carry this for me?'

'You can pay me what you think it's worth,' the porter replied. Piet gave him a R2 note and they embarked on the long trek across the parking area to the terminal. But when they reached the halfway mark the porter put the suitcase down and said: 'Mister, this suitcase has now become far too heavy for two rands!' The anecdote told one that Piet Marais the high-flyer and the lowly airport porter were not distanced from one another by rank, wealth or station in life, because they shared one important thing, a sense of humour.

* * *

There was another duty that kept me, as it had my predecessors, tied to my desk in Cape Town. Like all the other Directors-General, I had to appear annually before the parliamentary Joint Committee on Public Accounts, or JCPA, at which I had to give evidence in the form of answers to any questions the committee members might care to ask.

The questions usually concerned the Auditor-General's annual report on my department, and while I recognised how essential it was to have a democratic parliamentary institution acting as a watchdog over the spending of the taxpayers' money, it was not a body before which I would volunteer to appear for the pleasure of it.

Democratic procedures are often frustrating, and if they were to be scientifically evaluated for their effectiveness in problem-solving and decision-making they would probably score very low. But of course there are other considerations too, and I subscribe to Winston Churchill's statement that democracy is the worst form of government – except all the others.

The JCPA produced its own frustrations. At some of my appearances it felt as if I were the accused in a criminal case. On other occasions I felt like a humble servant being admonished by my master, who had been appointed by the voters – which is not to say that they were uncivil; they just didn't exactly approach me with kid-gloves. This was quite close to the truth, of course, and I simply had to accept the situation. I am not complaining.

The committee generally consisted of learned people such as lawyers and accountants, well-versed in the matters submitted to them for investigation. The common factor was that they were all politicians. And I suppose it is unavoidable, if not always easily noticeable, that party politics play a role in the proceedings of the committee.

It never really worried me. But the political style and techniques that members used to unsettle one another in Parliament were also used against any person appearing before the committee – to a lesser extent, fortunately, although for somebody like me, who was not used to this kind of fighting, it was bad enough. Sometimes I felt a bit bullied, because it was not possible to retaliate in the way the MPs do in Parliament. I tended to take everything very personally, because as DG I was the official responsible for my department's spending and I had to accept accountability myself. This was something I could not delegate.

Still, I should not complain. I was prepared to accept the task of being Chief of the Defence Force, and facing the waves of the JCPA was an occupational hazard.

There were, however, more meaningful frustrations: The Auditor-General's report was an open document, and political commentators seized on it immediately to make shocking revelations about the mismanagement of the taxpayers' money. But the rules and conventions did not permit the responsible director-general to comment publicly on such matters until he had appeared before the committee. This ruling was confirmed by a decision from the Speaker on 21 February 1979. Although it made sense to me, it was not pleasant: I was being criticised in public, along with my organisation, yet I had no right to reply.

Even so, I was convinced that the JCPA should never lose its watchdog function. In spite of the uncomfortable flak I faced at each appearance, I recognised the fact that it was an indispensable institution. Any person who had to appear before it had all my sympathy, but he simply had to sweat it out and face the consequences. There was just no other way.

However, one aspect needed further attention. For example, I could often find no other explanation for mistakes in the handling of stores and monies than the lack of sufficient qualified and experienced personnel. Unfortunately my predecessor and those before him probably found exactly the same problems and offered the same excuses, and one of the veterans of the JCPA, Mr Harry Schwartz, in fact told me in the committee that he was tired of hearing that excuse, as he had had to listen to it year after year. And he was probably quite right.

The causes of the shortage of qualified and experienced personnel followed a pattern. As soon as the personnel concerned had been trained and had accumulated some experience, they were lured away by the better compensation offered in the private sector. The ones who stayed on in the Defence Force did excellent work, because the force did not consist only of people who had been 'bought' on the manpower market; there were also those who were motivated by a desire to render service to their country. But there were not enough of them.

I know the generally accepted principle is that people in the employ of the State may not be on par with their private-sector counterparts as far as remuneration goes. For example, an accountant and a stores supervisor in the private sector will always be better rewarded financially than their opposite numbers in the public sector. But has the time not come to waive this 'principle'? Or do we want to entrust the taxpayers' money to the people who are left on the manpower market after the private sector has skimmed off most of the cream?

Now that we find ourselves in an era in which holy cows are being buried and long-standing concepts questioned, with new ideas being judged on merit and accepted where such merit exists, we should seriously reconsider this question: Why can the state, as an employer, not compete with other employers on the same terms when it comes to remuneration? And if there is nothing wrong with the principle, then we should change the system to eliminate any disparity which might exist.

This would naturally demand a fresh look at the auditing system. We had already made important changes under Auditors-General Joop de Loor and Peter Wronsley in my time, by moving away from mere accounting and regularity audits in the direction of performance and objectives audits. If it is eventually going to lead to a real productivity audit, we will have reached the point where the civil servant also has to 'produce'. And those who don't, will go the same way as those in the private sector who don't.

I will not argue with those who do not agree with me on this point, but then they should stop complaining that the civil service is not to their liking.

*   *   *

Parliamentary duties apart, one activity that always required attention was operations – which brings me to a sensitive subject: operations across the South African border. During the 1980s the Defence Force carried out cross-border operations against Umkhonto we Sizwe targets from time to time, usually in the form of successful raids by the Special Forces into countries like Mozambique, Zambia, Botswana and Zimbabwe. These operations were blitz attacks, a quick-in-and-out; sometimes they involved no ground troops but were pure air assaults.

In the earlier years MK had isolated bases of the same kind as SWAPO, with the possible exception that the MK bases accommodated smaller numbers. Then, as a direct result of SADF attacks, MK changed its system. Instead of a base in the bush or a camp outside a town, its operatives split up into small groups and dispersed themselves in apartments and houses in urban areas.

This was a good tactic which considerably hampered military action against them, because it was no longer possible to attack a concentrated group in one location. Besides, they now enjoyed the 'protection' of the civilian community in which they were hidden. Inevitably attacks on such targets would result in propaganda to the effect that we had bombed or raided civilians, which made action against them even more difficult.

However, they did not cease their actions against targets in South Africa. On the contrary, these actions increased in frequency and intensity. Seen from a security point of view, operations against MK had to be continued to prevent an escalation of attacks on farms and the use of mines and explosive devices. The cross-border attacks attracted a lot of criticism. Over the years various visitors to the country during interviews tried to pressure me into admitting that we had launched these operations with the specific aim of wrecking political initiatives and negotiations. I categorically denied it then, as I do now.

They pointed out, especially in the case of Angola, that operations took place just before or after international negotiations, and wanted to know the reason for this timing. But if one looks carefully at a political chronology, such as the one I produce later in this book – a continuous record of conferences, meetings and discussions like those of the General Assembly and Security Council of the UN, visits by representatives of the Western 'Big Five' and others, special envoys and so on – the matter becomes clearer. The fact was that it would have been almost impossible to have executed an operation which did not take place just before or after some political event or other.

Certain practical considerations have a big influence on the timing of an operation. A farmer will understand that if he does not get his seed in the ground at the right time, he may well have to wait until the next year. It is a matter of the natural rhythm of life, which will not be denied.

In South West and Angola we actually had to have separate designs for the dry and wet seasons. Certain operations could be carried out only during full-moon periods, and others during the time when there was little moonlight. If you missed out on the right moon, you had to wait 28 days – but your enemy was not going to wait for you. So MK activities increased, because its masters had no fear of international political condemnation.

I knew that cross-border operations could hamper negotiations, but that was never the motive. We made our recommendations from a security point of view, and after having considered the operational factors. Calculating the political risks was always the task of the politicians. I am not hiding behind anybody's political skirts when I say this. The Minister of Defence never told me to execute an operation with the intention of wrecking some political manoeuvre or other.

I must also add that to initiate an operation was not the exclusive right of the military. I mention this because I believe it might help to clear the air if this matter is seen in its true perspective. All the over-used and stereotyped expressions, like 'the SADF has done this or that' or 'the SADF's policy on this or that', created the impression that the Defence Force had its own independent policy and high-handedly acted as it saw fit. We did not! Our Defence Force, like any other, was an instrument of the State and acted within the current structures and policies of the State. One should keep this in mind, because the Defence Force is most definitely going to play its appointed role in the future of our country.

One can think this out for oneself: if farms are attacked, vehicles blown up by mines and bombs set off in busy commercial centres – with all the resultant damage and loss of life involved – then there will be pressure on the government concerned to take drastic action against the perpetrators.

We experienced this kind of situation as late as the end of 1992 and the beginning of 1993, when the Codesa constitutional negotiations were already well advanced. There was a series of incidents in the Eastern Cape and the eastern Orange Free State for which the armed wing of the PAC, APLA, accepted responsibility; in one such incident four people were murdered and 17 wounded when five men attacked the King William's Town Golf Club on 28 November 1992 with hand-grenades, rifles and petrol bombs.

The inhabitants of the affected areas urged the government in the strongest terms to act against APLA in the Transkei, or they would take the law into their own hands. But if any counter-operation had, in fact, been launched at the time, as the government had been urged to do, the propagandists would undoubtedly have claimed that it was done with the intention of wrecking the negotiations.

The 1992–1993 incidents were the latest of a long series of atrocities against civilians, some of them aimed at farms. On 14 October 1985, for example, a chicken farm near Bosbokrand was attacked by men armed with AK-47s, and on 13 February 1988 five infiltrators from Zimbabwe laid mines and attacked the farm of a Mr Fisher, 10 km west of Beit Bridge, with AK-47s, hand grenades and RPG-7 rocket launchers before crossing back over the border.

Landmines were often laid by cross-border infiltrators. Four children and two adults were killed, and two children and three adults injured on 15 December 1985 when their bakkie detonated a mine on the farm Chatsworth, 45 km west of Messina. Two black men were killed and eight injured in a mine incident near Davel on 25 May 1986. On 4 January 1986 Mr Hubert de Beer and his daughter-in-law, Elize, were killed and Mr Deon de Beer and Mr Danie Venter injured when their vehicle detonated a mine at Stockpoort, Ellisras.

Bombs and limpet mines were used on several occasions, a prominent example being the explosion of a powerful bomb in front of the Nedbank Plaza Building in Church Street, Pretoria, which killed 20 people and wounded 199. Two days before Christmas of 1985 a bomb exploded in a refuse bin at the Amanzimtoti Sanlam Centre, killing three women and two boys, and wounding 61 other people. On 30 July 1988 a mine exploded at a Benoni Plaza Wimpy Bar, wounding 55 people, one woman later dying of her injuries.

* * *

Another major point of criticism against cross-border operations was that South Africa used the Defence Force to destabilise its neighbours. Now, one might label the anti-infiltration actions of a target country as destabilisation or whatever terms suit one, but the results for the target country, from a security point of view, are good.

I have already mentioned, I think, such cases as Israel's neighbour, Jordan, and Zambia, which borders on eastern Caprivi, both of which forbade infiltration from their soil because they did not wish to bear the brunt of the retaliatory actions taken against infiltrators on their side of the border. Certainly Zambia's crack-down on exfiltration from its territory resulted in the cessation of the insurgency in eastern Caprivi.

When I was preparing the first edition of this book in the early 1990s a seasoned political analyst, who was normally critical of the then government, commented that, whether you called it destabilisation or not, cross-border operations had their advantages. His argument was that such operations against MK were a thorn in the flesh of the countries that harboured it. This was one of the main considerations which motivated Zambia's President Kenneth Kaunda to urge the ANC to enter into negotiations with the South African government.

To see his comment in the right context, we have to look at other chains of events that took place during the same period. To return for a moment to the wave of unrest during 1984–1986, we know that the crumbling of the administrative structures forecast for 1986 was thwarted by means of the emergency regulations and the security forces; the ANC came to the conclusion that the security forces could not be beaten, and said so.

During this period until shortly after December 1986, the so-called 'front-line states', in anticipation of an ANC take-over, came up with the most aggressive speeches they had ever hurled against South Africa. Then, when the take-over did not happen, they had to reconsider their strategies. One experience they did not want to relive was further cross-border operations into their countries. That inspired them, especially Zambia, to exert pressure on the ANC to use the opportunities for starting discussions with the South African government.

The effect of the cross-border operations and the failure of the attempts to bring the administration to its knees through unrest therefore played an important part in promoting negotiations and settlement politics.

* * *

Talking about allegations regarding cross-border operations, I would like to move on to the next instalment in the serial about accusations of violations of the Nkomati Accord.

As I have already said, the charges that South Africa continued to support Renamo just would not stop. However, one could detect a slow but sure turning of the tide. Influential Americans and Europeans visiting South Africa often requested interviews with me. Most of them were very critical of South Africa, but some of them, after a trip to Mozambique and having heard of more 'underground supply lines to Renamo', told me they did not believe the Mozambican stories any longer.

They asked me why we did not deny the allegations. I replied that my minister had done so on several occasions. They then insisted that we find other ways of proving our innocence. But how do you prove that you have not done something which you have not done? But okay, cowboys don't cry. I told them the following story I had heard from a German friend:

A man in a restaurant orders and receives a bowl of soup. The diner eats almost all the soup, then summons the waiter and in disgust shows him that there is a fly in the soup. The waiter apologises, removes the bowl and brings him a fresh serving. The man tucks in with relish, but when the soup is nearly finished, he calls the waiter and once again points out that there is a fly in the bowl.

Again the waiter apologises and offers to bring more soup, and this time the diner promises he will not complain again, as long as the waiter brings him another bowlful.

When the waiter has left, a man at an adjoining table – who has been watching this saga – taps the soup-eater on the shoulder and says: 'Listen, pal, when you've finished, could I borrow your fly, please?'

The moral of this story is that as long as you have a fly to put into the soup you will get more food. I began to believe that, as long as Mozambique could complain about the South African fly in its ointment (or soup in this case) it would have the sympathy and support of the whole world. The Mozambicans could not afford to rid themselves of the South African fly as long as they wanted more soup.

During the early 1990s the Mozambique government switched tactics, and, instead of accusing the government and the Defence Force, turned its attention to the private sector.

*   *   *

Meanwhile other things were happening on the other side of southern Africa, in the western theatre. The war that had been brewing up in Angola finally exploded during 1987. And it was not just any war, but the one which would lead to real negotiations about a Cuban troop withdrawal from Angola and the implementation of Resolution 435 in South West.

I now take up the story again on the spot where ice-cream floats were being served by Sampie and the Angolan alliance was being driven from Cuito Cuanavale by UNITA. The latter encounter was not the end of the campaign against UNITA, but the beginning.

The repeated offensives against Savimbi and UNITA had fallen into a distinct pattern. Every year there would be an attempt to drive him out of his base area at Jamba with the ultimate aim of destroying him completely, and every year it failed. I had often forecast that the day would come when the MPLA would fail for the last time – and then they would have to choose between total defeat or negotiations with Savimbi.

It was no secret that Chester Crocker became frustrated from time to lime. Every time he thought the MPLA was serious about talks on peace in South West, the Cubans and the Soviet-supported hardliners in the MPLA wanted just one more chance to destroy Savimbi militarily. Only then, they said, would they be prepared to talk. The following year, after another unsuccessful effort, they would come back with the same story. And so it went on, year after weary year.

I told Crocker I didn't believe their arguments. If the MPLA was going to win and eliminate UNITA as a factor, why would they want to negotiate? I am sure he didn't believe it himself. On the other hand, if the MPLA were really facing military defeat they should be willing to negotiate so as to bargain for the most favourable settlement. But Crocker stuck to his assignment, and persisted patiently with his diplomacy.

I had already initiated limited operational assistance to UNITA during

July 1987. We had ample confirmed information that the Soviets and Cubans were busy with an enormous build-up for a big war. Never-ending waves of Soviet transport aircraft carrying many tons of war material landed at Luanda, Lubango, Menongue and Cuito Cuanavale; a reporter from *The Times* newspaper of London commented that it reminded him of Afghanistan.

In the meantime Crocker carried on with his merry-go-round diplomacy; in mid-July 1987 he held discussions with the MPLA in Lusaka and once again departed full of misplaced hope. But now the South African Defence Force ceased to be the only organisation accused of destroying peace talks through military operations – it was the Soviets' turn. Within a week of the Lusaka discussions the Soviet-inspired Cuban-FAPLA advance through Cuito Cuanavale and other places began to roll. On 22 July 1987 a dismayed Crocker said the hope of a breakthrough in South West and Angola had been shattered. But he was wrong. The events that now followed would bring about the breakthrough from mock negotiations to the real thing.

That was what happened at high level. On the ground the big war had started, what Fred Bridgland aptly called in a book-title *The War for Africa: Twelve Months that Transformed a Continent*.

But, however important any matter might be, one seldom has only one special overriding priority to which all one's attention can be given. As I mentioned in Chapter 3, when dealing with the training of senior officers, such an officer should be able to work under pressure without isolating himself to the extent that there is no time for other important matters, and here is a good example.

The advance had already crossed the starting line when I had to divert my attention to other matters. Major-General Neels van Tonder of military intelligence came to see me one day with a suggestion that we go to Paris. I did not like the idea and told him impatiently that he had to persuade me that the trip would be cost-effective. So he mentioned about a dozen things that we had to go and do.

I was more stubborn than usual, and told him that under such circumstances I was not prepared to go. If a person gave me too many reasons I became suspicious; if he had given me only one good one I would have been more agreeable. He was justifiably upset. But a few days later he was back in my office. This time he listed three reasons for going. The very first of them persuaded me – the possibility that we could arrange the release of Major Wynand du Toit, who had been captured during an operation in Cabinda and evacuated to Luanda as a prisoner of war.

I immediately contacted my friend and colleague, Neil van Heerden, the Director-General of Foreign Affairs. Would he have any objections if I concerned myself with the issue? He was affable and even excited about the idea, saying: 'I'll welcome any effort by anybody who has a chance to get him out. We must try everything.'

Sometime in July Neels van Tonder, Johann Sonnekus and I left for Paris with the intention of persuading a major power, France, to play a role in Du Toit's release. France looked promising for a number of reasons. A Frenchman named Albertini was being held in detention by the Ciskei homeland government; the French Prime Minister, Jacques Chirac, and both President Francois Mitterrand and especially his wife Danielle dearly wished to have him set free, all for their own reasons. An acquaintance, a Mr Ollivier, had access to the Chirac government, and by way of this avenue we planned to propose that we assist them in trying to secure Albertini's release if they could arrange for Wynand du Toit's return.

There were two problems that would have to be resolved, however. Firstly, Neil van Heerden wanted to persuade President Lennox Sebe of Ciskei to free Albertini in an attempt to facilitate the acceptance of the accreditation of my namesake, Mr Hennie Geldenhuys, as the new South African ambassador to France.

The second problem became apparent as we discussed the matter over dinner with Mr Ollivier at his apartment in the 16th Arrondissement, and it was clear that approaching President Sebe would be the lesser of the two. Mr Ollivier was co-operative and enthusiastic when I explained our concept, but he noted that for him the difficulty would be approaching the Angolans without creating the impression that he was blatantly interfering in their domestic affairs.

Fortunately for us there were some favourable factors. Angola's President José Eduardo dos Santos planned to visit France towards the end of September 1987, so he would be keen to create a favourable climate for his visit. The government of the Netherlands had also brought pressure to bear on Luanda as the release of Wynand du Toit might mean the freeing of their national, Klaas de Jonge, who was being detained in South Africa – in fact, this was already under discussion by our Department of Foreign Affairs and the Dutch government.

I asked Ollivier if he could not present the case along these lines: he did not want to interfere in Angola's domestic affairs, but would like to discuss a French concern. The detention of Albertini was a matter of great importance to the French, and it should not be taken amiss that he wished to explore all avenues to get Albertini back. South Africa was of no concern to him, but if the release of Wynand du Toit could assist him in solving a French problem, he had to try all the options. From his point of view Albertini was all that mattered, and he would appreciate Angola's assistance.

I got the impression that he found my approach to be quite reasonable. And we enjoyed the dinner. That is how these things work in almost all cases: if you want to talk business, you arrange a meal.

We agreed on a follow-up meeting over breakfast the next morning, also at Ollivier's apartment. By that time I had telephoned Neil van Heerden from my hotel, reported back and asked if he could temporarily shelve his negotiations over Albertini to give me an opportunity to fully exploit the possibilities of reciprocal action by the French government. He agreed, and so at our second meeting I could confirm to Ollivier that South Africa would undertake to go all out to have Albertini freed if they would do the same in respect of Du Toit.

On a happy Friday, two days later, I was able to instruct Neels van Tonder to give a categorical assurance to Mr Roussin, Chirac's Chef de Cabinet, that Albertini would be set free if Du Toit was released as well.

It would take a long time and many discussions before this story was concluded, so in the meantime we went back to Pretoria ... and back to war.

CHAPTER 15

TWELVE MONTHS THAT TRANSFORMED A CONTINENT

Cuito Cuanavale – the myth

Five decades had passed since the first day I had opened my eyes. More than three of them had been spent in the Defence Force, and I had seen people and trends come and go. Dances like the Charleston and jazz music were before my time; so were the crooners and ballroom dancing my mother used to reminisce about. I came into this world in the swing era. Not that Kroonstad was what one would call a swinging town, but Cole Porter's 'Anything Goes' was the musical of the decade.

I went through World War II listening to the radio, and apart from the propaganda broadcasts there was Vera Lynn's 'I'll pray for you', and in South Africa a little girl named Eve Boswell, who was later to become world famous, comforted our ailing soldiers with 'I'll get by'. The Germans and English quarrelled over the rightful ownership of Lale Andersen's version of 'Lili Marlene'. But at all times Glen Miller stayed 'In the Mood'.

After the war, bikinis started decorating the beaches, while the juke-boxes began to shake, rattle and roll as Bill Haley and his Comets blasted out 'Rock Around the Clock'. And so on. But there were also people like Beniamino Gigli singing 'O Sole Mio'.

In the mid-1950s came the Teddy Boys, with their long, oily hair combed back into 'ducktails' (in South Africa the Teddy Boy clothes didn't really catch on, but the ducktails did, and so did sharp-pointed shoes). Everybody wiggled inside hula-hoops and women wore pony-tails. Then blue jeans and polo-neck shirts filled shop windows. The 1950s ended with women wearing the voluminous 'sack dress'.

When Mary Quant made her appearance in 1960 everybody started wearing what they liked; an approach that went well with the mania for dancing the Twist (personally, though, I stuck to flannels conserva-tive, blazers gentleman and ties sober). Twiggy was the rage. The most attractive style of them all – the mini – hit the fashion stage in 1965, but fashion reached an all-time low towards the end of the 1960s with unisex clothes.

The decade belonged to the Beatles, who inspired men to wear even longer hair, but it was James Bond who thrilled women with *Dr No* and *From Russia with Love.* John Kennedy told Germans, sincerely but incor-rectly: 'Ich bin ein Berliner', while Cliff Richard sang 'Thirty Days', which would later become 'Forty days' here in South Africa as national service and border duty took hold.

During the 1970s Simon and Garfunkel, Elton John and Kenny Rogers appeared on the scene. Everybody danced disco. At the home bases in South West I listened to Neil Diamond's 'What a Beautiful Noise'.

And so on. But there were also people such as Luciano Pavarotti ... People, fashions and styles came and went. The era of the old guard came to an end, and we watched them fade away: de Gaulle, Franco, Salazar, Meir, Adenauer, D F Malan. Others took over from them, and in turn handed over (voluntarily or otherwise) to yet another genera-tion of leaders, who were often no better than their predecessors, so that new dictators and one-party states arose. Then newer rising stars took over from *them.*

The colonies and possessions of the Third World – particularly in Africa – became independent. Small wars, cold and hot, broke out and then subsided in due course. It was peaceful co-existence and *détente* of a sort, and somehow the world survived

There was no lack of crises. The Yom Kippur War came ... and went. So did other crises. South Africa became ever more isolated from the rest of the world, and reacted by turning to its own resources, with considerable success.

Prime Minister Margaret Thatcher and President Ronald Reagan appeared on the international front, while increasingly geriatric Soviet leaders followed each other in quick succession, until a comparative youngster named Mikhail Gorbachev took the reins.

At this time there was an event which would change the course of southern African history, an event whose reverberations would echo in Moscow, Washington, Havana, Pretoria and in the assembly halls of the UN in New York: the fighting in Angola in 1987 and 1988.

We called it Operation Modulêr, which then became Operation Hooper and finally Operation Packer. In fact, however, these names were misleading, because they did not in the least signify strategic or tactical phases of the 1987-1988 fighting. They were allocated merely to indicate three main periods in which units and personnel were mobilised for operational duty and then demobilised again. Some of them were involved only in the first part (Modulêr), others only in the second (Operation Hooper) and so on. Other than that, the code names had no significance.

Actual operational phases overlapped these periods rather than coincided with them, so that commentators who later analysed the campaign's three 'duty roster shifts' ran the risk of coming to false conclusions. But for me and others, including the Air Force and the officers, non-commissioned officers and troops who were not relieved according to these time schedules, it was one on-going campaign.

I conferred regularly with commanders and senior officers in the field during this time; such discussions usually took place after they had briefed me on the course of operations in the preceding period, what the current situation was and what they were planning for the future. I also addressed the troops when outgoing units were relieved by fresh troops or demobilised.

On these occasions, towards the end of the campaign and during the period immediately thereafter, I committed myself to a firm promise.

But one can only comprehend the full meaning of the promise once I have told the story of the war:

South Africa had its own interests to defend. A major world power from Eastern Europe, the USSR, and a Marxist dictatorship from the Caribbean sphere, Cuba, got themselves heavily involved in southern Africa. These foreign powers joined forces with the MPLA, on a scale never seen before, to destroy UNITA in the Jamba area, once and for all.

If they succeeded and managed to establish military control in the south of Angola our operations against PLAN would once again extend from the mouth of the Cunene River in Kaokoland in the west to Mpalela Island in the eastern Caprivi in the east. The positive results for which we had sacrificed men and money for 14 years would be undone, and the peace which South Africa had maintained in South West would be seriously threatened once again.

There were also MK camps in northern Angola. They would probably be transferred to the south-east of Angola if Cuban/MPLA forces controlled the area. That would bring them right up to where the borders of Zambia, Zimbabwe and Botswana converged, and might create a new infiltration route to South African soil.

South Africa also shared certain interests with UNITA. That was no secret – the Minister of Defence made this clear in Parliament on more than one occasion. And so South Africa became involved. We undertook to supply armaments and troops to put UNITA in a more equable position *vis-à-vis* the advancing forces of the Cuban/FAPLA alliance. Savimbi did not have an air force, or weapons systems and troops able to effectively resist tanks, other types of sophisticated armoured vehicles and artillery which included missiles.

I will describe the campaign briefly, concentrating on my own observations, feelings and perceptions. Let me say immediately that because I was not a neutral spectator, observing from the sidelines, I can only tell the story from the point of view of South Africa's participation and my own involvement.

When you have read the whole story right up to the end of the campaign you might ask: What about Savimbi and UNITA? What did they do? The answer is: a lot. One hell of a lot. But naturally I am not writing about this war as seen from Savimbi's point of view, and so I shall not go out of my way to highlight his actions. This being so, please bear in mind that where I use terms like 'ours', 'the RSA', 'the SA Defence Force' and 'our commanders and troops', I am talking about the RSA/ UNITA alliance, and everything I say must be interpreted in that light. Because the fact is that the top leader group of UNITA and its troops achieved successes that will one day probably figure prominently in military annals.

The Russian-Cuban-FAPLA alliance launched offensives from two different directions. The offensive on the northern front started from Lucusse during April 1987, and was meant to divert attention from the build-up of forces on the Cuito Cuanavale front, which was supposed to have been happening unseen. The Cuito Cuanavale offensive was to be the main thrust aimed at conquering UNITA's general base area and headquarters' complex at Jamba (See Map 3).

UNITA fiercely countered the northern offensive with mobile, heavily armed regular forces, semi-regulars and guerrillas. They tackled their enemy from the front, from the flanks and from the rear, disrupted his supply lines and beat him off. After that the Cuban-supported FAPLA formations retreated to Lucusse and ceased to be a factor.

I say little about these operations because the South African participation was very small, amounting to no more than some preparation and training during 1986, in anticipation of the offensive, and the brief assistance of two medical orderlies. UNITA defeated the offensive in a solo effort and with few losses.

The real South African involvement was in the southern offensive, the main advance of which was along the general line of approach from Cuito Cuanavale to Jamba. The Cuban-FAPLA forces moved their 25 Brigade into the area in advance of the fighting, but the attack on Savimbi only started in all seriousness on 14 August 1987, when their 16, 21, 47 and 59 Brigades set off in the direction of Mavinga.

Mavinga was the stepping-stone to their ultimate target, Jamba, and to get to it they had to cross over to the southern bank of the Lomba River. This they planned to do by splitting the alliance forces in two, 16 and 21 Brigades taking one route and 47 and 59 Brigades another.

At this stage the South African Army's presence was quite small – one battery of 127 mm multiple rocket launchers, or MRLs, and one battery of 120 mm mortars, each with an infantry company drawn from

32 Battalion for its protection. There were also special-forces elements for specific tasks such as tank-hunting, clandestine reconnaissance and artillery fire control.

These elements, collectively called 20 Brigade, were commanded by Colonel Jock Harris until Colonel Deon Ferreira succeeded him on 5 September. His next higher commander was yet another Free Stater, Major-General Willie Meyer, who had recently taken over from Georg Meiring as GOC South West Africa.

The FAPLA advance was a very slow one, averaging about 4 km a day. They avoided the open veld, preferring to move through the thick bush, protecting their movement with armoured fighting vehicles and anti-aircraft gun batteries and ground-to-air missile systems which included Soviet SA-8s. Every day around 16h00 they dug themselves into well-camouflaged positions.

During August we decided to increase our support to Savimbi, so we reinforced 20 Brigade with 61 Mechanised Battalion Group, two infantry companies of 101 Battalion in Casspir armoured personnel carriers and one battery each of towed G5 155 mm field artillery pieces and 120 mm mortars. UNITA provided the overwhelming majority of the infantry assets, then and later; the total RSA/SWA contingent never exceeded 3 000 men.

During early September a team of our Special Forces partially destroyed a bridge over the Cuito River behind the forward enemy brigades in the sort of clandestine operation reminiscent of the daring deeds one sees in film and TV dramas.

Aided by UNITA guides, the 'Recces' cat-footed through and around the enemy troops until they reached the river, placed their charges behind the FAPLA positions and then withdrew by keeping on moving down-stream. During this phase one of them was attacked by a crocodile, which he fought off with his knife – if I remember correctly he stabbed it in the eye – although he had some permanent scars as a reminder (later I got hold of the knife, had it mounted on a plaque adorned with an appropriate engraving and presented it to him).

As a result of this operation the alliance forces were forced to use helicopters and later pontoons to ferry their supplies across to the eastern bank, causing a disruption of their logistical arrangements which later proved of benefit to us.

The destruction of the bridge was an example of the policy of aggressive defence the UNITA and RSA forces applied, successfully attacking the enemy's offensive actions, which resulted in some tough fighting at times.

During the end of August and early September 47 Brigade and a tactical group moved westwards around the source of the Lomba River and then turned east, in the general direction of Mavinga, but on 4 September we stopped these manoeuvres in their tracks, mainly by using the G5s and MRLS.

Then, just as our forces were fighting the Cuban/FAPLA advance to a standstill at the Lomba River, we found ourselves involved in the final act of a previous drama: two years after being captured in Cabinda, Major Wynand du Toit was set free in Maputo on 7 September, in exchange for 133 Angolan soldiers Savimbi had released and two Dutch citizens charged with terrorism in South Africa, Klaas de Jonge and Helena Pastoors.

The exchange was an extensive undertaking. There were small wheels within big wheels, and riddles that were solved by means of mirrors. It had become bigger and more complex than expected, and abounded with intrigues. A lot of people worked hard, cleverly and together to set it all up; I played only a very small part – a key mover was General Neels van Tonder.

It played out in a strangely unreal world, far removed from the dusty, lethal realities of the bushveld battlegrounds. Over *nouvelle cuisine* in Paris, the city of culture, you discussed the fate of people from different parts of the world who, for a variety of reasons, found themselves in detention in different parts of southern Africa. Then you went to Pretoria, where the jacaranda trees were showering the city with purple blossoms, and struggled with the usual round of annual transfers and promotions in the Defence Force, stock-taking and colour parades. After that you rushed off to the bush to Jamba to talk with your ally, the leader of a resistance movement, eat *caldeirada de cabrito com chindungo*, aka ragout of goat, flavoured with chillies, and swipe at the ever-present flies. Meanwhile your ally's opponent, President Eduardo dos Santos, made his personal Gulfstream aircraft available to ferry your long-captive fellow officer back to his own country. And at home wasps killed two of your parakeets … and Northern Transvaal won the Currie Cup at Ellis Park.

* * *

Things were simpler at the battlefront in the south-east of Angola, where the FAPLA forces were still making repeated attempts to cross the Lomba River. The first really purposeful one was launched by their 21 Brigade on 10 September, but it was beaten off with tremendous losses in the FAPLA ranks, one whole battalion being destroyed.

I remember two particularly interesting events during these battles. Late one afternoon two MIGs released two bombs over the area. They exploded at a considerable height above the ground, a thick column of smoke slowly sinking down to the ground afterwards. Concerned that it might be chemical dust, Deon Ferreira ordered his troops to evacuate the area and then sent in a team to test for chemical agents. The result was negative, and so he sent his troops back to their positions – just in time to repel 21 Brigade's determined attempt to cross the Lomba at first light the following day.

We saw it as an early indication of a possible use of chemical weapons, which we knew they had (and some time later UNITA troops were, in fact, treated for disorders caused by chemical poisoning).

Secondly, our new ZT-3 anti-tank missile was successfully used for the first time in operations by Major Hannes Nortmann and his men in beating off 21 Brigade; this sort of operation led to South African armaments gaining an international reputation for being reliable because they had been proven in battle, not just on some test terrain.

The second major FAPLA attempt to cross the Lomba took place on 12 and 13 September, with elements of 59 Brigade getting over and joining hands with 47 Brigade. After being attacked on 13 September and suffering very heavy losses, the remainder of 59 Brigade retreated to the north of the Lomba, while elements of 47 Brigade and the tactical group which had been involved withdrew westwards. Our total losses were two Casspir APCs and a Ratel armoured fighting vehicle.

From 14 to 23 September 21 Brigade made daily attempts to cross the Lomba. Each time it was driven back with heavy losses. In the beginning I could not understand how they could even think of trying to cross the river time after time in the same fashion and at the same place; the attacks looked like suicide missions. But there was a reason, as I shall relate in the next chapter.

Amid this succession of river-crossing attempts Deon found himself playing host to a batch of cabinet ministers who came to visit him at his tactical headquarters, among them F W de Klerk, Pik Botha, Magnus Malan and Barend du Plessis, then Minister of Finance; with them came Mr Dave Steward, the DG of the Bureau of Information.

They gathered round Deon's radio to listen in on one of 21 Brigade's dramatic assaults on the Lomba, a particularly interested listener being the flamboyant Pik Botha, who was intensely involved as always (earlier in the afternoon he had insisted on being allowed to try on an anti-chemical warfare suit).

But it was Barend du Plessis who caught my eye that day. Shortly after their arrival, a couple of Deon's men went to show the visitors where they were to sleep – and, what was even more important, the location of each one's fox-hole, in case of a possible bombardment of the headquarters.

Deon's men showed Barend du Plessis not one but three fox-holes. The first was a shallow little depression that was barely knee-deep, and the second a little more substantial, about hip-deep. The third was a proper foxhole, deep enough to feel quite safe in. He was told to choose one. But there was method behind the apparent generosity of his guides, as he discovered when he noticed that behind each fox-hole was a stick with a little home-made sign on it.

The shallow hole's sign bore the number 10, the hip-deep hole a 20 and the third a 30. Understandably puzzled, he asked them what the numbers signified. Easy, they said with mock gravity. If the Minister gave the Defence Force an increase of 10 per cent he could use the shallow hole, or he could have the second one if he made it 20, and ...

The minister chose the 30 per cent hole, but the Defence Force was still waiting for its increase when I retired in 1990.

Dave Steward didn't say anything at the time, but a few weeks later, before a meeting of the State Security Council, he recalled the visit and told me: 'What impressed me most was this: Colonel Ferreira right in the middle of a serious battle and you, the Chief of the Defence Force, are sitting 50 metres away. And what do you do? You leave it all in the hands of the colonel and you talk to the visitors. Your command culture interests me. It was an experience' (of course, neither Deon Ferreira nor I were doing the fighting).

The most decisive battle of the whole campaign took place on 3 October 1987, and later Deon told me:

Although I didn't physically take part in the battle, it was the best conventional attack in which I was ever involved ... It was an attack on the whole of 47 Brigade and the tactical group. They had air support, fire support from 59 Brigade and tanks. We didn't have close air support and no tanks, and they outnumbered us four to one.

I must take my hat off to Commandant Bok Smit and his men of 61 Mech Battalion who handled the attack, along with the gunners with their G5s and MRLS.

Our better equipment and soldiers apart, it was our timing that made the day. I have never seen such timing before: 47 Brigade wanted to cross the Lomba from south to north to join up with 59 Brigade. We knew it beforehand and engaged them on the way. We caught them in the open. They were totally destroyed – by any definition.

That was the turning point. Two hundred and fifty FAPLA soldiers were killed, and it was the end of 47 Brigade. Among the large number of weapons and equipment destroyed or captured were 18 tanks, three anti-aircraft batteries, two SAM-8 anti-aircraft missile systems of three vehicles each) and two SAM-9 systems, in addition to a variety of armoured personnel carriers and reconnaissance vehicles, infantry fighting vehicles, artillery field guns, a Flatface radar vehicle and 120 logistic vehicles.

It was the first time that a SAM-8 missile system had fallen into the hands of anybody not supposed to have it, and although it did not receive much media coverage, it was big news in military circles around the world.

Let us put this stage of the story in a broader perspective. A multitude of countries around the world suffered from ethnic, religious and ideological friction, terrorism and different forms of internal conflict. Emergency regulations were being applied in about 20 states (in many countries this was not necessary, as their normal laws were stringent enough). In *Beeld* of 30 October 1987, no less than 26 countries where war was being waged in some form or other were listed: Chad, Ethiopia, Nigeria, Sudan, Somalia, South West Africa, Uganda, Zimbabwe, Corsica, Cyprus, Northern Ireland, Spain, Yugoslavia, Burma, India,

Iran, Iraq, Israel, Lebanon, New Caledonia, Pakistan, the Philippines, Sri Lanka, Syria and Turkey.

And, of course, Angola, where the Cuban-FAPLA forces abandoned their offensive in what the Portuguese had dubbed the *terras do fim do mundo,* the 'lands at the end of the earth'. All their brigades, minus hundreds of fallen troops and huge quantities of destroyed war material, started a long but generally orderly withdrawal which eventually brought them back to near their original starting-point. We left them to their own devices and used the opportunity to regroup, replace troops and service our equipment.

From this point onwards I had only one consideration to deal with. We had completed our mission by totally breaking up the Cuban-FAPLA offensive, but we could not immediately leave the battle area, because in the short term we had to ensure that the new situation we had created would not be undone. This meant that we had to consolidate our gains and prevent the enemy force from regrouping and resuming its offensive.

But we could not assume permanent responsibility for maintaining the advantageous situation that we had established. This meant that we had to leave behind a scheme of things which would allow UNITA itself to take care of its defence in the event of another 'annual offensive', and that was what we intended to do. No more, no less.

This was classic doctrine. After a successful battle, you consolidate; you secure the captured area and clear it up to a determined 'line of exploitation'; you take the necessary precautions to deal with a possible counter-offensive, and if you leave the area, other forces take over from you to assume responsibility for its defence. In this case the line of exploitation was the Cuito River, and the force earmarked to take over the responsibility for the defence of the area was UNITA.

During this campaign, as before, we had to take an established pattern into consideration. In every cross-border operation we planned to accomplish our aims as quickly as possible, because there was always the danger that political pressure – by which I mean resolutions of the UN Security Council and international conferences – might bring the operation to a halt before we could achieve what we had set out to do.

Sometimes it also happened, however, as in the cases of Operations Sceptic, Protea and Askari, that the political pressure did not materialise as quickly as we had assumed during the planning stage. We then had more time than we had anticipated, and since we had no permanent presence in Angola we had to use this 'borrowed time' as best we could to create the most advantageous security situation possible while we were still there.

Political events can be unpredictable, but the indications were that we were already on borrowed time – or 'injury time', as we would say in rugby – and there was no way of knowing how much more of it we had left. What we *did* know was that if we wanted to leave behind a long-term favourable situation we would have to pursue the enemy up to the Cuito River, then reinforce it as an obstacle on which UNITA could base its future defence of the area. For the defence to be successful, we – and Savimbi – regarded it as imperative that a UNITA tank force be established by using the serviceable enemy tanks captured from FAPLA. And we had to do all this during the consolidation phase, which was of unknown duration.

During this phase the South African forces were reinforced with elements of 4 SA Infantry Battalion, extra 127 mm MRLs, a number of G6 self-propelled medium guns and a squadron of Olifant tanks – the first time since World War II that we had deployed tanks on operations.

Deon undertook some other operations while waiting for his new troops and equipment to arrive, among other things subjecting the Cuito Cuanavale airfield to a ceaseless bombardment by his G5s, which by mid-October had left it completely unusable. It was a hard blow for the Soviet, Cuban and Angolan pilots, because it meant that they now had to operate from Menongue, further to the west, and consequently could not cause as much damage as they would have liked. In the end they flew more than 1 000 sorties over the South Africans at this stage but hit only one G5, one supply vehicle and one water-bowser, and caused no loss of life.

It was an open secret that South Africa was involved in something with UNITA in the south-east of Angola, but we still could not yet release information to the press about the operation. This caused some embarrassment, because on 2 November I had to announce that 11 SADF and SWATF soldiers had been killed in encounters with PLAN three days earlier. Few people believed me, because the suspicion that the casualties actually had something to do with the UNITA-South African-Cuban-

FAPLA fighting was too strong. But I told the truth. There had been an unrelated operation initiated by the SWATF against a PLAN base just across the border from central Ovamboland, hundreds of kilometres west of the Cuito River; all 11 of our dead had been killed by a single mortar bomb, the insurgent death-toll being 150.

As soon as our fresh troops were in position they started to drive back the Cuban and FAPLA forces which were still east of Cuito. Successful battles took place on 9, 11, 13 and 17 November in which a total of 525 enemy troops were killed in action and 33 tanks were destroyed or captured. The result was that all the elements east of the Cuito that had taken part in the thrust towards Jamba had been driven back to within 24 km east of the river.

By mid-December FAPLA was still receiving reinforcements, including Cuban soldiers and T-62 tanks, which were deployed in the general Cuito Cuanavale area and thus also came under the fire of the G5s. The South African gunners with their towed G5s and later their self-propelled G6s were a decisive factor throughout the campaign.

UNITA provided the foot and motorised infantry for most of the operations and also protected our artillery positions and the objectives we had seized, while their protection of our supply lines was likewise of the utmost importance. UNITA also kept the enemy aircraft at a safe altitude with their Stinger missiles, which they had obtained from the Americans after the Clark Amendment had been repealed.

I announced on 5 December 1987 that we would start to withdraw our troops because they had completed their tasks, stressing that it would be a tactical withdrawal executed under operational conditions, and that further fighting could still take place. The troops scheduled to withdraw first were the elements that were not needed for safeguarding the area or assisting to form UNITA's tank force.

This was followed by another period of regrouping and equipment maintenance, because the national servicemen who were due to be discharged on 15 December 1987 had to be replaced. Towards the end of the month a UNITA force took Munhango, Savimbi's birthplace, using four T-55 tanks which had earlier been seized from the enemy.

The campaign entered its last phase with successful attacks by the UNITA/RSA forces on 13 January, 14 and 25 February 1988, which drove all the remaining Cuban-FAPLA forces over to the western side

Top and above: A captured Russian tank, the metal of which was melted down to make the South Africa Medal. PHOTO: *Paratus*

Left: Sappers (South African Engineer Corps) 'swept' 438 000 kilometres. Sweeping involves making a road or route safe by walking it on foot with a mine detector and investigating every alarm signal it sends out by hand.
PHOTO: *Stefan Sonderling*

Right: Lifting landmines by hand was painstaking and nerve-racking work.

Below: Members of Tiffies (Technical Service Corps).

Bottom left: Caprivi, characterised by baobab trees. PHOTO: *Stefan Sonderling*

Bottom right: The Puma – the workhorse of the airforce – over Ovamboland. PHOTO: *Stefan Sonderling*

Left: Members of Swaspes (South West Africa Specialist Unit) utilised dogs, horses and motorcycles to track down the enemy.

Below left: Ovambo and its Makalani palms. PHOTO: *Stefan Sonderling*

Below right: Kavango, inhabited by fish eagles and crocodiles. PHOTO: *Stefan Sonderling*

aokaland, haracterised by iffs, ravines and the ınene River.
ιOTO: *Stefan Sonderling*

KAOKOLAND   Ruacana   Oshakati   OVAMBO   Rundu   Mukwe   CAPRIVI   Katima Mulilo

KAVANGO

Sesfontein

Top: Operation Protea troops versus Xangongo, the province's football club champions.
PHOTO: *Sunday Times*

Below: Members of Swaspes with tracker dogs taking part in a parade in Windhoek in 1980.
PHOTO: *Stefan Sonderling*

Left, middle left and bottom: Anti-aircraft artillery, heavy military vehicles and tanks captured during Operation Protea in 1981 at Ondangwa.

PHOTO: *Gert van Niekerk* and *Citizen*

Below right: The Soviet Union SAM8 missile system captured by the South Africans – the first, if not the only time in the world.

PHOTO: *SA Defence Force*

Above: Martin Geldenhuys becomes Second-lieutenant (1983). PHOTO: *The Argus*

Below (l-r): Derek Auret of the Department of Foreign Affairs, Brigadier Neels van Tonder
Brigadier Johann Sonnekus and General Jannie Geldenhuys playing bridge on the pyramids
during international peace negotiations in Cairo in June 1988.

Above: General Jannie Geldenhuys, Heliopolous Cemetery, Cairo, visits the grave of a deceased relative.
PHOTO: *The Argus*

Below left: Jannie Geldenhuys and Chester Crocker, the US Assistant Secretary of State for Africa and
the chief facilitator of the international negotiations related to UN Resolution 435.

Below middle and right: Doug Watson (left), South African bowls champion bears a striking resemblance
Jannie Geldenhuys. PHOTO: *Beeld*

Top: Neil van Heerden, gifted diplomat and Pretoria's chief negotiator in Namibia's independence.

Below (l-r): Dr Niël Barnard, Jannie Geldenhuys, General Magnus Malan, Minister Pik Botha, Neil van Heerden and Derek Auret at the international negotiations in Cairo. PHOTO: *The Argus*

Top (*l-r*): Cuban Ulises Rosales Del Toro, Angolan Ndalu and Jannie Geldenhuys, Joint Commission, Havana.

Far left (*l-r*): Senor Carlos Aldana Escalante, General Prem Chand and General Ndalu.

Left: General Arnaldo Óchoa Sanchez – Fidel Castro's 'fall-guy'.

Below: General Geldenhuys's 'forty-days' party organised by his drivers, 1985-1990. PHOTO: *Paratus*

Top: Joint Commission, Havana. Mediator Chester Crocker (*left*) and host Fidel Castro (*right*).

Above left: 'Oom Kaspaas' Jorge Risquet, leader of the Cuban delegation's negotiating team. PHOTO: *The Argu*

Above right: FW de Klerk congratulating Jannie Geldenhuys on his retirement.

Opposite: The author with (*l-r*) 1 SSB Warrant Officers Jan O'Niel , 'Jan' Holliday and MA 'Piet' Booysens.

Top: Martin, Mariana, Jannie, Marié, Annamarié and Bruwer Geldenhuys. PHOTO:*Paratus*

Below: 1 SDB colour party. PHOTO: *Paratus*

of the Cuito, the only exception being a FAPLA presence in the Tumpo area, immediately east of the river.

At this point the setting of my story changes to a completely different scene. On Wednesday, 10 February, Corporal Arrie Jacobs and I were listening to the morning radio news while driving through Cape Town's suburbs from Wynberg to my office in the HF Verwoerd Building opposite Parliament, and heard that there had been a *coup d'état* in the Bophuthatswana homeland, and that President Lucas Mangope had been detained.

In the underground parking area I entered the lift and headed upwards to the Ministry of Defence on the 14th floor. There was another passenger in the lift, and at the third floor a third man entered. My two fellow passengers happened to know one another, and they exchanged the usual small talk as the lift bore us upwards.

One asked: 'How are you?'

The other replied: 'Ag, man, mercifully spared to keep on suffering!'

It made me think of something similar my daughter Annamarié had told me. In her version the answer was: 'By this time of day I've already come to accept my fate.' In this case 'this time of day' was nine o'clock in the morning.

When the doors of the lift opened at the 14th floor the oppressive atmosphere lifted immediately. The minister (P W Botha) wanted to see me straight away, and from that moment onwards I was in and out of his and Mr Pik Botha's offices all day.

What was evident – and, obviously, important – was that nobody actually knew what was really going on in Bophutatswana. So I did the customary thing and issued a warning order, setting a sequence of events in motion which soon brought an end to the attempted coup.

I flew to Air Force Base Waterkloof, where other SADF officers and I met with our opposite numbers from the South African Police, National Intelligence, Foreign Affairs and other interested parties. We exchanged information and began considering options and formulating plans. If we could reach the South African ambassador in Bophutatswana we would probably be able to find out exactly what was happening. Or we could try to contact the rebel leader and start a discussion …

In the end it was agreed that the best thing would be to go and look for ourselves. Lieutenant-General Johan van der Merwe of the SAP, Mr Derek Auret of Foreign Affairs, a few staff officers and I took off in a Puma helicopter and headed for Zeerust, where we exchanged information with our senior local representatives.

That done, we took off again and landed once more some distance beyond Zeerust at the command element of troops under Brigadier Du Preez Coetzee of Potchefstroom, who was heading for the Bophutatswana capital of Mmabatho. Again we pooled information and discussed possible courses of action before flying on.

When we reached Mmabatho we orbited it, decided it looked safe to land and came to earth at the residence of the South African ambassador, who put us fully into the picture; as he finished the first troops arrived, and we could start restoring order. Our first action was to free President Mangope from captivity at the sports stadium, which the troops accomplished by simply forcing the gates open and entering. Mr Mangope was freed unharmed, although a fellow detainee, Brigadier Jack Turner, the Chief of the Bophuthatswana Defence Force, had a wound in the foot.

The situation was a little confusing. People of all kinds were jumbled up together. By now the police task force had arrived, as well as members of the press, and supposedly rebel sentries were literally standing about among our Ratel AFVs and Eland armoured cars, whose crews paid them no heed.

Being still persuaded that it might be useful to make contact with the rebel leader, whoever he might be, I took a chance and walked up to one of the rebels to ask him where his commander was. No luck – he turned out to be as bewildered by events as Old Smokey, whom Chris Serfontein had captured during Operation Sceptic, only less dangerous. I advised him to hand his rifle to me, and helped him to make up his mind by removing the weapon from his shoulder in mid-conversation.

With President Mangope and Brigadier Turner safe, the police could set about clearing rebel elements out of the important buildings. It was a speedy and peaceful process, since the rebels had rapidly lost their enthusiasm when they spotted the SADF's Elands and Ratels.

Everybody then returned to the ambassador's residence, where PW and Pik Botha had now arrived, accompanied by General Malan. Derek Auret reported to the two ministers, Mr Mangope made a speech and P W Botha replied. Then drinks and snacks were served, and that was the end of the coup. The people who had come with me from Pretoria went back there, I got a lift back to Cape Town in the President's aircraft, and by 01h30 I was in bed.

Later that morning, as I travelled to my office once more, I thought to myself: *Just let me hear somebody else say 'mercifully spared to keep on suffering' today.*

* * *

In the meantime the war in Angola went on. I confirmed in a press statement on 20 February that a tactical withdrawal was in progress, but explained once again that it was being done under operational conditions and was therefore proceeding slowly.

As we had expected, the international politicking over Angola had now begun to generate momentum. Both Chester Crocker and Pik Botha exploited their opportunities, and in March 1988 they agreed on a package for a new peace initiative for the region.

From this we deduced that the time available to us for operational actions was nearly at an end, but that it would also be advisable to maintain a military presence east of the Cuito for the time being. There was still a possibility, however small, that the Cuban/FAPLA forces would grab one last chance to break out and improve their military position before the negotiations began. The Citizen Force 82 Brigade provided that presence.

The last battle took place at Tumpo on 23 March 1988 without changing the situation. FAPLA suffered considerable losses, but ours consisted only of three tanks which got stuck in a minefield. This much-trumpeted incident was FAPLA's sole 'success' of the war. But the fact remains that you can't score a try on your own half of the field!

On 30 April of 1988 a small combat group replaced 82 Brigade. Their task was to support the sappers who were still laying minefields on the opposite side of the crossing-points over the Cuito. In this fashion we continued to reduce our force levels to 1 500 or fewer sharp-end and support elements, to keep the occupied area safe together with UNITA. The existing FAPLA forces were concentrated at Cuito Cuanavale and Tumpo.

The results of the fighting between September 1987 and April 1988 were as follows:

Cuban-FAPLA forces (damage done by SADF and UNITA)		SA Defence Force (damage done by Cubans and FAPLA)	
Tanks	94	Tanks	3
Armoured troop and combat vehicles	100	Ratel infantry fighting vehicles	5
BM21/BM14 MRLs	34	Casspirs	3
D30/M-46 guns	9	Rinkhals	1
TMM mobile bridges	7	Withings	1
Logistic vehicles	389	Kwêvoel	1
Artillery, rocket and missile systems			15
Radars	5		
23 mm anti-aircraft guns	22		
MIG 21/23 combat aircraft	9	Mirage F1 fighter aircraft (one as a result of enemy action, one in an accident)	2
Bosbok light reconnaissance aircraft			
Helicopters	9		1

On the Cuban–FAPLA side 4 785 men were killed in action. This is a confirmed figure and does not include the deserters, the wounded and those who later died of wounds; the total figure was probably a few thousand more. On the South African side 31 men were killed in action and six more died of malaria. Once again, this is the real figure.

Many inferences can be drawn from this statistical 'scoreboard', but it does not tell of the friction behind the scenes which is unavoidable in any war. But the UNITA/RSA alliance functioned as well as could have been expected (and, in fact, better than expected). Tensions can arise between different elements of one force in peace-time and even more easily between allies in a war situation, but in this case it did not, although I showed signs of frustration which I regretted later on.

There was no doubt that we were working under time pressure. By now Mr PW Botha had already made serious requests on at least two occasions that we finish the job and get out of Angola. General Malan and I once had to go and see him in his office just before a meeting of the State Security Council, and on another occasion he stopped me in a corridor after an SSC meeting. This second time he was civil, but serious and firm, and when he had finished talking I had no doubt about what he did *not* want, which was a Vietnam situation. What this meant was that we had to accomplish our mission and then withdraw without further ado.

To put the discussion into perspective, I have to add that the perception existed that we had already successfully completed our mission. I can understand that, because we had indeed achieved our aim; but we still had to defend what we had achieved against possible follow-up attacks – and we had not yet progressed anywhere near to my expectations in establishing UNITA's tank force. On a few occasions I used harsh words about this which I later regretted.

Savimbi stayed calm, thanks to his deep insight, while I was in too much of a hurry. Looking back, I realise that I overlooked *friction de guerre*. As I said in the first chapter, everything in war is simple, but the simplest action is difficult to perform. To walk is simple; to walk in water is difficult.

An entrepreneur who wants to start a new business with a large number of heavy-duty vehicles will find it difficult to move his stock to his place of business, even in South Africa, and in addition we were fighting a war in the bush. How does one collect, in a short space of time, serviceable and semi-serviceable captured tanks scattered over an area consisting of thousands of square kilometres? There was no readily available tow-away service for tanks, even if such a thing existed, which it did not. This was the remote African bush, where there was no infrastructure; the Portuguese had not named it the 'land at the ends of the earth' for nothing. And how were we to find people in this totally undeveloped region with even the most basic aptitude for becoming tank drivers?

But I was being too impatient. Somehow it got done, and as you will see, the UNITA tanks later showed their worth.

*   *   *

At this stage it is necessary to look at the war at the ends of the earth in a wider context. There were, in fact, five 'wars' in progress: Operations Modulêr, Hooper and Packer; the propaganda war; the international diplomatic exchanges; the 'normal' war against PLAN and the UNITA–MPLA struggle in the rest of Angola.

The propaganda and international diplomatic encounters moved at such a hectic pace that it made one's head spin. For that reason I will give only a few flashes from which the reader can form a general impression of what was happening in these fields. First the propaganda:

- On 15 January 1988 the Angolan Minister of Defence alleged that 6 000 South African troops had attacked Cuito Cuanavale. The intention, according to him, was to capture Cuito Cuanavale to facilitate UNITA's penetration to the central highlands in order to prevent the reconstruction of the Benguela railway line.
- UNITA declared in Lisbon that it had encircled Cuito Cuanavale (it is possible that this statement resulted in some people thinking that the South Africans were making for Cuito Cuanavale).
- The official Angolan news agency, Angop, claimed on 22 January 1988 that FAPLA had shot down 40 SAAF aircraft.
- Two days later an Angolan spokesman, one Major Placido, said that there had been a concentrated South African attack on Cuito Cuanavale.
- President Dos Santos of Angola declared on 15 February that the South African forces in southern Angola had been increased during the previous three days by 6 000 troops.
- A few days later Angop announced that the South African troops now numbered 7 000.
- President Dos Santos added on 19 February that South Africa had lost 140 men, 6 aircraft, 47 tanks and various armoured cars during the previous 45 days.
- The Angolan Foreign Minister, Afonso von Dunem, declared on 17 April that more than 6 000 South African troops were preparing for another attack on Cuito Cuanavale. He said that they were only part of a larger South African force of 9 000 soldiers, 600 field guns, and 500 tanks and armoured cars which was deployed in Angola.

But the truth is:

- We did not attack Cuito Cuanavale. The central highlands and the Benguela railway line were not in our planning at any time whatever.
- We had deployed no more than 3 000 troops – not three times that number, as the Angolans claimed.
- We lost only the number of aircraft that I mentioned – not twelve times more, as claimed by Angola.
- The other allegations about our quantities of armament were likewise ridiculously out of proportion. Six hundred field guns!

How the Angolans could still think or claim as late as April 1988 that we wanted to attack Cuito Cuanavale is puzzling. It would have been practically impossible; it reminds me of a story that Lieutenant-Gen Jan van Loggerenberg, the Chief of the South African Air Force, once told me.

A motorist entered the town of Brits, if I remember correctly, and while trying to find the Post Office he accosted an old man in the street with 'Good morning, Oom.'

'Morning,' the oldster replied.

'Can you tell me how to get to the Post Office?' the motorist asked.

'All right, son, now you take this street and you cross the first robot. Then you cross the second robot, and at the third robot you turn this way, left. Then, when you get to the stream … no, that's wrong. Come back. Let's start at the beginning: You take this road and you cross the first robot, then you turn left at the second robot, and then when you get to the stream … No, that's wrong. Come back. Son, now you take this street, then you come to the first robot and you turn left, and then … uh … no, sonny boy, from this place where we are now, you can't get over the stream to get to the Post Office!'

We also had a stream to cross. A very big stream – the Cuito River. We lacked the wading capability of the Russian tanks, and we did not have the necessary bridges readily available. If we had wanted to reach Cuito Cuanavale during those last few weeks we would have had to position a sufficiently strong force west of the river ahead of time.

This was propaganda in action. In the same style, mentioning only a

few international political events, I will try to sketch a general idea of
the diplomatic activity:

- On 28 and 29 January 1988 Chester Crocker conferred with the
  Angolan government.
- Charles Redman, spokesman for the State Department, announced in Washington DC that Cuban and Angolan officials had
  affirmed for the first time that they had accepted the plan to with-
  draw all Cuban troops from Angola. George Schultz, the United
  States Minister of State, described it as an important development
  which held promise for a settlement in the region.
- Mr Pik Botha, the Minister of Foreign Affairs, was not very opti-
  mistic, but said on 11 February that South Africa would welcome
  progress made by Crocker on the deadlock.
- Afonso von Dunem stated on 14 February that the schedule for
  Cuban withdrawal would depend on whether the United States,
  South Africa and other countries would cease supporting UNITA.
- Pik Botha announced on 14 March, after having conferred with
  Chester Crocker in Geneva, that the Angolan government had ac-
  cepted in principle that a Cuban withdrawal from Angola should
  be linked to the independence of South West Africa (the South
  African government had always maintained that the SADF could
  not withdraw from South West Africa in accordance with UN
  Security Council Resolution 435 if the Cubans did not also leave
  Angola.)
- Boutros Boutros-Ghali, who became Secretary-General of the UN
  during the early 1990s, stated on 24 March that Dos Santos and
  Savimbi had declared themselves ready for personal discussions.

As I indicated earlier in this book, there are much fewer identifiable
dividing lines nowadays than before between phases of hostilities and
phases of diplomacy, between peace and war.

It was difficult to tell whether we had peace mixed with war, or war
mixed with peace. It was no problem to describe the war of 1987–
1988, as the hostilities were more prominent than the peace initiatives.
However, after November 1987, and especially during the first quarter of 1988, the peace efforts gathered so much momentum that they

often became more prominent than the war.

The focus started moving continually like a pendulum from war to peace and back again, and so I will describe it in that way.

War. From the battle of words I shall return to the 'land at the ends of the earth' to describe the conclusion of the battle of guns.

The war in the south-east of Angola had been decided. The offensive against Jamba had failed. The campaign did not end on a spectacular note; there was no final knock-out, just as the Gulf War did not end with a knock-out. But the drama of the conflict in Angola in terms of the Cuban and South African involvement had not yet ended. In fact, in western Angola a new drama was already building up.

Before telling that story, however, I expect that I had better give my answer to that frequently asked question: Who won the war over Jamba?

It is easy to answer this unnecessary question: We did – UNITA and South Africa – hands down. All the facts have now become available, and anyone claiming to speak with authority who gives a different judgement, does so with ulterior motives. The mission of the MPLA, Cubans and Russians was to capture Jamba. They did not. They never even reached Jamba. They did not even reach Mavinga or cross the Lomba River.

Our and UNITA's mission was to destroy the offensive against Jamba. We did just that – in fact, we did it *before* the attackers could even scale the first hurdle, the Lomba River. As a bonus we also pushed them back to west of the Cuito River, with the exception of one isolated spot at Tumpo, just east of the river.

This is the unquestionable truth.

After this the Soviets lost their appetite for the war in Angola. Only a few months later they told us that nobody could win it – the answer was negotiations. That showed that our long-standing conviction that the Soviets would have to abandon their military involvement in Angola sooner or later had begun to be proved true.

The Cubans were also fed up with the war. They told us that later. During 1975–1976 they had thought that they were going to Angola for a year or two. In 1988, 13 years later, they were still there, with no end in sight. The answer was ... negotiations.

The negotiations started in all seriousness, and on 22 December 1988 resulted in the signing of the now well-known tripartite agreement in New York. Our men had made it possible.

The agreement did not bring total peace to the region. The war between the Angolan government and UNITA continued unabated. Something still had to happen to force them to the conference table. And it duly happened. The MPLA's hard-liners wanted yet another try at conquering Jamba, so during March 1989 FAPLA launched six brigades in a new offensive aimed at Mavinga, this time without Cuban support.

They used the same routes and doctrines as during 1987 (this was nothing new – we had discovered many years earlier that Soviet-orientated forces used the same routes and tactics over and over again). They succeeded in crossing the Lomba and progressed till one brigade was less than seven km north of Mavinga. There they got bogged down, because UNITA now reaped the fruits of the preparations which had started as early as 1988. UNITA used its 23 captured T-54 and T-55 tanks with great success, and did it with absolutely no South African support, since by that time we had long since executed a formal and monitored withdrawal.

The UNITA forces cut FAPLA's supply lines to its forward troops and forced them to a standstill. They dug in and stayed in their trenches for 92 days, during each of which they were harassed by UNITA artillery bombardments. No back-up ever arrived, and on the 92nd day of this hell on earth they fled back to Cuito Cuanavale.

The brief high media profile of UNITA's successful solo defence, and the extensive high media profile of FAPLA's 92-day 'siege of Mavinga', brought the general reader and TV viewer under the impression that UNITA had been overrun. The media dust settled, and so UNITA's success passed quietly. But it had demonstrated in undeniable fashion that our long-term strategy for the 1987–1988 campaign – to enable UNITA to successfully defend the area without assistance – had worked as we had planned it.

FAPLA's failure caused even the MPLA hardliners to reconsider their position. Our long-held opinion that in time FAPLA would cancel its 'annual offensives' without reaching Jamba had also been proved correct.

The MPLA's failed attack on Mavinga was a major factor in bringing them and UNITA together round the conference table for serious negotiations. This resulted, two years later, in the signing of an agreement on 31 May 1991 at Estoril in Portugal. In the meantime the Angolans and especially the Cubans still continued a sustained and large-scale propaganda campaign to the effect that they had humbled the South Africans at Cuito Cuanavale.

Not everybody fell for the Cuban propaganda. Sharp and knowledgeable observers of the war knew better. For example, I had a talk once with some overseas generals, and one of them remarked that it was very clear that the Marxist alliance had lost, because the Cubans were bragging too long and too loudly that they had won. 'To quote Shakespeare,' he said, 'it is a matter of "the lady doth protest too much, methinks".'

Even so, many people believed the Cuban propaganda. The same thing happened with the allies' war against Iraq. In fact, the Gulf War serves as a very good and recent example as to how perceptions are formed and how people can argue over who won or lost a war.

We all saw Iraq biting the dust in no uncertain terms. But immediately after the cessation of hostilities the media carried reports of statements by Saddam Hussein and others that Iraq had won the war. Amazing. During TV interviews Iraqis very sincerely said they thought Iraq had won – although, thanks to the overwhelming international support for the allies and the domination of the Western media through CNN and the likes, this misperception was corrected within two days.

After that, however, certain other perceptions continued to persist, especially in some parts of the Arab world where impressions are not formed exclusively by the Western media. This was the sort of argument that persisted into the 1990s:

First person: 'Saddam Hussein lost the war in cowardly fashion. He didn't offer any visible resistance to the missile and air attacks. Before the land war really got going and before they really started to hurt one another, he chucked in the towel and yielded faint-heartedly without firing a shot.'

Second person: 'The mightiest power in the world, the USA, assembled allies from the other big powers in the world, the United Kingdom and France, with the best armaments they had at their disposal; it mobilised others – 27 countries in all; it secured the financial support of West Germany and Japan. And all of them together took the field against one single country, Saddam Hussein's Iraq – and they couldn't destroy him! He still rules Iraq, and his defence force is still intact. Saddam won.'

This dialogue is a clear illustration of how contradictory perceptions can be formed and that they can be sustained for extended periods. Long after the war, on 29 September 1991, *Rapport* wrote: 'Since [the war] Saddam has turned on the propaganda to make his population believe that Iraq really scored the victory "by remaining standing against 30 nations".'

We were hit by propaganda in exactly the same way. There were contributing factors: Our government's viewpoint was that the war was really an Angolan issue; that it was a war between Savimbi and his UNITA against the MPLA and its allies – the Soviets, Eastern Bloc countries and especially the Cubans. Although we had a real interest in the struggle, we only assisted UNITA. Whether one agrees or not, this was the policy. It was Savimbi's war and we were his ally – strictly speaking, the silent partner.

Owing to this state of affairs, the initiative in handling the media was in the hands of UNITA. The policy regarding liaison with the media was that UNITA would release information about the operations and would use every opportunity to propagate its cause and promote its image. The arrangement had the disadvantage for South Africa that on its part press releases could be issued only when we had to announce casualties. This created the impression that there was no good news, only bad – and this at a time when our forces were scoring one success after another.

The Cubans were another factor that contributed towards creating wrong impressions. Through the years the overall objective was to get them out of Angola. It was a challenge which Mr P W Botha regularly presented to us. Savimbi had also stated that to drive the Cubans out of his country was the most important single thing for which he was fighting. All other activities were to be considered against the background of this overall goal.

As early as the middle to late 1970s, when South Africa entered into discussions with the Big Five of the West and the UN, we had tried to put the issue of the Cuban presence in Angola on the agenda. The reaction of all the other parties always was, as Mr Martti Ahtisaari once put it, a 'non-starter'. In other words, if we insisted on having the Cuban question included in the agenda nobody would be prepared even to talk to us.

During the 1980s, however, three important developments on the international political scene had a significant impact on the SWA–Angolan situation: Reagan's election as USA president, the decision of the American government to support UNITA and the increased Cuban presence in Angola. To these could later be added the subsequent decision by the Americans to acknowledge that, in terms of Resolution 435, interdependence indeed existed between the withdrawal of the SADF from South West and a Cuban withdrawal from Angola. But the most important consequence of these developments was the fact that the Americans persuaded the Angolans and Cubans also to accept it as a valid item for the agenda. Now, for the first time, the departure of the Cubans became a real possibility.

This was the situation during the time leading up to the negotiations of 3 May 1988 in London. At this stage there was still no cessation of hostilities in the south of Angola. In other words, the prospect of getting the Cubans out of Angola and the preparatory moves to achieve this had started well before the war had officially ended.

This created a delicate situation in which public statements about the war had to be made with great circumspection.

In the first place, we had to be careful when announcing our successes, so as to avoid creating the impression that UNITA was playing second fiddle. Secondly, we had to consider the Cubans. It may sound simple, but we had already attracted criticism from Savimbi over media statements that we had made; at one press conference he said that we were hijacking UNITA's successes for ourselves.

However, we were compelled to publicise our successes because the Cubans had embarked on a big propaganda campaign in which they claimed glorious victories, as they put it, at Cuito Cuanavale; but once again we had to be very careful with our references to them, because it would have been extremely difficult, if not impossible, to persuade them to evacuate Angola if they had to depart in disgrace as a beaten force.

The popular international picture of the typical Cuban is that of a man with a Castro-type beard, in combat dress with a rifle over his shoulder, a cigar in his mouth and a clenched fist in the air; in short, a macho figure. It is not entirely a true reflection, because I have met many charming Cubans who do not fit this picture at all. However, it does contain some elements of truth, and to a large extent it is the image many Cubans have of themselves: A courageous Che Guevara figure in camo, liberating countries to bring communism; a revolutionary who supports anti-Western revolutionary movements all over the world and leads them to victory. How do you get somebody with such a self-image out of Angola if he is being humiliated in the process? We had to provide them with an honourable exit.

Everybody agreed a few months later that this was an accurate interpretation when the Cubans insisted that they would leave Angola only if it were to be an honourable withdrawal. The motto for the negotiation should be: 'There must be no losers.' Or, to turn it upside-down: 'There must only be winners.' In practical terms an honourable withdrawal meant a steady and orderly exit, following a formal, internationally acknowledged agreement, as opposed to a seemingly hasty and forced retreat as a result of the negative outcome of the war.

It was not as if there was complete and absolute silence about the Soviet and Cuban failures. During public speeches General Malan often described them in strong language. But the misconceptions remained for a long time, and those who find support for their political aims in boasting about the 'humiliating South African defeat at Cuito Cuanavale' still keep them alive.

* * *

After having told the story of the campaign and recalled the myth of Cuito Cuanavale, I can now come to the solemn promise I made to the commanders and troops I mentioned at the beginning of the chapter. I promised them that the truth of their victories would become known one day.

Our men gained one irrefutable success after the other. They performed feats of combat which will be recorded one day as unique in the history of the art of warfare. All this they did in a manner which bore witness to a force with character; of spirited fighting commanders wise in battlecraft; of men on the ground and in the air who showed guts, as one would expect of South Africans; of black, white, brown and yellow members of the South African Defence Force and the SWA Territory Force who did not flinch.

In a campaign in which a total of more than 40 000 troops on both sides participated, it is near to incredible that a handful of 3 000 South African and South West African troops could have played such a decisive role in changing the international course of events.

The war is long past now, and I do not want to be unduly nasty towards anybody in particular. I also have full understanding of the Cubans' desire to create a positive image regarding their involvement in Angola, internationally and especially back home. It was a stated condition to making their withdrawal possible and acceptable. They were in a difficult position – but they went too far with their propaganda. They, and those who liked to echo their stories, continued to strum the discordant tune about the 'humiliating South African defeat at Cuito Cuanavale' even after the beginning of negotiations, when the parties were supposed to create mutual confidence and an atmosphere in which there were no losers, only winners.

Crocker said that they and the Soviets and Angolans had tried their best to destroy UNITA, and instead had received a proper hiding (the sketches on Map 4 put the whole matter into its proper perspective).

If I were to describe the war in rugby terms, I could say that our opponents never came close to our goal line. That was Jamba. They could not even get over the halfway line. That was Mavinga. They barely crossed their own quarter line. That was the Lomba River. We were leading 50–0, and in the process of scoring a push-over try at the Tumpo in injury time when the final whistle blew for the end of the game. Now our opponents brag about having beaten us because they prevented us from scoring the last try, or because they might have won some line-out or other.

Or a boxer might put it this way: You have hammered your opponent – call him 'Punchie' – to pulp for 12 rounds. He stands, crouching against the ropes, his gloves tightly held against his face, trying to cover up anything that you may take a swing at. He barely survives to the last bell and, knees wobbly, is helped to his corner. Now, while Punchie sits there with swollen lips and eyes puffed closed, his manager says: 'We wuz robbed! My Punchie was undoubtedly the toughest of the two. The other guy tried his best to put Punchie down for the count, but Punchie defended brilliantly and survived. The other guy suffered great humiliation.'

But in this type of war you must not expect a knockout. You win by a technical knockout, or you win on points. We won by a technical knockout.

* * *

During this war my interpretations were sometimes questioned, which disappointed me intensely. A journalist once told me that in December 1987 I had said that we were about to begin withdrawing, but we were still in Angola long after that date – I had not told the truth. I replied that I had explained patiently from the beginning that the withdrawal would take time because, as I had pointed out, it was an operational withdrawal as opposed to a formal one. Then I explained to him what I meant by a formal withdrawal.

A formal withdrawal takes place when the belligerents reach a formal agreement. This agreement specifies the date and time at which a ceasefire will take effect and also determines how the opposing forces will break contact: each has to move back to be behind a certain geographical line at a certain date and time. One of the fundamental principles of such a formal withdrawal is that none of the parties should derive a strategic or tactical advantage from it. Then, once agreement is reached, a mechanism is established to monitor the entire process.

These rules do not apply in the case of an operational withdrawal. You must execute your withdrawal in such a way that your opponent does not gain advantage from it. He should not be allowed to undo what you have achieved. That is why an operational withdrawal is tactical by nature and not without fighting, and takes much longer. In any case, I added, I had issued a press release in which I explained all this. The journalist then questioned that I had, in fact, made such a statement.

It transpired later that I had issued the press statements on 16 and 20 February 1988. But on 20 February a bomb exploded at the Oshakati branch of the First National Bank, killing 20 people instantly and wounding many others (including the daughter of the Lutheran Bishop of Ovamboland, Cleophas Dumeni), six of them seriously. That same day also saw spectacularly newsworthy things happening during the flood disaster in the Orange Free State. All this naturally pushed my press release off the front pages, and in most cases out of the newspapers altogether. Incidentally, the matter was later resolved amicably between General Ian Gleeson and the National Press Union.

Where I and many other South Africans sometimes slipped up was in thinking that once you have released information it is the end of the story. But it does not work that way. One should provide the information on a more repetitive basis, as General Malan encouraged us to do. Perhaps it was this negligence on my part that prevented information I had released from making a proper impact. For example, during the campaign I said *inter alia* that the South African force levels from top to bottom never exceeded more than about 3 000 men. Perhaps I did not repeat that fact often enough. On the other hand the Angolans exaggerated our numbers *ad nauseam*.

My figures were not used, and even the authoritative *Jane's Defence Weekly* reported that between 6 000 and 8 000 South Africans were involved, while some publications even mentioned a figure of 10 000 – an indication that they had fallen for Angolan propaganda, or that their informants had collected information about our troop strength at a time when we were in the process of swopping contingents; or perhaps that they found it difficult to believe that 3 000 troops could have managed what we did. This information was then quoted by newspapers, which used those sources rather than the official numbers I had given.

But my facts were correct. We had to withdraw our last troops according to a formal agreement which was signed by General Willie Meyer, the GOC SWA, and General Cintra Frias of the Cuban forces on 22 August 1988 at Ruacana. We pulled out our remaining troops in 10 days at an easy pace, and the last of them were back by 31 August 1988.

The withdrawal caused us some embarrassment because we had so few troops left in Angola that we could not even muster 1 000 men to put on an impressive display, and so we were incapable of presenting the spectacle that the media had hoped to see.

* * *

My sons also made their contribution. Martin spent 1985 and 1986 at the Military Academy, but did not make the grade in his second year and had to go back to his unit, 32 Battalion. He participated in their operations during 1987 but also continued his studies in his spare time and was promoted captain at the end of that year. Bruwer started national service during August 1987. He went to the Infantry School, and was on operational duties during 1988.

Whereas I had much to tell about my immediate successors as GOC SWA Command, Charles Lloyd and Georg Meiring, and where they fit into this story, I have made only brief reference so far to the last of the line, Willie Meyer. So let me tell a story about him that illustrates his most outstanding characteristic: getting things done without any swagger or fuss. He was the GOC during one of the most difficult times in South West, and he showed his mettle again and again.

We had come a long way together by that time; he had been my chief of staff in South West during the earlier days. Willie was completely adaptable. Although he excelled as a commander in his own right – among others he commanded the School of Armour and Orange Free State Command before arriving in Windhoek as the last GOC South West Africa Command – he was also a commander's dream staff officer, intelligent, diligent and devoted. But you seldom saw him or heard him.

If I could be permitted to compare him with barbecue experts: one type puts up a big show with chef's cap, apron, displays of herbs and sauces and all the paraphernalia. He hustles and bustles and flamboyantly douses the flames that shoot up now and again. The other kind chats quietly, and you do not even notice that he is busy braaiing until he says the food is ready.

That was Willie Meyer. Everything was done without drama or demonstration, so much so that I always wondered how he managed to get everything done.

An aphorism from General Dirk Marais aptly sums up Willie Meyer's leadership style: 'When the best leader's work is done, the people say: "We did it ourselves".'

CHAPTER 16

IN THE WAKE OF THE WAR

Tinfoil and phoney mines

The events from here on consisted of a such an interwoven mixture of shooting and talking, at venues ranging from the SWA–Angolan bush to the capitals of the world, that the only way to present an accurate picture is to provide word pictures of each type of activity as it happened, to show how one affected the other and influenced the protagonists' actions and reactions.

War. The fight for Jamba was over. We had destroyed the Cuban/FAPLA advance at the Lomba River and pushed them back to the Cuito. We were consolidating, securing our results and strengthening UNITA's position in the terrain between the Cuito River and Mavinga, so that their forces would not need our help in maintaining the new situation that we had jointly created.

Peace. All these events now brought us much closer to the dramatic discussion on 3 May 1988 in London. But to arrive at the diplomatic drama in London from the military crescendo between the Lomba and the Cuito we first have to look at the scene through a wide-angle lens.

256

War. The first facet which the wider vision brings into the picture is the other wars which were simultaneously in progress – our on-going campaign against PLAN and the 'normal' war between UNITA and the MPLA in the rest of Angola. FAPLA had withdrawn many troops and weapons from elsewhere to reinforce the offensive against Jamba; with these forces now tied up at Cuito Cuanavale, UNITA started to gain more and more ground in other parts of Angola, including the Cazombo block.

The next aspect of the larger picture that comes into focus is the threatening drama in the west and south-west of Angola, which I have already mentioned.

The Cubans had started with the build-up in the west as early as November 1987, deploying their forces cautiously and non-aggressively in the vicinity of the Namibe railway line, then gradually moving them southwards. In the beginning the build-up had not drawn much attention because it had not seemed to be connected to the normal MPLA–UNITA conflict, the SWAPO campaign or the fighting in the south-east on which most people focused.

But then a number of events began to attract our attention. One of them was the discovery that General Arnaldo T Óchoa Sanchez – the Cuban commandante I mentioned when dealing with Operation Savannah – had been dispatched to Angola to take over the command in the west.

Óchoa had an impressive military record. He was a veteran of Fidel Castro's successful campaign to assume power in Cuba. Later he had been involved in the planning and conduct of the operations that had put the MPLA into power in Angola. During 1975 he had also commanded troops in Syria who were serving against Israel. He was the architect of the Somali defeat in Ethiopia, and for two years from 1983 commanded the Cuban forces in Nicaragua. He had also served in Afghanistan and Grenada, and on 1 January 1984 the Castro government's State Council had conferred on him the title of Hero of the Republic of Cuba and the order of Maximo Gomez.

The build up, based on the Cuban 50 Division, which was continuously being reinforced, now started a southward advance in the direction of Kaokoland in the west. The runways of the air force bases at Cahama and Xangongo were lengthened, and the ground facilities greatly and speedily improved.

The first deployments were all west of the Cunene River, but when we did not react, the Cubans also started to position themselves to the east, opposite Ovamboland (see Map 5). By January 1988 there were 3 000 Cuban troops just north of the South West border.

The southward movement continued, and by the end of May the forward Cuban units were positioned on a line running from Namibe through Chibemba, Cahama, Humbe, Xangongo, Cuvelai and Cassinga. Three combined Cuban–PLAN battalions, supported by tanks and artillery, were concentrated at Cahama, Xangongo and Mupa; by this time the force was nearly two divisions strong and was equipped with the most sophisticated weapon and radar systems.

We collected our information through the country's intelligence systems, but naturally also from the newspapers. The papers' information was fairly accurate, but they reported on this formidable force in a tone of alarm, as if one were supposed to shake with fear and choke with anxiety on reading it. In fact, however, it reminded me of the story of the East Germans who were supposedly poised to invade South West during the late 1970s. But not everything was mere military show business. This was not chess, it was war. On 18 April 1988 a Cuban force made contact with elements of our forces which were following a PLAN group, south of Xangongo. In the clash which followed we lost a major and a medical corporal. I kept General Malan informed about this and other events, and he in turn briefed the President, Mr P W Botha.

One should bear in mind that the Cuban generals had taken command of all operations in January, with Fidel Castro giving the orders. This meant that we always had to take the 'Castro factor' into account when assessing future Cuban intentions and actions (months later, when the Joint Commission to which I have already referred met in Havana, General Rosales showed me around the planning room, complete with clay models and maps, where Castro had made his decisions).

While this build-up was in progress, we naturally had to ask ourselves what the Cubans were up to. What was Óchoa thinking, and what were his instructions from Castro? Military Intelligence presented me with a useful staff paper on Óchoa. He was a shrewd man and a good strategist; I remember that he had a liking for special operations behind the forward line of enemy troops, and a predilection for unorthodox actions. The paper regarded his master, Castro, as unpredictable.

As regards Cuban intentions, there were a few alternative possibilities. One was that they wanted to split both our attention and our forces between south-east and south-west Angola to give them the opportunity to resume the offensive against Jamba. Another possibility was that they had accepted their defeat at the Lomba as a historical fact and were now searching for a victory at another place, even if it had to be inside South West. Information from overseas tended to support this hypothesis. It indicated that the least South African offensive action would be used by the Cubans as provocation to attack targets on South West African soil. SWAPO could then capitalise on these attacks with Cuban support.

I and a few others began more and more to believe that the Cubans had accepted that their allies had suffered a decisive defeat in the south-east, that they regarded the defeat as the turning-point not only of the campaign but of the whole drawn-out war, and that they would have to start negotiating.

However, negotiations often lead to troop withdrawals, something which one does not like to do while looking like a loser. Therefore the Cubans had to change the impression created by their defeat at the Lomba. Then, too, one prefers to negotiate from a position of strength. A threatening posture in the south-west would help to create this appearance, with the bonus that it would draw the limelight away from the south-east.

I told people close to me that although I agreed that we could not completely ignore other possibilities, my experience and gut feeling told me that this was probably the real alternative. Certain events supported this way of thinking. The Cubans had already started making intensive propaganda to the effect that they had achieved a heroic victory over the South Africans and UNITA at Cuito Cuanavale. At the same time, during late November 1987, they had put out feelers at the South African mission at the UN in New York regarding the possibility of negotiations.

At that stage General Malan had issued instructions which President Botha later repeated to me in his presence. According to the President, we had accomplished our mission and we had done it well, but he adhered to his point of view that we should not allow ourselves to be sucked into Angola and end up in a Vietnam situation. In the UNITA area we had valid reasons to become involved, but in the south-west of Angola we had an interest only in the Ruacana hydro-electric scheme and the water supply to South West.

The Cuban venture in Angola opposite Kaokoland and Ovambo was a new situation. We were not interested in picking a fight with the Angolans. Let the Cubans do what they liked; we would watch them closely and stay in contact, but we were not to start a new war. We must maintain our aggressiveness without being arrogant or cheeky, keeping cool and exercising self-restraint. But, Mr Botha added, if the Cubans were to put one foot across the border, we must hit them with everything we had. Ovamboland would become the new battlefield.

As usual, one knew precisely what P W Botha wanted. The Defence Force had always been very successful with operations in Angola and we had kept the war out of South West; but if war were to come to Ovambo, we would be fighting on our home turf. What a great inspiration and motivation that would be – not to speak of the other advantages!

But this discussion did not send me off on another military excursion. Instead of packing my pistol and going to war, I packed my paisley tie and went off to start talking peace. We were still assessing the Cuban intentions when I received orders in April 1988 to go to London as a member of a delegation headed by Neil van Heerden, who had been DG of Foreign Affairs for only 12 months; I was to prepare myself for negotiations with the Cubans and Angolans, Chester Crocker acting as the facilitator.

Peace. Thorough and systematic as always, Neil arranged a meeting or two in his office before our departure to exchange ideas in preparation for the negotiations, which were to start on 3 May. I remember that at the last of these meetings I laid heavy stress on the point that we should not be unduly influenced by Cuban propaganda or intimidated by them. We had won the war; the allegedly heroic FAPLA and Cuban victories at Cuito Cuanavale were pure and simple propaganda stunts.

I kept on turning over the issues in my mind. What was Castro up to? I believed that the Cubans wanted to publicise themselves out of the quandary in which the Lomba River disaster had landed them and into the phoney glory of the non-existent Cuito Cuanavale 'victory'. They wanted to scare us as we waited on the other side of the South

West border and talk fear into us at the conference table, followed by an international agreement and their withdrawal from Angola with honour.

But who knew? There was still the Castro factor. A real military victory would mean much to him, and so the possibility of a Cuban foray over the border could not be completely discarded. People told me in the lobbies of Brown's Hotel in London that we should not venture to clash with the Cubans; they would welcome it, and strike across the border with all their might. We could expect air attacks on Ruacana, Ondangwa and Oshakati as well as Rundu.

I now resume the story which I interrupted in the first chapter of this book, the meeting on 4 May 1988 when my Cuban counterpart, General Ulises Rosales del Toro, threatened me by saying that if we did not watch our step we would be overwhelmed by a destructive war.

One can keep one's options open, but sooner or later you arrive at the moment of truth. Then you have to make up your mind. For me that moment had now arrived. Was Rosales serious? Would the Cubans strike across the border? Did Castro want to have a go at the South Africans to beat them decisively and so bring an end to the war? Or was it all a bluff? It was then that I pulled my Pik Botha stunt on him and confronted him with the Boer War.

For him it was also the moment of truth, and after that we never again glared at each other in exactly the same way as before.

It was not all that easy. Operational events started to complicate matters on the very day of our informal threat session, and although it was the moment of truth, the fact was that we still did not really know exactly what the Cubans were up to.

War. Operational activities now had a direct influence on the negotiations. The large Cuban presence in the south-west of Angola, and the integrated Cuban–FAPLA–PLAN battalions, resulted in more frequent and bigger clashes between PLAN and the security forces – and the Cubans and FAPLA did not stand aside when that happened. The clashes with the Cubans which I have mentioned had already taken place on 18 April.

On 4 May, the day of my discussions with Rosales, a Cuban force attacked elements of 101 Battalion, the Ovambo battalion, which were conducting operations against PLAN south of Humbe in Angola. We lost six soldiers and four Casspir APCs, and one of our men was wounded and taken prisoner. He eventually ended up in a hospital in Havana, where he was treated for a serious leg wound. He was Johan Papenfus, and later I got to know him better.

The Cubans also suffered losses. Some of them were crushed by Casspirs in shallow trenches, and after the war a Cuban told Brigadier Chris Serfontein that we were crazy to make war like that.

A few days later there was another clash between Cubans and elements of 101 Battalion. As can be imagined, these incidents created an awkward situation between Rosales and myself, a situation which I had no option but to manage as best I could.

Peace. The negotiations of 3–4 May 1988 were not the end of the international political wrestling but the beginning of increased propaganda and diplomatic activity behind the scenes, in addition to military positioning. But one could already have forecast that the peace initiatives had generated a momentum which would never again be stopped. For example:

- Perez de Cuellar talked with the OAU at Addis Ababa on 27 May 1988, adopting a placatory mood.
- Reagan and Gorbachev conferred on 30 May. They said that a peace plan for Angola–Namibia must be drawn up before 29 September 1988 – the tenth commemoration of Resolution 435, and shortly before the American presidential elections (we arranged it for them, and the story of how we did it is told later in this book).
- President Castro addressed a conference of the non-aligned states on 2 June 1988. He threatened us.

War. While all this was happening the tension in the operational area went on increasing as the two kinds of operations in which we were involved – the 'normal' operations against PLAN and the Cuban advance southward, and our counter-actions – began to converge.

This situation brought about the last dramatic climax of our operations against the Cubans, on 26–27 June 1988. The run-up to this point took 10 days. On 16 May Commandant Jan Hougaard, who had his tactical headquarters at Ruacana (there was also a small force guarding the hydro-electric scheme's barrage at Calueque), began reconnaissance operations with men from 32 Battalion. A while later Jan's force was reinforced with three more 32 Battalion companies, which would also be used to play a delaying role, and a combat team of 61 Mechanised Infantry Battalion Group was deployed south of Calueque as a mobile reserve. The normal military infrastructure and force levels of Sector 10 at were, of course, in place as well at its headquarters at Oshakati.

Naturally I had issued the necessary directives to the Chief of the Army, the Chief of the Air Force and the Surgeon-General, each of whom had passed their own orders further down. I cannot remember the exact wording of my instructions, but I always tried to give clear orders which left the minimum room for doubt.

Orders usually work well in paper wars but not always in real life, and in this case we were in a very complex situation. The operations against PLAN, which was now integrated with FAPLA and the Cubans, had taken a new turn. I have already fully described the arguments around the Cuban intentions, and the tit-for-tat threats and posturing to gain a position carrying a certain message were more evident than usual. But you cannot tell your commanders to posture and pose. They must be given clear orders, and you have to discuss the orders you give with those who will be responsible for their execution. In this way a commander knows what he has to do, but he also knows what the intention behind the orders is. He can therefore use his own initiative with more confidence.

It was a tense time for Chris Serfontein, now the commander of Sector 10. At this stage we were still pumping water uninterruptedly from the Cunene at Calueque – there was no water in Ovamboland, and it was important to keep it flowing for as long as possible – and his mission, *inter alia,* was to delay the Cuban southward push for as long as possible and report on its progress, to try to make contact with the Cubans and to test their reaction, so that the intelligence picture could develop. But he was still not sure what the Cuban intentions were, and at this stage had no additional troops, so that he had to make use of 101 Battalion for offensive patrolling and 102 Battalion (the Kaokoland battalion) to develop a strongpoint at Calueque, which was under threat from a Cuban brigade dug in at Techipa in the west, about 40 to 50 km to its north-west; another Cuban brigade had taken up a similar posture at Xangongo.

It was here that South African ingenuity was demonstrated. The text-books contain many doctrines and methods of deception, including the use of phoney minefields, but they are not always easily applied in practice, and sometimes demand improvisation. That is what Chris and his men did – they laid a mineless minefield, complete with all the customary wire fencing and markers, and even a safe lane through it, But the mines in the holes they prepared were actually tin cans, and the three tanks they placed in prepared positions behind the minefield were made of plastic.

That was not the sum total of this display of smoke and mirrors. When members of the local population needed to cross the fake mine-field they had to pass through the usual control-points at the entrance and exit to the safe lane, and were then solemnly escorted through to the other side. All these activities were aimed at making sure that the existence of the ersatz minefield became widely known. And it worked. Much later, after our withdrawal from Angola, it took the Angolans three months to clear Calueque and re-occupy it, and they requested our assistance with clearing the minefield ... they were distinctly suspicious about the speed with which we obliged.

Because our forces in the area were so sparse, we decided to deploy additional troops to protect Calueque and deny the Cubans access to South West Africa through Ruacana. For this purpose we formed Task Force Zulu under Colonel Mieg Delport, consisting of a 32 Battalion battle group, three companies of 101 Battalion, 61 Mechanised Battalion group, a battery of Valkyrie 127 mm multiple rocket launchers, a battery of 155 mm G5 guns, a troop of G2 guns (the old 25-pounders) and a troop of 120 mm mortars.

Skirmishes took place. I have already mentioned the clashes of 18 April and 4 May 1988. In another action, south of Techipa, troops of 32 Battalion's E Company under Captain Maurice Devenish shot dead five Cuban sappers and a number of infantrymen, as well as the commander of four BRDM-2 armoured vehicles. Devenish lost a few Unimogs but suffered no personnel casualties.

This single paragraph is a cryptic description of what would be excellent material for an action movie. Devenish's very small group laid an ambush and then found themselves facing an overwhelming force of infantry, tanks and artillery. At one stage 12 men were missing for more than 24 hours, but by 16h00 next day all were safely back, thanks to thorough training and experience.

Operational intelligence now available to Chris Serfontein indicated that the Cubans were on the point of resuming their southward movement. Whether they intended to frighten us away from Calueque or to attack us was uncertain, and the threats, counter-threats, positioning and posturing led to a decision to mobilise various conventional Citizen Force units for service in South West Africa. This would not only provide for the necessary force levels in the event of an attack but would convey a message to the Cubans of what they could expect if, in fact, they decided to attack across the border. I issued an early warning order to the commanders of the selected Citizen Force units, and on 8 June announced the mobilisation.

In the meantime Mieg Delport had decided to use his artillery to carry out some serious disruption among the Cubans at Techipa before they started their advance, and also to deploy 61 Mech to delay them if they did move, as well as protect our artillery. One of those who joined 61 Mech while I was on my way to talk peace in Egypt was Major Hannes Nortmann, with a small combat team which included four of his own missile-armed Ratel IFVs.

All this brought us to 25 June 1988 – the eve of the last big armed encounter in which we would be involved in Angola. It would be the most extensive clash since 1976, and in the following two days would see one of the most brilliant operations in South African military history. But I was not there to see this, because I was on my way to talk peace in Egypt, my father's old stamping-ground during World War II, and so at this critical point my narrative shifts once again to the diplomatic scene.

Peace. At the Hyatt el Salaam Hotel in Cairo the next round of negotiations was about to begin. The various delegations followed a meandering route through the hordes of newspeople with their flashing, clicking cameras, their glaring TV lights and their occupational impertinence.

The scene reminded me of professional boxers moving down the aisle with their entourages, on their way to the ring for a world championship fight. Or of a rugby match: I brought up the rear, the last to take the field like fullback Gerbrand Grobler; Pik Botha right up in front like the Free State captain, Pote Human, and between us a crowd of jostling journalists, so densely packed that I arrived in the negotiation arena suffering from serious claustrophobia.

With great oratorical skill and superb acting Risquet launched a biting attack on the South Africans. Pik Botha could hardly wait to respond, which he did with alternating bursts of cool logic and transparent viciousness. Then we adjourned without any further ado, wondering what the next act would be like.

To the student of conflict and conflict management who is analysing the situation in terms of certain models, this debate would not appear to reflect a decrease of conflict, but rather a phase of intensification:

- You attack the representative of the other party in order to weaken his intellectual position.
- You bring emotional pressure to bear on the other side in accordance with the rule that states: 'play the man and you'll get the ball', while pretending to conform strictly to the rules of fair play.
- You subtly bend the rules of logic to deceive the other party.
- You elevate the other party's position to something big and then you attack that position as exorbitant and unrealistic. [*Instituut voor Organisatie Ontwikkeling*]

Such a debate is essentially a kind of intellectual violence. But the parties still believe that they can, in fact, settle their differences through discussion; this debate replayed itself in my mind's eye a few years later while watching the post-1990 Codesa speeches on TV and seeing Nelson Mandela gunning for F W de Klerk.

The first day of the conference came close to being a failure, its only usefulness being the momentum it gave the negotiation process. Everyone let off steam, but also got to know each other better.

Next morning things suddenly improved. It must be remembered that those were still the days when we talked in hushed tones of the Soviets, who were also active somewhere close by. We were given to believe that they had something to do with the clearing of the foul air. The leaders of the delegations probably knew what was happening behind the scenes – I was told later that Crocker's Soviet counterpart, Anatoliy Adamishin, had intervened.

Rosales and I had another session on the first evening, at which he delivered the same cautionary sermon as before, but in a more collegial tone than in London. It could be no other way, he had to act in step with Risquet's approach. I suppose it was planned that way, and that he was simply doing his duty.

During this meeting General Neels van Tonder, Brigadier Johann Sonnekus and I discussed the release of Johann Papenfus with Rosales and his officers. It was the beginning of a long, tedious and taxing process in which Neels and Sonnie displayed tremendous stamina, and eventually we got Papenfus back. We were also given the opportunity to visit South African war graves from World War II.

I think Cairo was the place where negotiation by means of a step-by-step approach started. It was also here that the idea caught on that the next step should be to reach agreement on a set of principles on which a total settlement could be based. When we dispersed, all the parties had agreed to meet again.

War. Another example of the South Africans' battle-craft and inventiveness at work caused serious embarrassment for the Cubans on Sunday afternoon, 26 June 1988, after the South African delegation had left Cairo.

Our commanders and staffs knew that around 17h00 on any Sunday afternoon all soldiers' preparedness was about zero. They also knew that the Angolan air force needed at least 60 minutes to react if they had not been placed on red alert, and that during the southern Angolan winter the light faded so fast that flying sorties were no longer possible after 18h00. Thus it would be possible to arrange for a sequence of events which would give us one hour in which to identify targets.

At last light on 26 June Jan Hougaard and a few of his men sent up a number of meteorological balloons carrying tin foil from a kopje north of Calueque. As the balloons soared into the air, a flight of SAAF Impalas carried out some mock manoeuvres. As expected, the reflections of the tin foil on the Cuban radar convinced them that an air attack was under way.

As they had hoped, the Angolan air force was not on red alert. The Cubans meanwhile activated their air defence system and launched six SA-6 ground-to-air missiles at the balloons. Our radar operators, artillery observation officers and members of a recce regiment who had been pre-positioned to observe the launchings from Techipa then plotted the launchers' positions and pounded them in the darkness for four hours.

The first salvo destroyed the Cuban artillery command post, which meant we could continue shooting without fear of counter-bombardment. Only one Cuban artillery battery responded: it fired about 10 shots and then also fell silent.

These serious losses did not stop the Cubans from setting off for Calueque, and Commandant Mike Muller's 61 Mechanised Battalion group was deployed to stop them.

Early next morning Hannes Nortmann and his force joined hands with one of Mike's companies under command of Major André Vermeulen, who took command of the combined combat team. About 08h00 tanks and infantry of the Cuban advance guard engaged Vermeulen's force and knocked out two of our Ratel-90s, killing the platoon commander, Lieutenant Meiring. In return Vermeulen's men knocked out a Cuban BTR-60 and a number of other vehicles, and inflicted heavy losses on the enemy infantry.

Hannes knocked out a tank and became involved with enemy infantry and RPG teams, which he held at bay with his tank's machine-gun in spite of being wounded in the neck and hand during the intense exchange of fire. Meanwhile two Olifant tanks from other sub-elements of Mike Muller's 61 Mech simultaneously hit another T-55 tank which was carrying a platoon of infantry, destroying both the tank and its passengers. The South African tanks then destroyed another BTR-60, and after about half an hour the Cubans broke contact and fell back northward.

Mike Muller read the battle brilliantly and handled the different elements of his force calmly and systematically. The result was that the Cubans did not resume the advance and retreated to Techipa, having lost 302 men, two tanks and eight other vehicles. The South Africans and South Westers now also withdrew.

Several South Africans distinguished themselves in this battle – in fact, all of them did, whether they were commanders, staff or troops. Kat Liebenberg told me how everybody participating in this operation had remained calm and aggressive but calculated. They had manoeuvred tactically, step by step, and done everything that one would expect of men on the field of battle. Outwitting the Cuban artillery, as I have described, was only one of many examples of deception and other combat techniques that were used. In anybody's book this denoted excellent battle-craft.

Then something happened which really hit me very hard.

Seven MIG-23s attacked the wall of the Calueque dam about 14h00 on 27 June. The eighth Mig veered off and bombed the water pipeline to Ovamboland; one of its bombs damaged the line and another missed, but exploded between a Buffel APC and an Eland-90 armoured car, where it killed eight men of 8 SA Infantry Battalion and three of 2 Special Service Battalion. The anti-aircraft troop of 32 Battalion with its 20 mm guns then hit two MIGs, one of which crashed on its way back to Lubango.

The Cubans exploited our loss during the air attack for propaganda purposes, claiming an important military victory, but the fact was that our operations on the ground effectively stopped the Cuban advance southwards; they had abandoned any intentions that they might have had of achieving military victories, because further losses and a repetition of the operations in the south-east would have made it impossible for them to withdraw from Angola with honour.

Friction de guerre had been good to us that day, but it had also dealt us a bitter blow. The general situation on 27 June 1988 was not, of course, as clear yet as I have described it here with the benefit of hindsight, and we continued to take the necessary precautionary measures.

The mobilised Citizen Force contingent became part of 10 Division, the conventional force in the area (as opposed to the anti-insurgency forces which continued with their operations). The division consisted of three mechanised battalion groups, a tank regiment, three armoured car squadrons and an artillery brigade commanded by Colonel Jean Lausberg, and it remained in place until the last South African forces were withdrawn from Angola on 1 September 1988. On a personal note, my son Bruwer was one of those who pulled out during August.

Peace. The Cubans made no further aggressive moves after 27 June, and no more major actions took place. We had reached the turning-point. From now on negotiations would continue on a serious note and at a hectic pace. But we still had to see it as something that was happening during the aftermath of the war in the south-west of Angola.

Strangely enough, the Cubans did not make anywhere near as much propaganda about this war as they had about the fighting in the south-east. One reason was that in the south-east it had been the Cuban/FAPLA forces which were on the offensive. But they turned this around. When the UNITA/RSA forces crushed the offensive and cleared the area up to the Cuito River, the Cuban propagandists presented the mopping-up operation as a pukka offensive which they had gloriously repelled, pretending that this was what the whole war had been about.

In this way they camouflaged their total failure to accomplish their mission. Crocker's comment on the episode was as follows: 'The Soviets and Angolans had laboured strenuously to smash UNITA, and had instead been thoroughly defeated ... How, then, did the fighting at Cuito become a heroic Cuban legend? By proclaiming to a credulous world that the town of Cuito Cuanavale – a town under MPLA control since 1976 – was the "prize" over which the entire campaign was fought, and then by crowing when you have managed not to lose it.'

In the south-west, however, there was no question this time of anybody else but the Cubans pushing southwards. And in the absence of anything resembling any real counter-offensive on our part, there was no opportunity for their propagandists to paint a picture of an alleged South African 'offensive' which had gone wrong. Instead they concentrated their propaganda on the strength and formidable nature of their force, projecting its 'big push' southwards as the approach of an unstoppable juggernaut. What it amounted to was that in the south-east they had had to use propaganda to cover up a defeat, while now they had to use it to instil fear and threaten us out of the war. For public consumption they depicted their manoeuvres as a brilliant strategic move which ended the war and forced negotiations.

However, it is not true that their 'big push' forced the start of negotiations. They had already tested the climate for initiating negotiations several months earlier, in New York during November 1987. According to Crocker, Castro had told him afterwards that the plan to extricate himself from the bad military situation in which the Cubans found themselves had already been made on 7 November 1987. In fact the first formal negotiations of the series had already started on 3 May 1988 in London, while the fighting in the south-west only ended on 27 June.

So the dramatically heralded Cuban advance to the south ended in an anti-climax, first halting and then petering out altogether. Rather than providing something to boast about, it brought them a certain measure of embarrassment, and we made no concessions in exchange for discussions.

If you make an objective assessment of these murky events and penetrate the mist of propaganda surrounding them (if you are willing to make the effort, of course) you will discover the true picture, which clearly shows the real crux of it all, namely the concept of 'linkage' – the connection link between the implementation of Resolution 435 and the withdrawal of Cubans from Angola.

The South African government would not change its position that implementation of the resolution and the consequent withdrawal of South African troops from South West was impossible until a satisfactory agreement could be reached on the withdrawal of Cuban forces from Angola.

Previously the linkage concept had received little or no recognition from the Western powers, and even less from the African states, resulting in the international political deadlock over South West and Angola which dragged from the 1970s into the 1980s and persisted until President Reagan appeared on the scene.

Reagan did away with the checkmate simply by acknowledging the interdependence between these two proposed actions, and linkage became a key point during his systematic and extensive diplomatic campaign concerning the Western powers, Africa, the Soviet Union, Cuba and Angola. The man who actually had to win all these parties over was Chet Crocker, and they gave him a hard time.

The battle of the Lomba on 3 October 1987, the turning-point in the south-east, had an almost invisible but decisive effect on the negotiations. Towards the end of January 1988 Cubans joined the Angolan delegation at Luanda for discussions with the US. They had already confirmed that they were prepared to negotiate their total withdrawal in exchange for the independence of South West Africa. Linkage had been accepted, even if initially it was expressed in well-chosen diplomatic verbal camouflage.

The Cubans did achieve one thing in the south-west of Angola: they managed to save their allies from further humiliation in the south-east through a campaign in which, it seems, they had not wanted to take part in the first place.

Now, with London and Cairo behind us, we faced the next three rounds of negotiations in New York, on Sal Island and in Geneva; and for me they would be the most crucial and exciting of all.

CHAPTER 17

THE UNITED STATES – A COMMON ENEMY

Nuances with finesse

The negotiations and politicking that now followed meant a lot of travelling. We became sick and tired of taxis, luggage, airports and aircraft; of the interiors of hotel rooms, limousines and conference halls; of waiting and strolling around; of packing and unpacking; of becoming hot under the collar and then cooling down again; of taking notes and doodling; of late nights and red eyes.

To pass the time I took refuge in playing bridge with Neels van Tonder, Johann Sonnekus and Derek Auret. Niël Barnard sometimes joined us, but his intellect was better than his bridge.

I take up the story of our diplomatic journey in New York.

We met at Governor's Island, New York, on 11 June 1988. The parties had reached agreement on the set of principles on which a complete settlement could be based, as envisaged at Cairo – the New York Principles.

These discussions inspired me to develop what seemed to me a useful line of thinking. I had already experienced the way in which the Cubans and Angolans had misinterpreted our intentions whenever we had launched an operation in Angola because they believed that in the main our efforts were directed not at PLAN but at Angola itself.

On each occasion they were convinced that our intention was to penetrate deeply into Angola. They once told me themselves that during Operation Protea they thought we were heading for a much longer-range objective; that we were going right up to Lubango! And during Operation Modulêr they publicly announced that we had our sights on the central highlands and the Benguela railway line.

They always vociferously exaggerated the size of our invading forces. After every operation they would accuse us of having stayed there longer than in fact we had. I do not know if they really believed it themselves – it might simply have been propaganda to make us the 'bad guys' and thus to gain international sympathy for themselves, the 'good guys'. Or perhaps they were starting to believe their own propaganda? Indeed, on a few occasions we had had to negotiate our withdrawal from Angola when we were on our way out in any case, or actually over the border already, as happened after Operation Askari.

In New York their tactics were suspiciously similar. It became clear to me that once again they believed, or pretended to believe, that we had stronger force levels than was actually the case, and that we were not already in the process of withdrawing, or, at the very least, scaling down. During the conferences they called on us every now and again to get out. To tell the truth, if they had not made it a point of discussion, we would have withdrawn on our own account, and probably sooner. In fact, General Malan had told me to withdraw in harsher tones than they did; not to mention President Botha. He had more authority than they had, and I was more scared of him than of them.

To withdraw or not was not the question, the question was how and when to complete it. We had never even considered a counter-performance from the Cubans and Angolans.

At Governor's Island the Cubans once again told us that they were not afraid of the G5 gun. It was inaccurate and did not really hurt them. But let it be silent, please! So I started to think along these lines: from what they said, one could conclude that they thought that we intended to continue fighting and to extend our presence in Angola, and that it was up to them to persuade us to stop shooting and leave.

In other words, we did not have to stop shooting and get out for nothing; if they wanted to achieve this through negotiation, then it was a matter of give and take, and surely we should be rewarded for withdrawing. I discussed the matter with our leader, Neil van Heerden, who agreed that I could enter into separate discussions with Rosales.

Thus it happened that Neels van Tonder, Johann Sonnekus and I had a brief conference with Rosales and his staff in my room at the New York Plaza Hotel. We had to cut it short to join the rest of the delegations at Governor's Island, but there Rosales and I continued the discussion in an anteroom.

During these military conferences I could make Rosales certain offers. We suggested a ceasefire, a gradual disengagement of the opposing fighting forces and a South African withdrawal (Neels and Sonnie worked it out for me). But, based on the principle that we had had to fight to get where we were and that they should not exploit our withdrawal to gain strategic and tactical advantage, they should undertake to reciprocate. For example, the battle area east of the Cuito must be cleared of South African and Cuban forces.

I got the impression that they were surprised by such a sudden proposal. They were also a little suspicious, probably because it had not been made in the mainstream of the negotiations and presented by Neil van Heerden himself. So they were cautious and would not commit themselves.

There was not enough time to take the matter any further, but all the parties agreed that the military components of the delegations would continue with the discussion during special future meetings, which would soon take place on Sal Island.

* * *

New York also produced some lighter moments. I suppose the Hudson River inspired my Angolan counterpart, Ndalu (Gen Antonio dos Santos Franca) to tell us the following story:

An Angolan, an American and a Cuban were standing on a river bank. Let us say they were himself, Crocker and Risquet. Crocker opens his briefcase and produces a long hot dog with mustard, peels off the paper wrapper takes a hearty bite. Then all of a sudden he chucks the rest into the river and it drifts away. The other two shout at him: 'What the hell are you doing?!'

He replies calmly: 'What are you screaming about? Here in the States we have millions of hot-dogs – it's no loss at all.'

So they continue talking. Suddenly Risquet produces a long Cohiba cigar from his briefcase, unwraps it carefully, goes through the whole customary rigmarole and eventually puts it into his mouth. He lights it, turns it around with the burning end upwards, inspects it and exhales with great satisfaction. Then without warning he flicks the cigar into the water. The other two grab him by his jacket, crying 'What are you doing? Are you mad?'

'Listen, chaps,' he says, 'in Cuba we have thousands and thousands of cigars; we won't miss this one in the least.' He looks at Crocker and starts talking again as if nothing has happened.

Like a bolt out of the blue Ndalu kicks Risquet in the pants, right into the water, and the Cuban starts to drift downstream, struggling and shouting.

Crocker gets the fright of his life. He grabs Ndalu by the shoulders and shouts at the top of his voice: 'Are you out of your mind?! The poor man will drown!'

'Ah, well, what does it matter?' Ndalu replies. 'In Angola we still have thousands of Cubans. This is no loss.'

I thought that Ndalu was taking a bit of a chance telling such stories, but I found later that he was a well-balanced person and that there was a very good understanding between him and the Cubans, and that they were not over-sensitive. They were full of jokes themselves.

Unlike some of his colleagues, Ndalu was not full of rhetoric, propaganda and pretensions. He was natural, soft-spoken and pragmatic, and I cannot believe that there was any person who could not get along with him.

* * *

In New York I sensed that a better understanding had developed between the Cubans and ourselves. In Angola and South West we were enemies. Here we were negotiating 'opponents'. But we could talk better sense.

On one occasion a Cuban asked me if we had flown to New York by South African Airways. I told him no, and described the long route via

Europe where we had to change over at various places, and how we had to make use of different airlines. So he wanted to know why we did not use SAA. I told him that SAA did not have landing rights in the States.

He was surprised: 'Neither have we!'

Then he said that he supposed I visited the States quite often. I told him that I had neither the money nor the motive to visit the USA. This visit was an exception, and in any case, being an officer in the SADF, I was not entitled to an American visa.

He got very excited: 'Neither are we!'

He said that it was exactly the same with the Cubans – they had no landing rights and were not allowed visas either. Then he carried on about all the other things that the Americans denied them and did to them. So we and the Cubans had a common enemy – the United States of America. Just imagine that!

The same sort of discussion apparently also took place between other South Africans and Cubans, and all of a sudden there was more mutual appreciation. It was certainly an upside-down world. It was difficult to know whether you should glare at a Cuban, smile at him … or shed a tear with him.

The New York Principles formulated at Governor's Island were an important milestone on the negotiation journey. The talks among the military in New York naturally did not draw much attention, since they were conducted on the sidelines, and the follow-up military discussions at Sal likewise took place without fanfares or floodlights. I noticed later that books and articles on this period and subject did not even mention the military conferences; but they were meaningful and did not take place without drama. The exception was Crocker, who gave this aspect considerable coverage in his book.

The special discussions at Sal took place in July, only a week or so after our return from the States. We were going to follow up on the proposals that we had initiated 'out of the blue' in New York, and the agenda would therefore contain such subjects as a ceasefire, the northward redeployment of Cuban forces and the withdrawal of South African forces.

As this conference was to deal with practical aspects, I decided to select more junior officers to accompany me as advisers. I did not believe in the tendency always to involve only senior officers, preferring people who were practically involved and know the most about a particular matter, irrespective of rank. I therefore took with me Colonel Eddie Viljoen, who was an operations staff officer, and Colonel Freddie Oelschig, an intelligence staff officer. Eddie still sported a lush bush-war moustache and Freddie a savage bush beard.

As is the custom during the opening of a conference, I introduced the members of our delegation to the other parties. If it was a strange experience for Eddie and Freddie to meet the enemy face to face, they did not show it.

On the third day at Sal I had the feeling that something strange was brewing amongst the Cubans, and what they were up to became clear when General Rosales suddenly came up with a surprising move. As we were about to take our seats for another session we were called to another room, where he and his delegation were gathered in a semi-formal type of formation with General Rosales first in the line-up.

In a friendly but stately style which had clearly been worked out beforehand, he introduced us to the second officer in the row, whom he had in the meantime ordered to report for conference duty, presenting him as a National Hero of the Republic of Cuba – a formal title in Cuba, something majestic. Since communicating through interpreters is often accompanied by a certain amount of confusion, I did not realise immediately what exactly was happening, but I met the officer – General Arnaldo Óchoa Sanchez.

But Óchoa left as suddenly and inconspicuously as he had arrived, and I later heard a rumour that when I had arrived there with Viljoen and Oelschig the Cubans had suspected me of trying to impress or even intimidate them with our hairy bush-fighters. That made them decide to bring in their own top fighter, Óchoa, as a counter to Eddie and Freddie.

This story provides an indication of the extent of the suspicion that still existed between us, and the tricks which were played as a result. It should therefore not come as a surprise that, in spite of the long discussions and hours of mental wrestling, we could not reach an agreement on a ceasefire, disengagement and the redeployment and withdrawal of our forces.

I suppose that is why the discussions at Sal Island did not make the books and articles. But I was quietly content with the meeting. I felt that we had planted a seed in New York that had now sprouted at Sal, and that the time would come for us to pick the fruit.

By the way, this meeting at Sal was not the alleged 'debaucherous conference' about which Crocker later created a sensation – that took place earlier, involved other principals and was not so much a debauch as a group of negotiators letting their hair down in rather too raucous a fashion after yet another round of highly stressful talks.

I am quite certain that if it were not for this link in the chain of negotiations we would never have achieved success at our subsequent talks at Geneva.

Months later a wooden box was delivered to my home in Pretoria. It was filled with tinned fruit juices and rum – a small gift from Gen Arnaldo Óchoa Sanchez.

* * *

A day or so after our return from Sal we were off again, this time to Geneva. For me this was without doubt the turning-point in the negotiations. Here the discussions of the preceding sessions reached a high point; knowing that the fate of countries and peoples was at stake tested one's moral courage.

The formal discussions took place between 2 and 5 August. Before every round of negotiations Neil van Heerden – whose methods and style I liked – would gather his team for what we called in-house meetings, to prepare ourselves for the up-coming session. Chet Crocker, on his part, usually arranged informal discussions with each of the parties before, during and after the formal negotiations, more often than not involving only the delegations' leader groups.

These informal talks usually took place during meal-times. I could not help putting on a mock serious expression and telling Neil that he should use his influence to have the pattern changed so that we would not have to talk serious business over meals. I pointed out that when saying grace we asked the Lord's blessing and that my mother used to caution us that if we were not cheerful and on our best behaviour at table, He would refrain from blessing the food; and this was probably why we sometimes suffered from indigestion! To my utter surprise he actually tried to change the arrangement, because he was sensitive to the small things in life.

This time, however, he did not succeed. It was now 31 July 1988, and before the negotiations were to begin we had to have a working meal with Crocker. During the eating and talking, and in view of our supposedly failed attempt at Sal, I asked Crocker how long it would take the UN to begin implementing Resolution 435 once the green light had been given. He replied that if one credited the UN with being capable of acting speedily, it should be able to do so within about three months.

So I did a quick mental sum: *Tomorrow is 1 August 1988, add three months and the answer is 1 November 1988.*

Later in the day Sonnie asked me why we did not propose a specific implementation date at the first plenary session, the full formal session of all parties, which was taking place next day. I said yes, brilliant –1 November 1988. We would then work backwards to arrive at the other dates: South African troop withdrawal, Cuban re-deployment and withdrawal, disengagement of forces and a ceasefire. That evening we put it to Neil van Heerden, Derek Auret and Niël Barnard.

More than a year later, I think, Neil invited all the members of his team, together with their wives or girlfriends, to an 'in-house' dinner at the State Guest House in Pretoria, where he gave a short intimate speech in which he thanked everyone for their contribution and recalled some of our experiences:

The negotiations around a settlement in Namibia and Angola proceeded through many phases and alternated between moods of optimism that a solution was close and stages of deep mistrust between the respective delegations.

General Geldenhuys and Brigadier Sonnekus came up with the suggestion, at the end of July 1988, in my hotel room during one of our countless late-night preparatory discussions, that we should simply propose a date for the implementation of the settlement plan to the other parties.

It would allay the mistrust on the part of mainly the Cubans and the Angolans and give direction to the negotiations, which at that particular point had reached a state of near-checkmate.

This proposal was submitted to the government and

approved, and the next morning, when we proposed in plenary that 1 November 1988 be the starting date for the implementation of the settlement plan, it had a dramatic effect on the whole meeting. There was an immediate request for an adjournment of the meeting. Our 'opponents' were clearly caught off-sides.

In the end this decision made an important contribution to an agreement being reached and which resulted in the independence of Namibia and the withdrawal of Cubans from Angola.

Agreement was reached on the Geneva Protocol during this round, and from a purely personal point of view I believe that this success was, to a great extent, the result of the wearisome work we had done in the side-halls at New York and especially at Sal Island. It included:

- A recommendation to the Secretary General of the United Nations that 1 November 1988 be earmarked as a date for the implementation of Resolution 435.
- Fixing 10 September 1988 as the target date for signing a trilateral agreement.
- Fixing 1 September 1988 as the deadline for Angola and Cuba to reach an agreement acceptable to all three parties on a schedule for the northward redeployment and the total withdrawal, in stages, of the Cuban troops from Angola.
- South Africa's assent to all its troops being withdrawn from Angola by 1 September 1988.
- An agreement that Angola and Cuba would use their good offices to restrict SWAPO to the north of the 16th parallel after the withdrawal of the South African troops (the latter was, in fact, completed before 1 September 1988).
- An undertaking by Cuba not to deploy its forces within specified geographical boundaries described in the protocol (this excluded Cuban forces from an area in the south-east of Angola.)
- The establishing of a Joint Commission to develop additional practical measures to build confidence and reduce the risk of unintentional incidents.

It became clear later on that in practice it was impossible to adhere to all these target dates. The resulting few months' delay, however, made no material difference to the content of the eventual agreement. This round put us, in Niël Barnard's words, in command of the moral high ground.

The border war and our subsequent intermittent entanglement with Angola had been dragging on from 1966 – 22 years. But it had taken just over a month to make a solid start on the road from war to peace. The last major clash with FAPLA and the Cubans was in southwest Angola on 27 June 1988; by the end of July and the beginning of August 1988 the path of negotiations towards peace had been clearly demarcated at Geneva.

* * *

It is to be expected that in this book I write about the people with whom I travelled along the road of war, but as the roads of war and peace crossed I also acquired some unexpected fellow travellers.

One of them was the bearded Jorge Risquet. Outwardly he reminded one of Fidel Castro in some respects, although he was shorter and sturdier in build. At the conference table he was all rhetoric and fiery emotion from beginning to end, so I found it quite amazing that in spite of the commanding and confident public image he projected he was sociable and indeed almost retiring in private.

Senor Aldana, who took over from him, was a cultured man with a keen sense of humour and an impressive intellect, self-effacing to the point almost of unobtrusiveness, yet with his feet firmly on the ground. One could not help but have respect for his professionalism. According to Neil van Heerden, he was an expert in the field of labour relations, which was, no doubt, why we found him such a proficient negotiator.

The Joint Commission met first in Havana, with the next meeting scheduled for Cape Town, and just before the adjournment of the Havana meeting Aldana asked Neil: 'How does one get to Cape Town?'

Neil's joking reply was: 'You fly east, and then you turn right.'

Aldana responded: 'Mr Van Heerden, are you sure – Cubans … turn *right?*'

During the same meeting Chet Crocker quoted the American admiral, Dick Walters, as having said: 'A person who does not recognise the value of flattery is one who does not get any.' I am not sure as to whether Aldana then tried to flatter Crocker, albeit ambiguously, but he remarked: 'I was always one of Crocker's most loyal opponents.'

I once sent Aldana a small South African national flag with an explanatory note, saying that the first time our national flag had ever been officially hoisted had been in Havana on 30 March 1928, two months before it was flown for the first time in South Africa and elsewhere on 31 May of that year. Mr Eric Louw, then South African trade commissioner in New York, had had the flag manufactured in time to fly at Havana during an international conference on immigration and emigration.

General Ulises Rosales del Toro was spartan in his eating and drinking habits. He kept himself neat and healthy, as becomes a soldier; he was loyal, courteous and quiet, did not seek the limelight and did not deviate from the rulings of the politicians. His appearance was that of a professional military man, nothing like the popular image of the bearded Cuban soldier in combat dress with a cigar in his mouth and a rifle slung over his shoulder. I got along well with him.

The cordiality of our relations once turned me into a minor smuggler of sorts on the way back from Geneva. When passing through one European airport's departure section, a few of the South Africans were singled out for special attention by the security staff. One of them asked me whether my luggage included any parcels given to me by anybody. Innocently I said no, and she let me through; it was only when we were already in the air that I realised I had been untruthful – the Cubans had given some of us a few packets of their coffee. I still wonder what the official's reaction would have been if I had said, yes, a Cuban had given me a parcel to take on the plane with me … But I can attest that there was nothing except coffee in those packets, because after we had flown back without any mishaps we drank it all.

I had first met our facilitator, Chester Crocker, some years before at the Zurich airport on 20 September 1981, when I was a member of a team under diplomat Brand Fourie which was involved in one of the first rounds of discussions in the new series of talks. Crocker and I were both waiting for our luggage, but he did not make any particular impression on me; it was only when he spoke that his hidden talent showed. I saw him only a few times after that, but I first got to know him better after May 1988.

At one time or another I have heard him described in a variety of ways: 'Oh, that bloody conservative'; or 'oh, he's a dangerous liberal'; or (by a number of US congressmen) 'he's arrogant'. But perhaps he was just an American and a man for realism; not the type of realism that necessarily suits his listeners, but the true article. Later, when it was all over, many conservatives resented him for what he had achieved in southern Africa, and some of his liberal opponents regarded him with malicious envy for the same reason.

I cannot think how anybody else could have played this role better, if at all. He was very practical for an academic; purposeful and systematic – good qualities for the type of negotiation we were involved in, because we travelled down many tricky roads and saw much beating about the bush.

Fortunately I had already retired from the service when he wrote: 'He [Geldenhuys] also had the disconcerting habit of doing crossword puzzles or falling asleep during Pik Botha's windier monologues.'

The other milestones in the series of formal negotiations were the discussions at Brazzaville on 24–27 August 1988, 6–9 September and 26–28 September; New York on 6–8 October; and Geneva on 11–13 October. All of these dealt with the northward redeployment and the phased total withdrawal of Cuban troops from Angola.

Agreement on the time-scale was reached at Geneva and afterwards confirmed in the formal bilateral agreement between Angola and Cuba on 22 December 1988. It dealt with the redeployment of all Cuban troops to north of the 15th parallel by 1 August 1989, and the 13th parallel by 31 October 1989, concurrent with the withdrawal of Cuban troops from Angola by 1 April 1989. In other words, 3 000 troops before the implementation of Resolution 435; 25 000 (50 per cent of the total) by 1 November 1989, the date of the general election in South West; and so on until they were all out by 1 July 1991.

The linkage between the various steps foreseen in Resolution 435 and the Namibian settlement plan, and the schedule for the redeployment and withdrawal of Cuban troops, was now clearly confirmed. It was an exceptional achievement, particularly when one recalls the near-universal rejection of the linkage concept in the past.

This series was followed by formal negotiations at New York on 22–24 November 1988 and Brazzaville on 1–3 December 1988. Agreement was reached on a new date for the implementation of Resolution 435 (1 April 1989); provision was made for the signing of the trilateral agreement between South Africa, Cuba and Angola; and for the bilateral agreement between Angola and Cuba concerning the end of the Cuban military presence in Angola, as well as a mechanism for its monitoring by the UN. The trilateral agreement was finally signed on 22 December 1988 in New York.

This did not mean the end of the talks, however. The parties still had to make the trilateral agreement work, and this function was assigned to the Joint Commission established by virtue of the agreement.

Somebody asked me one day what I had learnt from all the politicking and diplomacy. I responded by quoting a piece that I invented as a way to tease my diplomat friends and colleagues:

> It is more difficult to make peace than to make war. In war you try to deceive and outwit your opponent and he knows it; he tries to deceive and outwit you and you know it – which I think is quite an honourable arrangement.
>
> When you talk peace, the first thing that the parties do around the negotiation table is to establish mutual trust and confidence. Having done so, everybody starts to lie to everybody else – and you're not supposed to know it.

This is, of course, just a little joke that has no bearing on reality.

Then situations arise when the parties must agree because their masters insist that the talks not be derailed and that a favourable press statement is to be issued. In the meantime, however, one party says that the glass is blue and the other insists that it is green. Then they decide to agree that the glass is not yellow. They release a report to the press stating that the negotiations are still on track; there are aspects on which they agree, and although many problems still remain to be solved, they are cautiously optimistic; they have agreed to meet again. Whether the glass is yellow or not, to me it sounds much like the same language that one was hearing in South Africa during the early 1990s.

Neil van Heerden can talk straight, but he can also play this game of nuances with finesse.

Military men are internationally renowned for being at ease with their foes, or war opponents, if you like … like Major Edwards and General Manie Maritz, who considered calling a temporary cease-fire during the Anglo-Boer War so that they could play a game of rugby against one another at O'Kiep.

The South African Defence Force was likewise never filled with bloodthirsty hatred for its enemies. With very few exceptions – and definitely no meaningful ones – its approach was professional, scientific and businesslike. Sometimes I even got the impression that military enemies find it easier to make contact with one another than political opponents. So it surprised me when Crocker wrote: '… but getting these men [Rosales and myself] to communicate openly was a struggle.' Fred Bridgland, on the other hand, described our first meeting with the Cubans on 3 May 1988 in London as follows: 'The atmosphere was stilted and thick with suspicion. It took the military men to break the ice.'

The *Sunday Star Review Special* of 9 April 1989 wrote: 'General Geldenhuys, described by an American diplomat as "somewhat quiet, taciturn and reserved", took the initiative. Dressed in a blue-grey business suit, he walked over and introduced himself to his Cuban counterpart. He broke the ice. After that there were small, informal, and initially rather stilted meetings over drinks, dinner and coffee, the diplomat noted.'

I visited Windhoek after Namibia's independence. The permanent Secretary for Defence, Mr Frans Kapofi, received me in his office; also present was the Chief of Staff of the Namibian Defence Force – and my opposing commander many years earlier – General Dimo Hamaambo. Mr Kapofi arranged a small informal reception for me. Some of my officers and I swopped war stories with ex-PLAN commanders. A good spirit prevailed, and I really appreciated his gesture.

Some of my erstwhile colleagues, South Westers who had previously served in the SWATF, were also present, and I could sense that some of them were slightly uncomfortable. Possibly they thought that I took an unfavourable view of their decision to stay on in the Namibian Defence Force. But I made it clear to them that I did not even remotely feel this way. In fact, I told them that I supported them wholeheartedly. There was no question of resentment. They must serve their country without any reservations.

CHAPTER 18

A TRAGIC FIASCO

Flagrant contravention of the Geneva Protocol

I was now approaching the end of a long road. My contract as Chief of the Defence Force and Director-General of the Department of Defence would expire on 31 October 1990; I had less than two years to go. But much remained to be done. The war had finally ended and the most difficult negotiations over South West and Angola were also a thing of the past – but the road was still not running downhill. It had not even levelled out yet, and some of the biggest-ever intrigues imaginable lurked ahead.

Resolution 435 had still to be implemented. South West had still to become Namibia. The peace syndrome caught up with the war and overtook it, so that the scaling-down of the SADF had to begin even before the Cubans had withdrawn from Angola. And scaling down, which includes cutting back on your people, is an ugly thing that taxes one's emotions to the extreme.

The implementation of Resolution 435 generated its own drama. I have always said that it is difficult enough to conclude an agreement between warring parties, but to make it work – that is the big test. The story of the Lusaka Agreement is a case in point.

How does one make a peace-settlement plan work? In an interview with the editor of *Politica Internaçional* I aired my opinion in this regard with reference to another peace agreement which still had to be implemented, that between the Angolan government and UNITA, which was supposed to end their 17-year war with one another:

> The overall Angolan peace agreement and the documents in the ambit thereof make for heavy and formidable reading. They include the ceasefire agreement, including all its annexes, the Fundamental Principles for the Establishment of Peace in Angola ...
>
> The contents of the package spell one word, namely complexity – for the simple reason that it attempts to bring peace to a very complicated situation. Now, let me tell you, the multitude of papers will not make the agreement work.
>
> Success will depend on three equally important factors. First is the political will of the main parties, the Angolan government and UNITA, to make the agreement work. Second is the effective functioning of the Joint Political and Military Commission, and third, the continued involvement of their principal and, very important, the top echelon of the mediating country and observer-participants to the agreement, i.e. Portugal, the USA, the USSR and the UN.

This opinion was just as valid for the pre-implementation stage of Resolution 435. But it would soon become apparent that not all the parties' *bona fides*, at least in the beginning, were above suspicion because 'they (and others) expected false moves on the part of South Africa', in the words of *Politica Internaçional*.

Our fears were the exact opposite. As a result of previous experiences, we feared that SWAPO would start pulling tricks.

Our troop withdrawal cut our flow of information, making it more difficult than before for military intelligence to keep track of PLAN activities. But MI quickly adapted to the new situation, and information was soon received of PLAN manoeuvres in contravention of the agreements. According to the Geneva Protocol of August 1988 the South African troop withdrawal from Angola had to happen concurrently with an evacuation of all PLAN members in the border area to the north of the 16th parallel, the withdrawal to be completed by 1 September 1988. But it did not happen.

Other spokesmen for the Defence Force and I reported this threat to the successful unfolding of the peace process by way of the prescribed channels and to the committees and forums on which we served. But the situation continued unchanged. In fact, it worsened as D-day (1 April 1989) approached. In response I not only kept to the normal routine but created opportunities to focus attention on the dangerous situation that had developed. But no corrective action was taken.

I also informed Neil van Heerden. He took it further, but it seemed as if nobody wanted to listen to us. As I have already mentioned, I often got the impression that most people were only too eager to believe SWAPO propaganda, because it provided them with ammunition with which to attack South Africa. But if we had problems with SWAPO, I always felt our accusations were being rejected as unnecessarily alarmist, probably in the hope of derailing some peace policy or other.

Neil van Heerden presented our case in very strong terms at the Joint Commission, but it made no difference. In a 1990 report by the Africa Institute of South Africa, Pieter Esterhuizen wrote:

> ... PLAN guerrillas continued to roam the area between the border and parallel 16. South Africa's complaints were disregarded in the 5-power Joint commission and, presumably, perceived as alarmist ... The loopholes exploited by SWAPO and the laissez-faire approach towards this irregularity had been plain for months, even before the signing of the New York Accord. These mistakes were to be paid for in human lives ...

What Esterhuizen said proves the correctness of my intelligence concerns and actions at that stage. But he wrote it only very much later; while it was actually happening, I felt very much alone.

I had also instructed the South African component of the Joint Military Monitoring Commission to take the matter up with their Angolan and Cuban counterparts. This was yet another monitoring mechanism that had been established by agreement.

The other parties did not react and refused to investigate the information, as was provided for in the Geneva Protocol.

Every time I addressed the accredited military correspondents during the monthly conferences, or whenever I had contact with the media, I informed them of the violations and the dangerous situation that had developed. At the last monthly meeting that I conducted before the implementation date, in which Glen Babb of the Department of Foreign Affairs also participated, I told them out of sheer desperation that if they wanted to make a positive contribution they could publish the information to put pressure on the parties to stick to the rules. The media reported as follows:

- SWAPO is cheating, says Gen Jannie – Headline, *Die Transvaler,* 17/2/89 .
- Angolans not keeping pact: Defence Chief – Headline, *The Citizen,* 17/2/89.
- 'Angola and Cuba are allowing several thousand SWAPO fighters to operate … in violation of the cease-fire agreement, the Chief of the South African Defence Force, General Jannie Geldenhuys, said in Pretoria yesterday.'
- 'The Angolan government's apparent unwillingness to move SWAPO will be one of the hottest items on the agenda when the Joint Military Monitoring Commission (JMMC) meets in Luanda next week.'
- 'The Deputy Director of Foreign Affairs, Mr Glen Babb, said the Cuban-backed Angolan government had not honoured an undertaking to urge SWAPO to withdraw from southern Angola by September 1988. Mr Babb warned this put SWAPO in a position to interfere with the Namibian elections and could "affect independence".' – *Pretoria News,* 17/2/89.
- 'Angola must say now if it does not want to, or cannot, oversee SWAPO's withdrawal.' *Beeld,* quoting me on 17/2/89.

It is a pity that the press was not taken seriously I could only guess at the reason why this was so. I was actually very worried about what I had told them. It could have been interpreted as an indication that I was exceeding the boundaries of my responsibilities as a soldier. But I was not called to account. In fact, there was no visible reaction at all.

It still puzzles me that SWAPO's invasion, when it happened, was described by everybody as a surprise. The whole world expressed its shock over the invasion that came 'out of the blue'. How could it possibly have been out of the blue? I ask you!

The invasion started during the early hours of 1 April 1989, when the first wave of 1 600 heavily armed insurgents crossed the border at various places. The rest is history. A handful of South African Police and Air Force crews, together with elements of the SWATF and the SADF which were re-activated, saved the situation. On a personal note, one of them was my son Bruwer, who arrived at Ondangwa air base for deployment on 6 April, his twenty-first birthday.

The security forces wrote a chapter of courage and glory which make Rambo's adventures look like child's play, but also a chapter dripping with blood. Under the UN flag they shot more than 300 PLAN members for a loss of 26 of their own. As Esterhuizen later wrote, 'SWAPO had suffered one of their worst blows of a long war – after agreeing to a cease-fire!'

In the meantime South Africa suspended the implementation of Resolution 435 (it was not resumed until 19 May). A meeting of the Joint Commission was hastily convened and members worked non-stop through the night, discussing alternative appropriate actions to get the peace process back on track again. We met at Mount Etjo in South West and other places, and there was also a considerable flow of correspondence from the South African government to the UN. Esterhuizen wrote:

> While Secretary-General Perez de Cuellar, under immense pressure from SWAPO's friends, began to show signs of vacillating and wanting to compromise, the US State Department issued a hard-hitting legal analysis which left no doubt that SWAPO was the transgressor. The document also concluded that if Angola and Cuba had permitted the infiltration of insurgents into Namibia, they too were guilty of 'flagrant violation' of the Geneva Protocol. [Neil van Heerden had warned Angola and Cuba at the Joint Commission before the event.]

Various commentators offered different explanations for this tragic fiasco. Pieter Esterhuizen's was: 'As was to be expected, the trilateral monitoring mechanism created by the Protocol (the JMMC) failed like its predecessor in 1984.'

I do not agree with this. No sort of monitoring commission like those about which I am writing can prevent war, not to mention make war. Unless the governments in whose hands the commission is an instrument have the political will to maintain the peace and take the commission seriously, you can forget about it. This is the big lesson.

* * *

PLAN's incursion was just part of a bigger scheme. But even by itself it had a meaningful influence on subsequent events. Many people told me that it was to the advantage of SWAPO's opponents that the invasion happened, because, they said, SWAPO had damaged its image in London, Washington, Paris, Bonn and other places. That was true. But the Londoners, Washingtonians, Parisians and citizens of Bonn were not going to vote in the elections.

People who want to intimidate for effect must threaten, and then they have to demonstrate that they have the capability and the will to go through with their threats. This is exactly what SWAPO achieved *vis-à-vis* the bush voters of South West. For many people the results of the election in Ovamboland remain a mystery.

Among the people that I had forewarned of the danger of possible disruptions to the process were Mr Ahtisaari and General Prem Chand.

Prem, incidentally, was a lovable person and a real gentleman. He would do no one any harm, appreciated the beautiful things in life and was brimful of memories. Things happened to him, he said. He called it 'happenstance'. He had been part of India's transition to independence in 1948, and, like many other officers of his generation, was more British than the British of today. He made ample use of the British army jargon of a few decades earlier and executed his political masters' policy to the letter.

One of his memories of 1948 was of his dramatic involvement in the early part of the transition. He took over command from the British of the Gurkha Rifles Regimental Centre at Dharamsala Cantonment in the northern Himalayas in January that year. On the 29th of the month he attended a regimental centre commanders' conference in New Delhi and on the 31st he was in the city with his father when he heard that Mahatma Gandhi had been assassinated. He and his Gurkha driver travelled by jeep to the house where Gandhi had been living; in the confusion nobody stopped him, and he went inside; and so, while India reeled, Prem sat in Gandhi's bedroom and for half an hour watched over the remains of India's greatest modern national hero.

One of his many other recollections was sparked by the sight of the Union Buildings when he saw them at the end of a jacaranda-lined street in Pretoria. He was seized by a strange feeling of *déjà vu* – and then realised that he was thinking of another Herbert Baker creation – the bigger brother of the Union Buildings, which was the main secretariat close to the presidential residence on a hill in the centre of New Delhi.

Meanwhile the disastrous SWAPO incursion was not the end of the insurgents' irregularities. It was still fresh in everyone's minds when we picked up information of yet another threatening SWAPO violation. Naturally we were not believed about this one either.

Let me go back for a moment to 1980's Operation Sceptic, as I promised to do in chapter 9. Now, in 1989, after 1 April, we received reliable information that SWAPO was enjoying free movement in Angola, and that they were not being monitored according to the settlement plan and agreements. The insurgents had not even been compelled to hand in their weapons and armaments, including armoured vehicles of their mechanised force, that they still controlled. We lodged complaints. As before, SWAPO and the Angolan government rejected our allegations with contempt, indignantly denying that PLAN had ever had such a force.

Neil van Heerden received notes from governments of other countries, including major powers, in which our accusations were shot down as absurd on the grounds that PLAN had never used any such types of weaponry in any way. This attitude was completely at variance with the facts, either because these countries were favouring SWAPO or had fallen for its propaganda, hook, line and sinker and preferred the conventional wisdom that we had cooked up the information to wreck the peace process.

I therefore submitted a summarised dossier which contained suffi-cient detail about the history of their mechanised force, including an inventory of their armaments, training programmes, names of com-manders and much more. I was also in the fortunate position of being able to confirm that I had seen their mechanised force in the field my-self – complete with BTRs, 76 mm field guns and so forth. That enabled Neil to reply to the notes, and to the best of my knowledge we never heard from them again.

Nor did PLAN members cross into South West at predetermined en-try points, as prescribed in the resolution and the settlement plan. And that was not all – more and worse was to come; like the day the Chief of the Army, General Kat Liebenberg, brought me intercepts made on the radio net of transmissions by the Kenyan battalion of UNTAG. What it boiled down to was that the Kenyan battalion was to close its eyes to certain dubious PLAN activities.

Now, most countries practise radio and electronic interception. Those who don't either do not regard it as necessary or do not have the capability. And those who do it don't talk about it. The secrecy shroud-ing this method of collecting intelligence often caused embarrassment to ourselves and other countries. We regularly received military intel-ligence collected in this manner which would have had to be released some time or another, and in some appropriate format. But if ques-tions were asked about how we had obtained such information, we had to answer evasively or pretend that we had collected it by other means. And if somebody asked what evidence you had, you'd had it!

Even people with reasonable knowledge tell you that these methods are being used all over the world and everybody knows it; why are you so secretive about it? The answer is: although the enemy might suspect you of doing it, they do not know when you do it, for how long and on what nets, frequencies and callsigns. If they can answer those questions they can change their frequencies, call signs and, worst of all, their codes. Then you would have to spend anything from a few hours to perhaps six months to break their new codes.

Or, and this can be even more dangerous, they can plant false messages for you to intercept. The secrecy, as we all know, had fallen flat in respect of the Kenyan intercepts. It was in all the papers, which is why I feel free to write about it. Kat Liebenberg and I went to see Neil van Heerden and Niël Barnard, and together we went to General Magnus Malan and Mr Pik Botha. Mr Botha released the information, and the other parties immediately rejected it as fictitious. The last word in the news media was that I, or somebody else in the Defence Force, was allegedly producing false intercepts to wreck Resolution 435, or that somebody else outside the Defence Force had done it for the same purpose.

This was not only untrue, it was practically impossible to manufacture such evidence in the first place. The standing objection to my explanations was that I had failed to prove my case from the files of the accused, the Kenyan battalion, and secondly the question was asked: Why had the tapes on which the intercepts were made been 'destroyed'?

In fact the tapes had not been destroyed, just wiped – which, of course, was just as bad for us – and re-used, since the hapless signaller had not had the foggiest notion that those particular intercepts would cause such a sensation. Any person who wanted to produce such a volume of false intercepts with a ring of authenticity to it would have had to have the apparatus, the people able to operate it and detailed intimate knowledge of the Kenyan battalion's daily activities and transmission patterns. They would have had to be conversant with Swahili, speak Kenyan English with a Swahili accent and be proficient in the use of Morse code. Forget it!

When I retired two years later there was still not the slightest indication of any kind that anybody had done such a thing or even could have done it. And until today nobody can negate the possibility that there was another irregularity in the offing. In fact, after the 1 April fiasco I had forecast in an Austrian magazine *Zeitspiegel* that other breaches could still take place: 'In my opinion more problems may arise and the further implementation of Resolution 435 will not proceed without hiccups, but it will in all probability go the whole way to independence.' Nobody can deny that Pik Botha's disclosure *did* prevent another 1 April trick.

This was not a case of our wanting to impede the progress of implementation, as many commentators seemed to think. All we had in mind – take it or leave it – was to prevent a replay of the 'shocking' and 'surprising' incursion of 1 April 1989 by disclosing SWAPO's violations.

And so our operational involvement in South West came to an end. On 21 March 1990, precisely a week after Mikhail Gorbachev was made

President of the Soviet Union, South West Africa became an independent Namibia. And now one can see the nature and characteristics of our military actions in better perspective.

The war in South West was often depicted as child's play. On other occasions it was portrayed as a war of extreme dimensions coupled with extensive destruction and sorrow. Personally, I regard it as accurate to describe the war inside the borders of South West as a low-intensity insurgency war. As Willem Steenkamp wrote:

> It is an indication of the low intensity of the border war that during its course the population increased rather than declined and no part of the territory was laid to waste. It is remarkable, in fact, how little the struggle impinged on daily life in SWA/Namibia.
>
> South of the black tribal areas it was always barely noticeable except for the occasional urban bomb blast and a couple of small-scale SWAPO raids on white-owned farms in the midlands, and in places such as Ovamboland the regional economies actually benefited from the conflict; ironically, probably the greatest consequence of the war was the accelerated abolition of most segregation laws and the inclusion of blacks in the previously all-white administration, so that by 1988 the territory's internal government was mainly non-white.

However, if one limits the analysis of the war to South West, one is left with a distorted perspective of what was actually happening. You have to see it as part of a bigger conflict.

PLAN infiltrated South West mainly from Angola and Zambia. In Angola itself there was a much bigger and more intense conflict than the one in South West had ever been. In Angola the whole of the Benguela railway line, from the Atlantic Ocean to Zambia, was permanently put out of action. Angola's economy collapsed completely. UNITA operated from within Angola, and for all practical intents and purposes controlled areas as big as some European countries, or provinces of the RSA. At the border between Angola and Zambia UNITA even issued visas, and the International Red Cross liaised with UNITA at its seat in Jamba.

The Soviets, East Bloc countries and Cubans were involved on a large scale by any standard. The Cuban presence towards the end of 1988 exceeded 52 000. The situation in Angola cannot, even by the wildest stretch of the imagination, be compared with the situation in South West Africa. As a further complication, SWAPO's involvement in the MPLA–UNITA struggle led to South Africa clashing with Angolans during cross-border operations and, for strategic reasons, becoming involved with the MPLA–UNITA war.

The truth, therefore, is that the war alternated from a low-intensity insurgency campaign in South West Africa to a prolonged regional conflict with international involvement in Angola. Here it was of much wider dimensions and periodically reached peaks of very high intensity.

PLAN was good. We kept them running, sometimes 50 kilometres a day. They escaped and evaded extremely well and lived in desperate circumstances, but knew well how to survive. And if they were in trouble, they fought bravely and well.

During the 1970s and early 1980s commentators regularly made statements to the effect that after World War II all the revolutionary organisations had won their wars. Furthermore, they declared, nobody could stop such movements if they had the support of Soviet Russia and Cuba. But in our case it did not happen. We effectively reduced and isolated the insurgent-activated area to merely one part of Ovamboland, itself merely one region of South West Africa. We, the security forces, won the struggle on the field of battle.

CHAPTER 19

OFFICE POLITICIANS AND SENIOR GENERALS

So much information and so little knowledge

The fighting in South West was finally over. In Angola the government and UNITA still carried on with their civil war, but with our withdrawal the fighting across the border was no longer of any concern to us. We had entered a new era.

Our military performance in Angola could now be placed in perspective – and journalists were doing so; they now had much better access to information than before. One of the changed approaches in the new era was that it was no longer necessary for us to apply the same degree of restriction on the release of information about the operations of the previous years. Access to hitherto classified information was thrown open on a large scale.

All over the world the supply of information on military matters to the media has been a point of dispute for many, many years. I do not believe that the different parties will ever really make peace. Conflicting interests do exist; the media will always say they do not get enough information and the military will always say the media are insensitive to its security problems.

I would like to mention briefly a few aspects of the problem as I experienced it in the past. The first basic truth is: To threaten or to make war means conflict. Therefore, you have to consider the elements of conflict when you analyse the flow of information to the media during war.

In the case of armed conflict secrecy is actually an old and proven principle for successful campaigning. But secrecy can also relate to other principles, such as surprise. You will not be able to surprise your opponent if he can read about your intentions in his morning newspaper.

Many experts also list deception as a principle of warfare. The well-read Brigadier Blackie Swart, a task force commander during Operation Savannah, often said that 'war is deception'. Your opponent must be informed in a way which will guide him towards making incorrect inferences. In a basic sense it could mean that if you are strong, you must appear weak to your opponent; if you are weak, you must appear to be strong.

It is in this atmosphere, with journalists insisting on getting the news on the one hand, while the military, on the other hand, is reluctant to provide it, that the media more often than not complain they do not know what is happening. They said so again during the First Gulf War, although they were inundated with information.

That great journalist Lord Deedes once said, after giving the war correspondents all due recognition, that 'the fact remains that the ceaseless sound, the plethora of voices round the clock, sheds extraordinarily little light on what is actually going on.' Then he quoted the famous commentator Malcolm Muggeridge as saying that 'there is so much information, and so little knowledge'. In other words, the information contains facts and images, but these do not tell a story; there is a gap between the facts and the interpretation of the facts.

Sensitivity about the release of information is not peculiar to the military. One also finds it during other forms of conflict. I noticed that there is normally a free flow of information in the field of finance, economy and trade. But the moment boycotts and disinvestment start in all seriousness the situation changes dramatically. When South Africa moved into an 'economic and trade war' it had to be managed as a conflict situation, especially in regard to imports and exports. People to whom military secrecy previously probably did not make much sense suddenly changed their views. For example, Raymond Parsons, Director-General of the South African Chamber of Business, was suddenly heard to say on more than one occasion that the less information South Africa released about our imports and exports, the better.

But one must always bear in mind that the journalists are professionals. They also have principles, one of which is that what they are doing is in the public interest. They will always try to get their stories. It is their job, and you cannot blame them if they ask questions that you find difficult to answer.

By way of reflection I must say that I cannot complain about the questions the media asked me. In fact, what really caused me embarrassment were not the questions relating to the Defence Force – I suffered when questions of a non-military nature, especially political ones, were put to me. I tried my best, but I made mistakes.

Once during 1978 in Windhoek I was telephoned by my old diplomat friend from the AG's office, John Viall, a veteran of the International High Court days and the senior civil servant in South West. He told me about a news report in which I was quoted, and said: 'Pik [Botha] was looking for you all day long. So, now I'll give you his message. He wants to know who the hell do you think the Minister of Foreign Affairs is, him or you?!'

To get back to our military actions in Angola: with all the information made available after the war, many books, as well as magazine and newspaper articles, were published about the operations of the recent past. Books and publications like *War in Angola, the final South African phase,* by Helmoed-Römer Heitman, a correspondent for the authoritative *Jane's Defence Weekly,* and *The war for Africa, twelve months that transformed a continent by* Fred Bridgland, a correspondent for the *Sunday Telegraph* of London and *The Scotsman* of Edinburgh.

These and other publications were useful aids for evaluating our involvement in Angola, and especially the military aspects. But one should read these books and articles against the background of that time. Until the beginning of 1990 South Africa had a very bad image in the international world. Internally, too, a section of the reading public often had a poor impression of the government and its instruments. With regard to the Defence Force there was a great deal of negative talk about the 'securocrats' and the destabilisation of southern Africa.

Any writer who made a living from journalism would have had to take this into account, especially when writing in English for the international market. A writer could not really come out in praise of the South African Defence Force, because 'the business of every business is to remain in business', as the saying goes. The worst accusation that could be brought against a journalist was to be accused of being partial to South Africa or of relaying 'Defence Force propaganda'.

I believe that they were very much aware of it. They tried to protect their credibility in various ways. For example, in his foreword Bridgland says his publisher told him before he tackled the book that 'I [Bridgland] would be free to interview as many men as time, energy and money would allow. There would be no interference from top levels of the military or the government ... My own stipulation and that of my publisher was that there should be no question of the book being subjected to censorship by Pretoria ... These did not prove to be obstacles ...'

The advertising pamphlet for his book describes it as 'the unofficial story of the war through the eyes of the men who fought it, not those of generals and politicians hundreds of kilometres from the blood, sweat and dust.' Bridgland explains further: '... I subsequently pieced together the course of the war for Africa through scores of interviews with the fighting men. The only officer I interviewed above the rank of colonel was the Chief of the South African Defence Force, Gen Jannie Geldenhuys, who retired in November 1990.'

Seen against this background, it came as a surprise to me that both Bridgland and Heitman expressed themselves so strongly about who had won the war. Heitman says: 'The defeat inflicted on the FAPLA forces ... was so crushing that it changed the strategic situation beyond recognition.'

These and other writers, although describing UNITA and its allies as the undisputed victors, also take them to task in no uncertain terms. They lash out at the Defence Force, 'the generals' and 'politicians'. Well, one should always take criticism seriously. The writers offer valid arguments for their views. However, there are a few aspects with which I do not quite agree.

The first is that some other overall strategy might have delivered better results and that the campaign could have been handled in a different way. I suppose that, especially with the benefit of hindsight, one can always say things could have been done better, but I would like to query the approach of some writers. If they do not want to restructure the tactical run of operations on the versions of generals far away from the battlefield, they should also not try an analysis of the strategic course of a campaign that is based on the opinions of the fighters in the bush, far away from the strategic world.

The journalists created certain debatable impressions as a result of discussions they had had with junior members of the force about the 'bigger picture'. One was that if the ideas of the junior commanders had been put into practice our victory would have been even greater. Perhaps those field commanders were right, perhaps not. It is their right to express their views; it is a good approach which is part of our culture. We encourage people to air their views fearlessly, especially during debriefing conferences. Criticism coming from the bottom up is good, especially if you have won. If you have lost, it is bad. But the worst of all is when there is criticism from the top downwards. I have no such criticism.

One should appreciate the position of the field commanders. Some of them might only have participated in one part of the campaign and then gone back to the Republic with their troops.

During the campaign, of course, the junior commander regarded himself as responsible for achieving his particular mission, at the place where he found himself and during the time that he was there. How to do it successfully was his only concern – and so it should be. But a new commander and his troops, possibly straight from the Republic, might have had to take over the situation as the previous commander had left it and proceed from there.

Subordinate commanders were not relieved between specific operational phases of the campaign; somebody had to be responsible for continuity, to ensure that the operations to follow could be executed and that they would still fit in with the planned overall operational design. And that is the task of the higher commander.

As Montgomery said: 'This firm grip [of the senior commander] does not mean interference or cramping the initiative of subordinates;

indeed, it is by the initiative of subordinates that the battle is finally won. The firm grip is essential in order that the master plan will not be undermined by the independent ideas of individual subordinate commanders at particular moments in the battle.'

Another thing that was hinted at was that there was political interference in the operations. That was not true. Of course, from the overall perspective it is clear that politics played a dominant role by its very nature. Making war is a commitment of the political will. But I can bear personal witness that I received no political orders which meant interference with tactical decisions in the field. Perhaps some critics became confused by the grey area between tactical and strategic decisions, because political guidelines did have, as usual, an influence on strategic considerations.

The criticism of the South African government is actually ironic, because the clearest examples of political interference in this war were to be found on the Cuban-MPLA side! The most outstanding illustration was of course, Castro's handling of operations in Angola from Havana. But it goes further.

I promised earlier to tell why, in September 1987, the FAPLA forces very unwisely emulated the proverbial donkey and time after time thumped their heads against the fatal defensive wall of the Lomba River. Well, in a nutshell it was due to political interference. President Eduardo dos Santos, on the verge of a visit to Europe, wanted to arrive there with a military victory to his credit. That was why his troops had to try and try again to cross the Lomba, with tragic consequences each time.

Another theme of the criticism found in the world of books, political commentators and the news media was that of the stupid office politician or the senior general restraining the brave fighting general or commandant from destroying the enemy. It is an old and popular theme which is usually successful in arousing sensation, the most recent case being that of President Bush the elder, who supposedly stopped General Norman Schwartzkopf from destroying Saddam during the first Gulf War. I don't agree with that. Bush did as well as anybody in his position possibly could have.

Since governments make war without declaring war, it has lost much of its effectiveness in solving international disputes. War can be declared only if there is a strong political will plus a sound resolution by the government to commit itself. This requires sincerity, openness, courage and integrity.

When one country declares war against another it goes flat out to destroy its opponent and that opponent's capability to resist. Having done that, it subjects its enemy to its will and authority, and the dispute is settled. Then its publicly announced objective has been achieved.

When a country formally and openly declares war it must, however, realise that it can bring upon itself the mistrust, violent disapproval and possibly even the chance of action by the international community. It must therefore have a good case for which international sympathy exists, or it must be so powerful that it does not have to worry about international opposition. But declaring war will always be a momentous decision, to be taken with circumspection and integrity.

Nowadays, however, wars are being waged without prior formal declarations to achieve so-called limited objectives – in other words, the 'aggressor' does not aim to totally subject another country to its authority, it strives only to attain certain vitally important political goals, or perhaps temporarily safeguard its own national security. The war comes to an end when the limited objectives have been accomplished, or when regional or international political pressure leads to ceasefires and politically concluded peace settlements.

What frustrates the critics so much is that these wars end without all the international disputes having been settled in full, which often leads to further acts of violence.

From the sidelines I got the impression that Bush's political management of the military terrain was accompanied by insight and understanding. He handled the Gulf conflict brilliantly. He mobilised the whole American nation behind the war effort. In fact, he mobilised all of the international world that mattered to stand behind him. And, what is very important, he secured a legal base – a mandate to make war – from the Security Council, namely, please note, to eject the Iraqis from Kuwait and to reinstate the former government. Bush committed himself internationally and openly to this mission, to nothing less and to nothing more.

If Bush can be said to have made any mistake at all it was not holding Schwartzkopf back but possessing the wrong political objective – ideally he should have obtained a resolution from the Security Council authorising the allies to knock Saddam Hussein out completely and subject Iraq to their authority. I say 'ideally' because it is highly improbable that he would been able to secure such a resolution, even had he wanted to. As soon as the Iraqis had been ejected from Kuwait and the mission as described in the resolution therefore had been successfully accomplished, the war came to an end. Bush simply had no option except to honour his word. It was unthinkable that he should take matters into his own hands and act outside the mandate with the aim of totally overpowering Iraq and subjecting Saddam to his will. I do not dispute the fact that the war did not settle all the real long-term political disputes of the region, and left a situation full of remaining problems which could lead to renewed armed conflict within a few years. But this is a different matter.

The opinion of some of the Western media on this subject is well reflected in *The Citizen* of 18 March 1991, which said: 'We are beginning to wonder whether the United States and its allies went far enough in their battle against President Saddam Hussein.'

How far the operation went is irrelevant. What is important is how far the *political* decision went before the war started. Under the headline 'REGRETS OVER SADDAM TOO LATE', *Rapport* of 29 September 1991 stated: 'The American president, Mr George Bush, at this stage would probably like to tear out his hair because he forced Gen Stormin' Norman Schwartzkopf to abort his onslaught on the Iraqi capital Baghdad, a few hours before they would really have been in a position to overthrow President Saddam Hussein's regime.' But Bush did not constrain Schwartzkopf at the end of the war. He restricted his freedom of action long before the war had even started.

Nearer home, our aim in Angola was not to overthrow the MPLA's authority. We did not want to capture Cuito Cuanavale, get involved with Menongue and then create a Vietnam situation for ourselves. We wanted to help UNITA to repel the onslaught against them and enable them to defend themselves after we had left. Once we had achieved this objective, we had accomplished our military task.

Heitman read the situation well when he wrote: 'The 1987/88 campaign thus achieved its immediate aim and brought about a situation that offered interesting additional strategic diplomatic opportunities.

These were recognised and followed up, finally bringing about a settlement in south-western Africa that suited almost everyone. Quite apart from its tactical successes, therefore, the campaign of 1987/88 was a good example of how to use the carefully directed application of military force to achieve a political end – without so over-controlling the operation that it fails. The South Africans had come a long way since 1976.'

What more could we – and should we – have wanted to achieve than we actually did in 1987–1988? Bridgland wrote: 'Castro's dream of a Marxist revolution spreading from Angola to encompass the whole of southern Africa has become a poor music-hall joke, except perhaps in South Africa itself, where the ANC–South African Communist Party alliance had become by late 1990, along with Fidel Castro, among the last serious defenders of Marxist politics and economics in the world … It was the South African and Angolan men who fought the war for Africa against the Cubans and the MPLA who made it possible for Chester Crocker to secure his regional peace agreement.'

Heitman wrote that the key factor was the disaster which hit FAPLA in late 1987 and early 1988, which persuaded Moscow and Havana to reconsider their roles in this theatre. The campaign delivered conclusive proof that FAPLA could not stand against the South African forces on its own; furthermore, the successes achieved by a very small South African force had indicated that even Cuban intervention would not be able to stand up to them, unless Havana's forces in Angola were reinforced. This would require not only additional troops and equipment but also the creation of the technical infrastructure which was needed in a country like Angola to support a bigger force.

Notwithstanding the successful result of the campaign, commentators exercised their good right to query leadership styles. In this connection it is interesting to note the reflections of Thomas Pakenham, in his precise account of the Anglo-Boer War, on the styles of two generals, Redvers Buller and Louis Botha:

> What a contrast between the styles of the two Commanders-in-Chief. A British C-in-C was a *grand seigneur*, withdrawn behind a ring of ADCs, isolated even from his brigadiers. Botha's tent was open to the humblest burgher. It was an ordinary bell-tent,

captured from Symon's camp at Dundee and furnished with a packing-case and a stretcher chair. When an elderly burgher entered, Botha would give up the chair to him and sit on the ground. There he sat, as a procession of visitors tramped through the tent. He ate, drank, slept and wrote his official dispatches under their gaze. It won everybody's heart. Botha valued his privacy, but valued the confidence of his burghers still more. He took trouble with everything and everybody. He trusted in God – which of the Boers did not? – but left nothing to chance.'

Let us forget the two personalities for a moment and concentrate on the generals' styles. On the one hand we find the absolute maintenance of status and formalities in the field, and on the other a good-natured openness. From what I have been told, the Israelis probably lean towards the latter style. To them the task at hand is the most important thing. They do not go in for unnecessary ritual and shows of discipline; they are not interested in mere pomp and ceremony. To them it is taboo – they call it 'bullshit'.

I would say that nowadays the South African leadership style lies more or less between the two. It does, however, attract criticism to the effect that the presence of senior officers with battle groups during operations is unwise and unacceptable.

In recent decades it was General Viljoen who initiated the culture of senior officers being present, one way or another, during operations with task forces, battle groups or even combat teams.

I never led troops from the front. I never fired my rifle, shoulder to shoulder with the troops in the forward trenches, amid all the smoke, sweat, blood and flying shrapnel, and I would not argue that General Viljoen in his dauntlessness perhaps went too far in certain situations; but rather this way than the other way round.

The Army has a sound doctrine governing the best location for a commander during operations: He must place himself at a point from which he can best perform his duties. In other words, it depends on the officer's appointment, the function he has to perform and the nature of the operation.

Those few times when I was present during operations, however, I did not necessarily go there to carry out a specific task. I went there merely to be present and to observe. There are many reasons, in my opinion, why generals, or certain generals, depending on their appointments, should be present to observe during operations.

In the first place one should bear in mind that making war with volunteer career soldiers is one thing, but doing so with part-time soldiers and national servicemen is another. The public interest in the part-time soldiers is understandably much greater than it is in case of the career volunteers, and I believe that the nature of South African culture is such that it would be unforgivable, as the critics would put it, for generals to spend their time in their luxurious offices and to enjoy themselves after hours at cocktail parties in pretty uniforms, while the fathers, brothers, and sons of the people back home struggled and sweated in the bush, suffering wounds or perhaps even dying.

The nature of operations differs from place to place and from era to era. During World War II one might serve in the same regiment throughout the whole war, with the commanding officer getting to know every man under him. As a result a strong bond would develop between the commander, his staff and his troops. The same was true for much more senior commanders. Generals often had the opportunity to address all their troops on parade.

With the relief system in use in the South African army during the border war this type of continuity never existed. One had no hope of getting to know all of one's men, or even talking to them, because they were continually being replaced. It denied a senior commander the possibility of presenting himself, demonstrating his sympathy with his men and fostering a sound spirit of togetherness between himself and his commanders, staffs and troops.

The most and the least that he could do was tag along during operations. Then he could talk to the men. He could live under the same circumstances and experience what made life difficult for them, share in the success of victories and sweat blood with them when the going got tough.

A leader must be seen. A military leader is not like the normal business manager: he is responsible for his soldiers' weal and woe 24 hours a day. In an operational situation his decisions could mean life or death. In any case, who wants a factory manager who does not know what the production line looks like, or what happens there? It is also the duty of a commander, and especially a senior commander, to inspire his troops. He must promote the unique atmosphere and culture with the special values that he wants to see in the military organisation. And he cannot do that from a distance for too long.

Sometimes field commanders tried tactfully to keep me out of potentially dangerous situations, and in this respect a senior observer is probably a nuisance. It can also happen that one has an inhibiting influence on a commander, who might think that you are there to evaluate or criticise him, or that you might want to interfere. The overwhelming majority of our field commanders, however, had so much self-confidence that they were not in the least put out.

I was always careful not to interfere with subordinate commanders' responsibilities – although it happened that commanders told me straight out that it was comforting for them to know that I was in the vicinity. It did happen occasionally that they welcomed the opportunity to ask my opinion.

A high-level commander must beware of *fiction de guerre*, not to be confused with *friction de guerre;* it means having a fictitious impression of what really is happening during a war. He relies on the information that he receives. Much of the operational information he gets by radio or other means of communication, or by staff officers putting him in the picture through verbal briefings or written operational reports. But papers do not answer questions, and the cryptic style of operational reporting does not adequately describe the general atmosphere. It does not properly explain, for example, the influence of wind, weather and well-being on the practical execution of operations. Perception gaps and distorted impressions can be created in this way.

Remote and paper information can result in the making of wrong decisions. But if you are prepared to take the trouble to join an operation, even if it is only to observe and experience, then the same type of reports will mean much more to you later, because you can interpret them against the real background. You can put them into their true perspective and make better decisions in the office, if this is necessary.

Let us consider a hypothetical situation. You are at Defence Headquarters in Pretoria, or at 122 Plein Street (the former HF Verwoerd Building) in Cape Town, where you receive reports and briefings on an unrest situation in KwaZulu-Natal and the Witwatersrand. You form a certain impression of what is happening on the ground, after which you go and visit there. You talk with the senior commander, and together you and he talk to his junior commanders and troops. Perhaps there is an opportunity to see them in action. Now you get a different impression.

Back in Pretoria or Cape Town you receive more reports, but if you have to make decisions now, your judgement is greatly improved because you are not suffering from *fiction de guerre*. General Malan regularly visited subordinate headquarters, and another outstanding example of this sort of thing was the 1980s Minister of Law and Order, Mr Adriaan Vlok. If an unrest incident occurred he visited the scene if it was humanly possible. He would talk to the police and also to those disturbing the peace. Back in his office he could make certain decisions of which he might not otherwise have been capable, because his mind was not clouded by *fiction de guerre*.

If there is a degree of danger present during visits, you just have to use your discretion and be prepared to take calculated risks. Likewise, in a situation such as south-east Angola, where a sophisticated war was being waged, any general with a role to play must not have distorted impressions.

One such misconception I observed for the first time during Operation Savannah in 1975. The phenomenon became a pattern which recurred now and then until 1988. On a few occasions a sombre picture of developments in the war would be painted in Pretoria. Then I would go to Windhoek, and after a briefing the situation would not look quite so dark any more. Now I would go closer to the sharp end, say to Oshakati, and there the situation would almost look good. And when I arrived at the forward bases, I would find that everything was under control.

It happened a few times that worried staff officers would bring something to my attention. I would tell them that I didn't think the situation was quite as bad as it seemed, and that we should first go and have a look. Usually the situation turned out to be much better than expected, and we could make quick contributions to improve it (having said that, I am not trying to pretend that we never had serious problems that caused a great deal of stress).

This brings me to the next point of criticism against our high-level leaders – that our decisions had been unduly affected by the fear of losing human lives.

When you are a leader of men in an armed conflict, a unique factor distinguishing you from leaders in other fields is that the decisions you make can result in loss of life. This factor has a tremendous psychological influence on the decision-making process and the people concerned in it, especially the leaders who carry the responsibility.

Before the armed conflict in the Falkland Islands the United Kingdom mobilised its largest and most formidable air, land and naval expeditionary force since World War II, then set sail for the South Atlantic to evict the Argentinians. It appeared to me, however, that they procrastinated for a long time before the eventual decision was taken to give the command that really got the land battle going.

That occurred only on 20 May 1982, while the Argentinian invasion had taken place on 2 April. One explanation could be that there was nobody in the British cabinet or high command with much experience in taking decisions about sending people off to war and assuming responsibility for the consequences.

The first Gulf War was characterised by the same pattern of reluctance; newspaper headlines and extracts dealing with the period before the land war started tell the story:

- 'Officially, Bush had not even decided when he will decide ...'
- 'Bush dispatched Cheney and Powell to the Gulf to talk with Schwartzkopf and other allied commanders ... and they will give Bush their recommendations on whether the ground war should be launched and when' (*Time*, 18 February 1991).
- 'I don't want my men to die – US General Norman Schwartzkopf "Agony of fatal decisions"' (*Sunday Times*, 10 February 1991).
- 'Delay Gulf land attack plea' (*Citizen*, 11 February 1991).
- 'Tearful Bush tells of war order' (*Citizen*, 7 June 1991).

I believe that in similar situations the Israelis, for example, make such decisions more quickly. They attach the highest value to the life of a soldier, but they already have experience of the psychological torment involved.

When James Ambrose Brown's book *Retreat to victory* was published it also started a controversy over the question of whether Major-General Dan Pienaar's decision-making during World War II was unduly influenced by the high price he set on the lives of his men. His son denied such assertions.

After the 1987–1988 fighting in the south-east of Angola there were hints to the effect that South African generals had become over-sensitive to the possibility of losing lives during operations. The insinuations unsettled me. A person defending himself against such statements can easily be tagged as someone who is not sensitive to the loss of human life.

It is an emotional matter, and you are easily placed at one of two poles: Either you are sensitive to loss of life, or you are careless about it. Why cannot one place the highest price on every life and still have enough of the moral courage of one's convictions to take real decisions? Experience of this kind of psychological wrestling helps you to develop this frame of mind and mood, which I believe the senior South African officers of my time possessed.

It may perhaps seem noble to delay taking a decision in the hope that something will happen to change the situation, but the time that elapses can ultimately cause even more lives to be lost. You give the other side more time to prepare, and the chances of surprising and misleading the enemy become less and less.

As Montgomery says in his memoirs: 'The matter of decision is vital. The modern tendency is to avoid taking decisions, and to procrastinate in the hope that things will come out all right in the wash. The only policy for the military leader is decision in action and calmness in crisis: no bad doctrine for the political leader either.'

*　*　*

There remains one question about the fighting in south-west Angola: that I have left unanswered so far: What were the Cubans' real intentions there?

Well, a dramatic incident provided the answer, not long after the end of that episode. The man I met so briefly at Sal Island and who later sent me a box of canned fruit, fruit juice and rum, General Arnaldo Óchoa Sanchez, one of Cuba's most acclaimed national heroes, was arraigned before a tribunal in Havana on drug-smuggling charges. It was a transparently fake trial, and inevitably the verdict was 'guilty' and the sentence death

When the sentence was confirmed by Cuba's State Council on 9 July 1989 Castro delivered an address in which he gave his version of what had happened during the war. It confirmed what we had always suspected. Suddenly, as a result of these events and Castro's speech, sensational headlines appeared in the newspapers.

- 'Castro tells how his tactics ended Angolan war' – *Pretoria News*, 28 July 1989.
- 'Cuba executions spark suspicions about Castro' – *The Star*, 28 July 1989.
- 'Why Cuba's scapegoat general died at dawn – Fidel's fight not to lose face – Castro explains why Angola lost battle against the SADF' – *Business Day*, 27 July 1989.

From Washington DC, Simon Barber – a respected professional analyst who reported authoritatively on the American–Caribbean sphere – wrote for *Business Day*: '(Óchoa) was to preside over Cuba's last hurrah in Angola and the "heroic" defence of Cuito was therefore a vainglorious fraud, designed to cover a retreat that had already been decided. The 15 000 new troops who followed Óchoa came to save Cuban face, not the MPLA.'

Bridgland said: 'Nothing illustrated the Cuban crisis more aptly than the decision of a 47-man revolutionary military tribunal to shoot General Arnaldo Óchoa Sanchez, the soldier chosen by Castro to pull his chestnuts out of the fire in the War for Africa.

'For his efforts in Angola and elsewhere over the years Óchoa was one of only five officers to have been made a Hero of the Republic of Cuba. But scarcely a year after the Cubans and the South Africans fought their last battle on Angola Óchoa was put to death in 1989, by a firing squad, ostensibly for drug-smuggling offences of which he was found guilty at a bogus show trial.'

Business Day's Barber commented on Castro's speech as follows:

It is popular style to allege that Pretoria agreed to withdraw from Angola and Namibia as a spent force with its tail between the legs. This is not the analysis that emerges from Castro's version of events in his speech ...

In contrast, it is clear that Castro had already decided towards the end of 1987 that the MPLA was militarily and economically over the wall, defeated in the field and four years in the red with the insignificant 20 million dollars per year the Cubans apparently charged for their services. South Africa and UNITA had won effectively. For Castro there was only one way out – a unilaterally staged demonstration of military prowess and speedy departure homewards ....

The immediate aim with his address on 9 July was to denigrate Óchoa's role during the last year of the war by portraying him as lazy, incompetent, insubordinate and venal ... When Óchoa arrived in Luanda in November 1987, the Angolan army and its Soviet advisers were in headlong retreat after their rout at Mavinga ... On 15 November Cuba began to land the first of 15 000 reinforcements, amongst others 'our best pilots'.

'Everybody was asking us to do something,' Castro explained, adding, with thinly concealed contempt for his allies, 'we understood that even though we were in no way responsible for the errors that had led to that situation, we could not sit still and allow a military and political catastrophe.'

In the meantime there was panic and mutual recrimination at the Soviet–Angolan–Cuban operational centre in Luanda. 'Many problems had to be solved.'

Óchoa, judging from remarks last month by Cuba's Minister of Defence, Mr Raul Castro, Fidel's brother, during June 1989, was appalled by what he had found and apparently remarked: 'I had been sent to a lost war so that I will be blamed for the defeat ...'

The Angolans were no longer a factor in the war. On the other hand, the Cubans had secured their flank for the next move. It was the time for Castro's grand, solo stroke – the gesture that would save Cuban honour without the nuisance of Angolan incompetence.

On 10 March a new reinforced Cuban main force under Generals Cintra Frias and Miguel Lorente Leon was ordered to move from Lubango southward towards the Namibian border. 'The most important of all strategic operations had begun ...'

His major concern was that the South Africans would spoil his gesture by giving battle ... Castro merely informed President Eduardo dos Santos by telex that he had ordered his generals to 'place all forces on a state of maximum alert ... '

Although he did not play open cards with dos Santos, Castro was adamant that all other parties knew about his plans. 'We notified the Soviets ... we were warning everyone of the danger of the possibility that we might have to launch a strong attack in northern Namibia ...'

He cabled Óchoa: 'The first step must be a strong air attack against the camp, military installations and South African personnel in Calueque and its environs ... if the enemy's artillery can be located, strike it harshly.'

Twelve South Africans were killed in the air attack, the dam was hit and Pretoria 'raised a big fuss'. But the South Africans also 'restrained themselves militarily', just as Castro had hoped they would. 'We have given them our initial response. Now it is up to them to decide what to do and if they should continue the escalation ...'

It is not the story of a South African defeat. It is the story of an Angolan defeat and how, with considerable nerve and panache, the Cubans extricated themselves from it.

Crocker confirmed Barber's assessment. I definitely do not agree with Crocker on everything, but he still is one of the best people, if not the best, when it comes to writing with authority about this important period of war and diplomacy in the history of south-western Africa between 1980 and 1990. He was the man who listened to all sides, talked, cautioned and coaxed. He practised a great deal of restraint and did not take sides. He demonstrates this to an extent in his book: not by the fact that he is equally generous in handing out bouquets and backhanders, but rather because he gives everybody the same dressing-down. He certainly took a few digs at me, and said that our knowledge of Cubans was 'the stuff of comic books'.

As I have said many times, interpretations of these events depend largely on the person's political convictions. I have given my version, but we have also had others at regular intervals.

First there were the Cubans and Angolans, who announced to the world that they had won the war. Then came the professional journalists, who claimed the opposite. Then Castro came and qualified the earlier Cuban position virtually beyond recognition. Then I came with *my* account of the war.

As I was completing the original manuscript of this book in November 1992 the latest edition of the magazine *Insig* arrived with yet another version. On the outside cover was a sketch-map of Angola with a drawing of a tombstone and a wreath. The words on the gravestone read: 'Here lies the pride of the SA soldier (and the broken back of our economy)'. Inside is an article by Mr Jan Mellet under the heading 'ANGOLA – SA still licking its wounds'. Next to it is another article which is entitled 'Agony of a parent'.

By that time it was not difficult to know exactly what position *Insig* would adopt and how Mellet's version would be coloured. It is well summarised, in my opinion, by his choice of a quote from Stephen Ellis, written four years before, in May 1988 – before the war had ended, and long before Castro and all the others had disclosed meaningful and illuminating information and findings on the war: 'More than 6 000 South African and South West troops are dug in about forty kilometres south of Cuito Cuanavale and 400 kilometres from their base after they couldn't capture this strategic southern town. What the SADF had lost is the initiative and the belief that it could beat any black army.'

Amazing.

Then came the next version: the *Sunday Times* of 25 October 1992 published a report on Crocker's book about the same events, and presented a very different picture to the one in *Insig*, as if replying to it, under the headline 'Crocker: the big lie of Angolan war'.

Just about every week more and more of the truth came through, but up to the end of March and the beginning of April 1993 I was still encountering people who would ask me: 'Now, what *really* happened at the Lomba (Cuito Cuanavale)?' Then, when I had told them, they would ask: 'But what *really* happened?' And they would ask more questions, such as why we had withdrawn.

The answer is: We never wanted – and never tried – to keep a fighting force of any consequence in Angola on a permanent basis. It is a historical fact that we withdrew after every cross-border operation, and there was absolutely no reason why Modulêr-Hooper-Packer should have been an exception.

It illustrates the problem of creating perceptions by means of propaganda. Once a perception has been established one tends, even unconsciously, to take account only of the information that confirms your impression or fits into it. If the information does not suit you, you ask questions, and if the answers do not fit into your perception, you search for more questions to ask.

Anybody who does not want to accept that the Cubans launched a crafty and extensive propaganda scheme, and who wants to believe that the FAPLA alliance had clinched a victory, and keeps on asking questions to get confirmation for these views, will never accept my answers.

Such people will keep on asking questions such as: 'Why did you stop at Tumpo?' – the answer to which was that we had accomplished our mission and had already started to withdraw; the official clock on the scoreboard had long ago indicated that the game was over, and the political whistle had already announced the end of injury time – exactly as had happened so many times before.

They will keep on asking: 'What about our fighter aircraft's "technical deficiencies"?' Answer: Unlike sport, the playing field in war is never completely 'level' and the opposing parties never use the same standard equipment. In the armament technology race there is always one horse that pushes its nose ahead of the others, and then another one, and another and then perhaps the first horse again, and so on. It is usually, at any given point in time, a temporary arrangement.

In addition, it is so that cometh the weapon, cometh the countermeasures, then the counter-counter-measures, then the counter-counter-counter-measures, and so on. In my experience there was never a need to worry about a technology problem that could have put the result of the campaign in the balance.

But we did suffer a certain disadvantage that caused me conscious irritation, and about which few people talk. This drawback was the result of geographical chance, misfortune, *friction de guerre.*

The airfields at Cuito Cuanavale and Menongue from which the Soviet pilots, the Cubans and Angolans operated were very close to the battle area. By contrast we had to operate from Rundu and Grootfontein, which were much further away (see Map 2), and the disadvantages of doing so are obvious.

To name a few: In practice it took our ground-attack fighters such as the F1AZs 42 minutes from Grootfontein to the target area, which gave them just three minutes' fighting time. From Rundu it took our air-superiority fighters like the F1CZs 18 minutes, which gave them 17 to 20 minutes over the combat area. Our enemies, on the other hand, needed only 11 minutes to cover the much shorter distance from Menongue, which gave them approximately 45 minutes over the battle area.

If the geography had been the other way round – even if it had favoured neither side – it would have been a horse, or rather a course, of a different colour. Then we would have exceeded our proven excellence.

Whatever other questions may still be asked, whatever the answers given – it will not change the scoreboard ... or the result.

CHAPTER 20

REVOLUTIONARY POLITICS

Perceptions and misperceptions – 'the pig in the middle'

This chapter has remained almost unaltered since I wrote it in 1992. I have done so because in it I made certain observations and predictions about what would emerge from the South Africa of that time.

The country was then riven by dissension, often violent, particularly among the black political movements and parties, at the same time that those very parties and ones representing other races and interest groups were involved in the Codesa negotiations which aimed to forge a new South Africa out of the old one on whose behalf the SADF had fought the border war.

I leave it to the reader to judge the accuracy of my predictions and reflect on comments and observations made at a time of great uncertainty. Perhaps some insights will emerge which he or she will find useful, even after all the time that has passed and the things that have happened.

*   *   *

Having reached the end of the road which had led me through Angola and South West Africa, I could now shake the dust of war and peace from my feet. But in South Africa the thunderstorms and clouds of un-rest were pouring out scattered showers of political violence.

The use of violence in the form of terror to achieve political aims fol-lows a pattern. It was a phenomenon in Africa after World War II that many political parties, of which some were also resistance movements, had their own 'armed wings'. Everyone calls it by a different name to suit his politics.

In South West only one of the political organisations, SWAPO, had its own armed wing – PLAN. In South Africa we were in much the same position as in South West, although only the ANC's Umkhonto we Sizwe, or MK, was worth mentioning. However, one cannot in any way compare MK with military wings such as FAPLA of the MPLA, UNI-TA's FALA and SWAPO's PLAN in respect of numbers, capability, history, military achievement and armament. Be that as it may, as a psycho-logical factor and an implement to aid political efforts, MK could not be ignored.

As a result of its armed capability SWAPO had a decided political edge over the other parties in Namibia. SWAPO supported its politics to the end with the use of weapons or the threat that it would do so, and the same could happen in South Africa. But here the situa-tion has become more confused. The PAC's APLA has become more prominent on the news front. Whether it now actually possesses a big-ger capability than it had in the past, I cannot say. In the meantime armed organisations are also emerging on the right of the political spectrum. If you allow one party to have its own 'defence force' you cannot deny it to another.

If only one party has its own military capability, the chances are good that when arms are laid down you can have a bloodless period of transi-tion, as was the case in Namibia. If two parties have the capability, the possibility of some kind of civil war in the transition phase cannot be excluded – as in Angola. If more than two parties possess armed capa-bilities there is a prospect of anarchy. One could, perhaps, try to ignore them into insignificance. If that is impossible, it is an early warning sign that their intimidation is successful, and then you have to constrain that.

I am not altogether sure who is going to shoot who, but if this lot breaks loose, we will certainly reach the point where the Defence Force will have to assist the police once again. Therefore it is of vital importance that the Defence Force remains neutral.

It is definitely no longer the time for revolutionary movements and take-over strategies. It is the time for political parties and settlement politics. It would nevertheless seem, during 1992 and the beginning of 1993, as if the PAC, ANC and SACP are showing some reluctance to wave goodbye to armed wings, and one can see why.

For decades they lived in the atmosphere which prevailed in the Soviet Union, its satellite states and allies such as Cuba and Libya – an atmosphere created by dictators, one-party states and communism. The doctrines they practised for years were those of revolution and other violent forms of seizing power.

It is certainly not good for the extremely important politics of today still to hear incessantly about the maintenance of underground structures, the formation of defence units, mass action and 'the struggle continues'. This language belongs to revolutionary models. It creates suspicion exactly at a time when one wants to foster mutual trust. It makes me think of what the sovietologist Dr Jan du Plessis said many years ago:

> The top Soviet leaders used to talk about peaceful co-existence or whatever the nice 'in'-words of the time were; in the meantime, however, instructions were going out to the Communist Party or the KGB to divide, to cause friction, to start revolutions, to incite violence.
>
> The same pattern has occurred in Africa. The top figures say the nice things. Meanwhile the party, the military wing or the youth movement receives orders to commit violence. Even after this phase, when peace negotiations begin, the problem does not cease to exist.

After Angola and South West an officer told Fred Bridgland: 'We have won the war, but can we manage the negotiations?' It is difficult. Diplomacy is not the only alternative to war, there is also politics. But there are politics and politics. Communist-schooled revolutionary movements conduct a revolution through revolutionary politics and revolutionary warfare. But when the revolutionary war comes to an end, the revolutionary politics continue.

Call it political warfare, psychological warfare, street politics, propaganda or whatever else you like; it is in this field of revolutionary politics where politicians who are used to the Westminster brand of democratic politics normally find themselves awkwardly off-sides.

It is the politics of mobilisation and control of the masses, of enforcing stay-away actions, of boycotts and strikes. It is the politics of ultimatums, demands, claims and threats. It is the politics of creating perceptions through uninterrupted repetitions of accusations.

You do not have to like revolutionary street politics, but one thing is sure, you cannot ignore it, and you do not have to. It can be countered. If you do not counter it, the non-stop allegations create suspicion, and the suspicion creates impressions, and they become firm public perceptions which later cannot be changed.

However, in South Africa we have to cope with violence erupting from politically related unrest as well. Unrest also forms a pattern.

In 1984, 1985 and 1986 unrest – revolutionary by nature and aimed at the authorities – followed the inauguration of the tricameral parliament. The unrest that started in 1990, and which at the time of writing is still in full swing, similarly followed on political change. It was to be expected that we would experience a renewed wave of unrest after the coming to power of F W de Klerk as the new president, the release of political prisoners and the unbanning of political organisations.

In the beginning it was not of a revolutionary kind and was not aimed at the authorities. But this wave of unrest was also politically inspired, although in a different way.

The unity among black people, which was based on a common cause, namely to acquire political power, has crumbled. In the new dispensation, achieving blacks' aspirations became possible without the need to fight for it. As a consequence the black parties and politics-related organisations, in their endeavours to obtain political power, became fierce political opponents. This gave rise to polarisation, friction and violence; political conflict between factions began to include armed clashes.

The problem now was not so much that of national security but rather that of public safety. Most of the analysts use socio-political and socio-economic models to analyse a situation and make forecasts. Such models are valid, but others should not yet be discarded. The unrest of 1984, 1985 and 1986 neatly fitted more than one revolutionary model. After political reform, revolutionary incitement of unrest should go out of fashion.

But we can expect that unrest-related violence will spill over into the reforming transitional period. It may increase or decrease in intensity and frequency, but it will be there. Every political peak, referendum, election or whatever brings its own friction. It does not matter if it is a success or a failure. What is heartening for one is a serious disappointment to the other.

After the transitional phase of political reform we can expect a new wave of violence, one of a socio-economic and criminal nature. It will also probably be manipulated for political gain.

Sociologists claim that the population growth cannot meaningfully and timeously be checked. Economists say that we will not be able to reach the economic growth necessary to provide jobs for our population. Over a few years, consequently, we shall have to face the prospects of having thousands of young people, many of whom have only scanty education and training and lack the moral support of the family unit, who are unable to find jobs. Those who cannot be upgraded will probably have to be suppressed.

I am optimistic. Dr Wim de Villiers assured me that the economy will be able to provide enough work. I believe him. And Professor Laurie Schlemmer says that something can be done about the jobless youth. I believe him too. One consolation is that if extraordinary measures are necessary to suppress violence, they will be much more acceptable than before because the new government will be more widely regarded as legitimate.

The entry of right-wing radicals to the arena of violence became a serious problem during 1992. It can be contained on a manageable level, or it can break loose and become a serious threat to the negotiation process. But sooner or later the negotiators will have to return to the conference room. Through all this the role of the security forces remains vitally important.

I agree with those who say that sorting out unrest incidents is not the primary task of the Defence Force. But there are other aspects to this, and I would like to put the matter into perspective.

Those who were opposed to the use of the Defence Force in unrest situations propagated their cause very actively and emotionally through the mass media. Thus it happened that a general impression was created that it was negative and evil. Anybody who wanted to say anything positive about it did not count. You were out of step, you were promoting immoral doctrines. The emotions mobilised against the employment of the military seriously damaged neutral and objective approaches to the problem.

I would like to plead for fairness and rational thinking, because public opinion in this matter can greatly assist in solving the future problems of our country, or it can do a lot of harm.

I agree that the use of troops in internal unrest situations should be limited to the minimum, but it is also true that virtually all countries of the world provide for it in their legislation – and they make use of that provision.

The Defence Force, like most other government departments, does not have only one primary task. And in this respect our Defence Act is in line with international customs. The National Guard of the US has state and federal functions to protect life and property, and to maintain peace, order and public safety under conditions determined by law. It is regularly called up for such duties. In South Africa, too, troops have been used in unrest situations over many decades and by governments of different parties.

We should never regard the use of troops in unrest situations as completely taboo. The insistence on not employing troops has boomeranged on us before. At one stage during 1990 a variety of people and organisations almost pleaded for deploying troops in unrest-stricken residential areas. For example, newspapers reported that the Black Sash had come out in support of deploying troops in Natal. Troops were then used, and were praised for their actions. I received letters of appreciation.

On this occasion, just as I had done during previous waves of unrest, I formulated a personal message, printed on a card which was issued to each and every soldier performing unrest duties. By doing so I had made public my approach to the situation and the orders to the troops. It read as follows:

Fellow Soldier

Hundreds of people have already lost their lives in the renewed conflict in the black townships. Property, freedom and the right to a peaceful existence has been destroyed.

The people have the right to protection. We have been asked to assist in providing it.

During 1984 and the years thereafter you have been asked to deliver this service amid violence and chaos similar to what is at present happening in some areas.

This time, however, there are important differences – some of the people who previously insisted on your withdrawal from those areas, today plead for your presence – it is a tribute to you, the soldiers of this country.

Nowadays violence is often aimed not so much against the state to achieve political goals, but it is used rather to settle disputes amongst groups of the population.

Justice and good order is essential for stability and for the future of our country and all its people.

Be firm but friendly, determined but impartial; and above all, fair.

Respect the person and property of other people! I appreciate your valuable contribution.

Gen Jannie Geldenhuys.

My sons also received these cards. Martin, in the meantime, through war and all, had studied privately and passed the Military Academy's second-year exams at the end of 1987. He was now qualified to go back to the Academy in 1988 for full-time study to complete the final year of his degree course, and in 1989 was back at 32 Battalion. I bumped into him by chance a few times. Once was in Angola, when I had to attend to some matters at the Joint Monitoring Commission after the Lusaka Agreement; he was involved in the joint South African–Angolan patrolling. Another time was when he was on unrest duty in Natal.

Bruwer voluntarily signed up for 18 months' short service after completing his national service, and left as a lieutenant in December 1990. He, too, performed unrest duty in Natal.

I underwent training in unrest duties during the early years of my military career in the 1950s, while my uniform still smelt of the quarter-master stores, and we should continue to do so. We must not emotionally cut off our nose to politically spite our face. We must take care.

The problem is that during times of conflict propaganda is being used to create false perceptions for political gain, and in the following phase of reconciliation they are being kept alive, and are obstructing the peace process.

But I still believe in the basic ideal that it should not be necessary to use the Defence Force for such service. We must give the police the opportunity to increase their numbers. As far as possible they should be able to manage unrest themselves, at least during normal, and even short-lived abnormal, situations. During the early 1990s the police force is indeed far below strength in comparison with the police forces of other countries of the world.

The police need our sympathy and co-operation. They have to be neutral and treat all political parties alike. But there are parties and parties. They are not all like the Democratic Party in South Africa, the Conservative Party in the UK or the Republican Party in the US. Some parties have their own armed wings, their own intelligence departments and so on. What now? Should the intelligence community demonstrate the same lack of interest in them as in the others?

If the police turn up at a place of unrest before violence starts, they are accused of having caused the violence; if they arrive after the violence had begun, the accusation is that they purposely arrived late and could have prevented the violence through timeous action; if they arrive there just at the right time, their mere presence created the climate for violence, or they erred in some way or another.

In the Western world the security forces called upon to serve during situations of internal conflict are always the target of propagandists. It follows a pattern. In future we can expect that again there will be real objectors, pretentious objectors and supposed objectors from many quarters who will agitate against an allegedly 'unholy' or 'unjust' war. It is always the same. I think of the book by Desmond Hamill on the British security forces in Northern Ireland, which is aptly titled *Pig in the middle: The army in Northern Ireland 1969–1984.*

CHAPTER 21

THE END OF THE STORY

Ancient history and peace syndromes

Thanks to politics, propaganda and suspicion, different attitudes existed towards the role and image of the Defence Force in the aftermath of the border war. And so this penultimate chapter, too, remains largely as I wrote it in 1992, with South Africa still in transition, the present constitution as yet unwritten and the current external peace-keeping duties undreamt of.

* * *

It is unfair, in my opinion, to accuse the Defence Force of wittingly having gone all out to protect evil practices. Impressions have been and still are being created which do not reflect the true characteristics of the Defence Force. I do not believe that a single soldier ever joined the Defence Force with the purpose, or even the vaguest notion, of becoming a champion of evil.

The single most important theme of General Fraser's study, which was completed and officially accepted as far back as 1960–1961, was that the prevention or winning of a revolutionary war required 80 per cent political effort and only 20 per cent military activity.

The role of the 20 per cent military component in his formula must be clearly understood. Its purpose was to prevent a violent revolutionary take-over and maintain stability and public safety while political and constitutional solutions were being sought. Military solutions were not regarded as real solutions.

General Malan publicly supported the 80–20 principle over a period of 25 years. For example, at a banquet in Johannesburg on 20 October 1981 he said: ' ... the solution to a revolutionary terrorist war is only 20 per cent military. The main burden, that is 80 per cent, rests with the politicians'. His stated point of view was, in fact, used by many of his political opponents as ammunition with which to blast him, for example during the parliamentary debates of 23 April, 12 May and 16 May 1986.

My successors and I likewise publicly declared that it was our task in South West to create sufficient order, stability and safety so that internal constitutional development and international politics could follow the road to democracy and independence; and significant progress was made in this direction during that time.

The truth is that there is no bigger single group of South Africans with more experience of living in a country in an advanced stage of total democracy than our defence people who served with cheerful devotion in South West. From 1978 onwards South West was far ahead of South Africa in terms of political reform. The Turnhalle Conference was already functioning in 1977, 14 years before the Codesa negotiations started.

The biggest and toughest battles we ever fought in concert with the SWA Territory Force took place *after* the cornerstones of apartheid in South West had already been destroyed. As far back as December 1978 one-person-one-vote elections were held and the free democratic process was well on track. SWAPO had been invited to participate in the process, and one can't help but speculate about whether they would have done better or worse than during 1989 if they had accepted that invitation.

Some political commentators, usually ones apathetic towards the Defence Force, for a long time promoted the idea that the army should be a professional, in other words, voluntary, organisation. All right, let us hypothesise. If we had had a purely voluntary career army from 1948 onwards we would not have had national servicemen in it, representing the entire white political spectrum. We would not have had the Citizen Force and Commandos, which were equally representative of all the white political persuasions Actually this coverage was even broader, since all people of colour could volunteer for national service or the part-time components, and a great many did (even the regular component had many thousands of loyal non-white members by 1990).

So if we had not had that infusion of citizen-soldiers we might well have entered the 1990s with a purely Malan, Strijdom, Verwoerd and Vorster army. Would we not then have had a type of party-political army? Or what am I saying?

No, if the Defence Force was evil, it was no more evil than the government; and the reverse now applies as well. The principle that the Defence Force is subservient to the government of the day is one which applied in fact as well as in law from the earliest days. In this regard the following quotation from the Al Smith Feature Service is an apt one:

> War is an activity involving violence and passion.
> War is subject to the vagaries of human behaviour.
> War is essentially subordinated to politics.

The most fundamental element of Clausewitz's philosophy is that war is subject to politics, and should be. He says it many times and in many ways. But politicians are not always the best people to assist the military with their war problems – which they would not have had in the first place if it had not been for the politicians.

The Defence Force would have served the government if General Smuts had managed to achieve his post-World War II idea of incorporating South West into the Union of South Africa. The Defence Force would have served the government when the Odendaal Commission divided South West into sub-territories representing different population groups … if there had been any military duty to perform.

The Defence Force *did* serve the government, however, when there was a majority government in South West during the 1980s. In the 1990s, when this book first appeared, the Defence Force was serving the government in South Africa in the period of reform and transition.

During a joint sitting of Parliament on 1 March 1992 President F W de Klerk said: 'The government and I are proud of our security forces and their achievements. They saved the lives of many innocent people and bought time for South Africa through their successful counter-revolutionary actions over the years against conflict and terror. That is why we can now work full steam to get the new South Africa politically and economically going.' He said that he looked on the security forces as an indispensable element of a safe and stable future.

The employment and control of the Defence Force in a future government of the day will probably be prescribed by a law such as a constitution, which would in turn probably be maintained by an independent judiciary.

The country still needs the Defence Force, and will need it again in future. It does not seem as if much is coming out of the much-heralded 'new world order'. The question of whether the present African culture can support a democratic Africa has yet to be answered. While the new arrangement of blocs – the new Europe, the Americas and the Pacific Rim – draws much attention, we also cannot totally ignore the many forecasts that by far the largest part of Africa is dying. Many reasons are offered in support of this contention, one of which is its inability to use new technology in order to increase its well-being.

Because European and other countries need all their time and money to solve their own problems, Africa runs the risk of returning from its present prominent position in the international limelight to its former proverbial state of darkness. How long will it take before the rest of the world once more turns the spotlight on Africa and takes a fresh look at its many unexploited assets – and in the process causes new clashes of interests? And will such disputes be settled without the use of violence? In such a case, one should always bear in mind that a defence force is not there to protect a nation's interests only by waging war. It is also there to serve the national interest by preventing war and giving the nation a credible presence at any conference table at which it might seat itself.

After every conflict there are people who think that war serves no purpose, and in any case will never occur again; history proves that this is not how it has worked out until now. Before a war people are often enthusiastic over the idea. After a war people are often caught up in the syndrome that war is futile. It becomes a recurring cycle.

Somebody once told General Denis Earp, a former Chief of the Air Force and a Korean War veteran, that 'it served absolutely no purpose to have made war in Korea'. Now, before I describe his reaction, one should remember that Denis does not talk lightly on the subject of armed conflict. On 27 September 1951, during his stint in Korea, his aircraft's cooling system was shot to pieces. He had to eject and was captured near Kaesong. For 23 months and three days he was a guest of Red China, and was released only towards the end of August 1953, after peace had been concluded on 27 July of that year. And on 5 January 1982 his son, Lieutenant Michael John Earp, a Puma helicopter pilot, was killed in action on the border shortly after his twenty-sixth birthday. He was Denis and Beth Earp's only son.

But his reply was: 'How can you say that? After all, we saved a country, South Korea and its people, from communist domination that in other countries had caused so much grief and misery to so many people over so many decades. And look where South Korea is today – one of the most dynamic and prosperous industrial countries of the world. North Korea, its neighbour, by way of contrast, is one of the most miserable, cruel and suppressive of all the Stalinistic countries. It is also one of the poorest.'

Every year the South Koreans still express their thanks and pay tribute to South Africa and to our air force.

So what did we achieve in South West and Angola?

I have no doubt that SWAPO's goal was to seize power by force. In fact, they said so themselves and on many occasions. And they also tried to do it. Furthermore, I have no doubt that they would then have been seriously tempted to establish a one-party Marxist government, in the style of 1970s Mozambique and Angola.

Our military counter-measures prevented that. The mission of the Defence Force and the SWATF, as publicly stated, was to make a contribution towards giving South West its independence in the form of a democracy, by means of constitutional change rather than through a violent revolutionary take-over. That is what we achieved. Yet there are still people who say that nothing was achieved by the war.

Commentators' interpretations of the war depend on where they position themselves politically in respect of the war effort. Naturally I will be inclined to correct the 'distorted picture', as I see it. It was meaningful that we had kept the security situation stable up to 1988.

Although the intensity of the conflict increased, the security forces remained on the path of victory, while PLAN was losing ground. In the meantime FAPLA, on which PLAN depended heavily by that stage, was steadily losing ground against UNITA. In essence we bought time until 1988, creating a favourable situation for a political solution.

One would be unconsciously inclined to analyse the war years against the background and thought-patterns of the present situation, but in South Africa we took such a quantum leap during the early 1990s that now, only a few years later, it is only with great difficulty that we can do a proper job of thinking ourselves into the partly forgotten ancient history of the 1970s and 1980s. But to do that proper job we have to place ourselves back into the circumstances of the time. Cuba still believed in a military victory in Angola, and until 1989 the MPLA bargained on it. Within South Africa itself the ANC and the SACP believed that they were going to destroy the structures of the administration by December 1986, with matches and petrol-filled motor-tyre 'necklaces'. The so-called frontline states reached the peak of their political aggressiveness against South Africa during the same year. If a settlement had had to be negotiated under military pressure during the middle 1980s you can imagine how one-sided and excessive the revolutionaries' demands would have been.

As sovietologist Dr Wim de Villiers said at a conference on 3 November 1989: 'In 1975 South Africa stood almost alone in an environment where Marxism and one-party states were being established. But we won this third colonial war in Africa. We gained time for the rest of the communist system to fall to pieces all over the world.'

If it was not our strategy to gain a quick overall military victory, it certainly was to fight over a period in order to create a situation conducive to the favourable settling of political disputes. And that we did. If anybody finds fault with this approach I have to shoulder at least part of the blame.

There are also those who say that the war only foiled our diplomacy; that we caused South Africa's isolation; and that the war impoverished us. I always believed, and it has now been proved by recent history, that South Africa had absolutely no hope in any way whatsoever, war or no war, to be accepted by the international community of states while its domestic policy remained what it was.

During 1989 we did get a new government with a new policy. Political prisoners were released, banned organisations which included the SACP were unbanned. Even so, it takes years to get back, and it will never be complete until a new constitution and a new government are in place.

We would have been in a much worse position if we had not held the front. The mere cessation of the war would not have brought us back into the international world while apartheid was still in force.

It is also clear now that the war did not cause disinvestment and trade boycotts. Those problems would have remained even if the war had ended. The problem was politics. We did, in fact, conclude peace in 1988, and it made no difference to any boycott. Hopeful signs only appeared during 1990, when the political situation changed.

And still people say the war was unnecessary. SWAPO won the elections, not so? SWAPO did – it is true. But Namibia is a multi-party democracy with a sound constitution that only needs to be maintained. The representative distribution of parties in parliament is a good start. Friends tell me things are going well there.

Many commentators' predictions on the election results were hopelessly wrong. SWAPO collected 57 per cent of the votes and the moderate parties 43 per cent. The *Sunday Times* of 24 September 1989 reported that after a three-month opinion poll which concluded in June 1989, just before the election, the Arnold Bergstraesser Institute had found that 'if an election had been held in June the South West African's People's Organisation would have won easily with two-thirds of the votes.' The authoritative South African Institute for International Affairs, meanwhile, predicted that SWAPO would get something like 60 to 70 per cent of the votes.

Many other commentators' predictions on the election result were also hopelessly wrong, and so the results came as a shock to them. The analysts should have asked themselves where their information went wrong, or where their judgment had left them in the lurch.

In my opinion they were the victims of excellent SWAPO propaganda, not to mention *fiction de guerre*, and they ignored the influence of the security forces' successes.

I had always said that if the SWAPO fighters were to return to South West from the bush proud, neat and triumphant, they would clinch a large majority. But they came back first through a flagrant – and disastrously failed – violation of the settlement plan, and thereafter mainly as refugees.

Our endeavours enabled us to keep the war on the winning path until South West, Angola and South Africa were in the best position for constitutional transition to democracy. South Africa's bush and border war must be rated among the most successful wars of its kind since World War II.

In future South Africa will be cited as a good example of a country that waged war at low cost, even during an arms boycott. Indeed, the war was almost entirely financed from a normal defence budget which compared favourably with other budgets internationally.

An analysis of the total amount of money allocated to the Defence Force during the 10 financial years for which audited appropriation balance sheets were submitted to parliament by the Auditor-General (1977–1978 to 1986–1987), shows the following:

During these 10 years the defence allocation in real terms was an average of R7 173 million per year, which is slightly less than the R7 232 million for 1977–1978. In real terms the 1986–1987 defence allocation was 7.6 per cent higher than the 1977–1978 allocation, as opposed to the 37.6 per cent increase for the country as a whole.

Defence expenditure as a percentage of state expenditure decreased from 18.4 per cent in 1977–1978 to 14.4 per cent in 1986–1987. Defence expenditure as a percentage of the gross national product decreased from 4.8 per cent for 1977–1978 to 4.2 per cent for 1986–1987.

In real terms, at 1988 rand values, the amount budgeted by the Department of Public Works for the Defence Force decreased from R272 million for 1977–1978 to R197 million for 1986–1987 – a decrease of 28 per cent. Figures which I released on 1 April 1989 showed that the costs of our involvement in South West ran into R580 million per year, plus limited assistance to UNITA. The defence budget was less than 5 per cent of the gross national product. It compared favourably with countries such as the USA (6.5 per cent), the UK (5.4 per cent, Israel (14.8 per cent), and Mozambique (10.8 per cent).

The Defence Force provided SWATF with equipment and other stores against repayment. During the six years before independence the Department of Finance provided for additional budgetary assistance in respect of defence to South West; during the 1988–1989 book year it amounted to R80 million.

We were definitely not insensitive to financial matters. While I am on the subject of finance, and thinking back to the many taunts we had to endure about 'rich' senior civil servants enjoying such a 'good life', I cannot help but use this opportunity to mention that during my last few years in office a South African Airways Boeing captain was paid more than the Chief of the South African Air Force – and there were about 100 Boeing captains!

Towards the end of 1986 we formalised our productivity improvement programme with such success that during 1988 the SADF received a gold award in the competition run by the National Productivity Institute.

I conclude my review of the war with some final remarks on the Soviet effort. We believed that the Soviets' military involvement in Angola, together with other factors and other involvements, would exhaust them so much that eventually they would have to give it up.

During the late 1980s a certain aspect drew more and more attention: it is one thing to have the technological capability to manufacture armaments, such as the Soviet Union did; but it is another thing to use those armaments; and it is a totally different kettle of fish to use them thousands of kilometres away from home base while having to maintain them technically. And with every technological advance, maintaining them becomes more difficult.

I find it hard to make predictions in a fast-changing world and region. War is still raging in Angola, Mozambique is preparing itself for elections and multi-party politics, there is a new government in Zambia, the future of Zaïre is unsure and reform is taking place in South Africa.

I find it just as hard to look back and decide what the course of our region would have been if the South African government had followed a different policy in regard to South West Africa after the end of World War II. What would Namibia have looked like today if it had been an independence baby, born of the Cold War in 1950 or in 1960, or during the middle 1970s, when Angola and Mozambique became independent, or in 1980, when Zimbabwe became independent? I do not know. We know what Namibia looks like now. Given the historical fact that armed conflict started during the Cold War, we could hardly have done better.

The future may tell us that President De Klerk's speech of 2 February 1990, whether you were for or against it, was a more fateful event for South Africa than any other. But once again it is difficult to say what would have happened if it had been delivered at any other time during the Cold War.

Winners? South Africa and UNITA won the war. The MPLA and UNITA continue to fight. South Africa can work out its future in a climate free of the Cold War. The United States won the Cold War and got the Cubans out of Angola. The people of Namibia got peace, peacefulness and democracy – a rare phenomenon in this sub-continent.

* * *

My last glance at the war, however, is still not the end of the Angolan story. And it is a story with a moral.

Elections took place during September 1992 under UN supervision, after a peace agreement had been signed by the Angolan government and UNITA.

In the presidential election President Dos Santos led by a head, and in the general elections the MPLA won by quite a few lengths. Savimbi refused to accept the results, and the long war started up again. It was the same old story all over again – propaganda, propaganda, propaganda. South Africa again became the target. The Angolans alleged that they had shot down a South African aircraft giving support to UNITA. The last I heard was that South Africa requested Angola to provide substantiating evidence – and not another word was heard.

Another accusation was that South Africa assisted UNITA from Rundu in Namibia – although by now Namibia was an independent country, in full control of Rundu, and probably one of Angola's best friends. The next allegation was that South Africans were fighting on the side of UNITA and that more were being recruited.

As had happened earlier in the case of Mozambique, Angolans in Luanda told their South African confidantes not to bother about the accusations 'because we have to say these things for political reasons'. The problem with this was that so many people believed them. But then, in any case, reports reached the newspapers telling quite a different story: South Africans being killed and wounded while fighting *against* UNITA, defending government-controlled oil installations in Angola's war zone!

This brother-versus-brother peace-time war in Angola – *after* a peace agreement had been reached – is the bloodiest in the history of the country. I tend to think that the sponsors and overseers of the agreement should bear part of the blame.

One of the defects probably was that South Africa played no visible role in the negotiations – Minister Pik Botha once went to Angola to try to assist in saving the situation, but by then it was too late, and he was sent back. I hope that the peace process in our other neighbouring country, Mozambique, will not suffer from the same defect. Many people look upon Namibia's transition as a model, and I believe the success was due particularly to South Africa's involvement, rather than in spite of it.

While the war dragged on, the government and UNITA were playing the good-guy, bad-guy game. The government won.

For South Africa there are important lessons to be learned from all this as regards the planning and managing of peace and election processes. SAPA-Reuter and SAPA-AP reported in the *Pretoria News* of 8 October 1992 that 'Angolan Foreign Minister Pedro de Castro van Dunem conceded that 500 000 ballot papers – 12 per cent to 13 per cent of the votes – were invalid, but, he said, his government was "trying to identify the irregularities that had taken place".'

An SABC news bulletin of the time read:

> Portuguese observers who monitored the elections during December meanwhile allege that large-scale fraud had been committed. The spokesman of the group, Mrs Maria Antonia Paula, says the MPLA government was responsible for the wangling that took place before, during and after the elections.
>
> She says irregularities occurred with the registration of voters, and numbers of ballot boxes were transported without the observers of all the parties being present. Mrs Paula says the truth never came out because most of the international observers had left Angola before the results of the elections had been announced.

One should take note of these reports with a view to the future. According to another report, from UP in Lisbon on 26 November 1992, internal documents of the UN showed that 24 hours before UN representative Margaret Anstee declared the elections 'generally free and fair' she had been advised by her staff that there was proof of election fraud. The key document of 16 October 1992 states: 'It may generally be concluded that there were irregularities discovered in the electoral process which could have affected the overall outcome of the voting. In some cases, the volume of votes lost or gained by each candidate could, taken nationally, be so significant as to distort the final results.'

The same report alleges that Anstee took her decision with trepidation because the investigations of UNAVEM, the UN's group, generally supported the opposition parties' accusations. The deciding factor apparently was an expedient political decision, made in the office of the Secretary General, in view of the costs of a second round of elections should this one be annulled, and a desire to avoid international embarrassment.

At one stage Mr Pik Botha, speaking in Gaborone, expressed his concern about the possibility that the election problems could put a question mark over the legitimacy of the results. He requested the UN to provide additional personnel for the monitoring of the second round of elections. It never happened.

What really bothered me was that during this time the news media carried reports to the effect that various persons propagated the point of view that in the interests of peace the election results should be accepted 'whether they were free and fair or not'. I hope that 'elections and peace as soon as possible, and at all costs' does not become a widely held philosophy. It is too costly. It did not require special insight to forecast that the war – the most destructive in Angola's history – would resume.

An election can promote peace, or even be essential for it, but it is not a guarantee. In practice peace needs a sound base from which to take form. In early 1994, while listening to Margaret Anstee delivering a paper entitled 'Angola, what went wrong?', I realised that my warning against 'peace at all costs' elections was not far off the mark.

She asserted that the 'inelasticity' of the election date, which she had been unable to change, was one of the biggest problems. During negotiations it is essential, sooner or later, to fix certain deadlines. But these should be set with great circumspection, as deadlines often lead to deadlocks.

Was lack of time perhaps a major cause for the widely condemned *coup d'état* which was regarded as essential to get Bophuthatswana to toe the line? Or perhaps for the deadlock over KwaZulu?

Then there were elections in Kenya that came under suspicion. Mozambique and South Africa are also preparing for elections, and it would be irresponsible not to learn from the lessons of previous ones. South Africa cannot be compared to Angola, but the aspects that should receive attention during the planning and preparation are obvious. I have no reason to suspect that it is not being done. One can only imagine how the South African parties would react if a 12 per cent acknowledged irregularity occurred during the election without a mechanism having been provided to deal with such a contingency in a satisfying manner. The media can play a vital role here.

* * *

My story ends in an era of the most intensive flood of democracy and philanthropy that the world has ever experienced. The world of dictators and one-party states is crumbling. The Soviet Union is being democratised, as is most of Eastern Europe, the US is using the threat of sanctions to get Argentina and Chile to abandon the road of military government and to turn on to the road of democracy. One-party states in Africa are being squeezed into the multi-party and democratic crush-pen.

My story ends with the highest spring-tide ever of humanitarianism, righteousness and human dignity. The most extensive operations ever to feed the hungry of the world have been launched: Ethiopia, Somalia and Mozambique. The rights of the individual are being extended to the rights of the elderly, children, unborn babies and animals. Protection of the environment is the order of the day. Trade in ivory has been banned. The green rivulet of Green Peace is becoming a global flood which has increasing momentum.

The hot war was replaced by the Cold War; and the Cold War has been replaced by peaceful co-existence. The USA and USSR have become negotiation partners. The uncontrolled arms race has been turned around into a controlled arms-reduction process. South Africa has banned its bomb.

And yet?

And yet the Gulf War – in many respects the most destructive wave of violence the world has ever seen – still broke out! And yet the Yugoslavian wars broke out. We pray for peace and preach against war. But in the meantime violence rages. But it does not stop the peace syndrome. Now is the time for peace. That is the way the world wants it.

Although one should be fighting fit and employ combat craftiness when there is a war to be waged, one should not obstinately pursue battle when peace is being sought. The soldier who resists will find it hard to kick against the political pricks with his military boots. Just as certain syndromes come into play when nations decide to take up arms and make war, other particular syndromes emerge when nations decide to engage in negotiations to make peace. The prospects of peace bring into play dynamics that have their own impetus.

A soldier must fall in with the political decisions taken in this atmosphere – and with enthusiasm. His responsibility is to make war, at which time he needs maximum freedom of movement. The political leaders carry the responsibility when it comes to making peace: then they in their turn have to have maximum freedom of movement. When I had to make war, I did my best. And when I had to make peace, I did my best as well. But I was not wrong when I said that it was easier to make war than peace.

Patterns and models are sometimes used to study the transition from war to peace. One of these, in its crudest form, is that the victor disarms the defeated, dictates the conditions for peace, smells out the war criminals and writes a history.

If this model is used in the case of the South Africa of the early 1990s it would almost seem as if it is being applied the wrong way round. Ironically it was the ANC themselves who publicly told their militants that their claims should not be exorbitant, as the security forces had not been defeated in the field.

But the wrong model is being used. We are not so much in a transitional stage from war to peace as moving from an old political era to a new one. Other models should be used for the study of such a situation, even if it is common practice to blame war for everything and to find fault with those who were held responsible for waging it. In actual fact the real problem to be solved is not how to make peace between military enemies but how to do it between quarrelling political opponents.

It does not serve much purpose to look back. This is one lesson that we can learn from the new Namibian government. They did not yield to *Vergangenheitsbewältigung* (a German term meaning 'to manage the past through violent intervention') because, if you are obsessed with managing the past, you become blind to the favourable opportunities of the present, and you can end up with an unpredictable history and an uncertain future.

While the fault-seeking focus in South Africa falls on the war and warriors of the past, I would like to take a look at the current peace and peacemakers, whoever they may be, from a special angle, just to get another perspective. Making war is a way of settling clashes of interest. Making peace and negotiating, likewise, are processes for settling disputes. To make war is costly. What is the price of making peace?

During 1991 and 1993 we lost, on average, three times more policemen while they were containing *peace-time* political violence than the members of the Security Forces lost in South West and Angola while they were waging war with aircraft and artillery. And waging the peace is just as costly. According to various economists who have been quoted in the press, one day's mass action stay-away costs the country R300 million to R500 million or even more; in other words, the same as it cost to finance one whole year of making war in South West and Angola. Likewise, the amount of damage caused by currency fraud is being expressed in figures of hundreds of millions and even billions of rands.

In its report of 18 March 1993 on violence during 1992, as published in the *Pretoria News* of the next day, the Human Rights Commission stated that the death-toll as a result of politically related violence during 1992 had increased to 3 499. That means an average of 9.6 deaths per day, 35 per cent more than during 1991. The worst period of violence, as one could have expected, was just before the referendum of 17 March 1992.

During the war we held our collective breath every time we saw the SADF flash coming up on the TV screen during a news bulletin, because it heralded the announcement of a war casualty. Death from political violence has now become so bad, yet so generally accepted, that the *Pretoria News* keeps a routine scoreboard of the violence, like that for a weekly market report. I mention a few examples at random:

- This is too much – Deaths in political violence: midnight Thursday 26/11/92 to midnight Thursday 3/12/92 – 54; 12-week total since midnight Thursday 10/9/92 – 493.
- This is too much – Deaths in political violence: midnight Thursday 11/3/93 to midnight Thursday 18/03/93 – 14; 27-week total since midnight Thursday 10/9/92 – 898.
- Deaths in unrest: recorded from midnight Wednesday 30/03/94 to midnight Thursday 07/04/94 – 149; 82-week total since midnight Thursday 10/09/92 – 4 867.

According to the *Pretoria News* of 5 December 1992 the Commissioner of Police announced the previous day that more policemen had been killed during the year than in any single year during the wars in Namibia and Zimbabwe. *The Citizen* of 25 January 1993 quoted a spokesman for the police as saying that deaths were the most in one year since the establishment of the police force in 1913.

To kill a policeman in the United States is a serious issue. In Israel the government is prepared to cause grave international problems by taking military revenge if a member of the security forces is killed.

I have spent a considerable part of this book on military leaders' alleged reluctance to take decisions because they suffer so much emotional stress over loss of life, such as the 36 men we lost during the big war in the south-east of Angola from mid-1987 to mid-1988.

Well, the Defence Force accepted the responsibility for its war-time losses. Who is responsible for the peace-time losses?

The Citizen of 24 February 1993 quoted the psychiatrist Dr Merryl Vorster as claiming that the daily bombardment of crime reports during transition to the 'new' South Africa had caused the public to become insensitive and develop a general disregard for the value of human life.

She is right. It is possible that these figures bore rather than shock the average South African.

The figures did not shock me either, but for a different reason than the one mentioned by Dr Vorster. I had anticipated the violence because it was predictable. In fact, I forecast the violence during 1991 during at least three public seminars held under the auspices of one of our big banking groups.

I do not say this with any feeling of self-satisfaction. I mention it because when you anticipate something and it happens, you do not get panicky. Now is not the time to lose your head. Now is not the time to begin thinking with your heart. Now is not the time to arouse suspicion between people. Now is not the time to point fingers.

It is time to be strong in your belief, in your head and in your heart. Then we may walk the road of South Africa together.

* * *

As my story draws to an end, and as I reflect on the past years, I cannot help but be proud of the people of the Defence Force. Never since World War II has anybody come close to facing the full hitting-power of the South African Defence Force. During the civil war in Angola of 1975–1976 our force level was about 3 000 men, and again during the campaign of 1987–1988 in the country's south-east. With the unrest in South Africa between 1984 and 1987 our highest monthly average force level was 5 500. But this latter was a peace force.

When I look back I am proud of them all. From the generals at the top to the drivers at the bottom.

One of the most pleasant moments of my military career was when a big contingent of my drivers of the last number of years attended my 'Forty Days' party at very short notice. They had organised the occasion with the help of my personal staff shortly before my retirement.

The people of the Defence Force stood firm and worked hard to create a situation with opportunities. Many of them lived for it and some of them gave their lives for it. I have come a long road with them, and I will remember them.

Always remember that war is war and peace is peace.

When it is war and you reflect on the past, remember that it was peace then. When it is peace and you reflect on the past, remember that it was war then.

THE END OF THE STORY

It is not easy. But that is how we remember our soldiers of World War
II. Now we must remember our new veterans.

War is not only war. There is also peace. Peace is not only peace.
There is also war.

If you reflect on the past, remember that it was war and peace, peace
and war. That is difficult, but that is how it was.

I will remember our new veterans for walking with me along the road
of peace and conflict, of joy and stress, of the results of the friction of
war. Everything in war is difficult. If you want to repair your vehicles
you have to drag a garage along with you to the battlefield. If you want
to work during the night, you have to do so without light; or if you are
allowed to have light, you have to supply your own power. Then you
have to pack up and go and do it all over again at some other place.
That is how things go in war.

And on the journey through war a multitude of unforeseen incidents
can happen as a result of chance, and together they cause the friction
that makes everything in war difficult. As a result one never reaches
peak performance. Everyone who participates in war is subject to this
sort of chance, and it may mean bad luck. Everyone has the potential
to make excusable mistakes, and the least of these incidents can make
things go wrong for many people – even cause them to lose the war.

As they often say in rugby or cricket or other types of sport: we lost
because we made too many mistakes. That is so, but one must take care
with this philosophy. If you are only intent on not making mistakes you
do not try to score points yourself, you try to prevent your opponent
from scoring points. Eventually you do not play to win any more, you
play to prevent yourself from losing. And as a result you will lose.

One must be prepared to take calculated risks. Luck is on the side of
the audacious.

But everything does not depend on your making only a few mistakes,
or on your playing to win; it does not depend on fortune and misfortune. There is also another side. Clausewitz did not write only about
friction de guerre, he also argued that there were other factors – the quality of your people and the standard of their training. You do not lose
only because you make too many mistakes; you win because you do the
right things right.

If you do the right things right it can greatly compensate for the unforeseen misfortunes. That is why we won all our campaigns. Our people were top quality, and they were well-trained. Their tread was true, their fist was firm and their aim secure. Everyone played his part. Thanks to the standard of their training they underwent less stress; as a result of their muscle and bone they could handle the stress.

In this regard I quote from a newsletter of the Joint Staff Course Association: 'In their resistance to stress, in their ability to carry on when things go wrong, good officers are more easily distinguished from poor ones.'

That is how our people distinguished themselves; not only the officers but all of them.

I have heard speakers say 'everyone in the organisation is important' at so many occasions that I do not use such words myself. It has become such a commonplace expression that to me it has begun to sound too much like superficial motivation and cheap encouragement, as if it were merely a matter of good manners and something nice to say.

But if I do have to use those words now, I know what I am talking about, and I mean them. I have no need to motivate or flatter anybody. If I say that I thank every man and woman and pay tribute to them, I say it because I know it was the contributions of all of them that brought us victory. Arnold Glasow said: 'It doesn't take great men to do things, but it is doing things that makes men great.'

There were also those who did more than merely doing the right things right – certain persons and groups of persons were genial and brave. Heroes. But they did not perform in stadiums in front of spectators like a Springbok rugby hero who scores a decisive three points for South Africa, or the cricketer who runs up a match-winning century. Yes, we had them in the Defence Force too, and I want to praise them. The value of their contributions was immeasurable. But even they could not have applied their courage, genius and utmost devotion without the others.

Some courageous and excellent people were publicly acclaimed. But a multitude of others enabled us to win wars, each and every one of whom did his bit, and of whom we did not hear, including those who are not mentioned in this book. I also think of Elizabeth Albrecht of the Southern Cross Fund and others like her, and the thousands who helped them in making the troops' life a little more pleasant. This book belongs to all of them, and to all who believe in South Africa.

I see myself as one of many. Referring to the scores of generals with whom and against whom Napoleon had campaigned, someone once asked him who the best generals were. He replied: 'The lucky ones.'

There are people who are known as 'being smiled upon by the goddess of fortune'. Others are described as 'being haunted by the bird of ill omen'. People have told me that I was lucky. But there are those who argue that luck does not only follow on chance. You can create your own luck. The formula is to know what you want, believe that you can, be enterprising, seize the initiative and take calculated risks; and you must always work hard and cleverly.

But there are others who say that if you try to harness luck it evades you like quicksilver.

On the other hand, Frank Clark said: 'It's hard to detect good luck – it looks so much like something you've earned!'

Yes, I was lucky. But bad luck struck me, too.

My two sons were among the many thousands of people I have spent so much time talking about. Bruwer completed his national service plus 18 months of voluntary duty, while Martin joined the Permanent Force after his national service. Both served in 32 Battalion, one of the most active fighting units in the Army, and both lived to see the end of the war. But on 17 August 1991 Major Harper Martin Geldenhuys was killed in an aircraft incident at 32 Battalion's base at Pomfret. Chaplain Sidney Middlemost buried him there.

There is a truth which is bigger than the chance, fortune and misfortune about which I wrote so much – fate. God rules all destinies.

Thus, once again, I dedicate this book to all the thousands who served in the South African Defence Force and the South West Africa Territory Force – those who were injured or wounded, those who are dead and those who are still alive.

Napoleon, having fought with many nations and against many nations, inspired Madame Montholon to ask him which were the best soldiers. His reply was:

'Those who are victorious.'

CHAPTER 22

THAT WAS HOW IT WAS

Terries and Vorster's dogs

I love Namibia and am proud of its diverse population. The Namibians provide an example for all of Africa. Sam Nujoma was and is a colourful and controversial character. During the first years of this century there was controversy about him and friction in his SWAPO party, and thus in the government as well; but say about him what you will, he was a father-figure and leader to his followers.

Namibia is an excellent country in spite of personal friction and the usual political squabbles. The government is firmly seated and the op-position makes substantial contributions to the country's stability and welfare. The Namibians have a mature live-and-let-live political cul-ture. The average Namibian is proud but modest, friendly but purpose-ful. There is a prevailing atmosphere of harmonious co-existence that charms strangers.

One might ask where this friendliness and hospitable spirit comes from. The answer is that the Namibians are aware of their inner excel-lence; they know what they are and what they want. They achieve, but are proud enough not to be vain about their achievements. How did all this become possible after a serious war? Well, let us see.

The People's Liberation Army of Namibia, or PLAN, was our enemy from the early 1960s to the late 1980s. But how do things look from the perspective of the first decade of the twenty-first century?

In time of war – or 'armed conflict', if one prefers to call it that – you never praise your enemy. During the early skirmishes PLAN's 'cadres' damned our troops as 'Boers' and 'Vorster's dogs', and our troops had equally flattering names for them. We had certain knowledge, however, that they respected us, and for our part we used to tell one another that the 'terries' could fight well. So we respected one another, but discreetly.

PLAN and ourselves made war – with or without the presence of Russians, Cubans, FAPLA or UNITA – in the real sense of the word. We didn't play games; at the time the fighting involved tanks, aircraft and missiles, and both sides suffered casualties, among them senior officers. But after the war the discreet silence was broken, and each side quizzed the other with keen interest.

Soldiers on opposite sides during a war are often more approachable than the politicians. I think here even of General Manie Maritz at the siege of O'Kiep in 1902, while the Boer invasion of the Cape Colony was still in progress, who let his men persuade him to dispatch a written request to his opposite number, a Major Edwards, about a temporary cease-fire because they wanted to tackle the 'Rooineks' at a game of rugby!

In Namibia PLAN and the South West Africa Territory Force amalgamated. As was to be expected, the process did not take place without emotion and fits and starts. But it worked; it was vitally important that a significant element of the SWATF should be included in Namibia's new defence force.

After my retirement I had occasion to pay my respects to my former opposite numbers. The first time involved the Namibian Secretary for Defence, Mr Frans Kapofi, who then quickly arranged for me to meet his former bush commanders. Shortly afterwards, at an international conference on peace settlements at Midgard, near Okahandja, I met his successor, General Charles Namoloh, otherwise known as 'Ho Chi Minh'.

As is often the case at such occasions, there was one seminar-goer who was very fond of the sound of his own voice and keen to make an impression with his arsenal of high-flown words and academic knowledge. He launched a long speech at General Namoloh, full of resonant words that actually said very little; I do not believe that many people followed his line of reasoning or listened to him with any serious attention. Be that as it may, he concluded by asking General Namoloh's opinion.

General Namoloh immediately answered him by saying: 'I'm a guerrilla specialist. Ask General Geldenhuys, he's a professional – he'll tell you everything.' And I hadn't even understood the question! Everyone present chuckled – not at Namoloh or me, but at Mr Pompous.

Accompanied by 'Echo Victor' (General Eddie Viljoen), I met him again in 2006, by which time he was Minister of Defence, and then once more in 2007, when I paid a short visit to him and his successor as Chief of the Defence Force, General Martin Shaali. An atmosphere of mutual respect reigned, and once again they inquired after Generals Georg Meiring and Willie Meyer, and expressed their condolences about the passing of Colonel Des Radmore and Generals Deon Ferreira and Joep Joubert. In our turn we asked how things were with the former PLAN commanders whose *noms de guerre* were 'Danger Ashipala', 'Zulu', 'Bulanganga' and 'Chicken'.

Foot-soldiers and generals

In post-war Namibia there was no Truth and Reconciliation Commission like the one established in South Africa, simply a general amnesty. There are still question-marks about Namibian women and children who were under SWAPO control in Angola and remain missing, and in Angola itself there are still many graves in old African National Congress camps about which very little is ever said; but I have no doubt that on the whole the Namibian approach has worked out well for the foreseeable future.

By comparison, in South Africa we had the 'Promotion of National Unity and Reconciliation Act' (Act 34 of 1995), which did as much damage, if not more, than it did good. The commission never progressed further than a peculiar type of search for the 'truth'. The word did not even appear in the Act's short title, but that was its point of focus, and the process went shamelessly over to a one-sided pursuit of our people of the security forces.

Commissioners Archbishop Desmond Tutu and Dr Alex Boraine have admitted that they did not budget time for the promotion of 'national reconciliation and unity', as promised in the short title of the Act – not even when the commission's working life was extended. I know of no other institution of this kind anywhere in the world where a commission, and particularly that commission's amnesty committee, was so blatantly and unfairly loaded against the previous dispensation. In spite of this, Archbishop Tutu and Dr Boraine continue to plead for an end to charging 'foot-soldiers' and the start of prosecution of the generals; the researcher Charles Villa-Vicencio positively begs for it.

Let us examine these two elements of incitement against the norms of honesty and factual truth. Could someone please tell me the names of the 'foot-soldiers' who have been charged? If there were any, would one need more than the fingers of one hand to count them – or have I missed something here? For my part I can mention the names of five officers of general or flag rank who were charged and spent 18 months in the dock in Durban – General Magnus Malan (former Minister of Defence); myself; General Kat Liebenberg (former Chief of the SADF); General Tienie Groenewald; and Admiral Dries Putter – not to mention several others. Can you believe it! What can one say about the accusations made against them and myself?

The insane hate-filled criticism with which the frustrated ones still mercilessly and incessantly bombard the old SADF has the ability to hurt one – but then it makes one strong. When I handed in the original manuscript of this book in 1992, an editor insisted that I should add that the South African government sent the SADF to South West Africa for the purpose of maintaining apartheid!

With all due courtesy I told him gently that this was not the case, that I had been in command and knew what my directive had been. It had had nothing whatever to do to with apartheid, either directly or indirectly. My mission was simple, compact and clear: We were to create and maintain a situation within which a process of constitutional development could take place without hindrance. South Westers must decide on their future themselves.

But he refused to budge, and still insisted that I state that the Defence

Force had been in South West to enforce apartheid. Incredible!

In our time 'petty apartheid' vanished totally in SWA/Namibia – 20 years before the same thing happened in the RSA! And then 'grand apartheid' vanished as well. In Namibia we had to – and did – fall in loyally with the local legislation that had been passed by a majority black government, working and making war under extremely difficult political circumstances. At times we were accused of political bias from both the political left and the right ... which made me feel that we were on the correct path (it also happened at times that we were praised by both poles of the political spectrum).

I do not believe that the average South African of that time really understood our situation and what we achieved. Unlike the situation in South Africa, swapo and others were not banned organisations like the ANC/MK and the PAC. SWAPO would be holding its meetings and mass rallies inside the territory, while elsewhere we would be fighting its armed wing.

In the meantime we placed members of all the population groups under arms, and they appeared in public with their weapons. We trained and qualified officers and non-commissioned officers of all races, who enjoyed all the normal rights and privileges of their rank. There was no apartheid in the South West Africa Territory Force – and my witnesses to that statement number many thousands.

Political fever and extremist sentiment did surface from time to time, however, and we simply had to put up with it; I certainly did not enjoy seeing my name in large letters across a prominent building in Windhoek one morning, in a message to the effect that 'Vorster, Steyn and Geldenhuys are selling out the whites'.

And so, while critics in SWA/Namibia accused us during the changing 1970s of betraying the whites, a learned man in 1992 – 14 years later, before apartheid had vanished in South Africa – insisted that I acknowledge that we went to South West to defend apartheid!

Unlike the soldiers who were involved, politicians often still go unashamedly ahead with their political fights after peace has been concluded.

As I say, there are still people who give vent to their frustrations by attacking the old SADF. But perhaps that is now beginning to come to an end. Fairly recently the respected Dr Frederik van Zyl Slabbert speculated as follows: if the Cubans had achieved such a decisive victory at Cuito Cuanavale, why was the triumphant Cuban general executed by firing squad? And that was in 2006!

He did not, incidentally, ask two other related questions: if the Cubans had been winning so decisively, why did they call a halt while they were still such a long way from their objective, Jamba? Why did the other vanishing Cuban general, Del Pino Diaz, make a break for Florida? I and various informed writers, both local and overseas (Fred Bridgland, Chester Crocker, Simon Barber and Sir Robin Renwick, among others) had already asked these questions 14 years earlier, and answered them chapter and verse.

But it suited certain people not to believe us. The facts are that we repeatedly and decisively defeated a Cuban-allied force at the Lomba River, and near Techipa administered the final and permanent blows to a purely Cuban force. Some of the frustrated ones seek the truth in Havana, at the 'Hall of Castro Fame', because that is where they find what they want to hear. Others go to Miami, that nest of spies, to look for the other side of the story. That is a little better. Yet others seek the truth in Dakar, where there is a clone of the meaningless Havana version. Bridgland, on the other hand, sought the truth from (as he put it) 'scores' of troops and lower ranks who actually fought – and wrote a credible history.

According to the Freedom Park at Pretoria, which is supposed to honour the South African dead of all wars, 2 113 Cubans died in the 'liberation struggle'. But we can obtain the truth at first hand from those who fought and bore the responsibility: Colonel Deon Ferreira, Colonel Dick Lord, Colonel Chris Serfontein, Commandant Mike Muller and many others – *those who won.*

On the monument at Fort Klapperkop are inscribed the names of a total of 611 members of the South African Defence Force of all ranks who died in service between 1962 and 1994. Their names are enshrined in the roll of honour in Annexure A of this book, so that we may perpetually honour their memory.

When peace is declared, soldiers bury the hatchet, but politicians and their flunkies just carry on with their mud-slinging.

But – that was how it was.

SADF MEMBERS WHO DIED IN SERVICE 1962–1994

The South African Defence Force was the second of the three evolution-ary phases of South Africa's armed services. When the country attained Dominion status as the Union of South Africa in 1912 – one step short of full independence – it acquired its own military, the Union Defence Force. The UDF saw it through both world wars and Korea, and then in 1961 was renamed the South African Defence Force when the country became a republic and left the Commonwealth.

The SADF endured till 1994, when it was amalgamated with the armed wings of the African National Congress and the Pan-Africanist Congress, and the defence forces of the five autonomous black 'home-lands', the Transkei, Ciskei, Bophutatswana, Gazankulu and Venda. The new body was called the South African National Defence Force.

This list contains the names of all those who were on the pay-state of the South African Defence Force at the time of their death, irrespective of the place and cause of their passing. The names of members of the

SADF who died while on operational service – whether as a direct result of enemy action or from other causes (for example, aircraft accidents or disease) – are marked with an asterisk.

The list is based on a compilation by John Dovey (http://www.just done.co.za/ROH/), who obtained the data from the South African National Defence Force, and then collated chronologically, alphabetically and by rank-group. The resulting compilation was then compared with the inscriptions at Fort Klapperkop, which are collated chronologically and alphabetically only. A few names were then added to the final list.

1962

Heunis, J.J.S.   WO1   Army
Bischoff, J.S.   Air Mechanic   SAAF
Booysen, H.L.   Air Mechanic   SAAF
Burger, H.J.   Air Mechanic   SAAF
De Bruine, J.A.   2nd Lieutenant   SAAF
Foote, A.R.   Sergeant   SAAF
Gaylard, B.E.   2nd Lieutenant   SAAF
Jones, L.L.   Candidate-Officer   SAAF
Lawrenson, A.D.   Major   SAAF
Martin, K.L.   Lieutenant   SAAF
Van Zyl, J.J.C.   Lieutenant   SAAF

1963

Botha, A.L.   Signalman   Army
Helberg, J.J.   Signalman   Army
Mulder, U.A.   Signalman   Army
Runkel, J.G.R.   Private   Army
Taylor, I.L.   Signalman   Army
Visser, G.J.   Corporal   Army
Botha, H.A.   2ndLieutenant   SAAF
Brodreiss, M.A.   Corporal   SAAF
Chamberlain, M.A.   Private   SAAF
Coetzee, A.G.W.   Lieutenant   SAAF
Du Plooy, C.A.   2nd Lieutenant   SAAF
Hattingh, M.M.   Candidate-Officer   SAAF
Hattingh, P.J.   Air Mechanic   SAAF
Labuschagne, J.G.   Captain   SAAF
Mentis, R.H.   Private   SAAF
Schully, S.S.   WO11   SAAF
Sheasby, D.H.   Sergeant   SAAF
Silversten, T.H.   Captain   SAAF

Smith, G.J.   Lieutenant   SAAF
Strauss, D.I.   Candidate-Officer   SAAF
Taljaard, M.J.   Corporal   SAAF
Viljoen, C.P.   Corporal   SAAF
Vorster, M.C.   Captain   SAAF

1964

Agenbach, J.H.A.   Sergeant   Army
Du Plooy, C.M.   Rifleman   Army
Du Toit, J.A.   Bombadier   Army
Dummer, B.I.   Private   Army
Kies, J.F.   Rifleman   Army
Kotze, P.J.   Corporal   Army
Krogh, P.J.   Rifleman   Army
Potgieter, I.C.   Field-Cornet   Army
Prinsloo, A.C.   Staff-Sergeant   Army
Visagie, I.S.   Trooper   Army
Wepener, J.F.   Rifleman   Army
Brits, J.T.   2nd Lieutenant   SAAF
Kriel, J.F.   Corporal   SAAF
Rothman, L.J.L.   Air Mechanic   SAAF

1965

Brown, M.A.   Rifleman   Army
Burger, J.   Corporal   Army
Fourie, J.R.   Rifleman   Army
Kruger, P.F.J.   Private   Army
Newton-Thompson, A.M.   Rifleman   Army
Parsons, L.E.   Gunner   Army
Pullen, M.R.   Private   Army
Arnolds, J.A.   Seaman   Navy
Braaf, F.   Seaman   Navy

Farmer, J.G.   Seaman   Navy
Harris, H.   Seaman   Navy
Joubert, M.W.   Seaman   Navy
Newing, J.   Seaman   Navy
Presence, H.C.   Seaman   Navy
Rittles, R.   Seaman   Navy
Bolzern, J.R.   Air Mechanic   SAAF
Delport, J.J.   Air Mechanic   SAAF
Jarmain, R.L.   Air Mechanic   SAAF
Le Roux, J.J.   2nd Lieutenant   SAAF
Maxwell, J.J.   Captain   SAAF
Oltmann, R.J.   Lieutenant   SAAF
Schlesinger, L.B.   Lieutenant   SAAF
Schutte, B.J.P.   Air Mechanic   SAAF
Venter, J.A.   Air Mechanic   SAAF

1970

Coker, H.D.   Rifleman   Army
Grinyer, J.   Rifleman   Army
Latsky, S.A.J.   Corporal   Army
Leonhardt, P.A.E.   Rifleman   Army
Lombard, J.J.   Captain   Army
Mack, K.E.   Rifleman   Army
Marriott, R.N.   Rifleman   Army
Olyott, G.G.   Rifleman   Army
Theron, J.J.   2nd Lieutenant   Army
Vallero, M.F.   Rifleman   Army
Goosen, A.J.   Private   SAAF
Van der Merwe, H.S.   Corporal   SAAF
Van Deventer, P.J.   Candidate-Officer   SAAF
Van Dyk, G.H.   Major   SAAF
Van Heerden, J.F.   Commandant   SAAF
Van Sittert, J.   2nd Lieutenant   SAAF
Weyer, P.S.   Captain   SAAF
Bester, J.J.   2nd Lieutenant   Army
Englelbrecht, P.J.   Sergeant   Army
Loubser, J.W.A.   Major   Army
Morrison, D.A.   2nd Lieutenant   Army
Van der Merwe, P.S.   2nd Lieutenant   Army
Visser, J.G.J.   Trooper   Army
Beetge, N.   Major   SAAF
Blom, J.G.   Sergeant   SAAF
Euvrard, G.J.   Major   SAAF
Genis   Mc de G.   Major   SAAF
Grobler, R.N.   Corporal   SAAF
Hayes, E.L.   Lance-Corporal   SAAF
Henning, L.A.F.   Commandant   SAAF

Lamoral, H.H.A.M.C.   Major   SAAF
Lombard, D. DU. P   Captain   SAAF
Odendaal, H.O.M.   Candidate-Officer   SAAF
Prinsloo, W.A.   Major   SAAF
Snyman, G.N.   Captain   SAAF
Stork, J.   Corporal   SAAF
Tiedt, C.J.   Captain   SAAF
Van Rensburg, N.F.J.   Corporal   SAAF
Wasserman, G.H.   Private   SAAF

1972

Albrecht, W.   Rifleman   Army
Caddy, H.T.   Trooper   Army
Devenish, V.   Signalman   Army
Klue, M.C.   Sergeant   Army
Knight, J.P.   Private   Army
Labuschagne, C.D.A.   Private   Army
Roesstroff, A.   Rifleman   Army
Van den Heever, W.O.   Private   Army
Burger, J.D.   2nd Lieutenant   SAAF
Muller, L.G.   Private   SAAF
Warren, J.C.   Corporal   SAAF
Wienand, S.E.   Private   SAAF

1973

Beghin, K.F.   Private   Army
Boshoff, D.P.   Trooper   Army
Brits, A.J.   Captain   Army
Consatinou, C.   Private   Army
Fourie, R.   Rifleman   Army
Greeff, A.F.   Rifleman   Army
Hahn, K.   Rifleman   Army
Holm, J.G.   Rifleman   Army
Holscher, L.   Rifleman   Army
Kruger, J.M.   Private   Army
Langley, T.A.   Rifleman   Army
Leggett, R.   Private   Army
MacPherson, A.J.   Private   Army
Nelson, W.A.   Private   Army
Oosthuysen, C.F.   Candidate-Officer   Army
Pienaar, P.J.   Signalman   Army
Potgieter, J.J.   Private   Army
Potgieter, K.E.   Staff-Sergeant   Army
Steenkamp, L.P.J.   WO1   Army
Theron, H.C.   Private   Army
Van Heerden, J.A.S.   Trooper   Army
Van Heerden, M.C.   Rifleman   Army

Van Jaarsveld, P.P.   Sergeant   Army
Viviers, J.P.H.   Rifleman   Army
Weyers, D.Z.   Captain   Army
Wulfsohn, M.   Rifleman   Army
Kearns, I.W.   Able Seaman   Navy
Van der Merwe, H.   Able Seaman   Navy
Alberts, H.W.   2nd Lieutenant   SAAF
Antonis, B.M.   Captain   SAAF
Du Preez, H.   Captain   SAAF
Kolver, J.P.   2nd Lieutenant   SAAF
Marshall, L.J.   Captain   SAAF
Smith, C.L.   Captain   SAAF
Steinberg, J.J.S.   Major   SAAF
Van Zyl, F.R.   Captain   SAAF
Vice, C.R.   Major   SAAF
Yates, C.   2nd Lieutenant   SAAF

1974

Becker, A.G.   Corporal   Army
*Burger, W.J.   Staff-Sergeant   Army
Christello, A.M.   Rifleman   Army
Jensen, O.V.   WO1   Army
Kotze, J.A.   Trooper   Army
Marais, S.   Lance-Corporal   Army
Reynolds, W.J.   Corporal   Army
Van Rhyn, G.J.J.   Rifleman   Army
Voster, B.J.A.   Rifleman   Army
*Zeelie LWD, F.J.   Lieutenant   Army
Farmer, L.A.   Seaman   Navy
Bonthuys, J.H.L.   2nd Lieutenant   SAAF
Gouws, A.S.   2nd Lieutenant   SAAF
Human, J.H.   Private   SAAF

1975

Anderson, L.A.   Trooper   Army
Bate, A.T.   Rifleman   Army
*Beechey, N.R.   Corporal   Army
*Benson, A.J.   WO11   Army
Bessinger, L.W.   Trooper   Army
Chatwick, L.W.   Corporal   Army
De Beer, G.E.S.   Private   Army
Erasmus, G.J.   Rifleman   Army
Eybers, P.G.   Trooper   Army
Franzen, G.J.   Rifleman   Army
Hanekom, J.C..   Corporal   Army
Harmse, D.B.   Colonel   Army
*Holm HC, J.W.   Captain   Army

Human, D.J.   Sergeant   Army
Klopper, G.J.   Rifleman   Army
Le Grange, A.A.   Rifleman   Army
*Le Roux, D.B.   Trooper   Army
*Lombaard, N.   Trooper   Army
Lombard, A.A.   Trooper   Army
*Lotze, T. Du T.   Rifleman   Army
Mar, J.J.   Private   Army
*Marais, D.H.D.   Rifleman   Army
*Muller, G.M.F.   Gunner   Army
Neethling, B.   Gunner   Army
*Obbes, G.M.F.   Trooper   Army
Potgieter, M.C.E.   Corporal   Army
*Retief, M.C.E.   Gunner   Army
*Robin, C.J.   2nd Lieutenant   Army
Scheepers, L.J. de Wit   Rifleman   Army
*Schoeman, G.F.   Captain   Army
*Schonfeldt, A.J.H.   Rifleman   Army
*Senekal, G.A.   Rifleman   Army
Snell, D.B.L.   Corporal   Army
Steyn, N.J.   Sergeant   Army
Taljaard, D.J.   Captain   Army
Taljaard, J.J.   Corporal   Army
Teteko, R.   Private   Army
*Theunissen, M.J.   Gunner   Army
Tippet, D.   Sergeant   Army
Van Der Schyff, M.L.   Rifleman   Army
Van Der Walt, P.J.   Rifleman   Army
*Venter, B.   Rifleman   Army
Visser, N.J.   Major   Army
*Vollgraaf, N.J.   Trooper   Army
*Von Schmettau, U.K.   Sapper   Army
Vorster, D.J.   Rifleman   Army
*Wannenburg HC, F.G.   Sergeant   Army
Willemse, A.R.   Sapper   Army
Bes, H.J.J.   Able Seaman   Navy
Du Plessis, H.J.J.   Able Seaman   Navy
Clark, G.H.   Lieutenant   SAAF
Cox, J.H.   2nd Lieutenant   SAAF
Crause, J.J.   Sergeant   SAAF
Franklin, C.S.   2nd Lieutenant   SAAF
Labuschagne, D.J.   Sergeant   SAAF
Laidlaw, K.E.   Private   SAAF
Law, G.D.   Captain   SAAF
Pretorius, C.H.   Sergeant   SAAF
Thompson, E.B.   Lieutenant   SAAF
Uys, P.B.   Major   SAAF

SADF MEMBERS WHO DIED IN SERVICE, 1962–1994

Van Rensburg, P.B. Sergeant SAAF
Van Tonder, C.A.P. Sergeant SAAF
Williamson, K.A. Lieutenant SAAF

1976

Achpele, J.E.F. Corporal Army
*Aschman, J. Sapper Army
Backhouse, P.L. Rifleman Army
Bambo, J. Sergeant Army
Bantjies, J.G. Sergeant Army
Barnard, J.P.H. Corporal Army
Barnett, M. Corporal Army
Bekker, H.A. Rifleman Army
Blaauw, A.J. Rifleman Army
*Blaauw, L. Sergeant Army
Blom, A.J. Corporal Army
Bodill, T.D. Trooper Army
Booysen, T.W.A. Sergeant Army
*Brandon, D. 2nd Lieutenant Army
*Broodryk, A. Corporal Army
Bruwer, J.J. Rifleman Army
Cloete, J.S. Captain Army
Coetzee, H.J.S. Corporal Army
*Coetzee, I.P. Rifleman Army
*Conway, T.G. Corporal Army
*Korb (Corb?), J.W. Rifleman Army
Craul, M.G. WO1 Army
*Cronje, W.J. Trooper Army
Custard, L.W. Rifleman Army
De Bruin, D.K.M. Sergeant Army
De Swardt, M.P. Corporal Army
Delport, L.H. Rifleman Army
Dickens, C.R. Candidate-Officer Army
Du Toit, P.J. Sapper Army
Duvenhage, G. Captain Army
*Ehlers, C.F. Rifleman Army
Engelbrecht, B.K. Sapper Army
*Fouche, J.R. Rifleman Army
Gibbon, R.S. Corporal Army
*Henderson, C.H. Corporal Army
*Hinds, D.G. Lieutenant Army
Holland, C.D. Rifleman Army
Holtzhauzen, C.J. Gunner Army
Kidson, L.J. 2nd Lieutenant Army
Klingenberg, R.W. Rifleman Army
Kruger, W.J. Private Army
Leonard, T.P. Corporal Army

*Malan, J.H. Rifleman Army
Matendi, A. Private Army
Matoko, P. Private Army
*Medhurst, E. Rifleman Army
*Moss, H.S.L. Rifleman Army
*Muller, A. 2nd Lieutenant Army
Naude, D.A. Trooper Army
*Naude, J.F. Rifleman Army
Palmer, R.C. Rifleman Army
Pauley, C.H. Rifleman Army
Paulo (Roxo), D.S. Staff-Sergeant Army
Pearson, M.P. Corporal Army
*Phipson, P.V. Corporal Army
Potgieter, J.D. Brigadier Army
Pretorius, A.J. Rifleman Army
Pretorius, D.R. Rifleman Army
Pretorius, N. Rifleman Army
Rautenbach, A.J. Rifleman Army
Ribeiro, C.A.C Lance-Corporal Army
*Schoeman, B.J. Corporal Army
Small, N.T. Corporal Army
Smith, R.E. Trooper Army
*Snyman, P.W.M. Rifleman Army
Soeiro, P.G. Sergeant Army
Strydom, A.J. Rifleman Army
Swanepoel, J.A. Corporal Army
*Swanepoel, W.C. Corporal Army
*Swart, C.J. 2nd Lieutenant Army
Swartz, S.J. Rifleman Army
Van der Merwe, A.J. Private Army
Van der Westhuizen, H.J. Rifleman Army
*Van der Westhuizen, T.J. Lieutenant Army
Van der Westhuizen, T.J. Lieutenant Army
Visser, J.A. Rifleman Army
Von Brandis, J.H. Corporal Army
Whitter, D.R. Rifleman Army
Boucher, W.H. Corporal SAAF
Carter, R.H. Major SAAF
*De Wit, C.D. Captain SAAF
Geyser, I.J.J. Private SAAF
*Immelman, F. Captain SAAF
*Kellett, G.W. Sergeant SAAF
Rossouw, G.M.A. Captain SAAF
Van der Merwe, C.L. Corporal SAAF
Van Rensburg, M.A.J. 2nd Lieutenant SAAF
Van Rooyen, G.N. Private SAAF
Winterbottom, K.R. 2nd Lieutenant SAAF

1977

Analati, T. Rifleman Army
*Badenhorst, A. Corporal Army
*Badenhorst, J.C. Sergeant Army
Bango, M. Private Army
*Basson, J.J. Corporal Army
Baum, J.F. Rifleman Army
Bernado, A.D.B. Sergeant Army
Beukes, M.N. Rifleman Army
Bigalke, H.R. Corporal Army
*Bishop, E.C. Rifleman Army
Boma, J. Private Army
Bosch, M.D. Signalman Army
Botha, J.J. Rifleman Army
Bothma, J.J. Signalman Army
Bricknell, G.A. Rifleman Army
*Buys, D.L. Rifleman Army
Chuca, M. Private Army
Claasen, S.P. Corporal Army
*Clack, N.G. Sergeant Army
De Villiers, I.J.J. Private Army
De Vos, J.J.J. Rifleman Army
Deacon, G.A. Corporal Army
Deacon, G.A. Lance-Corporal Army
Desenga Private Army
Devereaaux, S.V.P. Rifleman Army
Dindo, B. Private Army
*Dossena, P.O. Corporal Army
Furstenburg, J.P.A. Sergeant Army
*Gagiano, K. Lieutenant Army
*Gildenhuys HC, W.H.B. Sergeant Army
Greef, G.P. Private Army
*Greyling, L.C. Lieutenant Army
Haarhoff, W.A. Rifleman Army
Hempstead, G.W. Rifleman Army
Henn, M.C. Rifleman Army
Holtzhausen, P.H.J. Rifleman Army
Hugo, W. Rifleman Army
Irvine, C.M. Private Army
*Jacobsz, A.M. Rifleman Army
Jones, S. Rifleman Army
Jones, T.J.L. Corporal Army
*Jordaan, H.J. Rifleman Army
Kambinda, M. Private Army
*Kemp, C. Sapper Army
*Keulder, G. 2nd Lieutenant Army

Kotze, C.H. Rifleman Army
Kotze, C.P. Corporal Army
*Kotze, C.R. Lance-Corporal Army
Kretzmann, L.D. Rifleman Army
Kruger, A.J. Sergeant Army
*Kruger, J.H.P. Rifleman Army
*Kruger, M.L. Sergeant Army
Langenhoven, G.F.M. Rifleman Army
*Lawrie, G.A. Lance-Corporal Army
*Le Roux, P.L. Lieutenant Army
Lemmer, M.G. Rifleman Army
Lensley, J.J. Private Army
Lentink, W. Private Army
Lourens, C.J. Rifleman Army
Luciano, J. Private Army
Marais, J. Rifleman Army
*Marx, W.C. Sergeant Army
Mathias, J. Rifleman Army
Mayo, E.L. Rifleman Army
*Mentz, M.J.D Rifleman Army
Minnaar, P.A. Sergeant Army
Muller, L. Corporal Army
*Myburgh, I.N. Rifleman Army
Myburgh, L. Rifleman Army
*Oberholzer, I.J. Rifleman Army
Oosthuizen, F.F. Rifleman Army
Opperman, J.A. Rifleman Army
Parvess, S.T. Private Army
*Pelzer (Pelser?), A.L. Corporal Army
Pietersen, W.J. Rifleman Army
*Ross, B.A. Rifleman Army
Ruaro, J. Private Army
Scannell, J.S. Rifleman Army
Shorty Private Army
Smith, A.J. Sergeant Army
Steyn, J.F. Rifleman Army
Steyn, L. Corporal Army
Strydom, K.C. Corporal Army
*Tesnar, C.M.A. Rifleman Army
Theron, D.P. Sergeant Army
Uys, H.J. Rifleman Army
Van der Walt, A.F. Private Army
Van der Westhuizen, C.H. Rifleman Army
Van der Westhuizen, E.P. Rifleman Army
Van Niekerk, R. Trooper Army
Van Niewenhuizen, W.J.J. Private Army
Van Noordwyk, C.H.J. Rifleman Army

Van Wyk Mouton, J.   Sapper   Army
Van Zyl, A.M.   Lieutenant   Army
*Van Zyl, A.P.   Corporal   Army
*Van Zyl, F.C.   WO1   Army
Van Zyl, P.K.D.   Rifleman   Army
*Venter, A.I.E.   Corporal   Army
*Viljoen, J.H.   Sapper   Army
Voges, G.J.   Sergeant   Army
*Walker, G.W.J   Corporal   Army
Wiese, B.F.   Corporal   Army
Wiggell, W.T.   Sapper   Army
*Wilcox, M.A.   Corporal   Army
*Wilters, D.H.   Rifleman   Army
Moolman, B.J.   Seaman   Navy
Bezuidenhout, D.   Captain   SAAF
Burger, D.P.   2nd Lieutenant   SAAF
Genis, G.   Candidate-Officer   SAAF
Kerr, J.M.C.F.W.   Major   SAAF
*Liddell, N.B.   Lieutenant   SAAF
Moody, B.L.   Major   SAAF
Purdon, J.M.   Lieutenant   SAAF
Sarbutt, P.C.   2nd Lieutenant   SAAF
Smith, K.N.   Captain   SAAF
Van der Merwe, W.A.J.   Sergeant   SAAF
Van Rooyen, G.H.T.S.   Commandant   SAAF

1978

*Backhouse, E.J.   Rifleman   Army
Benade, P.   Trooper   Army
*Biggs, K.J.   Trooper   Army
Borchardt, C.J.   Private   Army
*Bosch, A.   Rifleman   Army
Bothma, J.J.E.   Private   Army
*Bridgeman, T.M.   Corporal   Army
*Britz, R.N.   2nd Lieutenant   Army
Brtitz, W.H.C.   Private   Army
Burger, J.J.   WO1   Army
*Castle, P.J.   Lieutenant   Army
Cloete, A.W.   Rifleman   Army
*Cloete, J.J.H.   Rifleman   Army
*Conradie HC, VRM, J.L.   WO1   Army
Davis, T.   Corporal   Army
*De Amorim, P.P.   Rifleman   Army
*De Lange, H.W.   Trooper   Army
De Man, A.P.   Sergeant   Army
De Villiers, C.B.   Corporal   Army
*De Waal, J.C.   Rifleman   Army

*De Wilzem, C.L.   Lance-Corporal   Army
De Witt, A.J.C.   Colonel   Army
Dekker, N.M.   Corporal   Army
Dixon, A.D.   Private   Army
*Du Bois, P.J.   Corporal   Army
Du Plessis, J.C.   Rifleman   Army
Du Plessis, M.H.   Rifleman   Army
*Du Toit, J.H.   Lieutenant   Army
*Eayrs, C.J.   Sergeant   Army
*Elworthy, D.M.   Trooper   Army
Engelbrecht, H.S.W.   Private   Army
Engeldoe, G.J.   Rifleman   Army
*Erasmus, G.P.   Trooper   Army
Evert, V.C.   Corporal   Army
*Ferreira, J.C.L.   Rifleman   Army
*Forster, F.J.   Candidate-Officer   Army
*Fourie, H.B.   Rifleman   Army
Frans, J.   Rifleman   Army
*Ganhao, M.A.I.   Corporal   Army
Goosen, G.J.E.   Corporal   Army
Gordon-Bennet, A.   Corporal   Army
*Greyling, J.B.   Rifleman   Army
*Grobler, W.H.   Corporal   Army
Grundling, L.G.   Major   Army
Hattingh, A.   Gunner   Army
*Havenga, J.   Corporal   Army
Human, A.P.   Rifleman   Army
*Hunter, R.O.   Rifleman   Army
Instain, F.   Private   Army
Jonker, A.A.   Rifleman   Army
Jooste, J.C.   Private   Army
*Kaplan, M.   Rifleman   Army
*Koekemoer, N.J.   Corporal   Army
*L'Hoest, Y.M.   Corporal   Army
*Le Roux, J.G.   Rifleman   Army
*Leamy, S.   Corporal   Army
Lengner, P.M.   2nd Lieutenant   Army
*Lesch, L.J.   Trooper   Army
Lewin, A.C.   Signalman   Army
Loots, C.   Bombardier   Army
Louw, F.   Corporal   Army
Mandingi, N.   Rifleman   Army
*Meneke, C.I.   Lance-Corporal   Army
Meyers, W.D.N.   Rifleman   Army
*Nel, J.P.   Corporal   Army
Nel, M.A.S.   Sapper   Army
*Opperman, A.L.   2nd Lieutenant   Army

Paterson, D.W.   Rifleman   Army
*Pearson, S.D.O.   Rifleman   Army
*Phillander, J.B.   Corporal   Army
Porter, L.F.   Sapper   Army
Prinsloo, P.W.   Rifleman   Army
Remmington, H.D.   Rifleman   Army
Rieder, B.C.   Private   Army
Roman, A.   Rifleman   Army
*Schutte, J.J.R.   Trooper   Army
Sentefol, R.   Rifleman   Army
Shilemba   A   Rifleman   Army
Smit, C.H.   Gunner   Army
*Smit, G.J.   Trooper   Army
*Smith, F.J.   Private   Army
Smuts, W.S.   Trooper   Army
Strydom, S.R.   Candidate-Officer   Army
Swanepoel, H.   Rifleman   Army
*Swartbooi, W.P.   Corporal   Army
*Theron, C.J.   Sergeant   Army
*Truebody, H.C.   Corporal   Army
Van As, J.D.O.   Private   Army
Van den Boogard, A.   Corporal   Army
Van der Berg, J.A.   Rifleman   Army
Van der Bergh, A.J.   Gunner   Army
*Van der Merwe, A.D.   Trooper   Army
*Van der Merwe, H.G.   Sergeant   Army
*Van der Nest, C.F.   Rifleman   Army
Van Ellewee, A.J.   Captain   Army
Van Papendorp, B.V.D.   Private   Army
*Van Rooyen, N.M.H.G.D.S.   Private   Army
Van Rooyen, B.V.D.   Private   Army
Van Zyl, M.   Rifleman   Army
*Viljoen, K.P.   Rifleman   Army
Wienand, W.A.   Gunner   Army
Wolmarans, P.C.   Rifleman   Army
Bosman, C.   Lieutenant   Navy
Basson, C.H.   Private   SAAF
Brinkworth, A.H.   Captain   SAAF
*Els, A.P.   Major   SAAF
*Emberger, L.   Candidate-Officer   SAAF
Kidd, M.   Private   SAAF
Mare, P.M.D.   2nd Lieutenant   SAAF
*Poole, L.M.   Commandant   SAAF
Roe, L.A.   Corporal   SAAF

1979

Akaando, J.   Rifleman   Army

*Appelgryn, W.J.   Rifleman   Army
Atherton, P.W.B.   Rifleman   Army
Atkins, P.W.B.   Private   Army
Basson, G.J.J.   Captain   Army
*Bekker, C.D.   Rifleman   Army
*Bell, E.L.   Corporal   Army
Berg, F.L.   Rifleman   Army
*Bester, B.G.   Rifleman   Army
Botha, B.G.   Rifleman   Army
Buys, P.S.   Trooper   Army
Cahasa, P.S.   Rifleman   Army
Carroll, P.W.E.   Rifleman   Army
Cloete, J.C.   Rifleman   Army
*Coetzee, S.W.   2nd Lieutenant   Army
Conga, J.   Private   Army
*Coppard, G.C.   Rifleman   Army
Da Costa Miranda, A.R.   Private   Army
Daniels, A.R.   Rifleman   Army
*Daniels, J.   Rifleman   Army
De Beer, D.T.G.   Private   Army
De Beer, D.T.G.   Private   Army
*De Klerk, N.J.   Corporal   Army
*De Vos, W.A.   2nd Lieutenant   Army
Djalomien, M.   Corporal   Army
*Du Plessis, P.J.Z.   Rifleman   Army
Du Toit, I.M.F.   Gunner   Army
*Fourie, J.J.   Rifleman   Army
*Golden, D.C.   Rifleman   Army
Gotlieb, A.   Rifleman   Army
*Greyling, A.Z.   Rifleman   Army
Hanneman, S.P.   Corporal   Army
Howitson, J.A.A.   Captain   Army
*Jans, J.W.L.   Rifleman   Army
*Jordaan, J.B.R.   Rifleman   Army
Kastoor, L.M.M.   Rifleman   Army
Kirchner, B.F.W.   Sergeant   Army
*Kloosterziel, B.F.W. (J)   Sergeant   Army
Kotze, C.J.   Rifleman   Army
*Krog, C.G.   Rifleman   Army
*Louw, T.I.   Rifleman   Army
*Maritz, J.P.   Corporal   Army
Mitchell, J.J.   Rifleman   Army
Mocke, D.J.   Rifleman   Army
*Mostert, J.G.A.   Rifleman   Army
*Mukondu, S.   Rifleman   Army
Muller, D.M.   Corporal   Army
Mundy, D.M.   Private   Army

362

Mungunda, D.M. Rifleman Army
Mybergh, N.J. Rifleman Army
Nel , W.A. Rifleman Army
*Nienaber, F. Corporal Army
Njunge, D. Private Army
Odendaal, D.C. Rifleman Army
*Olivier, J.G. Corporal Army
Ortman, R.E. Gunner Army
Pavlakis, N. Rifleman Army
Perreira, L. Rifleman Army
Raaf, G.E. Trooper Army
*Rautenbach, G.J. Rifleman Army
Rix, G.J. Corporal Army
Roos, G.F. Rifleman Army
Ross, J.G. Candidate-Officer Army
*Roux, B.C. Sergeant Army
Saal, B.C. Rifleman Army
Samutiki, J.L. Corporal Army
Saunders, W.L. Rifleman Army
Schenck, P.A. Rifleman Army
Senekal, G.J.J. Signalman Army
Shangweni, S. Rifleman Army
*Snyman, F.W.J. Rifleman Army
Storm, D.J. Rifleman Army
*Stumbo, S. Rifleman Army
*Swart, H. Corporal Army
*Tchizonda, A.M. Rifleman Army
*Truter, J.L. Rifleman Army
Van Brakel, D.G. Rifleman Army
*Van Den Berg, F.C. Rifleman Army
Van Der Walt, B.J.C. Rifleman Army
Van Drutten, J.H. Rifleman Army
Van Heerden, D.J. Rifleman Army
Van Heerden, R.F. Sapper Army
*Van Vuuren, S.P.J. Rifleman Army
*Van Wyk, J.C. Captain Army
*Venter, E.A. Rifleman Army
Vermeulen, B.D. Corporal Army
*Victor, D.J. Rifleman Army
Wagener, D.J. Sapper Army
*Weitsz, F.J. Rifleman Army
Mallalieu, G.H. Lieutenant Navy
Britz, F.W.C. Major SAAF
Doyle, O.J. 2nd Lieutenant SAAF
Duncan, K.B. Lieutenant SAAF
Jordaan, G.J. Corporal SAAF
Marais, G.J. Lieutenant SAAF

Nel, L.G. Private SAAF
Osborne, N.D. Lieutenant SAAF
Retief, D.W.M. Sergeant SAAF
Silberbauer, M.C. Captain SAAF
Strydom, J.J. Captain SAAF
Velleman, P.D. Captain SAAF
Wahl, P.P. Lieutenant SAAF
Weideman, M.E. Private SAAF
Wolhuter, G.H. Corporal SAAF

1980

Abel, Q. Corporal Army
Ackerman, A.C. Rifleman Army
*Adonis, J.J. Rifleman Army
*Alberto, R. Rifleman Army
*Albino, B. Rifleman Army
Almeido, P. Rifleman Army
*Angelo, S. Rifleman Army
*Augusto, M. Rifleman Army
Babin, P. Corporal Army
Badenhorst, P.J. Corporal Army
*Balie, H. Rifleman Army
Barnard, G.J.A. Rifleman Army
Bonnet, P.J. Private Army
*Bosman, J.A.P. Rifleman Army
*Braz, S.D. Sergeant Army
Buys, J.L. 2nd Lieutenant Army
*Cabinda, J. Rifleman Army
*Caliango, A. Rifleman Army
*Calitz, J. Rifleman Army
Catto, C.B. Corporal Army
*Coetzee, M.C. Corporal Army
*Colling, H.B. Rifleman Army
*Cronje, S.M. Rifleman Army
*Da Costa, A.M. Staff-Sergeant Army
Da Trinidade, C.C. Rifleman Army
*De Beer, P.J. Rifleman Army
De Villiers, A.E. 2nd Lieutenant Army
*De Vito, R.N. Rifleman Army
*Deyzel, D.J. Corporal Army
Digombo, J. Private Army
*Du Preez, I.P. 2nd Lieutenant Army
Du Preez, I.P. 2nd Lieutenant Army
*Du Toit HC, J.J. Lieutenant Army
Du Toit, T.A. Signalman Army
*Eduado, A. Rifleman Army
Elifas, P. Rifleman Army

*Engelbrecht, E.C.   Corporal   Army
*Engelbrecht, F.   Rifleman   Army
*Erasmus, A.   Captain   Army
Erneste, S.D.   Rifleman   Army
Evans, D.J.   Lance-Corporal   Army
*Falkus, A.J.   Lance-Corporal   Army
Fhilipus, E.   Rifleman   Army
*Finnies, W.A.   Corporal   Army
*Fourie, J.H.   Rifleman   Army
*Francisco, J.   Corporal   Army
Francisco, J.   Rifleman   Army
*Fredericks, J.   Rifleman   Army
*Froneman, B.A.   Rifleman   Army
*Geddes, P.W.   Lieutenant   Army
*Geel, P.J.   Rifleman   Army
*Gericke, B.Z.   Sergeant   Army
*Goliath, D.   Rifleman   Army
Greyling, C.P.   Sergeant   Army
*Grobler, D.H.   Corporal   Army
*Grobler, L.   Rifleman   Army
Grundling, C.S.   Lieutenant   Army
Hardenberg, C.R.   Corporal   Army
Higrunda, B.   Rifleman   Army
Hills, J.J.   Gunner   Army
Izaks, N.C.   Rifleman   Army
*Jacob, P.   Rifleman   Army
Jacobs, H.J.J.   Sapper   Army
Janse van Rensburg, H.C.   Rifleman   Army
*Jewaskiewitz, A.   Lance-Corporal   Army
*Josef, T.   Rifleman   Army
Joubert, J.J.   Private   Army
*Joubert, P.J.   Rifleman   Army
*Kanunu, S.   Rifleman   Army
Kapuna, S.   Rifleman   Army
*Karupa, G.   Rifleman   Army
*Kaumba, J.   Lance-Corporal   Army
Kavatjana, C.   Rifleman   Army
*Kemp, G.J.   Rifleman   Army
*Klukoski, H.   Lance-Corporal   Army
*Koekemoer, J.P.   Rifleman   Army
Komengo, P.   Rifleman   Army
*Kruger, N.J.   Rifleman   Army
*Kruger, P.   Corporal   Army
*Landman, W.J.   Rifleman   Army
Lang, G.   Private   Army
*Langman, D.   Lance-Corporal   Army
*Lello, F.J.   Rifleman   Army

*Livingue, A.   Rifleman   Army
*Loubser, F.J.   Rifleman   Army
*Loubser, M.D.   Rifleman   Army
*Luyt, M.C.   Rifleman   Army
*Maass, J.J.   Rifleman   Army
Mac Lean, J.F.   Rifleman   Army
*Madden, A.J.   Rifleman   Army
Marais, A.   Sapper   Army
*Marcelino, C.   Rifleman   Army
*Miranda , J.   Rifleman   Army
Marinda , J.   Rifleman   Army
*Maritz, J.J.   Rifleman   Army
*Maritz, P.R.   Lance-Corporal   Army
Matamba, J.   Rifleman   Army
Matunda, J.   Rifleman   Army
Mc Ewan, J.E.   Rifleman   Army
*Miguel, J.   Rifleman   Army
*Mijburgh, C.J.   Rifleman   Army
Mindo, A.J.   Lance-Corporal   Army
*Muhenie, H.   Rifleman   Army
Mukweli, F.   Rifleman   Army
*Muller, C. de J.   Lieutenant   Army
*Muller, J.M.H.   2nd Lieutenant   Army
Murphy, J.K.   Major   Army
*Naude, A.D.   Lance-Corporal   Army
Naus, M.J.   Lance-Bombardier   Army
Netshidzivhani, N.A.   Rifleman   Army
Netshifhefhe, N.N.   Rifleman   Army
Nortje, C.J.   Rifleman   Army
Ntamshe, K.   Rifleman   Army
*Nyundu, F.   Rifleman   Army
Oarum, J.   Rifleman   Army
*Oberholzer, A.   Corporal   Army
Olivier, W.J.G.U.   Rifleman   Army
Oosthuizen, A.J.   Rifleman   Army
Oosthuizen, L.   Trooper   Army
*Oosthuizen, P.J.R.   2nd Lieutenant   Army
*Patrick, T.S.   2nd Lieutenant   Army
*Paul, G.A.   Rifleman   Army
Pfeffer, H.W.   Rifleman   Army
*Prinsloo, W.J.S.   Sapper   Army
Ralikwatha, M.B.   Rifleman   Army
Range, M.J.   Private   Army
*Redlinghuys, A.J.   Rifleman   Army
*Reynolds, N.J.   Rifleman   Army
*Scholtz, A.M.   Rifleman   Army
*Scholtz, L.A.   Rifleman   Army

SADF MEMBERS WHO DIED IN SERVICE, 1962–1994

*Schultz, B.E.   Rifleman   Army
*Sekopomashe, V.   Rifleman   Army
Shipago, I.   Rifleman   Army
Smit, M.J.   Rifleman   Army
Smit , W.H.   Lance-Corporal   Army
Smith, A.G.   Private   Army
*Smith , W.H.   Lance-Corporal   Army
Sophia, E.   Lance-Corporal   Army
Strydom, A.C.   Rifleman   Army
*Swanepoel, C.   Rifleman   Army
Swanepoel, P.J.W.   Sapper   Army
Taljaard, G.A.   Rifleman   Army
*Tjipuna, J.   Rifleman   Army
Tjisota, M.   Rifleman   Army
*Twi, D.   Rifleman   Army
*Uys, J.P.   Rifleman   Army
Vanala, K.   Lance-Corporal   Army
Van Aswegen, S.D.   Gunner   Army
*Van den Berg, J.F.   Rifleman   Army
*Van den Bergh, D.   Rifleman   Army
*Van der Linde, M.J.   Staff-Sergeant   Army
Van der Merwe, J.E.   Rifleman   Army
*Van der Merwe, J.S.   Rifleman   Army
*Van der Merwe, N.J.   Lance-Corporal   Army
*Van der Star, J.J.   Rifleman   Army
*Van der Vyver   D   Sergeant   Army
Van Der Walt, H.J.   Lance-Corporal   Army
*Van Der Walt, N.J.   Rifleman   Army
*Van Der Walt, P.   2nd Lieutenant   Army
Van Graan, J.C.   Sergeant   Army
Van Heerden, W.G.   2nd Lieutenant   Army
Van Niekerk, A.C.   Rifleman   Army
Van Niekerk, T.B.   Corporal   Army
*Van Reenen, E.N.   Rifleman   Army
*Van Rensburg, J.   Rifleman   Army
*Van Wyk, M.   Corporal   Army
*Van Zyl, C.   Rifleman   Army
*Van Zyl, R.S.   Corporal   Army
Vanala, K.   Lance-Corporal   Army
*Venter, G.J.   Rifleman   Army
*Warrener, P.W.   Rifleman   Army
Wasserman, J.H.   Corporal   Army
*Wiese, A.P.   Rifleman   Army
*Yenga, M.   Rifleman   Army
Henderson, P.J.   Able Seaman   Navy
Burger, J.J.   Corporal   SAAF
Cilliers, J.D.   Sergeant   SAAF

Gerber, G.P.   Private   SAAF
Hollis, P.H.   Lieutenant   SAAF
Lamprecht, D.F.   Sergeant   SAAF
Lautenslager, V.P.   Lieutenant   SAAF
Le Roux, E.J.   Lieutenant   SAAF
Leeuw, J.H.   Lieutenant   SAAF
Liebenberg, L.D.   Candidate-Officer   SAAF
O'Connor, D.   Lieutenant   SAAF
Roos, J.G.   Lieutenant   SAAF
Smit, P.F.   Lieutenant   SAAF
Stacey, C.   Sergeant   SAAF
Stanbury, D.G.   Lieutenant   SAAF
Swart, E.S.   Candidate-Officer   SAAF
Van der Wath, J.J.   Lieutenant   SAAF
Volkersz, S.   Lieutenant   SAAF
Wessels, C.J.   Lieutenant   SAAF
Zellor, M.J.   Candidate-Officer   SAAF
Badenhorst, H.J.   Private   SAGD
Bartie, C.G.   Lieutenant   SAGD
Pieterse, H.J.   Private   SAGD
Plateel, M.A.   Lance-Corporal   SAGD
Stanley, K.H.   Private   SAGD
Van Zyl, J.   Candidate-Officer   SAGD
Aspeling, F.   Lance-Corporal   Army
Beukes, E.J.   Rifleman   Army
*Blom, J.J.   Rifleman   Army
Booysens, F.F.   Private   Army
Botha, A.J.   Private   Army
*Botha, J.P.   Lance-Corporal   Army
Botha, M.C.   Trooper   Army
Briers, C.A.   Major   Army
Brindle, R.O.   Rifleman   Army
*Brooks, D.   Corporal   Army
Burger, B.F.   Corporal   Army
Burger, F.K.P.   Rifleman   Army
Catamba, A.   Rifleman   Army
Chamba, M.   Private   Army
*Chameia, F.   Rifleman   Army
*Chapman, P.A.   Corporal   Army
Coetzee, J.P.   Private   Army
*Coetzee, S.F.   Candidate-Officer   Army
*Cromhout, J.C.   Rifleman   Army
Cronje, K.J.   Rifleman   Army
Crous, J.A.   Rifleman   Army
*Dala , F.   Rifleman   Army
Dala, A.   Private   Army
Dala , F.   Rifleman   Army

*De Kock, A.J.P.   Captain   Army
De Lange, G.J.   Rifleman   Army
De Villiers, D.C.   2nd Lieutenant   Army
*Du Toit, J.C.   Corporal   Army
Elefanti   Private   Army
Elliot, G.D.   Rifleman   Army
Ferreira, T.J.   Rifleman   Army
Fourie, J.J.   Lieutenant   Army
Gingles, A.   Lieutenant   Army
Griffen, W.J.   Signalman   Army
*Grobler, H.A.J.   Lance-Bombardier   Army
Gwangwa, V.W.   Sergeant   Army
Haase, D.O.   Rifleman   Army
*Hadlow, M.S.   Lance-Corporal   Army
Hall, P.   Rifleman   Army
*Hanekom, J.W.   Trooper   Army
*Hansen, S.S.   2nd Lieutenant   Army
*Harmse, L.   Captain   Army
Harty, M.R.   Trooper   Army
*Harvey, G.J.   Rifleman   Army
Hassebroek, D.H.O.   Bombardier   Army
*Herbst, R.A.   Rifleman   Army
Hikab, F.   Private   Army
*Hutchinson, R.L.   Sergeant   Army
Jacob, B.   Rifleman   Leer
Janse van Rensburg, C.J.   Gunner   Army
*Janse van Rensburg, D.N.   Private   Army
Jessop, S.R.   Private   Army
*João, J.   Private   Army
*Joaquim, A.   Private   Army
Johannes, A.   Rifleman   Army
Jolliffe, C.P.   Corporal   Army
Jooste, W.L.   Private   Army
*Jordaan, H.K.   Private   Army
José, A.   Private   Army
Kotze, J.J   Private   Army
Kotze, J.J.   Private   Army
*Kruger, I.K.   Lieutenant   Army
*Kruger, P.   Lance-Corporal   Army
Lahner, D.F.   2nd Lieutenant   Army
Lamprecht, D.F.   Sergeant   SAAF
*Le Roux, T.R.   Private   Army
*Leach, B.J.   Private   Army
Levin, L.P.   Gunner   Army
Loubser, D.J.   Gunner   Army
Louw, D.J.   Private   Army
*Louw, J.A.S   Lance-Corporal   Army

Mac Intosh, R.J.L.   Private   Army
*Mokoena, M.S.   Rifleman   Army
*Maletta, I.   Lance-Corporal   Army
Martinus, J.E.   Private   Army
Matenjwa, S.   Private   Army
*Mc Alister, C.C.   Private   Army
Meyer, A.J.   Private   Army
Michael B   Rifleman   Army
Minnie, J.J.   Private   Army
Munro, D.G.   Private   Army
Myburgh, G.J.   Private   Army
Nel, E.M.   Trooper   Army
*Neveling, A.L.   Private   Army
Nortje, A.J.   Signalman   Army
Oberholzer, W.   Rifleman   Army
O'Connor, D.   Lieutenant   SAAF
Olver, H.V.L.   Lance-Bombardier   Army
*Park, J.K.   Lance-Corporal   Army
Paulo, D.   Private   Army
Pettit, E.A.C   Lance-Corporal   Army
Piek, S.P.   Rifleman   Army
Pienaar, W.J.   Trooper   Army
Pieterse, H.J.   Private   SAGD
Pieterse, P.J.   Private   Army
Plateel, M.A.   Lance-Corporal   SAGD
*Potgieter, J.L.   Rifleman   Army
Potgieter, R.   Sergeant   Army
Purdon, W.I.   Private   Army
Raubenheimer, W.F.   Trooper   Army
Richards, J.   Lance-Corporal   Army
Roothman, W.M.   Staff-Sergeant   Army
*Samba, A.   Private   Army
Schoeman, J.M.   Trooper   Army
Schoeman, L.B.   Private   Army
*Smit, F.C.   Private   Army
*Smit, J.H.   Rifleman   Army
*Snyman, E.M.   Private   Army
*Spies, W.   Lance-Corporal   Army
Stanley, K.H.   Private   SAGD
*Stapelberg, M.G.   Private   Army
Steenkamp, B.K.   Lance-Corporal   Army
Steyn, D.A.   Trooper   Army
Strydom, A.C.   Sapper   Army
*Suttill, I.   Sergeant   Army
*Swanepoel, P.   Lance-Corporal   Army
Taylor, C.P.   2nd Lieutenant   Army
Theron, J.C.   Colonel   Army

*Theunissen, K.   Private   Army

Tombo, F.   Rifleman   Army

*Truter, L.   Rifleman   Army

Van der Westhuizen, J.D.   Private   Army

Van Hamersveld, R.C.   Signalman   Army

Van Niekerk, M.J.L.K.   Private   Army

*Van Niekerk, P.A.   Private   Army

*Van Rooyen, E.D.   Private   Army

Van Rooyen, L.   Rifleman   Army

Van Schalkwyk, C.T.   Private   Army

*Van Staden, M.J.   Rifleman   Army

Van Wyk, D.J.   Rifleman   Army

*Van Zyl, G.   Lieutenant   Army

Van Zyl, G.   Lieutenant   Army

Venter, D.J.   Signalman   Army

Venter, I.P.   WO11   Army

*Venter, P.J.   Private   Army

Vermaak, C.J.   Private   Army

*Viljoen, P.J.   Rifleman   Army

Walsh, P.L.   Lance-Corporal   Army

*Wessels, L.T.H   Corporal   Army

Williams, A.R.   Private   Army

Williams, M.   Rifleman   Army

Williams, M.J.   Private   Army

Zwanepoel, E.   Private   Army

Malcolm, N.J   Captain   SAAF

1982

Andonio, F.   Rifleman   Army

Andonio, F.   Corporal   Army

Andreas, R.   Rifleman   Army

Ashford, E.J.   Rifleman   Army

Babtist, J.   Rifleman   Army

*Bambi, M.   Rifleman   Army

Bango, C.   Rifleman   Army

Bango, K.   Rifleman   Army

Barnard, E.J.   Rifleman   Army

*Barrett, R.H.   Rifleman   Army

*Beech, R.T.   Sergeant   Army

*Berry, P.D.   Candidate-Officer   Army

*Bester, H.P.   Corporal   Army

Bhayana, P.   Rifleman   Army

Bieldt, L.M.   Rifleman   Army

Buttland, B.R.   Rifleman   Army

Catumbele, D.   Rifleman   Army

Catumbele, D.   Rifleman   Army

Chivovo, R.   Rifleman   Army

Clerk, D.C.   Corporal   Army

Coetzer, J.A.   Colonel   Army

Comoxoxo, K.   Rifleman   Army

Conroy, J.   Sergeant   Army

*Croeser, D.P.   Rifleman   Army

Crossland, G.G.   Private   Army

Dala, F.   Rifleman   Army

Dala, F.   Rifleman   Army

*Dawson, W.R.   Rifleman   Army

De Beer, J.F.   Private   Army

De Bruin, P.J.   Sapper   Army

*De Klerk, A.   Rifleman   Army

*De Klerk, D.   Rifleman   Army

De Sousa, F.J.G.   Rifleman   Army

De Wee, P.J.J.   Lance-Corporal   Army

*Denge, D.D.   Rifleman   Army

Deysel, D.J.   Rifleman   Army

*Dimbo, J.   Rifleman   Army

Dimbo, J.   Rifleman   Army

*Drake, J.R.S.   Rifleman   Army

Du Plooy, G.B.   Rifleman   Army

*Du Preez, J.S.   Rifleman   Army

Du Toit, E.P.   Rifleman   Army

*Du Toit, J.D.G.   Rifleman   Army

*Dumba, E.   Rifleman   Army

*Dunn, R.G.   Rifleman   Army

*Everisto, C.   Rifleman   Army

Fincham, D.R.   2nd Lieutenant   Army

Fitzpatrick, T.N.   Rifleman   Army

*Forbes, A.   Rifleman   Army

*Fourie, H.   Trooper   Army

Francesco, L.   Rifleman   Army

Francesco, L.   Rifleman   Army

Francesco, L.   Rifleman   Army

*Geustyn, C.W.J.   Candidate-Officer   Army

*Gibbs, B.R.   Rifleman   Army

Gouche, G.G.   Lance-Corporal   Army

Groenewald, H.L.   Private   Army

*Harris-Dewey, M.A.   Corporal   Army

Hattingh, G.P.C.   Rifleman   Army

*Hoare, S.R.   Lance-Corporal   Army

*Hough, L.P.   Rifleman   Army

Jacobson, G.E.   Rifleman   Army

Jasva, J.   Rifleman   Army

*João, Y.   Corporal   Army

Jodt, A.   Rifleman   Army

*Jones, A.R.   Lance-Corporal   Army

*José, M.   Corporal   Army
Kademba, P.   Rifleman   Army
Kademba, P.   Rifleman   Army
Kakuru, T.   Rifleman   Army
Kapango, P.   Rifleman   Army
Kaputo, S.   O/Corporal   Army
Katibelo, D.   Rifleman   Army
Keen, S.L.   Rifleman   Army
*Kouswab, J.   Rifleman   Army
*Kruger, A.   Rifleman   Army
*Kruger, O.P.   Lance-Corporal   Army
*Kruger, P.   Lance-Corporal   Army
*Krull, G.W.   Rifleman   Army
Kuvari, V.   Rifleman   Army
Labuschagne, P.   Rifleman   Army
Landsman, H.   Rifleman   Army
*Le Roux, M.   Rifleman   Army
*Lombaard, E.P.   Corporal   Army
Lombard, J.T.   Rifleman   Army
Lourens, W.P.   Private   Army
Louw, J.   Private   Army
Ludick, W.H.   Private   Army
Lukas, D.   Rifleman   Army
Mahlio, M.J.J.   Rifleman   Army
*Mallon, S.P.   Rifleman   Army
Manuel, A.P.   Rifleman   Army
Manuel, G.J.   Rifleman   Army
*Marshall, J.T.   Rifleman   Army
Mason, M.   Rifleman   Army
Masonga J   Rifleman   Army
Maxwell, L.Z.   Rifleman   Army
Mbele, L.M.   Sergeant   Army
Mc Intosh, W.R.   Captain   Army
Mesonga, T.A.S.   Rifleman   Army
Meulemo, N.K.   Rifleman   Army
*Meyer, J.T.   Lance-Corporal   Army
Moerdyk, J.L.   Rifleman   Army
*Moody, C.A.   Rifleman   Army
Moolman, E.C.   Lance-Corporal   Army
Moses, R.   Rifleman   Army
Mostert, E.   Sergeant   Army
Muharukuo, M.   Rifleman   Army
Muhinje, K.   Rifleman   Army
*Mushanambango, F.   Rifleman   Army
Naikaku, H.   Rifleman   Army
Nando   Rifleman   Army
Nando   Rifleman   Army

Ndara, D.   Rifleman   Army
*Nel, D.   Rifleman   Army
Nel, D.J.   Lance-Corporal   Army
*Nel, P.J.S.   2nd Lieutenant   Army
Nemith, J.A.   Lance-Corporal   Army
Ngoma, M.S.   Lance-Corporal   Army
O'Neill, J.A.   Private   Army
Olyn, D.S.   Corporal   Army
Otto, M.D.   Corporal   Army
*Paulus, S.W.   Rifleman   Army
*Peterson, B.G.   Corporal   Army
*Peterson, M.   Rifleman   Army
*Potgieter, J.H.   Rifleman   Army
Reyneke, J.G.   Lance-Corporal   Army
*Rodricus, M.   Rifleman   Army
Rodriques, M.   Rifleman   Army
Rossouw, D.J.J.   Private   Army
Scheepers, J.W.C.   Rifleman   Army
Schwartz, G.J.   Rifleman   Army
Shilongo, O.   Lance-Corporal   Army
Spence, D.A.   Rifleman   Army
Steffens, A.I.   Private   Army
*Stewart, P.T.   Corporal   Army
Strydom, B.J.C.   Rifleman   Army
*Swana, P.   Lance-Corporal   Army
Swana, P.   Rifleman   Army
Titus, K.   Private   Army
Tjiharukua, K.   Rifleman   Army
Uys, C.   2nd Lieutenant   Army
Van den Berg, J.J.   Lance-Corporal   Army
*Van der Westhuizen, D.R.   2nd Lieutenant   Army
Van Heerden, I.J.   Private   Army
Van Heerden, W.E.   Rifleman   Army
*Van Heerden, W.E.   Rifleman   Army
*Van Jaarsveld, M.J.   Corporal   Army
*Van Niekerk, A.H.   Rifleman   Army
Van Rensburg, K.M.   Private   Army
Van Spronsen, R.P.   Private   Army
Van Staden, J.J.G.   Lance-Corporal   Army
Van Tonder, B.A.   Private   Army
Van Wyk, A.A.   Rifleman   Army
*Van Wyk, L.   Captain   Army
*Van Wyngaardt, A.F.   Sapper   Army
Van Zyl, J.A.   Private   Army
Vasco, N.   Rifleman   Army
*Venter, P.S.   Candidate-Officer   Army
Verrooy, J.   Rifleman   Army

368

Verwey, L.   Rifleman   Army
*Verwey, L.   Rifleman   Army
*Vilho, H.   Rifleman   Army
Weideman, A.C.   Lance-Corporal   Army
*Wessels, E.S.   Lance-Corporal   Army
*Wessels, J.A.   Sergeant   Army
*White, B.A.   Rifleman   Army
*Wolfaardt, B.J.   Rifleman   Army
*Wolmarans, A.   Rifleman   Army
Benjamin, G.T.   Able Seaman   Navy
Booysen, J.   Chief Petty Officer   Navy
Bothma, S.P.   Petty Officer   Navy
Brind, G.A.F.   Petty Officer   Navy
Bulterman, R.C.   Petty Officer   Navy
De Villiers, G.W.   Petty Officer   Navy
Koen, E.   Petty Officer   Navy
Lotter, H.   Petty Officer   Navy
Mc Master, R.A.   Petty Officer   Navy
Skeates, R.F.   Petty Officer   Navy
Smit, H.W.   Chief Petty Officer   Navy
Smith, W.R.   Petty Officer   Navy
Swart, P.R.J.   WO11   Navy
Van Tonder, W.M.G.   Chief Petty Officer   Navy
Webb, D.   Chief Petty Officer   Navy
Whiteley, M.B.R.   Petty Officer   Navy
Wium, C.J.   Petty Officer   Navy
Bondesio, M.A.   Major   SAAF
Brits, C.   Lieutenant   SAAF
Crafford, J.M.   Major-General   SAAF
*Dalgleish, K.G.   Flight-Sergeant   SAAF
De Villiers, J.I.T.   Captain   SAAF
*Earp, M.J.   Lieutenant   SAAF
Evans, D.W.   Candidate-Officer   SAAF
Goldstein, L.   Lieutenant   SAAF
*Grobler, C.N.   Flight-Sergeant   SAAF
Hughes, R.R.   Lieutenant   SAAF
*Janse van Rensburg, O.C.   Lieutenant   SAAF
*Kotze, E.   Major   SAAF
Niemand, A.   Flight-Sergeant   SAAF
Ostram, R.W.B.   Airman   SAAF
*Pietersen, C.W.   Lieutenant   SAAF
*Robinson, J.A.   Captain   SAAF
*Roux, A.G.   Candidate-Officer   SAAF
Steenkamp, D.J.   Corporal   SAAF
*Twaddle, J.G.   Captain   SAAF
Van Niekerk, D.J.   Major-General   SAAF
Williams, J.   Flight-Sergeant   SAAF

1983

Aboud, A.   Rifleman   Army
Atkinson, T.M.   Sergeant   Army
Augusto, J.   Rifleman   Army
Barrington, R.   Rifleman   Army
Beelders, G.F.   Corporal   Army
*Bezuidenhout, C.F.   Gunner   Army
Bezuidenhout, C.J.   Rifleman   Army
*Blignaut, G.D.   Lance-Corporal   Army
*Boshoff, G.M.   Rifleman   Army
*Bosse, J.   Gunner   Army
Botha, J. de K.   Corporal   Army
Bresler, G.   Signalman   Army
*Bruwer, J.A.   Corporal   Army
Burger, A.P.   Sapper   Army
*Claassen, K.   Lieutenant   Army
*Coleby, D.N.   Staff-Sergeant   Army
*Costello, M.A.   Rifleman   Army
*Couvelis, F.P.   Rifleman   Army
*Craemer, C.L.A.   Lance-Corporal   Army
*Da Silva, G.P.   Rifleman   Army
De Lange, J.H.   Trooper   Army
*De Villiers, J.   Commandant   Army
*Diedericks, J.H.   Rifleman   Army
*Du Randt, G.H.   Sergeant   Army
*Du Toit, B.J.   Rifleman   Army
Dula, D.   Corporal   Army
*Ede, R.A.   Corporal   Army
Engel, P.C.   Private   Army
*Engelbrecht, L.J.   Gunner   Army
Erasmus, R.R.   Private   Army
Fillipus, N.   Rifleman   Army
*Fourie, J.C.   Rifleman   Army
Frans, M.   Rifleman   Army
*Greyling, F.C.   Corporal   Army
*Griesel, F.M.   Rifleman   Army
*Hamtenja, S.   Rifleman   Army
Hamutenya, S.   Rifleman   Army
*Hanekom, P.   Rifleman   Army
Hanekom, P.   Rifleman   Army
Jacobs, T.   Rifleman   Army
*Janse van Rensburg, L.J.   Rifleman   Army
*Jonkers, K.   Lance-Corporal   Army
*Jordaan, A.   Rifleman   Army
Kanheto, T.   Sergeant   Army
*Kanheto, T.   Sergeant   Army

*Kasera, E.   Rifleman   Army
*Kativa, J.D.   Rifleman   Army
Kindness, C.W.   Lance-Corporal   Army
*Le Roux, G.P.   Rifleman   Army
*Liebenberg, P.M.   2nd Lieutenant   Army
*Liebenberg, R.H.   Captain   Army
Malan, A.P.   Corporal   Army
*Mande, A.   Corporal   Army
Manganhes, T.   Rifleman   Army
Milinga, R.   Corporal   Army
Milne, G.R.   Corporal   Army
Mkhosi, F.   Rifleman   Army
Moag, W.F.   Lance-Corporal   Army
Mostert, A.D.   Lance-Corporal   Army
Mostert, E.C.   Rifleman   Army
Mthembu, V.M.   Rifleman   Army
*Muller, J.W.   Private   Army
*Nambi, J.   Rifleman   Army
Nel, J.L.   Lance-Corporal   Army
*Niemand, N.W.   Rifleman   Army
Oliver, J.C.A.   Staff-Sergeant   Army
*Olivier, J.P.   Rifleman   Army
Oosthuizen, D.P.   Gunner   Army
Oosthuizen, Q.C.   Private   Army
*Oosthuyse, H.A.   Sergeant   Army
Phakati, L.   Rifleman   Army
*Philipus, N.   Rifleman   Army
*Pretorius, S.   Rifleman   Army
*Prins, D.   Rifleman   Army
Riem   Rifleman   Army
Ross, T.A.   Rifleman   Army
Salvador, A.   Rifleman   Army
Samson, J.K.   Rifleman   Army
Schoenborn, G.C.   Rifleman   Army
*Schronen, D.J.   Rifleman   Army
Shikandano, M.   Rifleman   Army
*Silverton, S.L.   Rifleman   Army
*Smit, A.M.   Rifleman   Army
Smit, L.   Rifleman   Army
*Smit, M.C.   Rifleman   Army
Steyn, J.   Rifleman   Army
Steyn, J.D.J.   Rifleman   Army
Steytler, G.L.   Corporal   Army
*Stols, J.J.C.   Rifleman   Army
Strauss, J.M.   Private   Army
*Thirion, A.J.B.   Rifleman   Army
*Tinda, J.   Rifleman   Army

Torre, P.G.   Corporal   Army
Trooperari, K.   Rifleman   Army
*Tucker, A.J.   Lance-Corporal   Army
*Uzzel, P.   Rifleman   Army
Van Bosch, J.P.L   WO11   Army
Van den Berg, J.G.J.   Private   Army
Van der Berg, J.G.J.   Private   Army
*Van der Merwe, J.L.   Rifleman   Army
Van der Westhuizen, J.A.   Rifleman   Army
*Van Eeden, P.F.   Rifleman   Army
Van Jaarsveld, T.   Rifleman   Army
Van Staden, E.J.   Sergeant   Army
Van Tonder, J.   Private   Army
Van Zyl, A.A.   Captain   Army
Van Zyl, F.C.   Lieutenant   Army
Viljoen, A.   Lieutenant   Army
Viljoen, G.   Rifleman   Army
Wessels, J.A.   Rifleman   Army
*Williams, O.C.   Lance-Corporal   Army
*Wolton, A.D.   Rifleman   Army
Ford, G.E.W.   Able Seaman   Navy
*Kemp, H.J.   Able Seaman   Navy
Mooi, N.   Chief Petty Officer   Navy
Chinery, B.C.   Lieutenant   SAAF
Haupt, W.   Airman   SAAF
*Henning, I.J.   Commandant   SAAF
Jacobs, L.   Lieutenant   SAAF
Janse van Rensburg, J.J.   Airman   SAAF
*Kirtley, W.L.   Airman   SAAF
*Nel, A.   Corporal   SAAF
*Ras, J.J.   Flight-Sergeant   SAAF
Short, T.D.   Lieutenant   SAAF
Terburgh, P.J.   Lance-Corporal   SAAF
*Walters, S.S.   Colonel   SAAF
Beard, P.A.   Private   SAGD
Cogill, J.   Private   SAGD
De Villiers, D.   2nd Lieutenant   SAGD
Human, J.B.   Private   SAGD
Kriel, W.E.   Private   SAGD
Welgemoed, S.W.   Private   SAGD

1984

Adams, J.R.   Sergeant   Army
Antonio, D.   Rifleman   Army
Arico   Rifleman   Army
*Aurelio, A.   Corporal   Army
Awino, K.   Lance-Corporal   Army

Badenhorst, J.J.   Gunner   Army
Badenhorst, S.   Rifleman   Army
Bekker, M.M.   Sergeant   Army
Bekker, R.W.   Lance-Corporal   Army
Boshoff, A.H.   Rifleman   Army
*Botha, P.   Corporal   Army
Brandt, C.P.V.D.M.   Captain   Army
Brierley, G.E.   Rifleman   Army
Briggs, R.P.   Corporal   Army
Brink, G.   2nd Lieutenant   Army
Byleveld, M.   Rifleman   Army
Cabriel, R.   Corporal   Army
Chiemba, K.   Rifleman   Army
Churchill, W.   Rifleman   Army
Clark, G.S.M.   Rifleman   Army
Conrad, S.H.   Rifleman   Army
Coram, C.J.   Rifleman   Army
Corrie, F.   Rifleman   Army
Crouse, G.J.J.F.   Private   Army
Da Silva, L.A.   Rifleman   Army
*Dala, J.   Rifleman   Army
Dala, J.   Rifleman   Army
Dala, L.   Corporal   Army
Dala, L.   Corporal   Army
Dala, L.   Rifleman   Army
Daniel, P.   Rifleman   Army
*De Beer, J.A.   Corporal   Army
*De Lange, G.E.   Rifleman   Army
*Dippenaar, C.R.   Rifleman   Army
*Douwrie, D.A.   Rifleman   Army
Du Plessis, P.J.   Corporal   Army
*Geen, B.   Rifleman   Army
Genis, W. de R.   WO1   Army
Gevers, U.L.   Recruit   Army
*Gouws, P.   Corporal   Army
Grobler, M.H.   Private   Army
Harms, O.B.   Rifleman   Army
Helberg, N.J.G.   Sapper   Army
Henn, A.J.   Rifleman   Army
*Heyns, H.A.   Rifleman   Army
Hildebrandt, R.F.   Private   Army
Inglis, K.   Rifleman   Army
Jacobs, A.C.   Rifleman   Army
Janse van Vuuren, F.H.   Trooper   Army
*Jepau, R.   Rifleman   Army
Jepua, R.   Rifleman   Army
July, L.   Rifleman   Army

*Kampanza, G.   Rifleman   Army
Kees, A.   Rifleman   Army
Klue, D.H.   Signalman   Army
Kruger, G.   Gunner   Army
Kruger, S.J.   Captain   Army
Kudumo, P.   Rifleman   Army
*Lennox, C.   Rifleman   Army
*Louw, D.A.   Rifleman   Army
Louw, E.J.   Major   Army
*Malongo, I.   Rifleman   Army
Marais, T.   Rifleman   Army
Maseti, T.C.N.   Corporal   Army
Matsetse, D.   Corporal   Army
Matthee, J.R.   Private   Army
Merrow, K.J.   Rifleman   Army
Nangalo, J.   Rifleman   Army
Nkada, M.J.   Rifleman   Army
Olivier, C.R.   Rifleman   Army
Parker, K.E.   Staff-Sergeant   Army
*Pearson, L.F.   Rifleman   Army
*Pretorius, J.L.   Rifleman   Army
*Pretorius, P.D.   Rifleman   Army
Randall, J.A.S.T.   Trooper   Army
*Roets, J.H.   Corporal   Army
Shiningivali, D.   Corporal   Army
Smith, H.J.   Rifleman   Army
*Steenkamp, W.T.   Lance-Corporal   Army
Strydom, J.H.   Rifleman   Army
Swartz, W.   Rifleman   Army
Taljaard, H.F.   Rifleman   Army
Taljaard, P.   Rifleman   Army
Terblanche, E.C.   Rifleman   Army
Terblanche, J.G.   Corporal   Army
*Theunissen, J.C.   Corporal   Army
*Tomes, A.L.   Gunner   Army
Uugwanga, J.   Rifleman   Army
Van den Dool, T.   Corporal   Army
Van der Merwe, D.S.   Rifleman   Army
Van der Merwe, H.F.   Rifleman   Army
Van Niekerk, D.L.   Corporal   Army
Van Vuuren, P.F.   Rifleman   Army
Van Wyk, J.   Rifleman   Army
*Venter, D.S.   Rifleman   Army
Verhoef, J.P.   2nd Lieutenant   Army
Vorster, G.D.   Lance-Corporal   Army
Ward, D.J.   Staff-Sergeant   Army
*Ward, D.J.   Staff-Sergeant   Army

Wasas, L.G. Rifleman Army
Wildschutt, J.J.J. Rifleman Army
Canner, C.J. Able Seaman Navy
De Jongh, S.H. Able Seaman Navy
Kok, J.H. Airman SAAF
Booysen, C. Private SA Med S
Maree, H.H.J. Lieutenant SA Med S
Ponder, S.S. Lieutenant SA Med S

1985

Anthony, P.H. Sergeant Army
*Antonio, P. Rifleman Army
Apollis, P. Corporal Army
Atkins, S.P. Rifleman Army
Borthwick, M.R. Lieutenant Army
Botha, P. Private Army
Bowers, D. Rifleman Army
Broekmeyer, R.A. 2nd Lieutenant Army
Buijense, J. Rifleman Army
*Chihamba, J. Rifleman Army
*Chipoya, Z. Rifleman Army
Coetzee, J.A. Rifleman Army
Cohen, P.C.F.D.P Sergeant Army
Cole, K.C. Sapper Army
*De Almeida, A. Rifleman Army
De Beurges, G.C.U.W.M 2nd Lieutenant Army
De Kock, S.F. Rifleman Army
Defransa, P. Rifleman Army
Difransa, P. Rifleman Army
Dougall, A.S. Rifleman Army
Du Plessis, D.G. Private Army
*Dumbe, L. Lance-Corporal Army
*Fernando, J. Rifleman Army
*Gabriel, I. Rifleman Army
*Galonga, K. Rifleman Army
Gobe, J. Lance-Corporal Army
*Gobe, J. Corporal Army
Goncalves, O.D.P. Rifleman Army
Gore, J. Corporal Army
Gould, P.N. Private Army
Gumede, M.G. Rifleman Army
Hall, J.P Corporal Army
Heathcote, C. Gunner Army
Helm, H.C. Trooper Army
Jack, C. Rifleman Army
Jacobs, H.I. Rifleman Army
*Jamba, J.E. Rifleman Army

*Joaquim, M. Rifleman Army
*Kahete, P.K. Rifleman Army
King, J. Rifleman Army
*Kinguelele, M.A. Lance-Corporal Army
Kotze, A.J. Corporal Army
*Liebenberg, R.R. Corporal Army
*Light, D.G. Lieutenant Army
Littrell, M.J. Rifleman Army
Louw, J.F. Scout Army
Luiters, W.R. Rifleman Army
*Marcel, N.M. Corporal Army
Matthee, D. 2nd Lieutenant Army
Mikael, H. Rifleman Army
*Muema, M. Rifleman Army
*Muheue, M. Rifleman Army
*Pearson, M.W. 2nd Lieutenant Army
*Pond, M.A. Corporal Army
Preuss, K. Private Army
Prinsloo, J.P. Private Army
Rautenbach, R.J. Gunner Army
Rudd, J.R.W. Rifleman Army
*Sachilombo, J.A. Rifleman Army
Schoeman, J. Corporal Army
*Smuts, N.W. Rifleman Army
Taljaard, P. Rifleman Army
Teffo, A.L. Corporal Army
Theron, P.J. Rifleman Army
Thompson, G.M. Rifleman Army
Uys, H.P. Bombadier Army
Uys, J.P. Major Army
*Van Breda, L.P. Corporal Army
Van Buisbergen, L. Corporal Army
Van der Merwe, W.S. 2nd Lieutenant Army
Van der Vyver, J.A. Major Army
Van Niekerk, D. Corporal Army
Williams, E. Rifleman Army
De Klerk, V.E.B. Seaman Navy
Els, F.B. Seaman Navy
Oosthuis, C.G.C. Chief Petty Officer Navy
Butler, W.S Sergeant SAAF
Clench, D.G. Corporal SAAF
Coetzee, L.J. Sergeant SAAF
Gouws, W.J. Sergeant SAAF
Hawkins, W.J. Sergeant SAAF
Knoetze, M.S. Airman SAAF
McLeod, C. Captain SAAF
Nell, B.A. Airman SAAF

Rodel, R.R   Lieutenant   SAAF
Wessels, J.P.   Major   SAAF
Dockerill, C.G.   Private   SA Med S
*Fidler, B.A.   Corporal   SA Med S
Lombard, M.S.   Lance-Corporal   SA Med S
Ruthven, G.S.   Lance-Corporal   SA Med S
Swain, G.G.   Private   SA Med S

1986

Badenhorst, C.   Rifleman   Army
Bergh, J.C.   Staff-Sergeant   Army
Botes, M.J.   Rifleman   Army
Bronkhorst, N.C.M.   Rifleman   Army
Carolus, F.   Rifleman   Army
Chilunku, T.   Rifleman   Army
Claase, J.N.   Corporal   Army
Clatke, A.B.   Recruit   Army
Cloete, C.J.   Captain   Army
Coad, W.J.   Sapper   Army
Conradie, I.   Private   Army
*Cook, R.A.   Sergeant   Army
Cooper, J.E.   Corporal   Army
*Cornelius, F.P.J.   WO1   Army
Dala, K.K.   Rifleman   Army
De Jager, J.J.   Recruit   Army
Delport, J.   Recruit   Army
Dolf, P.   Rifleman   Army
Du Preez, B.   Captain   Army
Du Toit, D.F.   Rifleman   Army
*Erasmus, A.H.   Lance-Corporal   Army
Fowler, D.J.   Rifleman   Army
Glinski, G.B.   Rifleman   Army
Goosen, W.   Commandant   Army
Hamman, J.F.   Recruit   Army
*Hochapfel, C.V.   Commandant   Army
Holland, T.R.W.   Rifleman   Army
Hood, S.R.   Rifleman   Army
Janse van Rensburg, J.G.J.   Rifleman   Army
Janse van Rensburg, T.W.   Corporal   Army
Knipe, R.A.   Rifleman   Army
Koekemoer, E.C.   Rifleman   Army
Kuyler, L.B.   Sapper   Army
Labuschagne, G.B.   Sergeant   Army
Labuschagne, J.H.   Lance-Corporal   Army
*Le Roux, A.M.   Lance-Corporal   Army
Lourens, I.J.   2nd Lieutenant   Army
Mahlangu, P.W.   Rifleman   Army

Malan, G.G.   Rifleman   Army
*Mariosu, D.   Corporal   Army
Marx, R.   Private   Army
*Mashavave, M.L.   Corporal   Army
Mauriocu, D.   Corporal   Army
Meisenheimer, P.J.J.   Corporal   Army
Mthimunye, G.Z.   Rifleman   Army
Nel, J.A.C.   Recruit   Army
Nelson, C. du B.   Recruit   Army
Nortje, G.F.   Sergeant   Army
Opperman, W.H.   Rifleman   Army
Pattenden, N.E.   Corporal   Army
Pedro, V.R.   Corporal   Army
*Pretorius, J.   Trooper   Army
*Renken, A.D.   Corporal   Army
Retief, D.J.   Private   Army
Schentke, G.E.   Sapper   Army
Schmidt, J.D.   Corporal   Army
Smith, P.J.   Corporal   Army
Snyman, J.H.   Private   Army
Sprowson, S.A.   Private   Army
Sterling, R.D.   Lance-Corporal   Army
Terblanche, B.   Major   Army
*Thomas, N.   Rifleman   Army
Tjenda, B.   Rifleman   Army
Van den Berg, J.P.   Sapper   Army
Van der Westhuizen, G.H.   Sergeant   Army
Van Niekerk, J.P.   Staff-Sergeant   Army
Van Schalkwyk, D.W.   Sapper   Army
Venter, C.M.A.A.   Rifleman   Army
Whiteley, M.T.   Corporal   Army
Pekeur, D.J.   Petty Officer   Navy
Bloem, E.M.   Flight-Sergeant   SAAF
Snaddon, D.L.J.   2nd Lieutenant   SAAF
Snyman, C.H.   Candidate-Officer   SAAF
Byrd, A.M.   Private   SA Med S

1987

Adams, W.   Rifleman   Army
*Alves, J.R.   2nd Lieutenant   Army
*Antonio, G.   Rifleman   Army
Barnard, J.   Rifleman   Army
*Batisda, A.N.D.   Corporal   Army
*Benecke, M.A.   Lance-Corporal   Army
Beukman, W.G.   Gunner   Army
Biet, S.R.   Gunner   Army
*Botes, D.   2nd Lieutenant   Army

Brissett, R.J.   Private   Army
Burger, W.P.   Rifleman   Army
Cainsford, C.   Recruit   Army
*Cassela, D.   Rifleman   Army
*Claasen, P.G.   Rifleman   Army
*Cloete, J.J.   Trooper   Army
*Cobbolt, D.C.   2nd Lieutenant   Army
*Concalves, J.   Rifleman   Army
*Dala, G.   Rifleman   Army
*Daniels, I.M.   Corporal   Army
De Bruin, F.   Rifleman   Army
*De Jager, F.   Trooper   Army
*De Klerk, M.M.   Lance-Corporal   Army
*De Rose, H.N.   Rifleman   Army
De Villiers, A.W.   Gunner   Army
*Digue, P.J.   Sergeant   Army
Docherty, C.G.   Rifleman   Army
*Dreyer, M.CM.   Lieutenant   Army
Du Plessis, C.P.   Corporal   Army
Du Preez, K.C.   Rifleman   Army
Du Randt, J.C.   Commandant   Army
Du Toit, C.J.   Corporal   Army
*Duvenhage, T.A.   Corporal   Army
Emmanuel, L.   Rifleman   Army
Engelbrecht, S.   Sapper   Army
*Ewels, W.V.   Rifleman   Army
*Fernando, A.   Corporal   Army
Ferreira, J.   Rifleman   Army
Fourie, C.A.   Private   Army
Hartzenberg, A.   Rifleman   Army
Henriksen, K.   Corporal   Army
*Hind, A.H.   2nd Lieutenant   Army
Howard, G.M.   2nd Lieutenant   Army
*Howes, J.M.   Rifleman   Army
Immelman, G.   Private   Army
*João, E.   Lance-Corporal   Army
Johannes, J.W.L.   Rifleman   Army
Jonker, A.   Corporal   Army
Julies, B.   Private   Army
*Kapepura, E.N.   Rifleman   Army
Kapinga, P.   Rifleman   Army
*Khumalo, A.A.   Rifleman   Army
Kilian, C.B.   Private   Army
Koopman, N.   Private   Army
Kriel, C.J.   Private   Army
*Kuyler, M.J.   Trooper   Army
Labuschagne, J.   Trooper   Army

Le Roux, J.A.   Rifleman   Army
*Light, R.M.   Lance-Corporal   Army
*Mananza, J.R.   Lance-Corporal   Army
Mansfield, P.   Lance-Bombardier   Army
Mariano, A.A.   Private   Army
Marlow, J.R   Recruit   Army
Masina, S.A.   Rifleman   Army
*Mauricio, F.   Rifleman   Army
Mbambo, A.D.   Rifleman   Army
Mbambo, S.E.   Rifleman   Army
*McCallum, A.D.   Captain   Army
*McGregor, M.W.W.   Corporal   Army
*Metcalfe, H.J.   Rifleman   Army
*Meyer, E.A.   Sapper   Army
Meyer, G.C.   Lance-Corporal   Army
Meyer, J.R.   Trooper   Army
*Mitton, M.J.   Rifleman   Army
Morris, R.   Sergeant   Army
Moyo, M.A.   Rifleman   Army
*Muehlenbeck, F.A.   Private   Army
Naude, A.J.   Private   Army
Ndlela, M.G.   Rifleman   Army
*Ntjamba, L.   Rifleman   Army
Nyamhunga, M.L.   Corporal   Army
*Olivier, N.S.   Corporal   Army
Oosthuizen, E.   Private   Army
Oosthuizen, H.A.   Lance-Corporal   Army
*Pedro, J.   Rifleman   Army
Pienaar, M.G.   Sergeant   Army
*Rademeyer, A.H. du B.   Captain   Army
Reynolds, P.B.   Private   Army
Riekert, A.G.   Rifleman   Army
Roman, S.L.   Lance-Corporal   Army
Sadler, A.T.N.   Private   Army
Scheepers, H.H.   Rifleman   Army
Schoenfeldt, B.J.   Private   Army
*Schutte, P.M.   Rifleman   Army
*Schuurman, J.M.   Rifleman   Army
Scott, R.A.   Lance-Corporal   Army
*Sebata, O.M.   Corporal   Army
*Sikote, F.   Rifleman   Army
Smit, F. du P.   Private   Army
*Sokola, B.   Corporal   Army
Sole, L.C.   Rifleman   Army
*Steward, A.   Private   Army
*Steyn, E.A.   Sapper   Army
Strauss, A.J.   Corporal   Army

*Strydom, H.L. Corporal Army
Stubbs, N.A. Rifleman Army
*Tchipango, W. Lance-Corporal Army
*Thom, A.M. Rifleman Army
*Tolosi, K. Rifleman Army
Uithaler, W. Rifleman Army
Van der Merwe, D.R. Rifleman Army
Van der Merwe, P.A. Major Army
*Van Heerden, J.C. Corporal Army
Van Heerden van Z J. Trooper Army
Van Loggerenberg, M.P. Corporal Army
*Van Rooyen, D.W. Rifleman Army
*Van Zyl, D.W.H. Rifleman Army
Venter, W.J.G. Corporal Army
Viljoen, M. Corporal Army
Viljoen, W. Rifleman Army
*Visagie, P.A. Rifleman Army
*Vocolo, J. Lance-Corporal Army
*Wetton, C.D. Rifleman Army
Zaayman, J.B. Corporal Army
Ziemkendorf, H. Trooper Army
*Zua, D. Rifleman Army
Zulu, P.J. Rifleman Army
Douglas, G.J.S. Lieutenant Navy
Mostert, J.J.B. Chief Petty Officer Navy
Glynn, R.W. Lieutenant SAAF
*Lan, D. Sergeant SAAF
Lucarne, C.A. Airman SAAF
Nelson, B.M. Captain SAAF
*Stapa, A.A. Captain SAAF
Vergottini, R.H. Captain SAAF
Vorster, B.J. Captain SAAF
Kilroe, C.D. Lance–Corporal SA Med S
*Redelinghuys, J.J. Lance-Corporal SA Med S
*Tamsen, E. Lance-Corporal SA Med S

1988

Bannell, M.S. Trooper Army
Barnard, J.P. Rifleman Army
Beneke, C.J. Private Army
Botha, J.N. Rifleman Army
Cambinda, A.L. Rifleman Army
Cornet, D. Rifleman Army
De Goede, C.A. Sapper Army
*De Lange, J. Signalman Army
*Diederichs, J.H. 2nd Lieutenant Army
Dilman, C. Rifleman Army

Dreyer, T.A. Rifleman Army
Du Plessis, J.C. Lance-Corporal Army
Du Toit, P.G.V. Lance-Corporal Army
Eduardo, Z. Sergeant Army
Ellis, S.C. Gunner Army
*Els, A.S.J. Rifleman Army
*Erasmus, E. Trooper Army
Ferreira, I.W. Gunner Army
Fletcher, A.M. Lance-Corporal Army
Gewers, N.C. v R. 2nd Lieutenant Army
Gobey, D. Corporal Army
*Groenewald, A.S. Rifleman Army
*Groenewald, P.H. Rifleman Army
Harker, J.B. Rifleman Army
*Hendricks, C. Bombardier Army
Herbst, P.J. Lance-Corporal Army
Horn, M. Staff-Sergeant Army
Hoy, B.A. Lance-Corporal Army
Khumoeng, M.I. Rifleman Army
*Kleynhans, J.H. Corporal Army
Koen, P.G.L. 2nd Lieutenant Army
*Koorts, E.P. Corporal Army
Lamb, G. Lance-Corporal Army
Lategan, A.S. Sapper Army
Lecuona, M.J. Lance-Corporal Army
Lelong, S.E. Sapper Army
Lones, D.A. Rifleman Army
Lotriet, J.A. Lance-Corporal Army
*Lotter, L.F. Major Army
Lubbe, A. Private Army
Magagula, F.A. Rifleman Army
Mahlakwane, A. Rifleman Army
*Maritz, G.M. Sergeant Army
Marloh, J. Private Army
*Marx, P.R. Rifleman Army
Matroos, P.D. Rifleman Army
*McCann, M.S. 2nd Lieutenant Army
Meiring, A. Gunner Army
*Meiring, M. 2nd Lieutenant Army
Molokomme, M.G. Rifleman Army
Moolman, L.J. Rifleman Army
*Moon, C.T. Lance-Corporal Army
Mpembe, M.J. Rifleman Army
*Msomi, S.B. Rifleman Army
*Ndinu, A. Rifleman Army
Nelson, R.I. Private Army
Neto, E.J. de S. Lance-Corporal Army

Ngubani, D. Private Army
*Nieuwenhuizen, V.V. Rifleman Army
Petersen, D. Corporal Army
Pienaar, H. Captain Army
Potgieter, D. Rifleman Army
Price, W.A.F. Lance-Corporal Army
Prins, R. Rifleman Army
*Prinsloo, A. Corporal Army
Prinsloo, A. Corporal Army
Prinsloo, A.P. Private Army
Renison, R. Sapper Army
*Rex, J. Rifleman Army
Roberts, K.A. Gunner Army
*Rudman, T.B. Rifleman Army
*Sachse, C. Sapper Army
*Scott, G. Trooper Army
Snyders, A. Rifleman Army
Stewart, G.M. Corporal Army
Stoop, S.P. Gunner Army
*Suter, M.C. Sapper Army
Swartz, N. Private Army
Thobejane, P. Private Army
*Tucker, N. Lieutenant Army
Van der Merve, J.P. Gunner Army
Van der Merwe, J.D.G. Corporal Army
Van der Westhuizen, H.J. Gunner Army
Van Dyk, P.L.H. Rifleman Army
*Van Heerden, M.J. Rifleman Army
Van Niekerk, W.F. Gunner Army
Van Rooyen, G. Staff-Sergeant Army
*Van Wyk, L.F. Lance-Corporal Army
*Van Wyk, W.A. Lance-Corporal Army
*Venter, H.J. Rifleman Army
*Venter, J.M.S. Rifleman Army
*Venter, V.Z. Corporal Army
*Vermeulen, N.J. Rifleman Army
Wama, P. Rifleman Army
Webb, I.M. Rifleman Army
*Weyers, J. Private Army
Wolfaardt, O.L. Trooper Army
Wolmarans, N.J. Rifleman Army
*Yeo, E.C. Corporal Army
Van der Merwe, W.S. Seaman Navy
Bekker, A. Colonel SAAF
*Every, E.R. Major SAAF
Marais, J.S. Airman SAAF
Nel, J.N. Amn SAAF

*Van Coppenhagen, J.W. Major SAAF
*Du Toit, P.G.V. Lance-Corporal SA Med S
Eichholz, L.J. Colonel SA Med S
Gerding, H.J.R. Lieutenant SA Med S
*Holder, J.R.G. Lance-Corporal SA Med S
*Jagga, R.V. Lance-Corporal SA Med S

1989

Antonio, M.S. Rifleman Army
*Carstens, H. Corporal Army
Coetzee, J.P. WO1 Army
Cooper, E.S. Private Army
Crowley, F. Sapper Army
De Freitas, D.E. Private Army
De Klerk, J.G. Private Army
Du Plessis, J.P. Private Army
*Els, C.P. Lieutenant Army
Gache, R.A. Rifleman Army
Hanslo, I.S. Private Army
Khuluse, T.M. Rifleman Army
Kriel, J.G. Signalman Army
Le Wack, C. Rifleman Army
Lukhelo, Z.A. Rifleman Army
Mackenzie, C.D. Private Army
Makatini, M.A. Rifleman Army
Mathebula, K.O. Lance-Corporal Army
Meerholz, C.A.J. Colonel Army
Moletsane, J.M. Lance-Corporal Army
Nghome, M.M. Rifleman Army
Patterson, R.E. Trooper Army
Rousseau, A. Signalman Army
Sibuyi, R.A. Rifleman Army
Swartz, P. Corporal Army
Thiel, R.E. Rifleman Army
Van der Merwe, A.B. Sergeant Army
Van der Merwe, H.S. Lance-Corporal Army
Bredenkamp, W. Lieutenant SAAF
Joubert, D. Lieutenant SAAF
Malan, P. du T. 2nd Lieutenant SAAF
Saayman, B.L. Lance-Corporal SAAF
Sheppard, R.S. WO1 SAGD

1990

Afrika, A. Corporal Army
Arendse, D. Rifleman Army
Baker, E. Trooper Army
Beech, W.R. Private Army

Boorman, G.G. Corporal Army
Bush, J. Rifleman Army
Campbell, A.V. Signalman Army
Chimongaia, C. Lance-Corporal Army
De Bruin, G.S. Recruit Army
De Villiers, C. Private Army
Dlomo, S. Lance-Corporal Army
Ferreira, L. Trooper Army
Fouche, J.J. WO1 Army
Fuller, A. Rifleman Army
Geduld, J. Rifleman Army
Haasbroek, P.G.J. Corporal Army
Hart, B. Rifleman Army
Heine, G.P. Rifleman Army
Jacobs, M. Rifleman Army
Joaquim, J. Rifleman Army
Khoza, A.M. Rifleman Army
Koekemoer, P.B. Gunner Army
Kotze, D.J.J. Lance-Corporal Army
Lourens, J.J. Rifleman Army
Louw, F.P. Rifleman Army
Maguire, C.A. Lance-Corporal Army
Malan, A. Rifleman Army
Mashile, T. Rifleman Army
Mathete, M.F. Rifleman Army
Mdaka, L.S. Rifleman Army
Mentoor, C.J. Rifleman Army
Mkhombo, M.I. Rifleman Army
Muller, M.C. Rifleman Army
*Palmer, F.J. Corporal Army
Pieters, W.J . Trooper Army
Pieterse, D.C. Private Army
Putter, L.F. Rifleman Army
Robertson, I.B. Private Army
Rochollz J .H. Recruit Army
Terblanche, J. Recruit Army
Van Rooyen, R. Private Army
*Van Wyk, S. Rifleman Army
Venter, H.W. Commandant Army
Wheeler, R.L. Signalman Army
Zondi, G.D. Rifleman Army
Zungu, T.C. Rifleman Army
Diggle, E. Lieutenant SAAF
Mc Guinness, S.J. Lieutenant SAAF
Krijger, E. Private SAGD
Lagesen, O.J.de V. Lance-Corporal SAGD

1991

Andrade, J. Rifleman Army
Augusto, J. Rifleman Army
Boyd, D.J. Lance-Corporal Army
Damnert, M.P. Gunner Army
De Koker, W. Major Army
Ferreira, F.M. Commandant Army
Geldenhuys, H.M. Major Army
Hein, M.W. Rifleman Army
Jeneke, F.J. Rifleman Army
Juskiewicz, A.M. Lance-Corporal Army
Kambinda, S. Rifleman Army
Khoza, M.B. Rifleman Army
Khoza, R.O. Corporal Army
Kruger, L. Sergeant Army
Makuwe, E. Rifleman Army
Mann, G. Gunner Army
Mdakane, M.P. Rifleman Army
Myburgh, R. Rifleman Army
Nel, J.F.L. Rifleman Army
Pietersen, W.C. Rifleman Army
Roesch, N. 2nd Lieutenant Army
Schillings, M. Lieutenant Army
Schutte, D. Lance-Corporal Army
Sekonjela, A.N. Rifleman Army
Shisari, J.S. Lance-Corporal Army
Sibuyi, B.A. Rifleman Army
Simbine, M.M. Rifleman Army
Swanepoel, M. Lance-Corporal Army
Swart, L.J. Rifleman Army
Tait, P.H.T. Lance-Corporal Army
Van der Merwe, P.A. Gunner Army
Van Heerden, B.A. Rifleman Army
Van Rooyen, S. 2nd Lieutenant Army
Miller, R.J. Major SAAF
Neuhoff, J.F. Lieutenant SAAF
Turner R .M. Major SAAF

1992

Adams, J. Rifleman Army
Beukes, C. Lance-Corporal Army
Bizeki, N. Lance-Corporal Army
Blankenberg, M.P. Corporal Army
Boorman, B. Rifleman Army
Du Toit, D.S.H. Rifleman Army
Elliot, C.D. Sergeant Army

Fourie, J.J.   WO1   Army
Grobler, G.J.   Recruit   Army
Johannes, J.   Rifleman   Army
Tavenga, K.   Rifleman   Army
Kekana, T.F.   Rifleman   Army
Khoathela, A.M.   Sapper   Army
Koekemoer, G.J.   Recruit   Army
Kubjana, K.T.   Rifleman   Army
Le Roux, J.J.   Lance-Corporal   Army
Lebepe, S.J.   Corporal   Army
Lourens, J.L.B.   Rifleman   Army
Lukhozi, S.   Rifleman   Army
Maborala, D.   Rifleman   Army
Mahasha, L.P.   Lance-Corporal   Army
Mahlaba, A.L.   Rifleman   Army
Mahlako, M.S.   Lance-Corporal   Army
Mahlangu, V.M.   Rifleman   Army
Makumu, M.A.   Rifleman   Army
Malaza, P.   Corporal   Army
Matlakala, M.P.   Corporal   Army
Mkhaliphi, J.D.   Rifleman   Army
Moloto, N.J.   Rifleman   Army
Motseo, M.J.   Rifleman   Army
Ngulube, D.S.   Lance-Corporal   Army
Otto, J.   WO1   Army
Peterson, C.V.   Corporal   Army
Pontes, T.   Rifleman   Army
Ponto, K.   Rifleman   Army
Pretorius, J.A.   Recruit   Army
Prins, A.   Rifleman   Army
Prins, J.P.   Rifleman   Army
Ruiter, A.J.   Rifleman   Army
Sambo, I.   Lance-Corporal   Army
Seerane, M.A.   Rifleman   Army
Shilenge, S.F.   Rifleman   Army
Steyn, R.J.   Rifleman   Army
Swarts, J.J.   Rifleman   Army
Thabete, N.Z.   Rifleman   Army
Titus, W.   Rifleman   Army
Valoyi, P.G.   Lance-Corporal   Army
Waterhouse, G.B.   2nd Lieutenant   Army
Watson, D.L.   Captain   Army
Zondi, S.B.   Lance-Corporal   Army
Kohne, R.D.   Lieutenant-Commander   Navy
Maphumulo, G.M.   Signalman   Navy
Gordon, B.J.   Private   SA Med S
Kladis, E.   Lance-Corporal   SA Med S

Malan, R.F.   Private   SA Med S
Oberholzer, F.P.   Private   SA Med S
Pohl, E.   Private   SA Med S

1993

Blignaut, J.H.   Rifleman   Army
Boer, S.   Rifleman   Army
Condo, R.G.   Rifleman   Army
De Waal, H.J.   Lieutenant   Army
Dixon, M.D.   Lieutenant   Army
Dube, M.   Sergeant   Army
Fingo, G.G.J.   Corporal   Army
Gaebolae, J.B.   Rifleman   Army
Gericke, R.E.   Staff-Sergeant   Army
Maduna, P.   Corporal   Army
Mans, C.Y.   Corporal   Army
Masha, M.J.   Signalman   Army
Masuku, J.M.   Rifleman   Army
Mbangu, J.   Rifleman   Army
Mekgoe, C.P.   Rifleman   Army
Mnusi, M.S.   Rifleman   Army
Montsho, J.T.   Lance-Corporal   Army
Mukelenge, M.   Rifleman   Army
Ndlovu, S.A.   Rifleman   Army
Nieuhaus, R.   Staff-Sergeant   Army
Nkwanyana, N.J.   Lance-Corporal   Army
Ntshalaka, M.E.   Rifleman   Army
Ntuli, S.N.K.   Sapper   Army
Nukeri, K.J.   Rifleman   Army
Opperman, F.J.   WO1   Army
Passen, H.   2nd Lieutenant   Army
Pati, I.O.P.   Gunner   Army
Petersen, P.   Rifleman   Army
Phillipson, T.T.   Captain   Army
Richard-Smith, B.   Lance-Corporal   Army
Robbertze, A.C.D.   Lance-Corporal   Army
Schotz, R.W.   Staff-Sergeant   Army
Scott, D.G.   Lance-Corporal   Army
Sigidi, M.   Rifleman   Army
Smith, P.J.   Rifleman   Army
Strydom, P.P.   Lance-Corporal   Army
Thomas, J.M.   Rifleman   Army
Van Zyl, G.   2nd Lieutenant   Army
Emmenis, G.C.   Airman   SAAF
Hamilton, G.D.   Major   SAAF
Ramsamy, P.   Corporal   SAAF
Rudnick, C.S.K.   Captain   SAAF

1994

Lekalakala, B.M.   Rifleman   Army
Makhatha, P.S.   Rifleman   Army
Mathonsi, G.R.   Rifleman   Army
Matwa, W.Z.   Lance-Corporal   Army
Mnisi, S.V.   Rifleman   Army
Mokgolo, P.J.   Lance-Corporal   Army
Myeni, M.J.   Rifleman   Army
Roux, F.P.S.   Captain   Army
Verwey, D.D.M.   Rifleman   Army
Esterhuizen, G.H.   Lieutenant   SAAF

CHRONOLOGICAL INDEX OF IMPORTANT EVENTS BETWEEN 1975 AND 1990 MENTIONED IN THIS BOOK

	Page no.	Date	Event: Political/ Diplomatic	Event: Military	Other events, and remarks
1	116	26 Aug 1966	SAP/SADF attack on On-gulumbashe	First armed clash with SWAPO	
2	85, 86	1973		SADF made responsible for security in SWA	Mil strategy p 84 incl 'General' and 'Specific' ops p 86
3	54–59, 62, 111, 158	1975/76		Op Savanna(h) – Angola	
4	57	1976/77	USA: Clark Amendment	SA troop with-drawal	
5	70, 83	26 Sept 1977	Talks Big Five Western pow-ers, Pretoria – no agreement		UK, USA, France, West Germany, Canada

	Page no.	Date	Event: Political/ Diplomatic	Event: Military	Other events, and remarks
6	70	1977	Appointment of AG in SWA: Mr Justice MT Steyn		
7	70	Sept 1977	Dirk Mudge resigns from NP and founds Republican Party		RP and other parties form Democratic Turnhalle Alliance (DTA)
8	70	25 April 1978	RSA govt accepts Western proposals for a SWA/Namibia settlement (also see serial 33)		Later becomes UN Resolution 435
9	95, 98, 146	4 May 1978		Op Reindeer	Cassinga, alias Moscow, and Chetequera, alias Vietnam
10	72	Aug 1978	Andreas Shipanga returns to SWA/Namibia		Resigns, and forms SWAPO–Democrats
11	108–112	23 Aug 1978		Cross–border field artillery and missile bombardment on Katima Mulilo from Zambia – 10 troops killed	Evening of UN General Philipp's departure
12	115–120	Mar 1979		Ops Rekstok and Saffraan	
13	123			'Fox' operations	
14	128	Feb 1980		Stopping of PLAN (SWAPO) infiltration: Tsumeb/Grootfontein/Otavi triangle	
15	95, 127–131, 154–155, 158, 235, 294, 311	10 Jun 1980		Op Sceptic	incl Smokeshell

	Page no.	Date	Event: Political/ Diplomatic	Event: Military	Other events, and remarks
16	145–147		**SWAPO** propaganda themes		
17	189	Jan 1981	Talks: RSA, SWA/Namibian parties incl. **SWAPO**, Western Five 'BAMTAZZ' states, under UN protection in Geneva		BAMTZZ: Botswana, Angola, Mozambique, Tanzania, Zambia, Zimbabwe
18	154	July 1981		Op Carnation	
19	190	12 Aug 1981			MK, Voortrekkerhoogte and Elsie
20	147, 154–158	23 Aug 1981	UN Security Council session 29 Aug 1981	Op Protea	
21	156, 163, 179	1 Nov 1981		Op Daisy	
22	156, 179	early 1982		Op Super	
23	157	Jul/Aug 1982		Op Meebos	
24	157	Feb–Apr 1983		Op Phoenix	
25	165–169	Dec 1983		Op Askari	Big Daddy, Koos Krokodil and FAPLA lieutenant
26	3, 144, 169, 170–174, 288, 326	Feb 1984	Lusaka Agreement		'Area in Dispute' and Joint Monitoring Commission created
27	181	Feb/Mar 1984		Dealing with infiltration over Botswana border	
28	202	1983/84	RSA tricameral parliament begins to function		
29	180–181	completed 28 May 1985		Clearing up of Kavango	

Page no.	Date	Event: Political/ Diplomatic	Event: Military	Other events, and remarks
30 174	29 June 1985		Op Boswilger	
31 177, 184, 185	1972, 1987		Shipanga's 'Massacred Village'	War, lies and semantics
32 204	1985/86	Russian general Konstantin Kurochkin becomes commander–in–chief in Angola and launches offensive against UNITA		Modulêr, Hooper and Packer begin
33 203	4 Mar 1986	PW Botha proposes 1 Aug 1986 for start of implementation of Resolution 435		Provided agreement is also reached iro Cuban withdrawal. Also see serial 8.
34 200	Middle 80s	Brazzaville shuttle		
35 215–219	Middle 80s		RSA cross–border lightning ops	
36 222, 223, 230	1986/88	The Wynand du Toit saga		
37 183, 226, 242, 274, 318	1986/88		Ops Modulêr, Packer and Hooper	
38 233–241	3 Oct 1987		SA forces achieve the decisive victories of the entire campaign at the Lomba River in SE Angola	Troops of Deon Ferreira, Bok Smit (61 Mech Battalion) and others destroy 47 Brigade etc. First–ever capture of Russian SAM-8 ground–to–air missile system
39 237–238	10 Feb 1988			Detention and freeing of President Lucas Mangope in Bopthutatswana

Page no.	Date	Event: Political/ Diplomatic	Event: Military	Other events, and remarks
40 256–258	Jan 1988		Prelude to Cuban offensive in SW Angola	
41 262–263	3–4 May 1988	London – inter-national talks (RSA, Cuba, Angola)		
42 262–263	4 May 1988		Cuban attack on elements of 101 Battalion	Cubans capture wounded Johan Papenfus
43 262	30 May 1988	Reagan and Gorbachev propagate peace plan		
44 265–267	25 June 1988	International negotiations at the Hyatt el Salaam hotel, Cairo. Hot air and intellectual violence	Prelude to SA forces' final vic-tory over Cuban forces in SW Angola	
45 268–269	June/July 1988		Mike Muller (61 Mech Battalion Group), Hannes Nortmann, André Vermeu-len and others defeat Cubans	Decisive victories of the entire campaign in SW Angola
46 269	27 June 1988		7 Cuban MIG–23s at-tack Calueque dam wall (SW Angola). 11 SA troops killed	Cubans use this incident to claim total victory
47 268	July/Aug 1988		Cubans aban-don offensive in SW Angola and withdraw to Techipa	

Page no.	Date	Event: Political/ Diplomatic	Event: Military	Other events, and remarks
48 273–275	11 July 1988	More nego- tiations, led by Chester Crocker, at Governor's Island: New York principles		
49 275, 278, 281	Middle July 1988	Sal Island: negotiation of cease–fire, northwards withdrawal of Cuban troops and withdrawal of SA forces from Angola		Psychological– warfare drama: Gen- eral Arnaldo Óchoa Sanchez, Col Eddie Viljoen and Col Freddie Oelschig
50 281–282	2–5 Aug 1988	Geneva. Turning–point of negotiations. Decision to recommend 1 Nov 1988 to Secretary– General as implementa- tion–date of Resolution 435		Provision made for joint monitoring commission (JC)
51 253	22 Aug 1988	General Willie Meyer (**GOC** SWA) and Cuban General Leopoldo Cin- tra Frias sign agreement		Troop withdrawal
52 285	24 Aug– 24 Nov 1988	Conferences determine pro- cess of imple- mentation of Res 435, ending with election– date for SWA/ Namibia		Brazzaville x 4, New York x 2 and Geneva (later becomes the Geneva Protocol)
53 246, 285	22 Dec 1988	Final signing of trilateral agree- ment New York		SA, Cuba, Angola

	Page no.	Date	Event: Political/ Diplomatic	Event: Military	Other events, and remarks
54	281–284	early 1989	Prelude to implementation of Resolution 435 and Geneva Protocol		
55	292, 293	1 April 1989		1 600 SWAPO members contravene cease–fire and shoot dead many people	Handful of police, 'Koevoet', helicopters and troops save the situation in the 'Nine–Day War' – last armed clash with SWAPO
56	292	19 May 1989	Resumption of implementation of peace plan		
57	318–323	1989 and later	Cold War propaganda and misinformation		
58	247	31 May 1991	MPLA and UNITA conclude Estoril Agreement (Portugal)		
59	176	7 Sep 1992		Failure of ANC/SACP/ COSATU alliance's attempt to overthrow president of Ciskei – 23+ people killed and 188 wounded	Compare with serial 55 – SWAPO's tragedy
60	335				SA defence budget during the Cold War

INDEX OF OPERATIONS

REFERENCES

Allen, Roy. 1980. *Sungong.* Windhoek: Gamsberg.

Armstrong, Sue. 1989. *In search of freedom: The Andreas Shipanga story, as told to Sue Armstrong.* Gibraltar: Ashanti.

Breytenbach, Jan. 1990. *They live by the sword: 32 'Buffalo' Battalion – South Africa's foreign legion.* Alberton: Lemur Books.

Bridgland, Fred. 1990. *The war for Africa: Twelve months that transformed a continent.* Gibraltar: Ashanti.

British Army. 1950. *Conduct of war.* British Army Pamphlet for Senior Officers.

Brookes, Andrew. 1975. *Photo reconnaissance.* London: Ian Allen.

Brown, James Ambrose. 1991. *Retreat to victory: A Springbok's diary in North Africa,*

Gazala to Alamein 1942. Johannesburg: Ashanti.

Collyer, J. 1939. *Die veldtog in Duits Suidwes-Afrika.* Pretoria: State Printer.

Crocker, Chester A. 1992. *High noon in Southern Africa: Making peace in a rough neighborhood.* New York: W W Norton & Company.

Du Preez, Sophia. 1989. *Avontuur in Angola: Die verhaal van Suid-Afrika se soldate in Angola* 1975–1976. Pretoria: J L van Schaik.

Dupuy, T N 1987. *Understanding war: History and theory of combat.* New York: Paragon House Publishers.

Esterhuyzen, Pieter and Leistner, Erich. (Eds.). 1991. *Namibia 1990: An Africa Institute Survey.* Africa Institute of South Africa.

Freeman, Chas W. 1989. *The Angolan/Namibia accords.* Foreign Affairs, Spring Edition.

Heitman, Helmoed-Romer. 1990. *South African armed forces.* Cape Town: Buffalo Publications.

Heitman, Helmoed-Romer. 1990. *War in Angola: The final South African phase.* Gibraltar: Ashanti.

Instituut Voor Organisatie Ontwikkeling. 'Process of Escalation of Conflicts and Roles of Third Parties' (document obtained from National Productivity Institute).

Militaria. 1989. Official professional journal of the SADF. Directorate of Public Relations. 19 February 1989, pp. 8, 9, 11.

Montgomery, Field-Marshal.1958. *The Viscount Bernard Law of Alamein, KG: The Memoirs.* London: Collins.

Pakenham, Thomas. 1981. *Die Boere-Oorlog: Vertaal deur Leon Rosseau.* Johannesburg: Jonathan Ball.

Politica Internacional. Accordos de Paz Para Angola. No.4 (Verao, 91 Trimestral), p. 65.

Raw, Wyatt Vause. 1988. *Flares: Fragments in discord.* Durban North: 54 Gleneagles Drive.

Retief, Bertrand. 1990. *Humor in SA Uniform.* Johannesburg: Perskor.

Sellars, Duncan W. 1989. *International Freedom Review.* Vol. 2, No.2, p. 47.

Snyman, P H R. 1989. *Beeld van die SWA gebiedsmag.* Pretoria: Directorate of Public Relations, SA Defence Force.

Steenkamp, Willem. 1990. *South Africa's border war* 1966–1989. Rivonia: Ashanti.

Tabois, Genevieve. 1938. *Blackmail or war.* 5th Ed. London: Wyman & Sons.

Westmoreland, William C. 1980. *A soldier reports.* Dell Publishing.

Zeitspiegel, Magazin für Entscheidungstarger No 5/4 JHG/89. 'War and Peace, The Caribbean-African Way'. Malek Druckerei Gesellschaft mbH.

SELECTED INDEX OF PERSONS' NAMES